Past Imperfect

Past Imperfect

French Intellectuals, 1944–1956

Tony Judt

UNIVERSITY OF CALIFORNIA PRESS

Berkeley / Los Angeles / London

Originally published as *Passé imparfait: Les Intellectuels en France, 1944–1956*.
© 1992 by Librairie Arthème Fayard, Paris.

University of California Press
Berkeley and Los Angeles, California

University of California Press, Ltd.
London, England

First Paperback Printing 1994

Library of Congress Cataloging-in-Publication Data

Judt, Tony.
    Past imperfect : French intellectuals, 1944–1956 / Tony Judt.
        p.   cm.
    Includes bibliographical references and index.
    ISBN 0-520-08650-3
    1. France—Intellectual life—20th century.   2. Intellectuals—
France—Political and social views—History—20th century.
3. Communism and intellectuals—France—History—20th
century.   I. Title.
DC33.7.J84   1992
944.082—dc20   91-42870
                                                        CIP

Printed in the United States of America
9   8   7   6   5   4   3   2

The paper used in this publication meets the minimum requirements
of American National Standard for Information Sciences—Permanence
of Paper for Printed Library Materials, ANSI Z39.48-1984. ⊚

Toute idée fausse finit dans le sang, mais il s'agit toujours du sang des autres. C'est ce qui explique que certains de nos philosophes se sentent à l'aise pour dire n'importe quoi.

Mistaken ideas always end in bloodshed, but in every case it is someone else's blood. That is why some of our thinkers feel free to say just about anything.

Albert Camus

Contents

Acknowledgments

This book was written while I was on leave in Stanford, California, as the guest of the Hoover Institution. I would like to offer my thanks to the director and fellows of that institution for their generous support and for access to their unrivaled library and archive holdings. My stay in Stanford was made possible by a fellowship from the John Simon Guggenheim Foundation. Research and reading at an earlier stage were conducted with the support of fellowships from the Nuffield Foundation and the Humanities Center of Stanford University. To all of these, and to New York University for granting me a leave of absence during the year 1990, my most grateful thanks and appreciation.

Some of the arguments developed in this book were presented as lectures, seminar papers, or articles in the course of recent years. They have thus benefited from the comments of many friends and colleagues, and it is a pleasure to acknowledge these contributions, too many to list in full. Helen Solanum read the whole typescript—twice! Her help and support have been invaluable.

I should also like to express my appreciation for the lively and intense discussions of some of the themes of this book that took place in my graduate seminar in New York, and for similarly provocative exchanges in Jacques Rupnik's seminar at the École des Hautes Études en Sciences Sociales, whose guest I was in the spring of 1989. Not the least interesting lesson of these experiences has been the marked difference in the way in which French and American graduate students approach problems of intellectual engagement. It is a pleasure to be able to report that there is much to be said for both cultural styles.

Finally, my thanks to my editor, Sheila Levine, for her enthusiastic support for this book. With her encouragement I have tried to adapt for a broader audience a text originally aimed at French readers. This has entailed some clarification of otherwise obscure references, an exercise from which the book as a whole has, I hope, benefited.

Introduction

For a period of about twelve years following the liberation of France in 1944, a generation of French intellectuals, writers, and artists was swept into the vortex of communism. By this I do not mean that they became Communists; most did not. Indeed, then as now, many prominent intellectuals in France had no formal political affiliation, and some of the most important among them were decidedly non-Marxist (Raymond Aron is only the best-known example among many). But the issue of communism—its practice, its meaning, its claims upon the future—dominated political and philosophical conversation in postwar France. The terms of public discussion were shaped by the position one adopted on the behavior of foreign and domestic Communists, and most of the problems of contemporary France were analyzed in terms of a political or ethical position taken with half an eye towards that of the Communists and their ideology.

This situation was not wholly unprecedented. During the thirties similar concerns had colored the stance of French intellectuals, and they would continue to do so, for some at least, until the early seventies. But the years 1944–56 were different. The Vichy interlude had served to delegitimize the intellectuals of the Right (who had played an important part in French cultural life between the wars), while the experience of war and resistance had radicalized the language, if not the practices, of the Left. The period after 1956 saw a progressive shift away from the concern with domestic and European radicalism, brought on by the emergence of anticolonial movements in the non-European world and the doubts and disillusion precipitated by Khrushchev's speech of February 1956, in which the leader of the Communist world attacked the crimes and failings of the Stalin era. The decade following World War II was thus unique in the near-monopoly exercised by the appeal of Soviet communism within the Left, in the importance of that appeal for a majority of French political thinkers, and in the enthusiasm with which the case for communism was defended.

Moreover, it was precisely in this decade that Soviet society expanded from its earlier containment within the frontiers of a distant and alien Russia and established itself in the territory formerly known as Central Europe. Where Lenin's revolution and its Stalinist unfolding could once be treated as something peculiar to a distant land, the experience of the People's Democracies brought communism literally closer to home. The postwar establishment of totalitarian government in Budapest, Warsaw, Berlin, and Prague, with its attendant repression, persecution, and social upheaval, placed the moral dilemma of Marxist practice at the center of the Western intellectual agenda. The interwar sufferings of Stalin's victims in collectivization, political purges, and mass population transfers could if necessary be ascribed to the trauma of modernization and revolution in a backward, historically barbaric society. The same could not be said in the case of Stalinism in Central Europe after the war, and apologias for communism, and by extension for Marxism as a doctrine of human liberation, were accordingly compelled to acknowledge and explain the immense human sacrifices now being exacted in the name of History and Freedom.

This book is about those apologias and their accompanying theorems, and about the men and women who espoused them in the years 1944–56. It is not a study of Communist intellectuals nor, except in passing, is it about the words and deeds of Communists. Its protagonists are those French intellectuals, some prominent, some obscure, some Communists, most not, who sought to "engage" themselves on the side of Progress at a time when that engagement exacted a heavy moral toll. From the privileged perspective of the last years of our century, the response of French intellectuals to these matters, the way in which they described their political and moral commitments, and the terms in which they explained and justified the practice of contemporary Stalinism seem strange and distant, echoes of a political and cultural universe from which we are now far, far removed.

So much is of course true of any society sufficiently far away, in time no less than in space. What distinguishes the writings of this period, however, is that they retain a power to shock and surprise. Even in 1991 we can readily agree with François Mauriac, writing in 1949, when he describes a contemporary justification of the Hungarian show trials as "an obscenity of the mind."[1] One reason for this is that some of those writing at the time are with us still. Another source of our capacity to respond to these writings is that they frequently came from the pen of men and women of considerable cultural standing, prominent nationally and internationally as novelists, philosophers, playwrights . . . and moralists. Their reputations may have dimmed with time but not to the point that we can read without discomfort of their insouciance in the face of violence, human suffering, and painful moral choices.

These matters have not gone unnoticed, in France at least. After Solzhenitsyn, after Cambodia, it became quite fashionable to turn the spotlight on French intellectuals and their erstwhile flirtation with Marxism. Indeed, one dominant theme in French intellectual life since the late 1970s has been the moral inadequacy of the French intellectual of the previous generation. Solzhenitsyn, after all, was not the first to describe in detail the Gulag and its attendant horrors. Artur London in 1968 had recounted the Czech show trials of the 1950s; before him there was Khrushchev himself, who in turn had been preceded by Victor Kravchenko and David Rousset in the forties, revealing in detail the workings of the "univers concentrationnaire." Before them had come Victor Serge and Boris Souvarine, and they in turn had been preceded by a host of revealing memoirs and analyses of the Soviet experience. How, in the face of all this literary evidence, not to mention the testimony of their own eyes, could intelligent people willfully defend communism as the hope of the future and Stalin as the solution to the riddle of History? Twenty years after World War II, more than a decade after the political persecutions and trials in her own country, the Slovak Jew Jo Langer was astonished to arrive in Paris and find herself confronted with a denial of her own experience, a refusal to accept the evidence of history, to abandon the myths and utopias of *bien-pensant* progressivism. Here, trapped in a time capsule of its own manufacture, was a genus that ought by now to have been defunct: "les intellectuels-de-la-gauche-française."[2]

Thomas Pavel has aptly described what happened to much of the French intellectual elite during the forties and fifties as a "refusal to

---

1. François Mauriac, *Le Figaro,* 24 October 1949. All translations from the French are my own unless otherwise stated. The original French quotations are given in full in the French edition of this book, *Un Passé imparfait.*

2. Jo Langer, *Une Saison à Bratislava* (Paris, 1981), 243.

listen."[3] To account for this failure it is not sufficient to acknowledge and describe the scale of the problem (although this is a necessary condition for such an understanding, one that was lacking until quite recently). This, however, would seem to be the limited ambition of most of what has been written on the subject to date. There are three reasons for this, and each one informs and circumscribes a different approach to its subject.

In the first place there has been the politically motivated desire to uncover the sins of the fathers. A spate of books published after 1975 sought to illustrate, often through selective quotation, the obtuseness and moral ambivalence of people like Jean-Paul Sartre, Simone de Beauvoir, Emmanuel Mounier, and their contemporaries, fiddling with their existential dilemmas while Budapest burned. This is easy to do—as we shall see, these people and many lesser lights alongside them wrote and said some quite astonishingly foolish things. The limitations on such an approach are considerable, however. It isn't enough, after all, to "kill the father"—you have to understand him, too. Otherwise, at the very least, you risk repeating his mistakes. Except in the most superficial sense, these are not works of history but, rather, exercises in character assassination. They don't explain *why* former cultural heroes held such silly opinions, nor do they help us appreciate just why, holding the views they did, they became and remained so prominent and respected. This sort of approach is also limited in its ability to explain just why modern critics, in many cases, once shared the opinions of the man they are now condemning.[4]

Secondly, the French in recent years have been treated to a remarkable series of personal memoirs and autobiographies from Parisian intellectuals. Here, the uneasy recollection of an author's *own* earlier commitments all too often colors his approach to this subject, and constrains it too, though in a different way. These works obviously describe very different personal trajectories and vary in quality and importance with the person of the author. But what unites so many of them has been the common search for exculpation, the urge to understand the political allegiance—to communism—that colored their youth and marks them

---

3. Thomas Pavel, "Empire et paradigmes," *Le Débat* 58 (January–February 1990): 172.

4. See, among many others, Jean Belkhir, *Les Intellectuels et le pouvoir* (Paris, 1982); M. A. Burnier, *Le Testament de Sartre* (Paris, 1982); J-M Goulemot, *Le Clairon de Staline* (Paris, 1981); Bernard Legendre, *Le Stalinisme français: Qui a dit quoi* (Paris, 1980); Serge Quadruppani, *Les Infortunes de la verité* (Paris, 1981); and Georges Suffert, *Les Intellectuels en chaise longue* (Paris, 1974), not to speak of the various works of the "new philosophers," notably André Glucksmann and Bernard-Henri Lévy.

still. In these memoirs, usually the work of men and women of mature years, there is a much more developed sense of history, of context, and of the ambiguities of political and moral choice than one finds in the essays of the young turks. They belong for the most part to the "Cold War generation," for whom communism was the "ineluctable question."[5] How, they ask, could I, being who I now am and understanding what I now understand, ever have said and done the things I am describing? What blinded us to things before our very eyes? And when and how did I see the light? Some of these memoirs are first-rate analyses of the historical moment through which the author passed—the earliest of them, by Edgar Morin, still in many ways the best. Those by professional historians are predictably better at grasping the wider picture, and they pay tribute, explicitly or by implication, to the pathology of this period, the quiet hysteria in which they all at some point shared.[6]

One has all the same an overall sense of inadequacy, sometimes even of bad faith. No one, after all, wants to admit that he or she was not only foolish but in some sense also duplicitous. And yet so many of these memoirs are led in that direction by an unavoidable paradox. Because intellectuals write, and thereby leave a record of their former opinions that cannot easily be erased, they are constrained in later years to admit that yes, they did say and do those absurd things. But it is not sufficient to draw a veil over those years and claim to have grown beyond the foolishness of youth. Even though we may not be the person we were, in a certain philosophical sense, we alone can take responsibility for the deeds of that former self. Hence almost every writer who was politically engaged on the Left in the postwar years claims now to have retained an inner identity not wholly aligned with the public one presented to the world and to friends on the Left. Claude Roy puts the point in a characteristic manner: "I voted for Jean-Jacques Rousseau and for Marx in the elections of History. But in the secret ballot of the individual, I opted rather for Schopenhauer and Godot."[7] Why did he not *say* so? Well, he did—after 1956. Others brought their personal and political identities into line at some earlier stage (if we are to believe what they say); a few waited until the sixties or even the seventies.

5. See Michel Winock, "Les Générations intellectuelles," *Vingtième Siècle* 22 (1989): 17.

6. Edgar Morin, *Autocritique* (Paris, 1958). See also Annie Kriegel, *Ce que j'ai cru comprendre* (Paris, 1991).

7. Claude Roy, *Nous* (Paris, 1972), 388.

That Claude Roy, like Emmanuel Le Roy Ladurie, Pierre Daix, and others, Communist and fellow traveler alike, should feel the need even after thirty years to claim for himself a little area of honesty and clear-sightedness is understandable and only natural. Moreover, Roy is certainly describing, and accurately, the experience of many of his contemporaries. But such an account, however honest, paradoxically inhibits any attempt to understand the source of their own beliefs, since it denies, against the evidence, that they ever really held them. As for those like Alain Besançon or Dominique Desanti—who do indeed admit that they thought what they wrote and believed what they thought—they obfuscate in a different way. Besançon, in defense of a youthful aberration that he does at least treat as such, claims that even after Stalin's death, "No one, or almost no one, was openly anti-Communist in France." Here, as with Roy, the author is telling the truth as it seemed to him—and it is part of the purpose of this book to show just why, in the circumstances of modern French political culture, anticommunism appeared to be excluded from the lexicon of nonconservative beliefs. But at the same time, Besançon is mistaken: there were a lot of anti-Communists in France, and some of them were on the Left. There were also a lot of non-Communists. Besançon is continuing to claim in his maturity what he and his peers asserted in their youth—that all of France was divided into Communists and anti-Communists and no one at the time could have been expected to occupy the space between. During the years in question, this was a real if highly partisan political and philosophical position, whose origins I shall be discussing in this book. But Besançon's deployment of it as an explanation and justification of his own contemporary choice is unfortunate—it does not do justice to his skills as a historian.[8]

These remarks bring me to a third inadequacy of existing accounts of recent French intellectual practice. Memorialists have stories of their own to tell, whereas historians are under a special obligation to understand the significance of time and place. In this case, however, there has been a certain conflation of tasks. The postwar context, domestically and internationally, is treated by many writers, historians, and memorialists alike as so overwhelming as to constitute an explanation in its own right. Events and choices, it is suggested, placed most reasonable men and women in a situation in which their actions (verbal and practical) were in effect overdetermined. This is a seductive view. After Hitler, after Pétain,

8. Alain Besançon, *Une Génération* (Paris, 1987).

after Stalingrad, who would not place their hopes in the communist dream? Reasonable people might differ as to the moment of their disillusion, but that the initial illusion was forgivable in the circumstances looks like a reasonable conclusion.

The inadequacy of this neutral historicist account is twofold. In the first place, its scope is too restricted. All three sorts of work discussed above—syllabi of errors, memoirs, and histories—share a common assumption: that the years 1944–56 represent something peculiar or aberrant about French intellectual life, an embarrassing diversion from the rational. They concede that those were also the years in which modern French high culture flourished and established a worldwide hegemony but treat moral aberration and cultural impact, when they do discuss them together, which is rare, as somehow unrelated phenomena. Thus M. A. Burnier indicts Sartre before the court of world opinion for his errors, contradictions, and lies but does not pause to reflect upon the significance of the fact that the world is indeed interested in his target.[9] Yet it is surely a matter of some relevance that when outsiders think of French intellectuals, they instinctively refer to the people and the writings of the very decade over which today's French thinkers are so keen to draw a veil.

In a similar vein, most histories of postwar intellectual engagement in France offer only exiguous accounts of its relationship to the intellectual experience in France *before* 1944 (or 1939) and the one that came after and is with us today. General intellectual histories of postwar France notice the antecedent practices of an earlier generation of intellectuals but make little sustained effort to explain the former in the light of the latter. Obviously, one can go too far in this direction. Some of the themes of French intellectual discourse that helped pave the way for the political positions I shall be describing—the attraction to violence, the uninterest in morality as a category of public behavior, the curious and repeated addiction to German philosophical style—could be traced readily enough back to Victor Cousin, 1793, Voltaire, and doubtless beyond. The *longue durée,* already hard to justify in social history, explains very little if anything in the history of public language and its political deployment. But between the restricted vision that sees in the world of postwar France the source of its own paradoxes and the view that would collapse those paradoxes into the centuries-long categories of French national history, there is surely room to maneuver. Thus,

9. Burnier, *Le Testament de Sartre.*

although this book is a study of the behavior of French intellectuals in a very specific historical moment, it also tries to draw on a larger understanding of France's recent past (and that of other countries too) in order to explain that behavior.

The second weakness of such histories concerns the even-handedness of the approaches described above, the reluctance to take or assign responsibility for positions adopted and things said. Everything becomes a matter of context, "the mood of the times." Now it is true that history is a discipline and a method that seeks to describe and, through description, to explain. It is not, should not be, an indictment. Nonetheless, there are degrees of disengagement in such things. Thus it is intuitively obvious to any reader that the historian of Nazism faces issues and dilemmas from which the scholar of medieval monasticism, for example, is usually exempt. In seeking to explain something that is intrinsically unattractive, to which the reader would normally respond with distaste, one is not excused from the obligation to be accurate, but neither is one under a compelling obligation to pretend to neutrality. With respect to the history of postwar French intellectuals, I too make no such pretense. The very importance and international prominence of French thinkers in the postwar world has placed on them a special burden, perfectly consistent with the claims made by Sartre and his peers regarding the responsibility of the writer for his words and their effect. It is the contrast between those claims and the actual response of a generation of French intellectuals when presented with practical situations and moral choices that is remarkable and requires explanation. Whatever the emotions of the time, they do not wholly explain; neither do they exculpate: "There is no soul so weak that it cannot, properly directed, acquire full control of its passions."[10]

What is more, this contrast, the failure of French intellectuals to fulfill the hopes invested in them by their admirers in eastern Europe in particular, together with the influence exerted by the French on intellectual life in other Western countries, had a decisive impact on the history of postwar European life. As I shall argue, the consequences of the attitudes described here were not confined to the years in question, nor to the lives and personal relations of the protagonists. In the history of French intellectual practice during the years 1944–56 there are to be found not

10. R. Descartes, *Les Passions de l'âme*, Part 1, Article 50, quoted in Leszek Kolakowski, "Responsabilité et histoire," part 2, *Les Temps modernes* 147–149 (May–July 1958): 279.

only echoes of earlier French and European experiences, but also the
seeds of our present condition. In this sense, then, a history of these
years is bound to be engaged with its subject matter. Whether I have succeeded in maintaining a balance between such engagement and the dictates of historical analysis, I leave to the reader to judge.

Previous essays into this terrain have not always been successful in this
respect. Thanks to Bernard-Henri Lévy in particular, it is now much
harder to pass a certain sort of judgment without appearing partial. In
his hasty little book on French "national" ideology, B-H Lévy used
selective quotation, atypical examples, and works torn from context to
hand down a condemnation of a number of French political and social
thinkers of the twentieth century.[11] I would not trouble the reader with
a reminder of this slim treatise were it not for the fact that despite a distaste for his methods, I believe its author to have been intuitively correct
in certain of his judgments. Some of the criticism addressed at him in
France was the product not of offended professional sensibilities but,
rather, of righteous indignation at his temerity in attacking the sacred
icons of France's cultural past—Charles Péguy, Emmanuel Mounier, and
others. But since he was in each instance right for the wrong reason, and
without proper evidence, Bernard-Henri Lévy's conclusions have been
dismissed by all serious intellectual historians. It does not follow, however, that those of us investigating some of the same matters should feel
precluded from passing down similarly forceful condemnations where
appropriate. In this book it will, I believe, be clear enough what I think
of Mounier and certain others of his generation. I have tried, though, to
treat such persons, if not as products of their time, then certainly as
deeply imbricated with it, and I have especially sought to give a full and
fair treatment of their writings.

In this there is some advantage to being an outsider, even if it is the
only benefit that accrues from such a position. A foreigner may also be
predisposed to raise matters that would not immediately concern a
French scholar. In this book I am interested, for example, in an aspect of
the modern philosophical tradition in France that has until very recently
aroused little comment in France itself, the marked absence of a concern
with public ethics or political morality. I am also curious to see just how
far and in what ways the French response to totalitarianism differed from
that of intellectuals elsewhere. And I am fascinated by what is to the outsider the peculiar shape of French intellectual discourse, the manner in

11. *L'Idéologie française* (Paris, 1981).

which the conversations I describe were conducted. Because they are framed in comparative terms—why was France so different?—these are the sorts of questions a foreigner might ask where a native would not.

These are also, perhaps, questions prompted by a peculiarly Anglo-Saxon tradition of intellectual history. In the spirit of that tradition, this book is neither a history of ideas nor a social history of French intellectual life. It aspires to cover territory common to both but can also be understood, in a simple sense, as the history of a conversation: the one conducted among themselves by a generation of French intellectuals and addressed to questions of "engagement," "responsibility," "choice," and so forth. In the context of the postwar years this conversation took the form of a complicated sequence of verbal actions, circumscribed by certain cultural and linguistic conventions and shaped by the world in which the dominant intellectual generation had been formed. The context—political, cultural, personal—is thus of some significance and accounts for the space devoted in the chapters that follow to the historical circumstances surrounding the writings that are discussed. But that discussion itself is largely textual in its form, seeking to locate in the language used and the positions adopted the determinants of intellectual attitudes and their source.

The design of this book flows from those concerns and from the problem that I set out to address. In part 1, there is a discussion of the intellectual condition in France at the moment of the Liberation, with some prior attention paid to the prewar context in which the experience of 1940–44 must be understood. This is more than just an exercise in scene setting: it is my contention that the experience of the thirties—and of defeat, occupation, and resistance—not only provides the context for postwar intellectual activity and concerns but helped shape the language and the assumptions within which that activity and those concerns were cast.

In part 2 there is a detailed account of the eastern European show trials of the years 1947–53, together with a discussion of the various ways in which French writers responded to them. The story of the trials and the reaction they aroused, or failed to arouse, is a unique occasion on which to see the intelligentsia of France engaging acute and problematic questions of justice, morality, terror, retribution, and the like, questions that pertained to the postwar European condition but also drew attention to France's own revolutionary heritage and its ambivalent ethical message. By using these trials (and to a lesser extent other contemporary events like the revelations concerning Soviet concentration camps) as a magnifying lens through which to observe French responses to sometimes agonizing moral and political dilemmas, I have tried to map out the complex intellectual terrain of these years, while keeping the focus sufficiently restricted to allow a close discussion of individual attitudes.

In part 3 the descriptive material of the previous section is analyzed and considered in the context of larger themes and traditions that shaped the French intellectual community. In part 4 I seek to assess how much the experience described in this book was unique to the French, and if it was unique, why; also why and with what consequences the attitudes of the years 1944–56 were forgotten or transformed in the period after 1956. The conclusion deals with the ways in which this particular French past is folded into contemporary French consciousness and asks how far and in what ways the intellectual condition in France has undergone fundamental transformation in recent years.

One final remark is in order. Authors are perhaps ill advised to explain why theirs is the book it is and not something else. But in the present case it may be worth emphasizing at the outset that this is not a general history of postwar French intellectuals. If it were, it would pay altogether more attention to some very influential and interesting people who are not much mentioned in the pages that follow. I have deliberately eschewed any consideration of the "great debates" of postwar French cultural life—that between Sartre and Camus, for example—and some of the most interesting books by Sartre, Camus, Merleau-Ponty, and others receive only a passing reference. Even Raymond Aron, who figures prominently in these pages, is present because of his perceptive commentaries upon the views of his contemporaries rather than for his own contributions to sociological theory and political ideas. This book is thus something different. It is not a history of French intellectuals; it is, rather, an essay on intellectual irresponsibility, a study of the moral condition of the intelligentsia in postwar France.

Thus the major protagonists of this book—Sartre, Mounier, de Beauvoir, Merleau-Ponty, Camus, Aron, and François Mauriac—do not represent their lesser contemporaries and are of course not typical of anything. But they were the dominant voices in these years—they controlled the cultural territory, they set the terms of public discourse, they shaped the prejudices and language of their audience. Their way of being intellectuals echoed and reinforced the self-image of the intellectual community at large, even those of its members who disagreed with them. The matters with which they chose to occupy themselves, at least until 1956, and the way in which they engaged or refused to engage crucial moral issues constitute a remarkable and very particular moment in the French intellectual experience. All that I would claim for this subject is that the themes I am treating here were absolutely crucial at the time and that the questions they posed then and pose today are at the very heart of modern French history.

PART ONE

The Force of Circumstance?

CHAPTER ONE

Decline and Fall
The French Intellectual Community at the End of the Third Republic

J'ai vécu les années '30 dans le désespoir de la décadence française. . . . Au fond, la France n'existait plus. Elle n'existait que par les haines des Français les uns pour les autres.

I lived through the thirties in the despair of French decline. . . . In essence, France no longer existed. It existed only in the hatred of the French for one another.

Raymond Aron

The Third Republic, it is said, died unloved. Few sought seriously to defend it in July 1940, and it passed away unmourned. Recent scholarship suggests this judgment may need more nuance as it applies to the general population, but so far as the intelligentsia were concerned, it remains a fair comment upon their disengagement from the Republic and its values.[1] Those who had sympathized with the Communists

---

1. See Jean-Louis Crémieux-Brilhac, *Les Français de l'an 40,* 2 vols. (Paris, 1990); Jean-Pierre Azéma, *1940, l'année terrible* (Paris, 1990); Pierre Laborie, *L'Opinion française sous Vichy* (Paris, 1990); René Rémond and Janine Bourdin, eds., *La France et les Français* (Paris, 1978).

were disillusioned by the compromises of the Popular Front, the refusal to intervene in Spain and, finally, by the party's about-face in August 1939, following the Molotov-Ribbentrop Pact. Socialists, so hopeful in 1936, had experienced a comparable loss of faith, accentuated by a division within the Socialist community over pacifism and the correct response to German expansion. To the Right there was the fear and loathing crystallized by the memory of the strikes of June 1936, bringing conservatives and reactionaries ever closer in a coalition cemented by anticommunism, increasing antirepublicanism, and an ever more confident and aggressive anti-Semitism. Intellectuals of the "center" were rare. Those few men who would speak after Munich in defense of the Republic and against fascism did so in the name of values that they continued to hold in spite of the Third Republic and its shortcomings but that they had mostly ceased to associate with that political regime and its institutional forms.

The notion that the Republic and the world that it represented were rotten and unsavable was widespread. Writing in 1932, in the first editorial of his new journal, *Esprit,* the young Emmanuel Mounier observed, "The modern world is so utterly moldy that for new shoots to emerge the whole rotten edifice will have to crumble."[2] For Mounier, the metaphor spoke above all to questions of sensibility, an aesthetic distaste for the cynical worldliness of late–Third Republic France; it did not commit him to any particular political position, and after an initial flirtation with Italian fascism (also on aesthetic grounds), he came out firmly against Nazism and was to be a critic of Munich. On the other hand, his vision of an organic, communal alternative to Republican anomie (Mounier and his generation reflected some of Durkheim's suspicion of modernity, albeit on rather different grounds) kept him and his colleagues in *Esprit* constantly critical of modern democracy. What was needed was a new elite to lead and renew a tired nation.[3]

Mounier's outlook was shared by many others, each in his own terms. Noting the seductive appeal of totalitarian systems, Denis de Rougemont confided to his *Journal* in 1938 the following reflection:

The first task for intellectuals who have understood the totalitarian peril (from right and left) is not to "join up" with some sort of anti-Fascism, but to attack the sort of thinking from which both Fascism and Stalinism necessarily grow. And that is liberal thought.[4]

2. Emmanuel Mounier, "Refaire la Renaissance," *Esprit,* October 1932.
3. John Hellman, *Emmanuel Mounier and the New Catholic Left* (Toronto, 1981), 82.
4. Denis de Rougemont, *Journal d'une époque, 1926–1946* (Paris, 1968), 374.

This was a characteristic response—fascism might be the immediate threat, but liberalism was the true enemy. Mounier and de Rougement were intellectuals of the Left (insofar as this distinction applied during the thirties), but what they were thinking was echoed on the intellectual Right. Jean-Pierre Maxence echoed their distaste for the mundane world of democratic France: "While most countries of Europe are being led towards greatness and adventure, our own leaders are inviting us to transform France into an insurance company."[5] All in all, the sensibility of the contemporary intellectual when faced with the condition of France was thus very much that of Drieu la Rochelle (an author admired on Left and Right alike): "The only way to love France today is to hate it in its present form."[6]

Separated as we are from the world of the thirties by the barrier of war and collaboration, it is easy to underestimate the importance and appeal of the intellectual Right at the time. Political weeklies like *Candide* (339,000 copies sold at its peak) had a wide audience. The daily *Action française* published 100,000 copies and had a much wider audience than that number would suggest. Indeed, the influence of Charles Maurras, the founder and guiding spirit of *Action française*, was immense, comparable in its impact on contemporary young intellectuals to that of Sartre a decade later. Maurras's particular contribution to contemporary alienation from the Republic lay in "his violent and contemptuous attitude towards his opponents,"[7] which formed a generation of writers in whom an aggressive distaste for the compromises of democratic politics became a commonplace. Like the Communist party of the postwar years, Maurras and his movement constituted a sort of revolving door through which passed a surprising number of writers afterwards associated with quite different political positions. Jean-Marie Domenach, a contributor to *Esprit* and later its editor, would admit some twenty years later to having been affected (albeit, as he put it, in "an intense, childish way") by the fascist mood of the thirties, and he was far from alone.[8]

5. J. P. Maxence in *Combat*, October 1936. Quoted by G. Leroy, "La Revue *Combat*, 1936–1939," in *Des années trente: Groupes et ruptures*, Actes du colloque organisé par l'antenne de l'URL, no. 5, University of Provence 1, 5–7 May 1983 (Paris, 1985): 129.

6. See Drieu la Rochelle in *Combat*, April 1937. See also Emmanuel Mounier, reviewing *Gilles* in *Esprit*, April 1940; "La France d'avant-guerre avait besoin de muscles et d'un peu de sauvagerie," quoted by Michel Winock in *Nationalisme, anti-sémitisme, et fascisme en France* (Paris, 1990), 371.

7. Julien Benda, *Belphégor: Essai sur l'esthétique de la société française dans la première moitié du vingtième siècle* (Paris, 1947), 209.

8. Thus Jean-Marie Domenach: "J'ai vécu, de 1934 à 1939, d'une manière enfantine et intense, la vague fasciste qui secouait alors l'Europe," quoted from an interview with *L'Express*

The gleeful *schadenfreude* with which right-wing intellectuals would greet France's downfall in 1940 was echoed in muted form in the feelings of people who were themselves by no means on the Right. For many Catholics, who took no responsibility for the deeds and misfortunes of a republican political system that had devoted time and effort to expelling them from its midst, 1940 was at best a well-merited tragedy, if not a punishment for the sins of the past three generations. But even for their erstwhile opponents the event also had redeeming dimensions, an apocalypse half-welcomed, deliverance through catastrophe from a political and moral system they could no longer defend. Left and Right alike felt a distaste for the lukewarm and were fascinated by the idea of a violent relief from mediocrity.[9] Robert Brasillach, who was to be executed at the Liberation as the symbol of intellectual collaboration and who in the thirties wrote pointed, often scabrous columns for extreme right-wing papers, frequently expressed his reluctant admiration for the hard Left. Himself drawn to fascism, he could appreciate the appeal of Moscow to his opponents; as he would note, reflecting on the experience of the interwar years from the perspective of 1940: "It was a time when everyone looked to foreign countries, seeking there . . . warnings and examples."[10] The disaffected, antibourgeois tone of the reactionary intellectual echoed and sometimes even inspired that of progressive contemporaries: the "nausea" of Drieu's *Gilles* at the prospect of France's old ruling class has more than a little in common with that of Sartre's Roquentin.

This crossing of the lines, the intersection at the extremes of radical sentiments from Left and Right, did not begin with the thirties. Proudhon and Péguy were icons for the syndical Left and the neo-monarchist Right alike because they had addressed, in their very different ways, the limitations and frustrations of parliamentary republicanism that had occupied the thoughts of earlier generations as well.[11] It was in the 1920s that Georges Valois had unsuccessfully attempted a combination of nationalism and socialism in a movement to be devoted to attacking individualism, liberalism, and the parliamentary regime, and among those who

in 1959. See Eric Werner, *De la violence au totalitarisme: Essai sur la pensée de Camus et de Sartre* (Paris, 1972), 41, n. 1.

9. Claude Roy, *Moi, Je* (Paris, 1969), 215.

10. Robert Brasillach, *Notre avant-guerre* (Paris, 1941), 204.

11. Ibid., 163.

had initially been attracted was Paul Nizan. Even before World War I Édouard Berth (in *Les Méfaits des intellectuels*) had proposed something similar, a union of Left and Right against democracy and "for the salvation of the modern world and the grandeur of our Latin humanity."[12] The difference after 1932 was that a new generation of intellectuals adopted these vague ideas and tried to give them tangible form and programmatic content.

This generation has now been consecrated in the historical literature as that of the "nonconformists" of the thirties, representing a special mood and outlook.[13] Just how new or original it really was is perhaps open to question—Nizan, by then a committed Marxist, described it as a middle-class elite, distilling half-understood "thick foreign philosophical currents."[14] But however superficial its contribution to political or philosophical speculation, it most assuredly shared a common sense of the need for renewal and expressed a widely held longing for something new and confident. Between 1930 and 1934 there appeared a steady flow of books, pamphlets, clubs, plans, journals, and circles, all peopled by men and women in their twenties and thirties; some came from the political Right, others from the Left (like the *Révolution constructive* and *Plan* groups within the Socialist party and the Confédération générale du travail), though most made a point of asserting their indifference to existing political divisions and organizations. Few of these movements and periodicals survived the early thirties (*Esprit* is the most important exception), and much of what they published neither deserved nor acquired a wide audience. There were also important distinctions among them (not always clearly seen at the time): Mounier and his circle sought to construct a new morality, antibourgeois and spiritually refreshed, while others saw capitalism as the problem and worked to devise alternative social and economic programs for national renewal. What they shared, however, was what François Mauriac (in a different context) called "an idea at once just and tainted":[15] the nation was in a parlous condition and only wholesale change could save it. This condition of France was taken to include, and in part to derive from, its republican and democratic forms, its emphasis on the rights of the individual at the expense of the duties

12. Quoted in Winock, *Nationalisme, anti-sémitisme, et fascisme,* 252.
13. See Jean-Louis Loubet del Bayle, *Les Non-conformistes des années 30* (Paris, 1969).
14. Nizan, quoted in Hellman, *Emmanuel Mounier,* 73.
15. According to Mauriac, Drieu, like others, "sentaient vivement que le concept de nation, au sens étroit que les Jacobins français lui donnaient, était atteint." *Journal,* vol. 4 (Paris, 1950), 25 September 1945.

and interests of the community. Hence the ease of communication across traditional political barriers and hence, too, a certain ambivalence in the face of antidemocratic challenges, at home and abroad.

These challenges only surfaced openly in the wake of the events of 6 February 1934, for many young intellectuals on Left and Right the moment at which their aesthetic and philosophical leanings were shaped into political commitment. With the Popular Front of 1936 there came a further exercise in sentimental education, the moment at which those of the Right parted company definitively from the "socialist and Jewish" Republic. On the Left there was a momentary truce, as many of the "nonconformists" of the early thirties placed their hopes in the promise of radical social transformation from above. With the failures of Blum's government and its heirs there came a renewed alienation from republican politics, this time definitive. By 1938, the common sentiment of French intellectuals is described (and echoed) in Arthur Koestler's characteristically disabused commentary: "What an enormous longing for a new human order there was in the era between the two wars, and what a miserable failure to live up to it."[16]

The end of the thirties was marked, furthermore, by the growing significance of pacifism.[17] From the early twenties, the desire for a secure peace had marked the whole of the French community, exhausted and drained by its "victory" in the war and collectively sensitive to Paul Valéry's famous rumination on the fragility of civilizations. The intellectual community of the 1920s expressed its war-weariness most forcibly in a collective retreat from political affiliation, but even those on the Right or Left who remained politically involved shared a universal longing for an end to military involvement. The Right sought to achieve this through the illusory strength of the French armed forces, the Left through the hunt for collective security. Indeed, writing in the late twenties, Albert Thibaudet remarked, "Today one could say that 'socialism equals the search for peace.' One is a Socialist by virtue of the priority given to this problem over all others."[18] But by the thirties, lines that had once been clear were again blurred. The Communists, until 1935 adamantly opposed to any form of national defense, were from then until August 1939 the most ardent and consistent proponents of antifas-

16. Arthur Koestler, *The Yogi and the Commissar* (New York, 1945), 102.

17. See, notably, Antoine Prost, *Les Anciens Combattants et la société française, 1914–1939*, 3 vols. (Paris, 1977). See also André Delmas, *À gauche de la barricade* (Paris, 1950).

18. Albert Thibaudet, *Les Idées politiques en France* (Paris, 1927), 203.

cism (before joining the integral pacifists once again in their opposition to any "capitalist" war). The Right, while remaining in principle as Germanophobic as ever, was confused in its allegiance by a sympathy for Hitler's Italian ally and by a virulent hatred of the post-1936 Republic, led by outsiders with interests of their own that risked embroiling France in a war she did not need. Most intellectuals, like the political parties of the center-left, were cruelly divided. Some, the followers of Alain or heirs to an older socialist emphasis on antimilitarism, moved from anti-Fascist committees into unconditional opposition to war at any cost. Others, a small minority, shared Raymond Aron's precocious understanding of the nature of Nazism and the way in which Hitler's accession to power had altogether changed the terms of political choice.[19] And a considerable number found themselves somewhere in between: witness the paradoxical condition of a Bertrand de Jouvenel—half-Jewish, a friend of Blum's and against the Munich compromise but a member in 1936 of the neo-Fascist Parti populaire français and attracted by the theme and appeal of order and stability.[20]

These intertwined and contradictory positions, adopted by various people or by the same people at different times, often in the midst of confusion and moral uncertainty (Blum's famous "cowardly relief" at the news of Munich was probably typical of many), are inadequately captured in the notion of *commitment* or the opposition between democratic and undemocratic affiliation. Certainly, *commitment*, or *engagement*, was the term of choice for many contemporaries. But it fails to distinguish between Left and Right—or else, when making the distinction, exaggerates it. More to the point, it implies a discontinuity between the active engaged intellectual of the early and mid-thirties and the apparently disillusioned, disengaged cynical stance of all but a few in 1940. What is lost here is the idea of engagement as an end in itself—the notion, common to intellectuals of the 1930s and 1940s alike, that there was some sort of existential imperative to be involved; the specific direction of that involvement was less important—in politics as in battle, "on s'engage et puis on voit." Moreover, the emphasis on engagement versus disengagement fails to catch the continuing commitment of intellectuals in 1940 and after, as we shall see. But whatever the nature of that engage-

19. Étiemble, too, was tempted to follow Drieu, sharing his scorn for Left and Right alike, but was fortunate enough to be disenchanted by Hitler and Munich. See Étiemble, *Littérature dégagée, 1942–1953* (Paris, 1955), 193. See also Jean-François Sirinelli, *Génération intellectuelle* (Paris, 1988), 640.

20. See Bertrand de Jouvenel, *Un Voyageur dans le siècle* (Paris, 1979).

ment, it was not committed, and had for some time not been committed, to the democratic Republic.

The uncertainties and variations in intellectual life during the thirties also help explain the relative unimportance of the Communist intellectual. In marked contrast with what was to come, communism did not yet exercise an irresistible charm for the thinking classes. Like fascism, Soviet communism's strongest suit was its condemnation of bourgeois society, in its rhetoric and in its actions; indeed, then as for decades to come, Communist rhetoric was suffused with just that concern with corruption, decay, and renewal that colored the writings of the thirties "nonconformist" intellectuals. But its practical positive appeal was still limited:

The intellectual leans toward communism because he smells the scent of death hanging over the bourgeoisie and because capitalist tyranny exasperates him. . . . But Communism then requires of him that he subscribe to a program and methods that seem to him respectively stupid and ineffective.[21]

With the withering away of the Popular Front, the Communist party and its syndicalist allies lost much of their recently acquired mass support, to the point of being little better off at the outbreak of war than they had been in 1934. Out of tune with the pacifist sentiments of the nation in 1938 and 1939, accused by former supporters like André Gide of having hidden the truth about the Soviet Union,[22] embarrassed by the Moscow show trials, and alienated from a radical intellectual constituency by their very moderation during the Popular Front years, the French Communists by 1940 exercised little appeal for most intellectuals. Although some came to the party's defense during its persecution by Daladier in the *drôle de guerre*, the *volte-face* that precipitated this official harassment of the Parti Communiste français (PCF) not only lost the party most of its remaining support but alienated it from some of its most influential intellectual adherents. Had men like Paul Nizan and Gabriel Péri not been killed in the war and Occupation, they might well have returned to haunt the PCF in its postwar bid for cultural hegemony.

The dramatic events of 1940 thus found a French intellectual community in a political disarray symptomatic and reflective of the social and physical disarray of the nation itself. Even those who remained faithful to

21. Emmanuel Berl, *Mort de la pensée bourgeoise* (1929; reprint Paris, 1970), 97–98.
22. André Gide, *Retour de l'URSS* (Paris, 1936).

the Republic would be so shaken by the events of that year that they would be driven to reflect on the disaster, finding in it evidence of a corruption and decay they had not previously understood.[23] It is worth noting that among those who did remain loyal, who were ostensibly immune to the mood of the thirties, were a disproportionate number of intellectuals from an older generation. Those on the left who had come of age at the time of the Dreyfus Affair retained a loyalty to republicanism in its classic shape, whatever their growing criticisms of the practice of politics in Republican France. The younger generation, the one for whom it was war, not the defense of the rights of man, that had been the formative moment in the collective experience, was much more likely to prove sensitive to the appeal of pacifism and/or fascism.[24] This is a point of some significance, not so much for the thirties themselves as for what would follow. For not only was Vichy initially appealing to many in this younger generation, but it was this same cohort that emerged after 1944 as the dominant group within the intellectual community. Born between the turn of the century and 1913, they lacked any collective experience of successful democratic politics. They had also never had the occasion to unite, in good faith and with clear conscience, in defense of democracy and rights. All their political experience consisted of *opposition* and disaffection.

1940, then, marks not so much a break between a democratic and an authoritarian regime as the consummation of a process of moral decline and cultural alienation shared by many and articulated by a new generation of intellectuals in the last decade of the Republic. For many, Hitler's lightning victory constituted the verdict of history, a judgment upon the inadequacy and mediocrity of contemporary France, much as Stalingrad would later be seen as history's (positive) verdict upon communism. Many past and future democrats shared the view that, though hardly a "divine surprise," the accession of Pétain and his "National Revolution" provided an opportunity to begin the reconstruction of the nation along lines drafted in the course of the debates of the 1930s. Henri Massis, an intellectual of impeccable conservative credentials, could have been speaking for many from all points on the spectrum when he wrote in December 1940 that the task now was to deliver the French from "the appalling abuse of trust to which they have fallen victim; it will be neces-

23. See Léon Blum, *À l'échelle humaine* (Paris, 1945); and Marc Bloch, *L'Étrange Défaite* (Paris, 1946).
24. See Sirinelli, *Génération intellectuelle,* 463ff.

sary to re-learn how to use words truthfully, to restore to them their meaning and their value."[25]

If it is true, as Albert Camus noted in October 1944 that "a world ended" in June 1940, it should not be supposed, therefore, that this was a source of regret to many.[26] This is not, however, something one can easily discover from the memoir literature that deals with this period. Those who would go on to collaborate or abstain from public life are naturally inclined to minimize the pleasure they felt at the overthrow of the Republic, even though for many of them the war with Germany had been but an interlude in the much longer and more important conflict between the French. But the memoirs of those who had the good fortune to emerge on the victorious side in 1944 are not much better. There is something fundamentally disingenuous about Claude Roy's suggestion, for example, that he lived the years 1935–39, ideologically speaking, as an "insomniac" trying to find a comfortable spot in bed.[27] He may have sensed that his true home did not lie with the men of *Action française* and *Je suis partout* with whom he was then sharing column space; later he would have the same experience with his new Communist friends. But uncomfortable or not, it is odd that his three-volume memoirs offer little echo of the enthusiasm with which his fellow right-wing intellectuals greeted the ignominious collapse of the Republic. Others among his contemporaries slide across the space between the collapse of France and the establishment of the Resistance some years later with similarly selective recollections.

This is an understandable human response to complicated and contradictory experience. But for the historian it leaves the moment of 1940 in shadow. This is in part the result of treating the events of the spring and summer of 1940 as the beginning of Vichy, the Occupation, and (by extension) the Resistance. On the contrary, they are best seen as the closing sequence in the intellectual adventure of the interwar decades, an experience composed of various shades of hope—positive, negative, forlorn, and ultimately lost. Intellectuals who had made a career out of describing and condemning the inadequacies of the Republic came face to face in 1940 with the fulfillment of their earlier demands for its overthrow. It is not really surprising that most of them, once they got over

25. Henri Massis, *Au long d'une vie* (Paris, 1967), 149. The passage quoted was written at Uriage in December 1940.

26. Albert Camus, in *Combat,* 7 October 1944.

27. Roy, *Moi, Je,* 21.

the shock of the defeat itself, saw in the National Revolution some hope for the future. This was especially and predictably the case for those who, during the early thirties, had espoused ideas about central planning, social organicism, new moral orders, and an end to divisive emphasis on the individual. To take a stand against Pétain at this early stage would not only have required considerable foresight, not to speak of courage; it would also have meant a willingness to defend, albeit in some modified form, the very values with which the deceased Republic had been associated.

That was not an attitude widely found in France at this time among any group of the population, and there is no reason why it should have prevailed to any greater extent among intellectuals. If "a certain number of Frenchmen were already weary by 1940," there is no reason to exempt the intelligentsia.[28] To understand the impact of the years 1940–44 upon French intellectuals, it is thus important to have in mind the point of departure for that experience, which shaped the terms in which Vichy, the Resistance, and the postwar revolution would be understood. With respect to liberalism, democracy, the rights of man, and the heritage of republicanism, it was very, very difficult in 1940 to imagine, much less proclaim, a case for the defense. What was missing was a commonly agreed-upon language in which to express and advocate such matters. The very men and women who might now have undertaken the task of rebuilding an ethos of democratic politics were in no position to do so for purely practical reasons. But that would pass. What endured, and colored so much that followed, was the sense of being politically inarticulate, of having been deprived—of having deprived oneself—of the ideological and linguistic means with which to construct a morally defensible polity. It has been charged against the writers and thinkers of the 1930s that their arguments, directed against the prevailing regimes, offered no guidance to others on how to react to political or moral dilemmas—the rise of Hitler, the crisis of appeasement, the advent of Vichy. This is true, but perhaps a little beside the point. The real problem was that these intellectuals provided no such guidance to themselves.

28. Camus, *Combat,* 7 October 1944.

CHAPTER TWO

In the Light of Experience
The "Lessons" of Defeat and Occupation

En somme, nous avons appris l'Histoire et nous prétendons qu'il ne faut pas l'oublier.

In sum, we have discovered History and we claim that it must not be forgotten.

Maurice Merleau-Ponty

The experience of occupation and resistance in the years 1940–44 transformed the French intellectual community and accelerated the transfer of status and authority within it. An older generation, already thinned out by the first war, saw its ranks further diminished as a result of collaboration, deportation, and death. There were, to be sure, certain notable exceptions. François Mauriac and Jean Paulhan, central figures in the French literary community well before the thirties, would be prominent in the postwar intellectual and political world for a decade at least. Georges Bernanos, although he would never recover either his style or his influence of earlier days, nonetheless cut a distinctive figure in the polemics of the forties, following his return from wartime exile. But others—Gide, Maurras, and their contemporaries—had now been passed over, their place occupied by a new generation with very different sensibilities. This should not be taken to imply that the older authorities were no longer being read (as late as 1953, André Malraux was still the preferred reading of the students at the École Normale Supérieure),[1] but theirs was no longer the dominant *public* voice; they no longer set the terms of intellectual communication.

There are limits to such generational distinctions. Malraux, after all, was born only four years before Sartre, Aron, and Mounier, the new generation of which I am writing. But he, despite his relative youth, was as much a prewar figure as writers twenty years his senior; he had been active in the political battles of the thirties, a literary giant even before the young "nonconformists" had taken central stage. Thus, World War II for Malraux represented no political or moral awakening—indeed, he sat it out for the most part in comfort and safety on the Côte d'Azur, entering the active resistance at a relatively late date.[2] Above all, Malraux, who had passed through a philo-Communist stage in the mid-1930s, was not only not tempted by the revolutionary possibilities of the postwar era but was from the outset a committed supporter of de Gaulle. This alone, despite his continuing literary audience, would place him a little to the side of the mainstream intellectual world, at least until the end of the forties, after which he would be joined, though for reasons of their own, by men like Raymond Aron and later still François Mauriac.

The unusually rapid transfer of intellectual authority from one generation to another is a frequent consequence of war, since war not only kills people but also changes the direction of public taste and concern. Something comparable had taken place after the Franco-Prussian war and again after World War I, and after World War II France was far from unique in seeing the emergence of a new and younger cultural leadership; in Poland and Hungary, for example, not only the intellectual but also the political world, decimated by the Nazis, was occupied by new, youthful activists. Indeed it was they who were largely responsible for the initial enthusiasm with which communism and thoroughgoing social revolution were welcomed in their countries.[3] Any account,

1. Pierre Bandet, in *La Revue de Paris,* March 1953, quoted by Jean-François Sirinelli, "Les Normaliens de la rue d'Ulm après 1945: Une Génération communiste?" *Revue d'histoire moderne et contemporaine* 33 (October–December 1986): 586, n. 71.

2. See the jaundiced views of Clara Malraux, *Le Bruit de nos pas,* vol. 6, *Et pourtant j'étais libre* (Paris, 1979).

3. For example, Geza Losonczy was twenty-eight years old at the Liberation and was already an experienced senior politician in Hungary by the time he was killed for his part

then, of the postwar formation and shape of an intellectual community, in France as elsewhere, must begin in 1940.

It is not always easy to distinguish in the biographies of prominent postwar figures the precise circumstances or motives that impelled them to take a particular political or philosophical stance. Writing from the vantage point of 1945 and beyond, they often collapsed the years 1940–44 into a single experience. Placed in the path of history by the impact of combat, prison, German occupation, and intellectual or physical resistance, they recognized at the Liberation that their prewar concerns, notably those that had kept them aside from political engagement or public action, could no longer be recaptured. For some, such as Jean-Paul Sartre and Maurice Merleau-Ponty, this was a philosophical insight before it became a political choice; for others, like Mounier and his fellow Catholics, it was—or seemed to be—a natural extension of their earlier spiritual critique of interwar society. What few were willing to admit was that this lesson had been learned, not in 1940, but only in the course of the years that followed. Not only did the intellectual resistance and the accompanying historical self-consciousness, so much in evidence in 1945, *not* begin in 1940, but the fall of the Third Republic was in fact followed by a brief but important period of illusion and even optimism.

Those who sought to recover something positive from the defeat of France had first to give the new order a meaning beyond that imposed on it by German force. The events of 1940 had to be recast as an occasion to transcend old divisions, to remake France, and not simply as an opportunity for revenge on the defeated Republic. With a greater or lesser degree of good faith, this is how pro-Vichy intellectuals of the nonfascist variety presented to themselves the opportunity of 1940, and it helps explain why men who would later join the intellectual resistance to Pétain and the Germans were at first swept along by the fantasy.

The best, because best-intentioned, example of the ambivalence that characterized initial responses to defeat can be found in the brief experiment at Uriage. The outlines of this first French attempt to establish a training ground for a new moral and political elite are well known.[4] The group that came together in the autumn of 1940 with the ambition of building a new and exemplary community, something halfway between

---

in Imre Nagy's government. See Anna Losonczy, interviewed by Pierre Kende in *Nouvelle Alternative*, 11 September 1988.

4. See Pierre Bitoun, *Les Hommes d'Uriage* (Paris, 1988).

a scout camp and a *grande école,* carried distinctive echoes of ideas and attitudes of the early 1930s. It was dominated by a younger generation of Catholics—soldiers, scholars, and teachers—and gave priority in its lectures and daily activities to ideas of responsibility, hierarchy, and national renewal. The emphasis on a specifically Christian renewal was accompanied, as it had been a decade earlier, by a markedly critical attitude towards the bourgeoisie and the late unlamented "bourgeois" Republic. Mounier and other writers from *Esprit* were prominent among the early lecturers, but also present was a new group from whom would emerge important public figures in the Fourth and Fifth Republics, including Hubert Beuve-Méry, the founder and first editor of *Le Monde,* who would later bring to his new publication some of the ideals and quite a lot of the sanctimonious confidence of the Uriage community.

The ambivalent aspect of the Uriage experiment, which lasted little more than a year, lay in its acceptability to Vichy. Indeed, the new regime and the Uriage activists shared a symbiotic relationship. With the exception of the Communists, these left-wing Catholics (the description is slightly anachronistic but not inaccurate) constituted the only group with a clear social and cultural identity to survive 1940 in a recognizable form; indeed, there is a certain significance to the fact that both Mounier and the Communists sought official permission to continue printing their journal under the new regime—Mounier being accorded the right to do so. Although the growing insistence at Uriage on themes of freedom and morality eventually brought it into conflict with the Vichy authorities, the early concern with a remaking of the national soul echoed the language of the National Revolution. Mounier's rather Delphic concept of "personalism" favored values—like service, leadership, efficiency, and community—which some prominent officials around Pétain sought genuinely to apply to French public life.[5]

Moreover, this sort of language also addressed a parallel sensibility within the secular community and even within the political Left. Léon Blum, after all, had similar criticisms to offer of the spiritual shortcomings of the Third Republic and his own and his party's role within it: one of the themes of *À l'échelle humaine* was the need for a liberated France to give itself a stronger executive power, to rid itself of the traditional distaste for control and direction that had undermined Republican government. The representative institutions of the bourgeois republic had failed the nation, Blum would write, and his views were shared by a

5. See Gérard Lurol, *Mounier I: Genèse de la personne* (Paris, 1990).

goodly number of younger Socialist intellectuals who emerged in the Resistance.[6] Thus the Uriage group spoke to a widespread sentiment and might be said to have combined for a brief period the concerns of the Left within the National Revolution and the moderates of the nascent intellectual resistance. This point is captured symbolically in the reading matter favored by the leadership at Uriage, which ranged from Proudhon to Maurras but took in Marx, Nietzsche, and Péguy, among others, along the way. Any and all critiques of bourgeois materialism were welcomed, while democracy in all its parliamentary forms was a source of steady condemnation and ridicule.[7]

Where the intellectuals at Uriage eventually parted company from the Vichy regime was in the latter's increasingly collaborative stance and the growing evidence that the National Revolution was at best an illusion, more likely and increasingly a cynical facade for persecution, dictatorship, and revenge. But it is important to note that the illusion of finding a third way between fascism and liberal democracy was *not* abandoned. As late as February 1941, by which time articles in *Esprit* were already being heavily censored and some of the original Uriage activists had gone underground, Emmanuel Mounier was attacking the newly formed Christian Democrats (that Catholic element within the Resistance that would eventually coalesce into the Mouvement républicain populaire— MRP) for their overemphasis on democracy. Placing the "defense of democracy" at the masthead of opposition and renewal was, he wrote in a letter, "uncreative" and inflexible.[8] From then until his death in 1950, Mounier would remain suspicious and critical of the MRP and its ideals, preferring to retain the high ground of moral renewal rather than descend to the level of democratic political struggle, with all that this implied about a return to the ways of the Republic.

For Mounier's non-Catholic contemporaries the early Vichy experience offered less hope of change or national rebirth, but they did share with the men of Uriage the sense that 1940 had changed the rules of the game. Before 1940, even the most engaged intellectuals could see themselves as isolated actors, making private choices and expressing preferences and objectives that were theirs alone and that they were free to adopt or abandon at will. The very relationship between writing and action had hitherto been fortuitous—only rarely, as with Malraux or

6. See Blum, *À l'échelle humaine* (Paris, 1945).

7. See Janine Bourdin, "Des intellectuels à la recherche d'un style de vie: L'École nationale des cadres d'Uriage," *Revue française de science politique* 4 (December 1959): 1041.

8. See Mounier, "Lettre à Étienne Borne," 22 February 1941, in *Oeuvres,* vol. 4 (Paris, 1961–63), 694–95.

Antoine de Saint-Exupéry, were writers living, or appearing to live, the demands of their literary creations. With the defeat of France all this changed. Writers and artists were no longer free to say, publish, or perform whatever they wished. They risked, always in theory and often in practice, persecution and punishment for their ideas. Many of them were brought face to face for the first time with the need to think through the relationship between their private thoughts and their public lives; in the midst of a humiliating national tragedy, even the most solitary writers could not help but feel affected by the fate of the community.[9]

It does not follow that the shape of intellectual life in wartime France was constantly colored by real dangers and the sort of clarity such dangers can bring to even the most clouded mind. Only a few of the men and women who are the subject of this book were ever exposed to real risks during this period; indeed, those who went to the most trouble to theorize this situation tended to be the ones whose position was least exposed and whose careers were least affected. But this does not diminish the significance of their interpretation of the times. What Sartre in 1945 would call being "situated in one's times" was something all could feel. Whatever was now going to happen would in a sense be their responsibility, especially if they chose to abstain from choice by pretending to an irresponsibility that no longer existed.[10] It is not clear just how much intellectuals actually felt "suddenly situated" from the very start, but even if it is an *ex post facto* account of their condition it is not for that reason false.[11]

Being a part of History—having no choice but to respond to your circumstances and take charge of them—meant breaking with the aesthetic impulse of some thirties intellectuals to be "wherever the crowd isn't,"[12] and it meant taking seriously the idea of evil, the possibility that human existence might hang in the moral balance and must be defended and reclaimed. Once again, it should not be supposed that no one had thought of this before 1940,[13] but as we have seen, the intellectual

9. See, for example, Raymond Aron, *France libre* (London), 15 June 1941.

10. "Jamais nous n'avons été plus libre que sous l'occupation allemande," Jean-Paul Sartre, *Les Lettres françaises*, 9 September 1944; see also Simone de Beauvoir, "Oeil pour oeil," *Les Temps modernes* 5 (February 1946), especially 814ff.

11. In *Qu'est-ce que la littérature?* Sartre writes of having had his eyes opened by the crisis of 1938—"du coup nous nous sentîmes brusquement situés." This seems a little doubtful. See *Situations,* vol. 2 (Paris, 1948): 242–43.

12. See Drieu la Rochelle, "Récit secret," quoted by Louis Bodin in *Les Intellectuels* (Paris, 1964), 70.

13. According to J-M Besnier, *La Politique de l'impossible* (Paris, 1988), Georges Bataille at least did not need Hitler and the impact of his war to awaken him to the existence of evil. See p. 234.

ethos of the late thirties precluded the sort of ethically grounded political defense of freedom (at least in the republican form in which the French had hitherto conceived of it) that such a stance might entail. After the fall of France, however, and especially after 1942, when excuses for collaboration or compromise became harder to find, intellectuals would find themselves discovering in the very act of political disobedience the freedom they would later defend. The dilemma between "being" and "doing," which had seemed so significant before the war, collapsed. To do was to be: no longer a universal consciousness vested in a singular self, the intellectual was bound within the organic community and there presented with apparently simple choices, all of which entailed action of one sort or another.[14] Being part of the common purpose, accepting as one's own the meaning given to a collective action, offered certainty in place of doubt: the intellectual resister took on a mantle of confidence and shed the cloak of insecurity that had shrouded the previous generation.[15]

Why did some intellectuals find this confidence and others not? For some people, the explanation lies in their disillusion with the initial expectations placed in Vichy; others never harbored illusions in the first place but could only be brought to defend what became the values of the resistance once they had recovered from the shock of defeat and had been sufficiently moved to protest the policies and practices of occupiers and collaborators alike. A third category, which should include men such as Merleau-Ponty and Sartre, seem to have been waiting for some such moment all their lives, so enthusiastically did they welcome the chance to be part of a romantic commitment whose scope and meaning would transcend, transform, and give practical effect to their earlier writings. The chance was welcomed mostly in theory, however; in practice only a minority of intellectual resisters saw real action of any sustained sort, whether in the Free French armies, the armed resistance, or clandestine networks of all kinds. For most of the rest, it was the association with the community of resisters that counted, the sense of being part of something larger than oneself—a circle of dissenting writers, a resistance group, a clandestine political organization, or History itself.

This sense of being part of something larger than oneself also had a politically radicalizing effect. In part this was the inevitable outcome of

14. Maurice Merleau-Ponty, "La Guerre a eu lieu," *Les Temps modernes* 1 (October 1945): 64.
15. See Merleau-Ponty's letter to the journal *Action* 74 (1 February 1946).

the one-sidedness of domestic resistance politics and the increasingly reactionary and repressive nature of government policy. With the passage of time, and at an accelerated pace after 1942, people forgot their dislike of the Republic and concentrated instead on the crimes and sins of the regime that had replaced it. In effect, the French had now been engaged in a civil war that by 1944 had lasted eight years, and the participants on the winning side were led by the force of their own experience to rethink their commitments and state them in ever starker forms. The absence of any possibility of compromise (and, later, of any need for it) encouraged the emergence of a political and moral vocabulary keyed to absolutes— the absolute defeat of one's adversaries, the nonnegotiable demands of one's own side. Once it had become clear that there was nothing to be retrieved from the Vichy experience, resistance intellectuals of every kind devoted their attention instead to constructing the future, taking it as given that one began with a tabula rasa.

Curiously, this did not mean abandoning once and for all the Republican past, since the national political imagination and contemporary circumstances offered few alternative sources for a rethinking of France. On the contrary, the lost illusions of 1940 helped cast the once-despised Third Republic in a better light. True, as Camus put it in August 1944, the Resistance had not made so many sacrifices only to resume the bad habits of a country "which had been preoccupied so long with the morose contemplation of its own past." That past, the France of Monsieur Herriot, of boutiques, *bureaux de tabac,* and "legislative banquets, a France without obligations or sanctions," which had made of the words *député* and *gouvernement* symbols of derision, was gone and should not be revived.[16] But, as an anonymous editorialist noted in the clandestine journal *Après,* published in Toulouse, "A few years of the French State and the Vichy dictatorship will have sufficed to endear the Republic to those who had no love for her in the past."[17] Compared with what one had just seen, heard, and experienced, the Republic did not look so bad.[18]

16. Albert Camus, *Combat,* 24 August 1944.

17. See Camus, *Combat,* 27 June 1945, and the editorial in *Après* 2 (July 1943), quoted by Henri Michel and Boris Mirkine-Guetzévitch, *Les Idées politiques et sociales de la Résistance* (Paris, 1954), 87.

18. François Mauriac, on 15 March 1945, commented with reference to "nos anciens adversaires" and their incurable phobias: "La haine de la démocratie, une peur animale, une peur viscérale du communisme, l'attachement aux privilèges de l'argent et aux régimes qui mettent la force brutale au service de ces privilèges, l'injustice à l'égard de la classe ouvrière." See *Journal,* vol. 4 (Paris, 1950).

Intellectuals who had identified with the Resistance, then, emerged from the war years with an oddly paradoxical sense of themselves and their purpose. In the first place, the experience was of interest and value to them precisely to the extent that it denied the previous isolation of the intellectual condition and merged it with the actions and movement of a whole society. Yet at the same time their engagement on the side of a historical movement as intellectuals bequeathed to them a special sense of duty, the obligation to articulate and pursue what they understood to be the lessons of the war years, both in politics and in their own professional activities as responsible intellectuals. Second, they had undergone a political radicalization very unlike that of the thirties, since it was shorn of ambiguity and ulterior motive, and yet the local form of political life to which that radicalization now committed them resembled the same Third Republic that most of them had shunned just a few years earlier—the continuity with the Third Republic accentuated by de Gaulle's insistence on treating the Vichy regime as nothing more than an illegitimate interlude. The years of resistance and clandestinity (for some) had obscured these paradoxes, but they would emerge with embarrassing clarity as soon as the war was over.

Superficially, Resistance-era intellectuals were divided in many ways. On the one hand there were the Catholics, themselves split along political lines and also by generation: the intellectual and cultural gulf separating François Mauriac from the *Esprit* circle, for example, was quite unbridgeable. Then there were the unattached intellectuals soon to be associated with Sartre and *Les Temps modernes*. Beyond these there were the "politicals"—Socialists, Communists, and Gaullists—beyond them an important if disparate group of intellectuals whose distinctive identity was formed in the Resistance itself, men like Claude Bourdet and Albert Camus. In practice, most of these people had experienced the Resistance years in one of two ways. If they had been part of the organized Communist or Gaullist movements, they inclined towards a collective view of the recent past, seeing the organizations and activities of the years 1940–44 as a paradigm for a better France. On the other hand, as individual resisters or as members of movements more loosely shaped (and often resolutely nonparty political), the rest tended rather to recall the war years as a sequence of *individual* choices, exemplary and binding upon themselves, but above all a private experience, lived in public. The implications of this distinction would be felt in later years in the uses to which wartime memory was put and the causes it could be made to serve.

There were, however, two aspects of the war years that were common to all. One of these was well expressed in a speech in 1945 by Albert Camus:

The hatred of the killers forged in response a hatred on the part of the victims. . . . The killers once gone, the French were left with a hatred partially shorn of its object. They still look at one another with a residue of anger.[19]

This seems to me a remarkably acute observation. The civil war did not come to an end in 1944; it simply lost its external targets and shape. In the writings of all French intellectuals of those years there lurks a hidden and half-admitted fury. It would be too easy to treat this as the redirection of self-hatred and insufficient to ascribe it to straightforward motives of resentment and revenge. Many of the angriest men and women may have been overcoming feelings of inadequacy: there was an occasional inverse correlation between the publicly stated desire for vengeance and any marked record of heroism or physical engagement; but they do seem to have been speaking, in their way, for the emotions of the nation. Pursuing a line of thought already characteristic of the later Third Republic and now shaped into a moral language by the struggle against Vichy, they divided all experience, all choices—indeed, all of humanity—into binary categories: good or evil, positive or negative, comrades or enemies. A natural and normal practice in time of war, this angry Manichaeanism continued to mark France long after the resolution of the conflict with Germany.[20]

Another universally shared sentiment was urgency. Urgency to join the winning side in 1944 ("so many were afraid, at that point, to miss the bus of history"), but also the desire to make up for lost time.[21] This was true at the personal level, with many intellectuals frenetically writing and publishing their way into a literary or journalistic career, and it is in large measure accounted for by the fact that most of the prominent figures of the intellectual community were still not much over thirty years of age. But it also marked the political and social thought of the day and the policies and positions derived from it. Having rediscovered their faith in certain truths (if not transcendent, at least self-evident), the French intelligentsia were in a collective hurry to see these applied. Once again

19. Camus, speech at La Mutualité, 15 March 1945, reprinted in Camus, *Actuelles*, vol. 1 (1950; reprint Paris, 1977), 116.

20. See Paul Wilkinson, *The Intellectual Resistance in Europe* (Cambridge, Mass., 1981), 265.

21. Pierre Emmanuel, "Les Oreilles du roi Midas," *Esprit*, December 1956, 781.

extrapolating from the Resistance years, the only experience of collective action most of them had ever known, unaffiliated intellectuals looked upon inaction as the worst of all options. Indeed, like the generation of the thirties, they saw revolution, in this case the continuation and completion of the experience and objectives of the Resistance, as the only solution, the only way to prevent France from slipping backwards. But unlike their predecessors, or in some cases themselves at an earlier stage, they were now in a position, if not to make a revolution, at least to impose upon their own society the language and symbolism of urgent and wholesale upheaval.

Curiously, the political ideas and programs of the Resistance itself were not notably revolutionary. Rather, they were implicitly radical in content and in the context of French social and political history, but they were expressed for the most part in remarkably mild language.[22] Some of them consisted of the continuation of the social program of the Popular Front, others proposed significant legal and political innovations, and some even sought to pursue and perfect certain administrative and institutional reforms inaugurated by Vichy itself. One can ascribe this low-key approach to the need for compromise between different political parties and movements, or to the search for a consensus around which to reunite a divided nation. Whatever the causes, the consequence was a series of proposals and ideas remarkably moderate in their overall tone. Most of the people speaking for the Resistance certainly saw the Liberation as an opportunity for dramatic economic changes, for more and better planning and socially controlled distribution of goods and services. But beyond that goal and vague calls for political "renewal" there was no consistent and clearly articulated Resistance vision.

One reason for this moderation was the desire to avoid overly programmatic designs: easily drawn up, as easily abandoned. François Mauriac probably spoke for many when he noted in August 1944, "We know all too well the uselessness of these panaceas, these hastily typed fantasy programs,"[23] even if his own rather exalted perspective took insufficient account of the practical problems facing the new governments. Perhaps even more representative is the opinion of Claude Bourdet, reflecting a few years later on the remarkably nonideological nature of the Resistance, in which he played an active part:

Clandestinity, and then prison, sharpened in most of us the sense of the certain collapse of a whole society . . . but they did not lead us to think in plans or schemas; the Resistance had learned to rely on a combination of voluntarism and empiricism: un-French approaches, but which had succeeded elsewhere.[24]

A further source of this moderation was the total concentration, at least in the internal Resistance, on fighting the enemy. A large part of the initial program of the Conseil national de la Résistance (CNR) was concerned with practical problems to be faced in the daily struggle, with longer-term solutions to France's chronic weaknesses to be addressed once the battle was won.[25] The Resistance, intellectuals and politicians alike, had no shared background experience, no common view of the future and its possibilities. The Resistance program was primarily a moral condition and a bond of experience and determination. Something better had to come from the sacrifices of the struggle, but the shape of that vision was left to individuals and political groups to articulate. If there was a general sentiment it was probably something along the lines of Camus's desire for "the simultaneous instauration of a collective economy and a liberal polity."[26]

In these circumstances, it might be thought, the wider hopes vested in the Resistance were doomed from the start. This may be so—certainly in France, as in Italy, the dream of a single all-embracing party of the Resistance, breaking old political allegiances and committed to nonpartisan national reconstruction, never really got off the ground. But even before the disillusion of 1945, political reality had intervened. It was in 1943 that Jean Moulin allowed (some would say encouraged) the reformation of political parties within the CNR, largely to appease those who resented the presence of Communist political networks in their midst. Thus the main organization of the Resistance fostered the reconstitution of the major parties of the defunct Republic, with the notable addition of the MRP. This return to party politics occasioned some comment and disapproval, but it was not until later, seeing the ease with which postwar France seemed to have slipped into the comfortable old

24. Claude Bourdet, in *L'Observateur,* 21 August 1952.
25. See Jacques Debû-Bridel, "La Quatrième République est-elle legitime?" in *Liberté de l'esprit,* October 1952, 220.
26. Camus, quoted by Jeanyves Guérin, *Camus et la politique* (Paris, 1986), 231.

clothes of its predecessor, that intellectuals directed criticism at the parliamentarians for betraying the ideals of a united national renaissance.[27]

Of all the newly reemergent political parties, it was the Communists whose appearance mattered the most for the intellectual community. This is not because the Communist party could count on a significant membership among the *haute intelligentsia*—quite the contrary: the impermeable, deathless commitment of an Aragon ("My Party has restored to me the meaning of the times / My Party has restored to me the colors of France") was only ever a minority taste. But for many younger intellectuals, not only had the party redeemed itself in action since 1941, but it represented in France, both symbolically and in the flesh, the transcendent power and glory of Stalin's Soviet Union, victorious in its titanic struggle with Nazi Germany, the unchallenged land power on the European continent and heir apparent to a prostrate Europe. A sense of having experienced the prelude to an apocalypse was widespread among those for whom the Occupation had been their formative political experience. Older left-wing intellectuals might vote Communist and even place their hopes in a Marxist future, but they could not wholly forget the Molotov-Ribbentrop Pact, nor even the troubling Soviet domestic record of the thirties. Younger ones, however, ignorant of the past or anxious to put it behind them, saw in the party a political movement responding to their own desire for progress, change, and upheaval.[28] Thus Pierre Emmanuel could write in 1956:

I dreamed of an ideal Communism through fear of real Communism, fascinated as I was, like so many others, by the imminent apocalypse rising out of the chasm into which Europe had just been swallowed up.[29]

It helped that communism asked of its sympathizers not that they think for themselves, merely that they accept the authority of others. For intellectuals who sought so passionately to melt into the community, communism's relative lack of interest in their own ideas was part of its appeal.

Moreover, and it was the most important part of the attraction, communism was about revolution. This was the source of some confusion: intellectuals dreamed of revolution in the immediate and in the abstract,

---

27. See Michel and Mirkine-Guetzévitch, *Les Idées politiques et sociales de la Résistance*, 33.
28. Jeannine Verdès-Leroux, *Au service du parti* (Paris, 1983), 100ff.
29. Emmanuel, "Les Oreilles du roi Midas," 781.

while Lenin's heirs dutifully maneuvered on the terrain of tactical practice, where revolution in the future could always justify passivity in the present. But these crossed purposes, even when conceded, had no impact upon the commitment of intellectuals to the idea of revolution itself, even if they led to occasional ingenuous criticisms of the PCF for its lack of insurrectionary fervor in the years 1945–47.

For most postwar French intellectuals, the term *revolution* contained three distinct meanings, none of which depended upon the Communists or their doctrine. In the first place, revolution, it seemed, was the natural and necessary outcome, the logical *terminus ad quem* of the hopes and allegiances of the wartime years. If France in 1945 was to go in any direction at all, it would only be propelled there by a revolution:

If we call ourselves revolutionaries, it is not just a matter of hot words or theatrical gestures. It is because an honest analysis of the French situation shows us it is revolutionary.[30]

We should not take too seriously Emmanuel Mounier's claim to have undertaken an "honest analysis" of the contemporary French situation, nor suppose him as free of "hot words" as he imagined. He had, after all, been proclaiming the need for "revolution" ever since 1932. But the difference in 1945 was that the cumulative experience of the defeat, Vichy, the horrors of occupation and deportation, the sacrifices of the Resistance, and the revelation of France's decline made it seem realistic to believe in a coming moment of catastrophic and total change, in a way that had not been the case before 1940. Not only could reasonable people now believe in the likelihood of utter collapse and destruction, but it seemed irrational to imagine that major change could be achieved in any other way. If French history from 1939–45 meant anything, it seemed to warn against believing in the possibility of progressive improvement and human benevolence.

Second, revolution meant order: in this respect intellectuals and Communists were in agreement. It had been a commonplace of the cultural critiques of the early thirties in France that capitalism and bourgeois society were a version of the Hobbesian vision of nature, a war of all against all in which the strong emerged victorious and all nonmaterial values were doomed. A new order was thus called for in the moral and the social realms alike. But disorder, after 1945, described not only the

30. Mounier in 1945, quoted in Anna Boschetti, *Sartre et "Les Temps modernes"* (Paris, 1985), 239.

unregulated mediocrity of the Third Republic but also the unjust and arbitrary authority of foreign and domestic fascist power. Order, in contrast, would be the condition of society after a revolution of a very particular sort, one deriving its political coordinates from the lessons of history and its moral imperatives from the recent experience of political struggle and engagement.

Third, and this was Sartre's special contribution though it expressed the views of many others at the time, revolution was a categorical imperative. It was not a matter of social analysis or political preference, nor was the moment of revolution something one could select on the basis of experience or information. It was an a priori existential requirement. Revolution would not only alter the world, it constituted the act of permanent re-creation of our collective situation as the subjects of our own lives. In short, action (of a revolutionary nature) is what sustains the authenticity of the individual. In the early postwar years Sartre, at that time still committed to his writing, would seek to deculpabilize himself and his social class for their intrinsic social marginality by claiming that writing *was* action. By revealing it transformed, and in transforming, it revolutionized its objects, a view that is seen at its most developed in *Qu'est-ce que la littérature?*[31] Later, of course, he would abandon this indirect approach and commit himself to direct action, or as direct as his personal limitations allowed.

The abstract and protean quality of revolution thus described meant not only that almost any circumstance could be judged propitious to it and any action favorable to its ends; it also meant that anything that qualified under the heading "revolutionary" was necessarily to be supported and defended. The Manichaean heritage of the Resistance did the rest—to be on the side of the good was to seek the revolution; to oppose it was to stand in the way of everything for which men and women had fought and died. Within France this reductionism could do relatively little damage, since the threat of real revolution after 1945 seemed to be ever diminishing. Thus it cost little to be for the revolution and was hardly worth the effort to be against it, in this abstract form. But elsewhere in Europe the impact of war and real revolution was still being felt, and there one's stance on the meaning of revolutionary language and acts really mattered.

This topic is central to the theme of the present book and it will be dealt with more fully in later chapters. But because the dream of revolu-

31. See Sartre, *Situations,* vol. 2.

tion was so pervasive in the discourse of postwar intellectuals, it is worth noting the moral price that was exacted. The case of Mounier is exemplary, precisely because he and his circle were not attached to any political movement, had few if any foreign entanglements, and represented in their own eyes a moral position purer than that of their contemporaries, beholden to no one and driven only by a wish for spiritual renewal and a love of truth and justice. Writing in 1944, Mounier urged on the French community a thoroughgoing spiritual and political revolution, whatever the cost. All revolutions, he wrote, are "full of ugliness"; the only question is, "Should the crisis come to a head, and if so as soon as possible?" We are engaged in radical upheaval, he insisted; we cannot go back now. As for a precipitous historical transformation, "the only way to neutralize its risks is to complete it." The French have the chance, he went on to suggest, to abolish human suffering and lay the basis for happiness and something more besides. This challenge cannot be met by a "parliamentary democracy of the liberal, chatty sort but . . . must be organically resolved by a real democracy, with firm structures."[32]

All this sounds harmless enough, a typical article of its time, combining an invocation of revolutionary possibilities with general political prescriptions drawing on the language of the thirties nonconformists. But buried just below the surface one can already detect the "omelet" thesis, the belief that a sufficiently important historical advance is worth the price we may have to pay to bring it about. Mounier stated this idea a little more openly in an article published two years later,[33] but it is rendered explicit in the editorial commentary published by *Esprit* on the occasion of the Prague coup in February 1948. Because this, the last Communist takeover in central Europe, made little pretense of representing the desires of the majority or of responding to some real or imagined national crisis, Mounier's response to it is illustrative of the moral price he was driven to pay in order to sustain his faith in the intrinsic value of revolutionary action. It is worth quoting at length:

In Czechoslovakia the coup masks a retreat of capitalism, the increase of workers' control, the beginnings of a division of landed property. There is nothing astonishing in the fact that it was not undertaken with all the ceremonial of a diplomatic move, nor that it is the work of a minority. None of this is unique to Communism: there is no regime in the world today or in history that did not

32. Mounier, "Suite française aux maladies infantiles des révolutions," *Esprit*, December 1944.

33. Mounier, "Débat à haute voix," *Esprit*, February 1946, 76–77.

begin with force, no progress that was not initiated by an audacious minority in the face of the instinctive laziness of the vast majority.

As to the victims of the Prague coup, the Czech socialists and their social-democratic allies, Mounier had no regrets. The social-democrats in particular he described as "saboteurs of the European Liberations." Their cause is lost, their fate richly deserved—"they belong to a dead Europe."[34]

Mounier and his colleagues on *Esprit* are significant precisely because they did not claim to share the Communists' worldview. But a revolution was a revolution, its goals *ex hypothesi* laudable, its enemies and victims in principle the servants of the past and the enemies of promise. One source of this favorable prejudice, and it is a point that has received wide attention in recent years, was the problematic status of the term *revolution* in the history of French political thought and language. One hundred and fifty years after Saint-Just, the rhetorical hegemony exercised by the Jacobin tradition had not only not diminished, but had taken from the experience of the Resistance a renewed vigor. The idea that revolution—*the* Revolution, any revolution—constitutes not only a dramatic break, the moment of discontinuity between past and future, but also the only possible route from the past to the future so pervaded and disfigured French political thought that it is hard to disentangle the idea from the language it has invested with its vocabulary and its symbols.

Thus it comes as no surprise that Mounier and his generation adopted such a vision and the venerable language that accompanied it. The disdain felt by Simone de Beauvoir, for example, at all mention of "reformism," her desire to see social change brought about in a single convulsive moment or else not at all, was a sentiment she shared not only with her contemporaries but with *fin-de-siècle* socialists, Commune-era feminists, and the Blanquist fringe of French socialist thought throughout the previous century.[35] As the last and most enduring of the myths of the Enlightenment, the idea that an intrinsically evil order could only be replaced by one founded on nature and reason, revolution was always likely to become a dominant passion of the intellectuals, in France as in Russia. The special quality of the postwar era was the

---

34. Mounier, "Prague" (editorial), *Esprit,* March 1948.

35. See de Beauvoir's comments throughout her writings from this period, notably in her memoirs, *La Force des choses* (Paris, 1963).

immediate possibility it seemed to offer for the enactment of this last great historical drama.

It is this which made all the more poignant the rapid disillusion of those years. Indeed, almost before the revolutionary moment seemed to have come, there were those who could already sense its passing. As early as December 1944 an *Esprit* editorialist lamented that there was nowhere to be found in France the smack of firm and new political authority. In the same journal, Jean Maigne drew readers' attention to the dead and deported Resistance leaders and the mediocrity of the political chiefs now emerging: "We see all of a sudden that the Resistance is but a shadow of itself."[36] In some circles a certain dolorous pleasure was taken in proclaiming the hopelessness of the situation, even as the same writers called for change and upheaval. But in this case the sentiment really was widespread. By 1947 it was universally believed that the Liberation had failed. The best-known symptom of this was the failure to follow through on the purge of collaborators and tainted political and eco-nomic leaders.[37] The demand for justice, or vengeance, had been integral to the revolutionary vision of Communists, intellectuals, and even some within the political center; a final settling of scores with France's past was the necessary condition of a better future. Even those like Jean Paulhan, who thought that the purge had been a hypocritical exercise in private revenge, conceded that as a movement for revolution-ary change the Liberation had lacked the courage of its convictions and represented a lost opportunity.[38] In January 1947 François Mauriac, perhaps recalling his own hopes of 1944 and his biting condemnations of the Third Republic, noted sourly, "Everything is beginning again. Everything remains hopelessly unchanged. . . . The Third Republic lives on; it is the Fourth that is dead." Who, as Camus lamented a few weeks later, "today cares about the Resistance and its honor?"[39]

The revolutionary hopes invested in the liberation of France and the rapid disillusion that followed so soon after are an important part of a

36. Jean Maigne, *Esprit,* December 1944, quoted in Jean Galtier-Boissière, *Mon jour-nal depuis la Libération* (Paris, 1945), 81; see also the editorial in *Esprit,* December 1944: "Ce que l'on cherche partout en vain c'est une doctrine politique neuve et ferme."

37. For detailed figures on the French *épuration,* see, for example, Hilary Footitt and John Simmonds, *France, 1943–1945* (New York, 1988). Whereas in Norway, Belgium, and the Netherlands the numbers of persons sentenced to prison for collaboration varied from 400 to 640 per 100,000 inhabitants, in France the figure was only 94 out of 100,000.

38. Jean Paulhan, *Lettre aux directeurs de la Résistance* (Paris, 1952).

39. François Mauriac, *Journal,* vol. 5 (Paris, 1953), 28 January 1947; Camus, *Combat,* 22 March 1947.

number of stories about contemporary France. They cast a revealing light upon the emphasis that was placed in the first postwar years upon "the honor of the Resistance," the need for a vengeful justice, and the half-acknowledged desire to prolong by all possible means the certainties and harmonies of the resistance experience itself. This entailed on the one hand reconstructing that experience as something both more significant and more decisive than it had been, and on the other extracting from it political and moral positions that could then be applied in other situations and to other conflicts and choices. Had the actual experience of resistance and liberation been more decisive, had the Fourth Republic been the child of something more recognizably decisive and radical by way of birth pangs, things might have been different. As it was, the intellectual community in postwar France remained unhealthily fixated upon its wartime experience and the categories derived from that experience, with significant and enduring consequences.

CHAPTER THREE

Resistance and Revenge

The Semantics of Commitment in the Aftermath of Liberation

La Résistance a fait de nous tous des contestataires dans tous les sens du terme, vis-à-vis des hommes comme vis-à-vis du système social.

The Resistance made us all disputatious in every sense of the word, toward men as toward the social system.

Claude Bourdet

We have become familiar with the "Vichy syndrome."[1] We should not, however, neglect its *doppelgänger*, the syndrome of Resistance. After the war, it suited almost everyone to believe that all but a tiny minority of the French people were in the Resistance or sympathized with it. Communists, Gaullists, and Vichyists alike had an interest in forwarding this claim. By the end of the forties, amidst growing disenchantment with the Fourth Republic, there emerged a new sensibility critical of *résistantialisme* and cynical about the whole wartime experience. Promoted by a younger generation of "alienated" apolitical writers, this rejection of the

1. Henry Rousso, *Le Syndrome de Vichy, 1944–198–* (Paris, 1987).

myths of heroism and sacrifice gained currency and credibility because of the skepticism of genuine former resisters like Mauriac, Paulhan, and Camus regarding the exaggerated claims that had been made for the Resistance and the uses to which the power of the victorious side had been put after 1944. After 1958 and the return to power of the Gaullists, a modified *résistantialisme* became once again the order of the day, the better to claim for the president and his movement a nationwide and retrospective legitimacy. Since that time a degree of historical perspective has entered into discussions of the subject, assisted by the passage of time and a new generation of professional historians of the period. But there is still nothing to compare, for the history of resistance in France, to the myth-breaking synoptic studies of Vichy that began to appear in the 1970s. The historiography of the subject still echoes, however indistinctly, the early official accounts, which treated the war years as though they consisted largely of the activities of a national Resistance and the repression it elicited.

The initial postwar myth claimed that although the fighting Resistance may have been a minority, it was supported and assisted by "the mass of the nation," united in its desire for a German defeat. Only Laval, Pétain, and their henchmen felt or acted otherwise. This was the official Communist position.[2] It was largely echoed by the Gaullists, who insisted in their turn that the Resistance had been the natural reflex of a nation faithful to its historical traditions; the "insurrection" of the summer of 1944 was singled out as "a popular tidal wave surpassing in its dimensions all such uprisings in our past."[3] Although there were from the start those who acknowledged how small and isolated resistance had been,[4] their voice was drowned by the chorus of mutual admiration. In a book published in 1945, Louis Parrot would write of the "pure heroism" of Aragon and his wife Elsa Triolet, the "audacious courage" of Paul Éluard, and the "subtly dangerous game" played by Jean-Paul Sartre, practicing "open clandestinity" in the face of the occupying authorities.

2. But not just the Communists. According to Jean Lacroix, "Le régime de Vichy a été une entreprise de trahison contre la France: il a été senti et vécu comme tel par le peuple français." See Lacroix, "Charité chrétienne et justice politique," *Esprit*, February 1945, 386.

3. Jacques Debû-Bridel, "La Quatrième République est-elle légitime?" *Liberté de l'esprit* (October 1952): 220. See also Claude Morgan, in *Les Lettres françaises*, 16 December 1944, who admitted that the fighting Resistance was a minority but claimed that behind it there had stood "la masse de la nation."

4. Yves Farge, for one, who was in a good position to know. He is quoted to this effect by Mauriac in *Journal*, vol. 5, 31 August 1946.

This is drivel of course, but it is at least ecumenical drivel: everyone was good.[5]

In order to put Vichy behind in this way, postwar France resorted to a strange self-induced amnesia, strange in that it took place in broad daylight, so to speak, and in the face of common knowledge of the truth. At one and the same time, France undertook to purge itself of the most obvious collaborators, while putting behind it the memory of the indifference or ambivalence of the majority. Last-minute resisters, Communist intellectuals who had openly advocated collaboration until July 1941, writers who had suddenly discovered in de Gaulle virtues they had previously sung in Pétain were welcomed into the community of resistance with hardly a dissenting voice (as in the case of Paul Claudel, who wrote in 1944 a poem of praise for de Gaulle almost identical to the one he had composed for Pétain just two years earlier). François Mauriac's suggestion, even before the end of the war, that real Pétainists were better than false freedom fighters went unheeded.[6] Later on, in the heat of the Cold War, the investigation of credentials was undertaken with greater vigor, but by then the motives of those undertaking the investigation were already suspect in the eyes of their opponents. The preference of the critic Étiemble for the openly neo-Nazi Lucien Rebatet over what he called the "Stalino-Nazi Claude Roy" now sounded more like a skirmish in the ideological battles of the fifties than a genuine effort to establish the truth about the affiliations of an earlier decade.[7]

This "exercise in suppression of memory"[8] succeeded in reestablishing the credentials of the nation, but at the cost of building into postwar life an element of bad faith. The *résistantialiste* account of 1940—that it had been the work of a corrupt minority, an act of treason by a defunct and desperate political elite—not only demanded an act of collective amnesia on the part of the intellectual community (what, then, of the aspirations of the intellectuals who had gathered so hopefully at Uriage?) but bequeathed to the country a thin and implausible account of its own recent history. This is one of the reasons why the Resistance fell into disrepute within such a short time. By 1951 mention of it, if we are to

5. See, for example, Louis Parrot, *L'Intelligence en guerre* (Paris, 1945).

6. François Mauriac, *Figaro*, 17 October 1944.

7. Étiemble, "Lettre ouverte à Jean-Paul Sartre," in *Arts,* 24–30 July 1953; and "Les Deux Étendards," in *NNRF,* March 1953.

8. J-H Roy, "Les Deux Justices," *Les Temps modernes* 33 (June 1948). This was an unusually perceptive commentary on the role of the purge in effacing 1940 and Pétainism from the national memory.

believe Camus, provoked nothing but "derisive laughter."[9] Because the myth was, understandably, cultivated with special assiduity by the Communists, there was a certain conflation after 1948 between anticommunism and a skeptical attitude towards the Resistance experience. Those who were not openly cynical were at best ambivalent. When the succession of amnesties after 1949 brought in their train a series of publications by lesser lights of Vichy, anxious to defend their past and reenter the political nation, the predictable backlash provoked only skepticism and ultimately rejection. For Jean Paulhan, to identify oneself with resistance had now come to be a matter not of pride but embarrassment.[10]

Communist hyperbole clearly distinguished party intellectuals from the non-Communist variety but in the quantity of their rhetoric not its quality. Communists like Claude Morgan or Georges Cogniot used the resistance complex relentlessly: not only are you with us or against us, but to be against us is to "collaborate" with the forces of Capital, to "betray" the masses.[11] To criticize the party is to join a long line of enemies beginning with Trotsky and passing through Jacques Doriot and Marcel Gitton to Pétain (and on, after 1948, to Tito). Heirs to the mantle of resistance but also to a chauvinist rhetoric once associated with the nationalist Right, Communist writers addressed themselves to their audience in language calculated to offer no moral or political refuge. This was nothing new, tactically speaking. As early as 1927 Léon Blum had warned against the uncompromising, cynical manipulation of sentiment and allegiance that characterized Leninist discourse.[12] What *was* new was the condition of the audience, receptive and exposed.

The source of this unique vulnerability on the part of France's postwar intellectual community is to be found less in wartime experience itself than in the vocabulary, the moral language that it had inherited from this experience. The endless litany of Resistance-era references to renewal, purification, and struggle had formed a network of linguistic symbols that the Communists manipulated with practiced ease, the more so in that this radicalized political lexicon substituted for revolution itself. Seeking real change, intellectuals for the time being had to

9. Camus, preface to Jeanne Héon-Canonne, *Devant la mort* (Paris, 1951), reprinted in *Actuelles,* vol. 2 (Paris, 1977), 25–29.

10. Paulhan, *Lettre aux directeurs de la Résistance* (Paris, 1952), 9.

11. See Georges Cogniot, "Chroniques internationales," *La Pensée* 27 (November–December 1949): 119.

12. Blum, quoted by Jeannine Verdès-Leroux, *Le Réveil des somnambules* (Paris, 1987), 236–37.

satisfy themselves with a symbolic alternative. The thesaurus of postwar intellectual communication consisted of six overlapping tropes, any and all of which could be pressed into service to shape and describe the postwar situation and the choices it presented to the individual.

The first of these concerned *violence*. Everything about themselves was presented to contemporary thinkers in terms of conflict—the "struggle for peace," the need to "act decisively," the division of historical experience into winners and losers. This language had a history, rooted in a conception of political division as something consummated in terror and death. During the 1930s the rhetoric of personal and collective violence had been largely the monopoly of the intellectual Right, but we have already noted the influence of the Right, through Maurras, on many later left-wing thinkers. The war and Resistance did the rest, making it difficult for many, especially younger writers, to think of public life except in neomilitary terms—attacks, battles, movements, liaisons with the masses, and so forth.[13] If Stalinism seduced, it was as much through the subliminal appeal of its paramilitary tactical language as through the charms of its dialectic.[14] Totalitarianism of the Left, much like an earlier totalitarianism of the Right, was about violence and power and control, and it appealed because of these features, not in spite of them.

Mention of seduction and control brings us to the second category, the *sexual*, almost homoerotic dimension of contemporary intellectual rhetoric. This sort of thing is more commonly thought to be the province of the aesthetic Right: Brasillach, among others, was fascinated by the fine display of handsome young men at the Nuremberg rallies. But sexual imagery was widely disseminated in the postwar language of the Left, too. The Communists once again were past masters at this. In Claude Morgan's early postwar novel *La Marque de l'homme*, the would-be collaborator (female) is tempted to yield to the charms of (German) seduction, illustrating a view of collaboration as an activity essentially restricted to and indulged in by women influenced by the strong masculine appeal of the dominant occupier. This association of collaboration with the female gender was a widespread myth of these years. It both symbolized the collective consciousness of national weakness and projected it onto others, in this case women. From the Communist point of

13. On military metaphors of the time, see Claude Roy, *Nous* (Paris, 1972), 408.

14. For examples of this, see Elsa Triolet, *L'Écrivain et le livre, ou la suite dans les idées* (Paris, 1948); and Marc Lazar, "Les 'Batailles du livre' du Parti Communiste français (1950–1952)," *Vingtième Siècle* 16 (April–June 1986).

view it also helped emphasize the particular resistance qualities they sought to promote—comradeship, virility, strength—and politics.[15]

In this the Communists were far from alone. Sartre used his essay on collaboration, published in August 1945, to draw a composite picture of the typical collaborator, distinguishable from others by his "realism, his rejection of the universal and of the law, by his preference for anarchy and his dream of iron controls, his taste for violence and plots, his femininity, his hatred of men."[16] This is Sartre at his most characteristic: not only does he treat collaboration as essentially feminine in nature, but he also manages to pass on to the collaborator those very traits—respect for authority, admiration of violence—that best describe his own psychic longings. The Sartrian binary aesthetic—masculine heroes seeking control of their existence versus feminized victims (of both sexes) collaborating in their own servitude—is already on display in this early piece of writing. The later tendency to prostration in the face of the heroic masses had yet to reveal itself, however: for the Sartre of 1945, the masses presented themselves as essentially feminine in the face of strong would-be seducers from either camp—"they agree to submit, they wait to be forced, to be taken." Even Mounier, whose retiring personality and style make him an unlikely protagonist in this instance, found in radical politics a very special virtue. One might think, he wrote in 1944, that violent upheaval could be inimical to those whose task it was to reflect upon society and its needs, but this was not at all the case. The "spirit of revolution" (Michelet) was for Mounier a "robust spirit [that] virilizes the very intelligence that it appears to compromise."[17]

In this brief dictionary of French intellectual tropes, the third is the concept of *treason,* to which was usually appended the lesser theme of cowardice. Appropriately enough, Julien Benda reissued his classic *Trahison des clercs* in a new edition in 1946, to which he appended a preface that makes opulent use of words like *treason* and *imposture* to denounce his opponents within the erstwhile resistance community; Paulhan was a special target for his insistence on the human right to err.[18] But whereas Benda's original use of the term in the edition of 1927 addressed the intellectual temptation to wander from the path of rigor and truth in

---

15. See, for example, Claude Morgan, *La Marque de l'homme* (Paris, 1944); and Vercors, *Le Silence de la mer* (Paris, 1942).

16. Sartre, "Qu'est-ce qu'un collaborateur?" in *Situations*, vol. 3 (Paris, 1949).

17. Emmanuel Mounier, "Suite française aux maladies infantiles des révolutions," *Esprit*, December 1944.

18. Julien Benda, *La Trahison des clercs* (Paris, 1946), preface.

the pursuit of political objectives, he and his postwar contemporaries now meant by *treason* something close to the opposite—an insistence upon following the dictates of one's own conscience even at the price of breaking ranks with one's political allies. Trading on his own reputation and the symbolism of the Resistance, Benda wrote widely on this theme in the next few years. His argument can be briefly summarized: to abstain (from choosing one's class-identification, one's political alliances) is to betray. The intellectual has a duty to throw in his lot with history and the masses. In going his own way (not to speak of choosing the other side), he betrays not only his natural constituency and community but his own calling.[19]

In a curious inverted way, this was a position Benda shared with Sartre.[20] For Sartre, the condition of the intellectual is one of treason virtually by definition. He lives in a permanently traitorous condition, and the nearest he can come to "authenticity" is by realizing this and by choosing his treason. The intellectual who throws in his lot with the people, with revolution and history, in betrayal of his class and vocation, at least gives his life a meaning. Any backsliding from this commitment constituted not only a personal failure but an act of existential cowardice. This position seems to have been shared by most contributors to *Les Temps modernes,* even when they took subtly different political positions. Desertion from the "workers' camp" was just that, desertion, and it made of you a "coward."[21] In this overheated context, one can begin to understand why the Communist vocabulary, which at a distance of forty years sounds at once inflated and empty, had some real appeal. Tito, after 1948, became first a traitor, then a coward, then ever more traitorous, and finally a "traitor from the very start." Whatever one thought of the particular case of Yugoslavia, the language employed for the purpose of expelling it from the community of *bien pensants* touched a chord in its intended audience. Looking ahead, we can already detect the dilemma to be posed by the anticolonial movements of the fifties. Who betrayed whom when one refused to support France in its treatment of colonized populations? Was it right to obey a government that betrayed France's true interests, in 1955 any more than in 1940? When the journalist

19. Benda, "Le Dialogue est-il possible?" *Europe,* March 1948.

20. On the way in which the theme of *treason* links Benda and Sartre, see Pascal Ory, "Qu'est-ce qu'un intellectuel?" in Ory et al., *Dernières Questions aux intellectuels* (Paris, 1990), 16.

21. Louis Dalmas, "Réflexions sur le communisme yougoslave," part 3, *Les Temps modernes* 55 (May 1950): 1961.

Claude Bourdet began his campaign in defense of Henri Martin, the first of many such, it was natural that he should seek in the language of betrayal the basis for a new opposition. From then until the final defeat of the OAS, French political life would be constantly disfigured by charges and countercharges of treason, political and moral alike.[22]

After treason, and as its natural companion in the thesaurus of post-war intellectual communication, came the fourth trope, *collaboration*. As a term of opprobrium this became so universal after the war that there is little point in offering examples of what had become a standard figure of speech. Its presence here is meant to suggest, however, that its use was not at all limited to the identification of people who stood accused of sympathizing with Vichy or the Nazis. It is the metaphoric uses to which it was applied that make it of special interest. Thus, to take one instance, from 1947 and with growing frequency in the half-decade to follow, all sympathy for American policy, all expression of support for Anglo-American interests, in France or abroad, was stigmatized as "collaboration," and the United States cast, by analogy, as the "occupier." The campaign against the Marshall Plan (by no means limited to the PCF) took as its central plank the thesis that the plan was the first stage of a peaceful occupation and takeover of France, and that collaboration with it in any form was to be condemned. Paul Fraisse in *Esprit* drove home the implication of this terminology by calling for a new "resistance."[23]

Collaboration, it seemed, was a state of mind, not merely a particular political or social choice. All democratic societies, Sartre asserted, harbor "collaborators" in their midst, even (especially) when the collaborator does not realize his (or her) own condition. The solution was not to identify and execute a few "traitors" but to make a revolution.[24] In a manner reminiscent of the still unknown Gramsci, collaboration was treated as a form of sociohistorical pathology, the condition of acceding to the hegemony of an authority or ruler. One was in this sense "occupied" by the ideas and interests of others (it will be seen here why Sartre and others so readily treated the collaborator as feminine and her "occupier" as male). The only solution was rejection (in the medical

22. See Claude Bourdet, *Combat,* 27 January, 31 January, and 4–5 February 1950. See also Paul Sorum, *Intellectuals and Decolonization in France* (Chapel Hill, N.C., 1977), 152–54.

23. Fraisse is quoted by Pierre de Boisdeffre, *Des vivants et des morts . . . témoignages, 1948–1953* (Paris, 1954), 7.

24. See Sartre, "Qu'est-ce qu'un collaborateur?"

sense): the social body could free itself from the condition and temptation of collaboration (whether with Germans, Americans, capitalists, or
its own weaknesses) only by rebelling against its condition. Once again,
the solution was revolution.

To rebel is to be against. The fifth terminological obsession of the
postwar intellectuals was thus in this generic sense *resistance,* the condition of being anti-something. Like collaboration, and for the same reason, the metaphor of opposition, of being against one's condition or
that of other people, permeated all political conversation. Like the fascination with violence, it has its origins in the habits of an earlier time;
being against the world around them was what constituted the common
bond of the interwar generation discussed in chapter 1. It might be
objected that ever since the early Romantics this self-appointed status of
the radical outsider rejecting the present in the name of something better
or merely different represents the condition of youthful opposition in
the modern world—whether bohemian, nihilist, surrealist, or existentialist. But after 1945 there was an important difference. The "antis" were
not youthful outsiders, they were the dominant cultural group. To be
sure, they sought to identify with social groups that they saw as true outsiders; with Sartre, they sought to share with the working class its "duty"
of contesting and destroying, finding their own historicity in the workers' world-historical role.[25] But they took up this position from the cultural center, as editors of influential dailies and periodicals, as prominent
columnists and writers, as the leaders of opinion and the representatives
or moulders of intellectual and political fashion. The insider-as-outsider
but in permanent rebellion at their own status.[26] The appeal of the
Communists (and of de Gaulle as well), was that they not only spoke for
the nonintellectual masses but existed for the express purpose of opposing and overturning the status quo. It was for this reason, above all, that
although you could not be with them for their own reasons, you had to
march with them for yours.

In this way of thinking, all experience, all of society, was necessarily
divided into two irreconcilable parts, whose differences could not be
bridged by good intentions, nor by a resort to Kantian universals. And
so the last, the most embracing of the styles of thought inherited from

25. Sartre, *Qu'est-ce que la littérature?* in *Situations,* vol. 2 (Paris, 1948).

26. This argument differs, albeit subtly, from that presented by Annie Kriegel. See
"Résistance nationale, antifascisme, résistance juive: Engagements et identités," in Karol
Bartosek, René Galissot, and Denis Peschanski, eds., *De l'éxil à la Résistance* (Paris, 1989).

the lessons of the Occupation, came to this: life consists of a series of encounters with an *enemy*. Everything was classified in Manichaean terms: Communists/capitalists, Soviet Union/United States, right/wrong, good/evil, them/us. *Tertium non datur*. It was once again Sartre who gave this idea its most rarified expression. Hell being other people, one found one's own identity through one's enemy, through the opposition of others; thus, it was better to choose that identity than have it imposed from the outside. But no one needed to resort to existentialist metaphysics in order to share and understand the basic principle. The imaginative exercise of empathy, the wish to understand the reasoning of those with whom one disagreed, was not widespread among French intellectuals in the aftermath of liberation. The point, after all, was not to understand the world but to change it, and for that one did not need to know what the Other felt or thought but only who it was.

Such an account of contemporary styles does not, of course, exhaust the points of view to be found in postwar France. For every Benda, Mounier, Sartre, or Bourdet there were those who fought back against this etiolation of the spirit.[27] But theirs was not the dominant voice. They were, precisely, fighting back against a powerful tide. And the intellectuals with whom we are concerned had other sources of authority and support beyond their newly found prominence. The language I have been describing antedated the use to which it was put during and after the Resistance episode; extremist terminology, a weakness for terror and verbal violence, and the temptation to divide the world into simple exclusive categories had long marked the discourse of French politics in ways that do seem to be uniquely French. Although Lenin and his heirs made a very important contribution, introducing into French political life terms of abuse hitherto confined to the Russian lexicon, "traitors," "salauds," "slimy rats," and the rest found a comfortable and familiar home in the menagerie of French polemic.

The conjunction of intellectual and political treason, the assimilation of disagreement and betrayal, also sat easily with the dominant interpretive schema in the historiography of the French Revolution. In the work of Albert Mathiez and Georges Lefebvre especially, the formative years of modern French political culture had been cast as a drama of conflict and irreconcilable opposition. The history of France from 1789 to 1799 (not to speak of the century that followed) was taught at every level as a

27. See, for example, Henri Lévi-Bruhl, "Refus d'un dilemme: Réponse à M. Julien Benda," *Revue socialiste* 20 (April 1948).

struggle between unassimilable opposites, with frequent references to treason, betrayal, and exclusion. This was as true for Catholics and the Right as it was for Republicans and the Socialist Left; indeed, the inter-war monarchist version of modern French history was nothing so much as a mirror image of the dominant Jacobin account. In this respect, the experience of war and occupation, of civil conflict and resistance, added little to the collective national sensibility but, rather, reinforced it at all its sharpest and most divisive points.

If the recent French experience contributed something of its own, it was a special sense of urgency and personal involvement in these matters. Many of the most adamantly *résistantialiste* of France's postwar intellectuals were compensating for what in retrospect they may have felt had been shortcomings in their own role during the war. This is a matter that requires sensitive treatment, since it is all too easy to accuse Mounier, Sartre, and others of having been heroes after the fact. It is not given to many to be brave and clear-sighted even at the best and most obvious of moments, and Vichy was a complex and cloudy experience for most people. In any case, intellectuals are not commonly thought of as the stuff from which heroes are made. That there were exceptions is famously the case. From Claude Bourdet to Marc Bloch, not to speak of numerous Communists, the French intelligentsia could boast a remarkable record of collective courage. But even prominent intellectual resisters, although they undertook clandestine work that exposed them to real risks, at the same time managed to live through the war in superficially normal ways. This applies to Mauriac, Paulhan, Vercors, and many others.

What strikes the historian, however, is how easy it was during those years to do or say things that, in retrospect, constituted a kind of muted acceptance of the Occupation and a willingness to work in and benefit from it. Paul Éluard and Elsa Triolet, postwar Communist heroes both, had no compunction about publishing their poems and other writings in journals approved and censored by the Occupation authorities or with publishers whose lists were tainted by the presence of collaborating authors. Sartre's career advanced apace through the public wartime performances of his work, and it is not very convincing to read Simone de Beauvoir telling us that the writing and producing of *Les Mouches* was "the only form of resistance open to him."[28] Indeed, de Beauvoir herself passed briefly through the services of occupied Paris's *Radio national*.

28. Simone de Beauvoir, quoted in Herbert Lottmann, *The Left Bank* (Boston, 1982), 193.

Louis Aragon, the postwar scourge of collaborators and backsliders, published *Les Voyageurs de l'Impériale* under German censorship and with German authorization. The Resistance credentials of Emmanuel Mounier consist largely of the refusal to continue publishing *Esprit* after the first months of 1941, which did not prevent him from writing in 1947 an essay in which he unashamedly identifies himself with the Resistance in its most partisan and active form.[29]

It was often these same people who took the most rigid and extreme positions in the coming years. Making up for lost time? Feelings of guilt assuaged through a commitment they had been unable to make when it mattered? A gnawing sense of having missed the opportunity to act, followed by a frenetic search for compensatory activities (verbal and otherwise)? It is easy to speculate and would be pointless to pass judgment. The point at issue is the curious urge, in the Liberation and thereafter, to be on the cutting edge of events, to pass up no occasion to be on history's front line, never to be outsung in the liturgy of radicalism. Having comported themselves in ways not altogether consonant with their later image, many of France's more prominent intellectuals would spend the following years obsessed with the need to avoid making the same mistake again.

The issue of comportment is interesting. Most people who were punished after the war for their behavior during it were held to account not for their deeds but for their "attitude," usually as it was recorded in print or on paper. From the intellectual perspective, this made sense. Since writing and reading are actions of major social significance, the words that one had pronounced in the public place carried special weight at times of momentous political choice. As Sartre put it in an unsigned but characteristic article in the still clandestine journal *Les Lettres françaises*:

Literature is no innocent song that can accommodate all regimes, but asks in itself the political question: to write is to assert freedom for all men; if a work of literature is not duty-bound to be a free action demanding its recognition as such by other freedoms, then it is just unworthy chatter.[30]

The experience of occupation and resistance, however one had behaved, thus taught the overwhelming importance of choice and commitment

29. Mounier, "Y a-t-il une justice politique?" *Esprit*, August 1947, 230: "Nous avons tous tué et violenté, directement ou indirectement, nous tuerons et nous violenterons encore, si nous voulons poursuivre notre devoir d'hommes, qui vise au delà de la vie."

30. Sartre, *Les Lettres françaises,* 14 March 1944; also quoted in Boschetti, *Sartre et "Les Temps modernes"* (Paris, 1985), 81.

and the weight that would attach to the way in which one expressed these. Indeed, as a political education, the experience of resistance (and even deportation) taught little else. Those whose behavior had been morally or politically impeccable were free, in later years, to use their credentials as a springboard from which to offer a more nuanced judgment upon their peers. But for others, the best way to establish such credentials, as it turned out, was to turn the full force of their self-ascribed moral authority upon their enemies and never to flinch from the firmness of their position, however uncomfortable and ultimately untenable their perch. The first sign of this syndrome, which would in due course be directed towards national and international political causes, came in the months following the Liberation, with the move to purge the land of the enemy within.

> *Vengeance is pointless, but certain men did not have a place in the world we sought to construct.*
>
> Simone de Beauvoir

In the circumstances of postwar France, the drive to expel from the community all those associated with the Vichy years was understandable and irresistible. The last months of the Occupation had been the worst, both in material deprivation and in the punishments and revenge exacted by the Germans and the Milice for the growing audacity of the Resistance. The mass murder of the citizens of Oradour took place in June 1944. But even before then the Conseil national de la Résistance had made clear, in two of the first demands of its original charter, that the liberation of France would be followed by legal and economic sanctions against those who had collaborated. The shape and extent of those sanctions remained undefined, but as the war drew to an end it was clear to all that there would be a demand for revenge: "France must first of all pass through a blood bath."[31]

In itself, the concept of a purge was unproblematic—French history since the Revolution is studded with such things, undertaken after the fall of a regime and usually confined to the wholesale replacement of officials or the selective punishment or exile of politicians and ministers from the losing side.[32] The most recent such exercise had actually been undertaken under Daladier, in October 1939, when the interior minis-

---

31. Edouard Herriot, quoted in Maurice Larkin, *France since the Popular Front* (Oxford, 1988), 124.
32. The scale of the purge that followed the defeat of the Commune of 1871 was thus exceptional.

ter, Albert Sarraut, had sought to pursue a nationwide purge of Communists in the wake of the Moscow Pact. Thus there was no lack of precedent, even if one does not include the dismissals and exclusions undertaken by the Vichy regime itself. What was lacking, on the other hand, were the legal and institutional bases for the sort of housecleaning now proposed.

Serious crimes of collaboration could be prosecuted under Article 75 of the 1939 Penal Code for "intelligence with the enemy," and most major collaborators were indeed charged under this article.[33] But Article 75 only really addressed the crime of treason, and it was thus necessary to introduce other categories of offense to cover the larger number of people to be prosecuted. Hence the introduction of retroactive legislation. Here too there existed a precedent, if only in the form of Vichy's own laws of 1941 and after. But that was hardly a model of jurisprudence to which postwar constitutional lawyers could turn for assistance. Instead there was invented the crime of collaboration, something short of treason but distinct from mere passive acceptance of the Occupation and its demands.[34] The shape of the new jurisprudence can be gleaned from the Ordinance of 26 December 1944, which determined the crime of collaboration after the thing itself had largely ceased to exist. In this ordinance occasional personal weakness and ambivalence are equated with active and deliberate political or economic engagement, leaving very little room for discussion of questions of intentionality, responsibility, or scale.

If the definition of collaboration was so inadequately drafted, this was in some measure because events had overtaken the niceties of constitutional or legal practice. Of the approximately 10,800 executions without trial that took place in France during the course of the Liberation, 5,234 had already happened before the Allied landings. Some of these had been preceded by a trial (about one-quarter of them), but most were exercises in summary judgment, by no means all of them the work of genuine Resistance units. By setting up, within the limits of the contemporary moral and military situation, a formal basis for judgment, the French authorities of this period sought to take punishment out of the

33. See Pierre Guiral, "L'Épuration administrative dans le sud-est en 1945," in *Les Épurations administratives: Dix-neuvième et Vingtième Siècles* (Geneva, 1977).

34. This was also the case in other countries. For comparable "reprisal laws," also retroactive in effect, on the model of Nuremberg, see *International Congress of Jurists: Discourses and Protocols* (West Berlin, 1952), notably the contribution of J. Stransky on Czech postwar purges.

hands of autonomous and often competing organizations and return it to the state. In this they were reasonably successful. Official trials for collaboration or treason were held from 1944 until the beginning of the 1950s; and tribunals, courts of justice, and the high court would eventually sentence to death nearly 7,000 people (3,900 in absentia). Of these, fewer than 800 were eventually executed.

In addition to those prosecuted for treason or collaboration, a further 50,000 government employees were "investigated" at the Liberation, of whom 11,343 lost their jobs or were otherwise punished. But most of these would eventually return to government service following the amnesties of January 1951 and August 1953. (By contrast, it should be recalled that Vichy had unceremoniously sacked 35,000 *fonctionnaires* as politically unreliable or otherwise "unsuitable," and with no hope of later redress.) In general, the amnesties, the first of which was declared in 1948, reduced rather rapidly the number of people who stayed in prison. An initial 32,000 persons were incarcerated, but that number was down to 13,000 by December 1948, to 8,000 by the following year, and to 1,500 by October 1952. At the end of the Fourth Republic, there remained in French prisons just 19 persons sentenced for their wartime activities or writings.[35]

For most sectors of the population, the sanctions applied for collaboration were relatively mild. This was partly a result of de Gaulle's determination to avert national bloodletting and to reunite the nation under a strong central authority. That, it was felt, could best be achieved by punishing quickly and harshly the most obvious figures, national and local, and then by applying the law with moderation and restraint to the larger pool of potential victims, the better to reconcile them to their defeat. There were so many tens of thousands of persons who were indictable under the new legislation that a consistent and rigorous application of the law would have been not only counterproductive but probably impossible. But in one sector these considerations did not apply in the same way, and the result was a rather different configuration to the experience (and memory) of the *épuration*. This is the purge of the intellectuals.

The treatment of writers and artists who had collaborated was notoriously unfair—not so much because some of them did not deserve the punishment they received (many did), but because it was so selective.

35. See Larkin, *France since the Popular Front;* Rousso, *Le Syndrome de Vichy 1944–198–;* and François de Menthon, "L'Épuration," in *Libération de la France* (Paris, 1976).

Many intellectuals who had published in the collaborationist press redeemed themselves by their later part in the intellectual Resistance and then turned with a vengeance on their former colleagues. More generally, intellectuals were singled out for much more attention than was ever given to lawyers, generals, businessmen, and high civil servants whose services to the occupying authorities had been unquestionably more significant. Moreover, distinctions were not always drawn very consistently between those who had actually said certain culpable things or advocated criminal activity, and those who had merely honored the publications of the occupying regime with their presence, without saying anything of particular note.

There were a number of reasons for the severe treatment of the intellectuals. In the first place, as de Gaulle later noted in his memoirs, in literature as in everything else, talent is a responsibility. The capacity to express a point of view in a way calculated to convince others, the skill in dressing up an unacceptable act in respectable moral clothing, confer on the writer a power but also a duty. The abuse of such responsibilities calls down on the guilty party greater blame than would attach to someone who merely reads the writer's words or acts upon them. That is why newspapers and their erstwhile owners and editors were so severely sanctioned at the Liberation, losing not only their names and their positions but also the very property itself. This process was further fueled by the desire of Resistance intellectuals and journalists to secure for themselves scarce resources in newsprint, printing plant, and space; but although the same might have been true of aspirant entrepreneurs in other fields, no other industry was so harshly penalized for its wartime allegiance.[36]

Secondly, collaboration-by-the-pen had a distinct advantage over other sorts of collaboration from the point of view of the jurist. It left an unambiguous record, open to examination and cross-examination. An individual could deny that he or she ever worked for the Germans or for Vichy or could claim that such work was a cover for clandestine opposition. Such a claim was hard to disprove, and if the accused could obtain corroborative evidence or a friendly witness, it was hard to secure a conviction, once the first flush of field justice had passed. But an article, a letter, a book, play, or poem could not be denied. The decision to let one's name appear in a tainted journal or on the list of a publisher who accepted

36. See Pierre Assouline, *L'Épuration des intellectuels, 1944–1945* (Paris, 1985); and Charles de Gaulle, *Mémoires de guerre* (Paris, 1959), 135ff.

German censorship or (worse) who published openly collaborationist writers was an error that could not readily be undone. This was especially the case in a time when words, as it was now asserted, had *mattered* so. It was not always a crime to say or write the wrong thing; but neither was it a matter of no consequence, a weightless act of no moral meaning.

The main reason for the especially contentious shape of the purge of intellectuals, however, was that it was undertaken by intellectuals themselves. This meant that the significance to be assigned to a person's words was now being weighed by men and women for whom words were everything and who were seeking, both philosophically and in the political realm, to establish the historicity and centrality of intellectual choice. By magnifying the importance of the writer-as-collaborator in their account of the Occupation, they were also staking out a larger territory for themselves. If collaborating intellectuals were important persons who deserved to be judged for their words, then intellectual resisters could make the same claim, both for their role in the war years and for their place in postwar society.

The literary community was not the only one that set out to police itself. For example, an academic council sat in judgment over suspect teachers and in 1945 drew up a list of those to be purged.[37] But the self-policing activities of writers were the most prominent, the most public, and the most obviously arbitrary. Formally, there existed two official bodies, both of them emanating from the Comité national des écrivains (CNE), which had been formed in the Resistance. Both operated under the terms of the Resistance ordinance of May 1944, which established a framework for defining procedures for purging "les gens de lettres." The Commission d'épuration of the CNE had the task of deciding who among the names it investigated was "more or less compromised," as distinct from those who were subject to the law and found deserving of "indignité nationale." The latter would, in principle, be the concern of the courts; the former would be named by the commission. It was then for writers, artists, scholars, journalists, and others to decide whether they wished to be associated with these people in any way. Such a boycott, if successful, would effectively expunge "guilty" people from the intellectual community, since newspapers would not print their articles; publishers would not take their books; and theaters, film studios, and orchestras would deny them work.

37. See Sirinelli, *Génération intellectuelle* (Paris, 1988), 559 n. 68.

Among the initial members of this commission were Jacques Debû-Bridel, Raymond Queneau, Paul Éluard, Gabriel Marcel, and Vercors (Jean Bruller). There was also established a Comité d'épuration de l'édition, with Jean-Paul Sartre sitting on it as the representative of the CNE. His fellow committee members included Vercors, Pierre Seghers, Francisque Gay, Jean Fayard, and Duran-Auzias, among others, together with a representative of the provisional government.[38] These examining bodies, though clearly partisan, were not drawn exclusively from any one side or interest group within the intellectual community. During the autumn of 1944 they put out a series of lists, placing those whose names appeared there in the uncomfortable position of being presumed guilty until proved innocent. There was some internal dissent within the CNE over the makeup of these lists. On 16 September 1944 *Les Lettres françaises* (not yet the Communist-dominated weekly it was soon to become) presented its own list of suspects, which it distinguished from that of the commission by insisting that it had no official status but simply denoted people who were "professionally repugnant" to CNE members. But on 27 September the CNE unanimously voted to clarify matters somewhat by announcing that anyone who supported Pétain after the occupation of the southern zone (in November 1942) was a prima facie candidate for national indignity.[39]

At this point, the published lists of names included everyone from Robert Brasillach and Pierre Drieu la Rochelle, active collaborators by any standard, to Pierre Andreu and Jean Giono, whose sin was at best that of omission, of having failed to make a clear break with the Vichy regime and its goals.[40] Indeed, at its peak, the formal list of persons declared "undesirable" by the CNE (after certain names had been removed with much effort and lobbying) consisted of some 148 men of very different hue, few of whom could be formally accused of any specific crime. During the years 1945–1947, the list was intended primarily for internal consumption, as a guide for others. But it exposed editors, writers, and publishers to all manner of pressures and temptations, moral and financial, while doing nothing to draw a line under the memory of the war years. If anything, it made matters worse, since it was notoriously the case that some categories of person had suffered more than others. Publishers came away remarkably unscathed, despite the fact that most

38. For membership of these committees and commissions, see *Les Lettres françaises,* 30 September 1944 and 7 October 1944.
39. *Les Lettres françaises,* 16 September, 7 October 1944.
40. See, for example, Pierre Andreu, *Le Rouge et le blanc, 1928–1944* (Paris, 1977).

of them had done well from wartime production of books.[41] Of the major French publishing houses, only the name of Bernard Grasset was to be found in the final CNE file, yet his list was not notably better stocked with suspect authors than that of Gallimard or Denoel, for example. Here, despite the later efforts of the Commission nationale interprofessionelle d'épuration, which took over responsibility from the Comité d'épuration de l'édition, the interests and affiliations of the major figures in the CNE prevailed. Aragon, Sartre, and others were certainly not going to cast their *own* publishers into the flames, with all that would imply for their own wartime presence on contaminated lists.[42]

The situation thus described placed all the cards in the hands of the most adamant, the most vocal, and the most extreme members of the intellectual community. From its very first post-Liberation reappearance, *Esprit* took the lead in the demand for a thoroughgoing purge, of intellectuals and everyone else: "Enough of this poison flowing through our veins . . . for this we must do whatever is necessary, however brutal."[43] The *épuration*, Paul Fraisse asserted in January 1945, was not just a matter of punishing collaborators but *all* those who were responsible for the climate that had allowed collaboration—anti-Communists, right-wing politicians and thinkers, big business, anti-Semites, and anglophobes. More than a liquidation of treason, the purge should be a revolutionary social and political act.[44]

Fraisse found support on the far Left. Claude Morgan, the editor of *Les Lettres françaises,* noted that the war was not yet over. Why, then, harbor doubts about the punishment of intellectuals? They are responsible for deeds they either provoked or else implicitly approved.[45] Referring here to the cases of Brasillach and Henri Béraud, recently tried in the courts, Morgan anticipated de Gaulle:"The more talented they are, the more they are guilty." In time of war, the execution of such men was simply a part of the war effort—"Do we want, by sparing traitors in the name of some so-called liberalism, to risk the return of such horrors?"[46]

Such a position could perhaps be defended in good faith. But it helps to understand it if we recall how much the purge was an opportunity for

41. Pascal Fouche, *L'Édition française sous l'Occupation* (Paris 1988).
42. See appendixes in Assouline, *L'Épuration des intellectuels;* and Herbert Lottmann, *The Purge* (New York, 1986), 235ff; see also Vercors, *Les Lettres françaises,* 20 January 1945.
43. Editorial, *Esprit,* December 1944.
44. Paul Fraisse, "Épurons l'épuration," *Esprit,* January 1945.
45. Morgan was responding to an article on the subject by Jean and Jérôme Tharaud that appeared in *Figaro,* 15 January 1945. See *Les Lettres françaises,* 24 February 1945.
46. *Les Lettres françaises,* 13 January 1945.

the settling of a variety of scores, personal and professional. Among those whose names appeared on the CNE lists and in the pages of *Les Lettres françaises* were many unknown mediocrities. But also there were Henri de Montherlant, Charles Maurras, and Céline, together with prominent essayists and social commentators like Jacques Chardonne and Anatole de Monzie. Some of these people were being punished as much for what they had said and stood for *before* the war as for their errors and actions during it. A new generation was clearing the ground behind it and trying to show just how complete the break with the past would be. This was all the more the case for those who had once been admirers or followers of the very men they were now expunging from their midst. Claude Morgan and Jacques Debû-Bridel, like Emmanuel d'Astier de la Vigerie and Claude Roy, had been Maurrassiens until the Resistance remade them as patriots of a different color.[47] The pacifism for which Jean Giono was criticized after the war had been but the extreme expression of a sentiment widely shared in the younger generation, and the Pétainist illusion of a man like Bertrand de Jouvenel was certainly no worse than that of Mounier. The difference had to do with luck—and timing.

Sometimes the purge was put to cruder personal uses. Aragon made a halfhearted attempt to smear André Gide in the pages of *Les Lettres françaises* (while it was still the semi-official journal of the CNE), seeking to exact revenge for the latter's influential *Retour de l'URSS* of a decade before. In this case the attempt failed, because of Gide's standing and iconic significance. But lesser writers fell victim to such activities and would harbor resentment for many years to come. As everyone realized, however, the true test of the motives and ethics of the purge came in those cases where the activities of the accused were not in doubt and where everything depended on the degree of responsibility one should attach to words and ideas. The *locus classicus* for such a test was the trial of Robert Brasillach, which would set the terms of reference for much of what was to come.

As a symbol, a representative of intellectual collaboration, Brasillach was almost too perfect. After a gilded youth that took him from the École normale supérieure to *Je suis partout*, he moved comfortably within the literary and journalistic circles of Occupied France, writing, speaking, and visiting Germany in the company of other collaborators. Born in 1909, he was of the same generation as Merleau-Ponty, Mounier, and

47. See Claude Roy, *Moi, Je* (Paris, 1969), 193.

the rest, but unlike them he had not abandoned his youthful interest in the extreme Right. He never made any effort to hide his views, which included a virulent and often expressed anti-Semitism. Although it became fashionable after his death to cast aspersions upon his gifts as a writer, contemporaries of all parties had credited him with a major talent; he was not just a gifted and dangerous polemicist but a man of acute aesthetic insight and real literary talent. In short, an intellectual, *première classe*.

Brasillach was tried in January 1945 and found guilty of treason, of "intelligence with the enemy." His was the fourth such trial of a major collaborating journalist: December 1944 had seen the cases of Paul Chack (a journalist with *Aujourd'hui*), Lucien Combelle (director of *Révolution nationale*), and Henri Béraud (a contributor to *Gringoire*). But Brasillach's talent far exceeded that of the other three, and his case was of much greater interest to his peers. In his trial, it was established at the start (with Brasillach's agreement) that he had been pro-Vichy and was anti-Communist, anti-Jewish, and an admirer of Maurras. Not that these traits were unique to the accused; during the trial Brasillach remarked that anyone seeking to read an anti-Semitic, anti-national tract at least as vicious as anything he had ever written had only to turn to Louis Aragon's poem, *Feu sur Léon Blum*![48] The issue, however, was this: was he a traitor? Had he sought a German victory, and had he assisted the Germans? Lacking practical evidence for such a charge, the prosecutor placed the emphasis instead upon Brasillach's responsibility as an influential writer: "How many young minds did you, by your articles, incite to fight the *maquis*? For how many crimes do you bear the intellectual responsibility?" In a language all would understand, Brasillach was "the intellectual who betrayed."[49]

Brasillach was found guilty under Article 75 and sentenced to death. He was thus not punished for his views as such, even though these were much cited during the trial, notably his editorial in *Je suis partout* declaring, "We must separate ourselves from the Jews *en bloc* and not keep the little ones."[50] And yet it was clearly for his views that he was to die, since his whole public life consisted of the written word. With Brasillach, the court was proposing that for an influential writer to hold shocking opinions and advocate them to others was as serious as if he had followed through on those opinions himself.

48. See Jacques Isorni, *Le Procès Robert Brasillach* (Paris, 1946).

49. Maître Reboul, Commissaire du Gouvernement, quoted by Isorni, ibid., 137, 159.

50. Robert Brasillach, editorial, *Je suis partout*, 25 September 1942.

A petition was circulated, largely by the efforts of François Mauriac, to seek clemency in Brasillach's case. Among the many who signed were Mauriac himself, Jean Paulhan, Georges Duhamel, Paul Valéry, Louis Madelin, Thierry Maulnier, Paul Claudel, and Albert Camus. Of the opinions of Mauriac and Paulhan we shall have occasion to comment at a later point. The presence of Maulnier is no surprise,[51] and the signature of Claudel is worthless as a moral guarantee. But Camus's support is instructive. He only agreed to add his signature after long reflection, and in an unpublished letter to Marcel Aymé, dated 27 January 1945, he explains his reasons. Quite simply, he opposes the death penalty; but as for Brasillach, he "despises him with all my strength." He places no value on Brasillach the writer, and, in his words, would "never shake his hand, for reasons that Brasillach himself would never understand."[52] Even Camus, then, was careful not to support a case for clemency on anything other than grounds of general principle (and indeed the petition itself referred only to the fact that Brasillach was the son of a dead hero of the First War).

Those who refused to petition for clemency for Brasillach also felt constrained to explain themselves.[53] Simone de Beauvoir attended the trial—it was the event of the month—and offered an existential justification for his execution: for our life to have meaning we must take responsibility for the evil that we do. Brasillach's virtue—she was impressed with his performance in the dock—was just this, that his life was all of a piece. His political attitude was "situated" in his life. But because he thus "assumed" his past, he must die for it: "he demanded . . . to be punished." There was something to be said for this position—Brasillach was what he had always been, a gifted, cynical, anti-Semitic critic and man of letters of the Right. But to suggest that this was enough to condemn him to death was to embark on dangerous, uncharted territory.[54] De Gaulle rejected the petition, and Brasillach was executed. Other writers against whom much the same sort of charges might have been made—Combelle, Céline, Rebatet—were more fortunate, either

---

51. Thierry Maulnier (J. Talagrand) was a friend and contemporary of Brasillach from his school days.

52. Camus's letter is reprinted in Jacqueline Baldran and Claude Buchurberg, *Brasillach ou la célébration du mépris* (Paris, 1988), 6–7.

53. For Claude Roy's vacillation and his decision not to sign, see Jean-François Sirinelli, *Intellectuels et passions françaises* (Paris, 1990), 151–52.

54. See Simone de Beauvoir, "Oeil pour oeil," *Les Temps modernes* 5 (February 1946): 828–29; and de Beauvoir, *La Force des choses* (Paris, 1963), 36.

because they were less well known, because they were out of the country, or because the death of Brasillach somehow closed a particular episode of the *épuration*. Writers would be condemned, whether to prison or national indignity, for their views in the months and years to come. But after Brasillach, no one would be executed for what some still felt was a crime of opinion.

The division within the intellectual community over the Brasillach case echoed differences of opinion within the CNE that had been present almost from the start. Although it was not until January 1947 that Paulhan, Duhamel, Jean Schlumberger, Gabriel Marcel, and the Tharauds resigned from the CNE, leaving it as little more than a Communist front, they had been at odds with its more radical spirits for months.[55] Whereas the CNE had treated its lists of tainted writers as amounting to a public sanction, Paulhan and his colleagues had tried to insist that the "index" of collaborating writers was a guide and implied no judgment, nor had it any standing in law. Paulhan was afraid that the mood of the times (he was writing in 1946) amounted to "a sort of (little) revocation of the Edict of Nantes."[56] The official CNE position, restated in response to Paulhan's misgivings, was that the intellectual community (as "represented" by the CNE) differed from the judiciary in that it could pass *moral* sanctions on those responsible for "the irreversible harm done to the nation."[57] The standing of the CNE in these matters was defended by Jean Cassou, its co-president, who insisted, "The CNE makes no claim to exercise any imperium over the world of letters. . . . It is neither a Holy Office nor a Committee of Public Safety. It is content to serve as a memory."[58]

This defense of the CNE was perhaps more revealing than Cassou intended. It was indeed a "souvenir," an attempt to retain intact the binary certainties of the Liberation and the authority of the intellectual Resistance in new and very different circumstances. By 1946 that was not easy. Most people wanted to put all that behind them, and the responsibility of the intellectual, whether for evil, as in Brasillach's case, or for good, was clouded by altered political divisions. Although there were real moral and ethical issues in contention within the intellectual community, they were already complicated by the partisan echoes of the

55. Details can be found in Jean Galtier-Boissière, *Mon journal dans la Grande Pagaille* (Paris, 1950), 49.

56. See Jean Paulhan, *De la paille et du grain* (Paris, 1948), 57.

57. See *Les Lettres françaises*, 22 November 1946.

58. Jean Cassou, *Les Lettres françaises*, 10 January 1947.

coming Cold War. To see more clearly what was at stake in the intellectual purge, we have to return to the Liberation and to a sustained exchange of views between two of the Resistance's authentic moral voices, François Mauriac and Albert Camus.

Divided by just about everything else—age, class, religion, education, and status—Camus and Mauriac shared a postwar role as the moral authorities within their respective Resistance communities. Each had a formidable perch from which to address the nation (Mauriac in his column for *Le Figaro*, Camus as director of *Combat*), and both men from the outset brought strikingly similar sensibilities, however differently expressed, to their writings. Camus, echoing the masthead on his newspaper, saw his task as helping France to move from resistance to revolution and never missed an occasion to urge on the nation a radical renewal of its social and spiritual structures. Mauriac, in contrast, remained an essentially conservative man, brought to the Resistance through ethical considerations and separated from many in the Catholic community by this choice. His postwar political writings often have the feel of a person for whom this sort of polemic and partisan engagement is distasteful, who would rather be above the fray but who has been compelled to engage himself by the imperative of his own beliefs. No doubt this was, by the fifties, a cultivated style as much as a natural disposition, but it rang consistently true.[59]

In 1944, Mauriac and Camus disagreed publicly, and at times pointedly, over the conduct of the purge. For Camus, in the months immediately following the Liberation, France was divided into "men of the Resistance" and "men of treason and injustice." The urgent task of the former was to save France from the enemy that dwelt within, "to destroy a still-living part of this country in order to salvage its soul."[60] Shorn of its metaphorical camouflage, this meant that the purge of collaborators should be pitiless, swift, and all-embracing. Camus was replying to an article in which Mauriac had suggested that a rapid and arbitrary justice—the kind in which France was now engaged, with tribunals, special courts, and various professional commissions d'épuration—was not only inherently troubling (what if the innocent suffered along with the guilty?) but would pollute the new state and its institutions even before they had formed.[61] For Mauriac, in turn, Camus's reply sounded like an

59. See Mauriac's views over these years in his *Mémoires politiques* (Paris, 1967), various *Journaux, Bloc-Notes*, and other writings.

60. Camus, *Combat*, 20 October 1944.

61. Mauriac, *Figaro*, 19 October 1944.

apology for the Inquisition, saving the soul of France by burning the bodies of selected citizens. The distinction Camus was drawing between resisters and traitors was illusory, he argued; an immense number of the French had resisted "for themselves" and would form once again the natural "middle ground" of the political nation.[62]

Mauriac returned to these matters in December 1944 and again in January 1945, at the time of the trials of Béraud and Brasillach. Of Henri Béraud he wrote that yes, the man was punishable for what he wrote; given the weight that his fanatical polemics had carried in those terrible days, he deserved ten years in prison and more. But to accuse him of friendship or collaboration with the Germans was absurd, a lie that could only bring discredit on his accusers.[63] Camus, in his turn, did not directly address this last issue (as we have seen, he was shortly to sign a petition on behalf of Brasillach, after giving himself a sleepless night on the question), but he did comment on Mauriac's increased tendency to invoke the spirit of charity in defense of the accused in these trials. Whenever I speak of justice, he wrote, M. Mauriac speaks of charity. I am opposed to pardons, he insisted; the punishment we demand now is a necessary justice, and we must refuse a "divine charity" that in making of us a "nation de traîtres et de médiocres," will frustrate men of their right to justice.[64] This is a curious response, a mixture of realpolitik and moral fervor. It also hints that there is something weak-kneed and unworthy about the exercise of charity or mercy in the case of condemned collaborators, a feebleness of the soul that threatens the fiber of the nation.

At this point, in early 1945, much of what Camus was saying could have been said by Mounier or de Beauvoir or even Morgan, except that Camus said it better. What distinguished Camus was that within a few months the experience of the purge, with its combination of verbal violence, selectivity, and bad faith, led him to change his mind in a quite remarkable way. Without ever conceding that the purge had been unnecessary, he was able to see, by the summer of 1945, that it had failed. In a much-quoted editorial in *Combat* in August 1945, he announced to his readers, "The word *épuration* is already painful enough. The thing itself has become odious."[65] Camus had come to see just how

62. Mauriac, ibid., 22–23 October 1944, 26 October 1944.
63. Mauriac, ibid., 4 January 1945.
64. Camus, *Combat,* 11 January 1945.
65. Camus, ibid., 30 August 1945.

very self-defeating (in his sense) the purge had become. Far from uniting the nation around a clear understanding of guilt and innocence, crime and justice, it had encouraged just the sort of moral cynicism and personal self-interest he had sought to overcome. Precisely because the activities of the purge, especially that of intellectuals, had become so degraded in the public eye, the solution was now exacerbating the very problem it had been intended to resolve. The *épuration* in France, he concluded, "had not only failed but fallen into disrepute." If French society was unable to distinguish between pacifism and collaboration in its treatment of past errors, then its spiritual renaissance lay far away.

Camus never came around wholly to Mauriac's point of view. Mauriac, for example, had from the very start taken a more distanced position than Camus would ever adopt, preferring to see the guilty escape rather than the innocent punished. He also, and in this he was truly unusual, rejected the suggestion that Vichy was somehow the work of a minority or an elite. The "double-game" that marked the Vichy interlude was that of peoples and nations everywhere, he insisted, the French included. Why pretend otherwise? And his vision of a reunited France was closer to that of the Olympian de Gaulle than the partisan intellectuals of the domestic Resistance:

Should we try to re-create national unity, with those of our former opponents who did not commit unforgivable crimes, or should we, on the contrary, eliminate them from public life, according to methods inherited from the Jacobins and practiced in totalitarian lands?[66]

Mauriac, in other words, began from the principle of forgiveness, in all but the worst cases (and even in these he advocated moderation), whereas Camus and his colleagues sought justice, or revenge, or both.[67]

But by 1945, they were moving towards the same conclusions. Of all possible purges, wrote Mauriac, France was experiencing the worst, which is corrupting the very idea of justice in the hearts and minds of the population. Later, as his polemics with the PCF grew bitter and the dividing line between them grew wider, Mauriac would claim that the purge had been a card in the Communists' hand, an asset they refused to abandon. But he was honest enough to concede that at the time he

66. Mauriac, *Journal,* vol. 4 (Paris, 1950), 30 May 1945.
67. Curiously, Mauriac attacked Léon Blum in May 1945 for *his* moderation on just this subject. Blum understandably asked why it was that he alone should not benefit from M. Mauriac's concern for charity. Details of this polemic are in Jean Galtier-Boissière, *Mon journal depuis la Libération* (Paris, 1945), 269.

might have been premature in calling for forgiveness and amnesty; in a France torn by hatred and fear, some sort of score-settling had perhaps been necessary, though not the one that took place.[68] In other words, Camus might not have been as mistaken as Mauriac had once thought. By 1948, however, it was Camus, long since disabused of the prospects for revolution and already uncomfortable in the intellectual community of which he was still a leading member, who had the last word. In a lecture to the Dominican community of Latour-Maubourg, he reflected on the hopes and disappointments of the Liberation, on the rigors of justice and the requirement of charity. In the light of events, he declared, "In our quarrel, it was monsieur François Mauriac who was right."[69]

Of course, it was not that simple. As Mauriac himself would note in his *Mémoires,* the purge was a "necessary evil."[70] Even if one remained within the confines of the world of the intellectual and the writer, the problem of collaboration had to be faced. The wartime French press, a worthy successor to the putrid journalism of the thirties, was in Camus's words, "the shame of this land." Men like Brasillach or Georges Suarez had not only pursued their racist and political vendettas in the advantageous circumstances of the Occupation, but they had openly advocated the undertaking of what amounted to war crimes. A fine judicial distinction might exist between such language and the crime of treason, but in the overheated atmosphere of the Liberation, the surprise is not that the two were sometimes confused but that this did not happen more often. It has been well observed that collaborationist intellectuals, unlike Fascist intellectuals before the war and Stalinist ones after it (in France at least), were in a position to have their enemies killed. This could not be so easily forgotten in 1945, nor should it have been.[71]

The other complication is this. Some of the most clear-headed and morally honest of the critics of the purge, men like Jean Paulhan, had a tendency to see the whole problem in almost excessively aesthetic terms. Noting that it was frequently the most gifted of the collaborators who were being punished most severely, just because they had been most prominent and perhaps most influential, Paulhan defended them in ways that made it seem almost as though their talent should be an excuse for their actions. This was the same distinction drawn by Claude Morgan

68. Mauriac, *Journal,* vol. 5 (Paris, 1953), 9–10 February 1947.

69. See Camus's lecture, reprinted in *Actuelles,* vol. 1 (Paris, 1950), 212–13.

70. Mauriac, *Mémoires politiques,* 179.

71. See J-M Goulemot, "L'Intellectuel est-il responsable?" in Ory, *Dernières Questions aux intellectuels,* 83.

or Charles de Gaulle, but in reverse. Talent, genius, has special rights, which can on occasion excuse moral failings, according to this reasoning; did it then follow that mediocre writers who had collaborated should be punished, since they lacked the excuse of literary gifts?[72]

Paulhan also attacked what he saw as the new and convenient notion of writers' "responsibility," as though a writer or thinker had any more (or fewer) rights and duties than any other citizen. Once again, this point looks reasonable enough but showed a lack of appreciation of the special circumstances of the moment. For Paulhan, like Mauriac, sometimes confused the right to err with real criminality. It was one thing to deny that intellectuals who had erred in judgments or opinions were some-how therefore "responsible" for the evil world in which they found themselves, but quite another to collapse the whole of Vichy into one huge "error." Here, too, the advocates of charity and moderation were doing exactly what they accused their opponents of doing, only in reverse. Whereas Mounier or de Beauvoir or Morgan or Jean-Richard Bloch treated errors and human weakness as a crime, Paulhan and Mauriac were inclined to see in all but the most bestial crimes of Vichy a massive but forgivable human misdemeanor. In this quarrel no one had a monopoly on wisdom, but the advocates of *épuration* did have some incontrovertible historical evidence on their side. If Mauriac was right, and for the most part he was, it was only because his moral antennae were more firmly attached and better tuned than those of his younger Resistance comrades, not because he had any better grasp of the tragic dimensions of the moment.

The purge did not really come to an end. It dragged on for years, a "running sore," a disease, as Mauriac put it, to which one becomes accustomed and of which one does not speak.[73] By the late forties, few had a good word to say for the experience: Dominique Desanti, in one of her reptilian pamphlets written to order for the PCF, claimed that the truly rigged trials were not those now taking place in eastern Europe but the trials of the Liberation in France.[74] The general feeling was that no one had emerged from the episode looking good—even Laval was now widely acknowledged to have been the victim of a judicial murder. The French had spent time and energy in a widely trumpeted exercise in domestic housecleaning, and yet 75 percent of the judges who had

72. For a criticism of Paulhan's argument, see Jean-Richard Bloch, "Responsabilité du talent," *Europe*, August 1946, 29.

73. Mauriac, *Journal*, vol. 5, 28 March 1946.

74. See Dominique Desanti, *Masques et visages de Tito et des siens* (Paris, 1949), 214.

presided over this exercise had held office under Vichy, the very institutional marsh they were supposed to be draining. Worst of all, there was a gnawing sense that the purges had been carried out not in the name of justice but rather on the principle of winner takes all. No one, it seemed, had heeded the warning sounded in Lyon by Yves Farge, the newly installed commissioner of the Republic, in October 1944: wrong opinions, he insisted, should never be punishable; a suspect is not necessarily guilty; above all, a pure man always finds a purer man to purge him.[75]

The comparison with 1793–94 comes readily to mind, when one reflects on this drive to cleanse society of its domestic foes, to punish the past. But it should be recalled that the Jacobins of the Year Two were not only in the middle of a revolution, they were also at war. Moreover, the inflexibility of a Saint-Just, the totalitarian democratic arguments of a Robespierre, had the virtue of originality. Deployed in 1945, they have the air of doctrine, even of routine. What is more, and perhaps worse, many of the intellectuals who pressed for a cruel justice in 1944 and the years that followed knew that their arguments were frail and depended for their credibility on the accident of victory. Just one year after the end of World War II, Maurice Merleau-Ponty would make an explicit parallel between the trials of the Liberation in France and the political trials of the thirties in Moscow. In both cases, he acknowledged, the individuals in question were blamed for their "comportement." Their motives were irrelevant. Put differently, Brasillach and Bukharin might as well have had the same opinions, or none at all, since these did not enter into the question of their guilt. "Objectively," they were guilty, Bukharin because he fell foul of the self-determined interests of the Workers' State, and Brasillach . . . because his side lost. If the Resistance wins (and it did), a collaborator is a traitor. If not, not.[76]

There is a terrifying simplicity about this line of reasoning.[77] The purge, it asserts, was revenge, but revenge given the status of "objective" justice by the chance and happy outcome of the war—an outcome, it should then be noted, with which France had little to do. Quite how this fits into a schema of historicity and responsibility is unclear. What is clear is that it points to a vacuum at the heart of public ethics in France;

75. Yves Farge, 15 October 1944, quoted in Lottmann, *The Purge,* 105.

76. This, in essence, is the argument of Merleau-Ponty in *Humanisme et terreur* (Paris, 1947).

77. Elegantly formulated by Sir John Harington in seventeenth-century England: "Treason doth never prosper, what's the reason? / For if it prosper, none dare call it treason."

at a crucial moment, the victorious intelligentsia of the Resistance were unable to rise to the needs of the nation. Neither the crimes that they ascribed to their enemies nor the punishments they advocated were grounded in any common ideal of justice, nor any general principles of morality. The only universally acknowledged category of human experience on which all could agree was the primacy of the political, an understandable lesson to have brought away from the past decade of French history but tragically inadequate. In a situation where judgments about good and evil, right and wrong, moral and immoral, were on everyone's lips, the substance of those judgments was reduced in every case to the political and the ideological. Once we have appreciated that, and to do so will require a brief detour into some aspects of contemporary French thought, we shall be in a better position to account for the errors of judgment of the coming years.

CHAPTER FOUR

What Is Political Justice?
Philosophical Anticipations of the Cold War

*Sartre's maxim, "Man is responsible for the whole of humanity"
strikes me as being the formula par excellence of modern sophistry
and false morality.*

Nicola Chiaromonte

The absence, in postwar France, of any consensus about justice—its meaning, its forms, its application—contributed to the confused and inadequate response of French intellectuals to the evidence of *in*justice elsewhere, in Communist systems especially. With no common agreement as to the criteria, if any, to be applied in the critique of arbitrary political authority, progressive thinkers were ill equipped to recognize, much less defend, individual victims of ideological realpolitik. To understand why this was so, we must turn our attention to the contemporary philosophical context, and existentialism in particular. By no means was every one an "existentialist"; as we shall see, there was a strong but complementary element of neo-Catholic moral reasoning that also resonated in some of the writings of the period. But existentialism articulated in

75

an acute form the philosophical fashion of the time and reflected many of the assumptions and linguistic habits of intellectuals who would not normally have associated themselves closely with Sartre, Merleau-Ponty, and their school. A skeptical rejection of both conventional rationalism and the optimistic neo-Kantian heritage of the academic French tradition had already marked a generation of young thinkers, who now found in the experience of war and occupation apparent corroboration for their views.[1] French history, it seemed, confirmed in the most irrefutable manner the categories of German thought.

The impact of German philosophy on the French is well documented. From Victor Cousin to Celestin Bouglé, young French philosophers customarily spent a year or two in a German university, absorbing the heady ideas they found there.[2] Thus there was nothing unusual about the fact that Aron, Sartre, and their peers had gone from the École normale to Berlin at the beginning of the 1930s and returned smitten with modern German thought (except that Aron would return to France more affected by the frightening political climate than his friends, who managed to ignore it).[3] Their interest was then sustained and directed by the famous series of lectures offered by Alexandre Kojève in Paris during the thirties in which he reinvented and interpreted Hegel for French audiences. The latter included, at various times, Aron, Merleau-Ponty, Jacques Lacan, Georges Bataille, Raymond Queneau, André Breton, Alexandre Koyré, and Hannah Arendt, among many others;[4] in short, the cream of the interwar French intelligentsia.

Kojève's reading of Hegel placed an overwhelming emphasis upon the master-slave relationship, in which each comes to know himself through the actions and presence of the other. For the slave, this was a situation only to be overcome by action, by a struggle for truth (that is, self-recognition), which necessarily entailed the destruction of the authority

1. Despite his other disagreements with them, Camus concurred with Sartre and Malraux in this at least: "Il faut d'abord poser la négation et l'absurdité puisque ce sont elles que notre génération a rencontrées et dont nous avons à nous arranger." See *Actuelles*, vol. 1 (Paris, 1950), 112.

2. See Jean-François Sirinelli, *Génération intellectuelle* (Paris, 1988), 355; see also, more generally, Vincent Descombes, *Le Même et l'autre* (Paris, 1979).

3. Sirinelli, *Génération intellectuelle*, 364; and Raymond Aron, *Mémoires* (Paris, 1983), especially 131–61.

4. See J-M Besnier, *La Politique de l'impossible* (Paris, 1988); Michael Roth, *Knowing and History: Appropriations of Hegel in France* (Ithaca, N.Y., 1988); Kerry Whiteside, *Merleau-Ponty and the Foundations of an Existential Politics* (Princeton, 1988); George Lichtheim, *Marxism in Modern France* (New York, 1966).

and claims of the oppressor. This was not an option for the slave (or the master, come to that); it was his very condition—he *must* struggle for acknowledgment. This awakening to a realization of one's circumstances was an inevitable outcome of the given human situation—"History," and more particularly the violence that Kojève claimed was its very essence, would bring the slave face to face with his situated condition. The practical lesson of such a heady doctrine amounted to this: whatever happens in human history, and especially those events that seem most terrible and total, has the ineluctable result of furthering the unfolding of the master-slave dialectic that *is* the meaning of that history. Whatever is, therefore, must have meaning.

It has been well observed that there was no basis in Kojève's teaching for the rejection of any historical act or epoch, however prima facie meaningless or obscene. Like Carl Schmitt, he opened up the possibility for rendering anything respectable, even Nazism, whose very success might be construed as the verdict of history. Kojève and his followers, unlike Schmitt's, did not draw this conclusion. On the other hand, as we shall see, they were defenseless in the face of analogous claims made by the defenders of Stalin. Within a purely philosophical universe, this was the ironic consequence of their unconcern with other branches of German thought itself, for Kojève and most of his audience not only excerpted and adapted Hegel, they also drew a veil over competing strands within his own national tradition. German neo-Kantians, like Austrian positivists, were little known in France; in exile, they went to Britain, Australia, and the United States, so that what had once been a major stream of central European (and Jewish) social and ethical theory became "Anglo-American" philosophy, leaving to the French the other heritage, that of Hegel, Nietzsche, and Heidegger.[5]

Why the French should have been so receptive to this particular branch of German thought is a problem beyond the scope of this book. Clearly, though, it cannot be attributed simply to the accident of exile and contact. A more profitable line of argument might begin with the nineteenth-century French emphasis upon positivism and science, which left modern French philosophy rather on the margins of the philosophical revolution of the early twentieth century. When Paul Nizan and his contemporaries rebelled against the "guard dogs" of bourgeois thought in the 1920s, their target was the comfortable neo-Kantianism of Bouglé

---

5. See Thomas Pavel, *Le Mirage linguistique: Essai sur la modernisation intellectuelle* (Paris, 1988), 185–86.

and his generation, which they found no more convincing or attractive than the positivism it had replaced in the university and which lacked even the positivist virtues of a feeling for history and process. The only countervailing alternatives were Bergsonian "creative evolution," the crude materialist Marxism of the day, or the memory of an enthusiasm for Nietzsche that had flickered briefly during the 1890s.[6] Any one of these might have served well enough in the years after World War I, when positivism and neo-Kantianism alike struck such false notes in the face of carnage and destruction, but whatever their emotional appeal they all lacked epistemological sophistication. It was this complexity, together with some attendant political implications, that the imported German philosophy of the thirties could provide, incorporating in its appeal all the counterofficial trends in indigenous French thought (including surrealism, with its hyperrational and destructive ethos) but going much, much further. To an interwar generation short on political sophistication but already committed to the rejection of optimistic social theorems, here was a "concrete" philosophy that could address private and public anxiety and offer, at least in theory, a resolution to the crisis of the modern world.

It was Maurice Merleau-Ponty who best captured in his own work the philosophical spirit of the times, including its profound contradictions and limitations: the tensions later evident between his phenomenological principles and his marxisant conclusions are simply the fully worked-out form of defects present from the first in French political Hegelianism. In Merleau-Ponty, situation was everything. The body is situated in its world just as people are situated in their history. This described for him not only the given condition of humanity but also the terms of human self-perception—we can only perceive ourselves as situated, in our body and in a physical and historical context. It follows from this that we are always relative, to something and someone. This intersubjectivity—the duality of subject-object that is Merleau-Ponty's abstracted version of the master-slave dialectic—is thus the essence of our situated condition, the source not only of conflict but also of whatever knowledge and understanding we possess. But because this is a condition common to all persons, the mutual conflict and perception in fact

6. These years happened also to see the development of Gabriel Marcel's own early version of existentialism, but this was a taste and language still largely confined to Catholic thinkers.

create a common bond and thus open up at least the possibility of community and harmony. History is not a war of each against all.

Here there are two difficulties. If Merleau-Ponty accepted the Kojève version of Hegel (and he certainly did so in his earlier writings) and thus agreed that the dialectic of self-recognition through struggle was the central historical force, why should he believe that this struggle would ever end? On what grounds could he be politically, as distinct from metaphysically, optimistic? From within the dialectic, there were none. But Merleau-Ponty imported into his thought (smuggled might be a better word) the distinctly historical category of the proletariat, rather as Marx had done. This alien presence in French philosophy was doubly problematic. If, as Merleau-Ponty insisted, *all* human existence contains within itself a potentially harmonious intersubjectivity, what would the proletariat (or, as we shall see, those who spoke for it) add to the story? And what was it in principle about the proletariat that would invest it with the capacity to introduce harmony through its own role in the conflict of subjectivities?

The second difficulty pertains to these same matters. Merleau-Ponty seems from the beginning to have harbored secret Kantian tendencies, which would surface in partial form in his post-Marxist writings of the fifties. His arguments in defense of a possible human harmony and in support of a political system that claimed to be striving for it imply the necessity of universal ethical values, and of historical goals that derive their legitimacy from those values. In other words, and unlike Kojève (or Sartre), Merleau-Ponty did not deny the ultimate commensurability of values or claim that these could only be derived from whatever experiences and sufferings it suited the historical Spirit to vouchsafe us. But this left him in a deeply contradictory posture, claiming, on the one hand, that conflict is intrinsic to humanity but, on the other, that conflict is in principle resolvable and would be resolved in ways to which we would, as human beings, attach judgments of value. It also left him in the uncomfortable position of making statements concerning what he held to be the truth of the human condition, while simultaneously asserting that no one situated person can absolutely distinguish truth from falsehood, right from wrong.[7]

Unlike Merleau-Ponty, Sartre was not troubled by such contradic-

---

7. See Merleau-Ponty, *Humanisme et terreur* (Paris, 1947); see also *La Phénomenologie de la perception* (Paris, 1945) and *Sens et non-sens* (Paris, 1948).

tions, nor did his philosophical writings seek to develop these arguments with the same consistency or depth.[8] Indeed, Sartre's *philosophical* thought during the thirties and early forties was quite devoid of political or social implications. His account of perception derives from the same sources as that of Merleau-Ponty but is far more resolutely subjective. According to Sartre, we only have access to "reality" through our perception of it, and it only exists by virtue of that perception. The conclusion must be that even our own existence is only the result of someone else's perception. We thus have meaning in this world only to the extent that this meaning is ascribed to us by others (who create for us, therefore, such identity as we have). Clearly, this is a condition of unfreedom (and also of un-consciousness), and the struggle for freedom is therefore a struggle between persons for the control of perception. To put it in the unmistakable language of the author, every "en soi" collides with another "en soi," since each is a sovereign and "total" source of meaning about the whole of experience. The logical incompatibility of these conflicting "gazes" means that struggle is not only the permanent and universal condition of mankind but also never to be overcome. All subjectivities remain totally separate and doomed to infinite and unresolvable collision.[9]

Thus there is no reason in principle why people should not be politically radical, nor why they should not be engaged, in the Sartrian sense. But each personal political act, each exercise in commitment, is bound to be a purely personal choice, with no transcendent or universal significance; and it has as much chance of bringing us into conflict with others as it has of contributing to harmony. For the early Sartre was a thoroughgoing nominalist, in whose thought there is no space for social categories or shared moral objectives.[10] Even love falls within the terms of the conflict thus described, with each partner seeking above all to appropriate the freedom of the other.

In these circumstances, however, engagement, whatever its social justification, becomes part of the struggle: not a struggle for freedom or rights or justice, but the struggle to assert oneself against the asserted selves of other people. To engage is to be free in this at least; it gives a person a place within history and not just within the perceptions of other

---

8. As a rule, philosophers found Sartre slippery; playwrights thought him didactic. But each supposed him to be a genius at the other activity.

9. Sartre, *L'Être et le néant* (Paris, 1943).

10. Hence Sartre's views on Jewish identity and the nature of anti-Semitism. See his *Réflexions sur la question juive* (1946; reprint Paris, 1954).

persons. In contrast with Gide, for whom the very "gratuity" of literature is what gave it interest, Sartre sought to place as much weight as possible on the literary act, so as to give to its author an existential gravity otherwise lacking. The conflict with others must continue, endlessly, but at least some autonomy, some freedom will have been self-created, "pour soi." In his later writings, Sartre would align himself much more with the "progressive" position, according to which some parts of this human condition were in fact capable of being overcome and resolved through violence and in the company of the proletariat or the victims of colonialism. In doing so, he would be more politically plausible but less philosophically consistent; but then the virtues of consistency were never uppermost in the Sartrian canon.

More even than those of Merleau-Ponty, Sartre's contemporary opinions precluded any attention to questions of ethics or morality. This point is sometimes obscured by his own constant reiteration of the demands of morality and the need to generate a properly existentialist ethics. But his failure to produce such an ethics was not simply the result of a loss of interest or lack of time. A Sartrian ethics would have been intrinsically inconceivable, as he must have realized. If we only exist in the eyes of others, then all judgments about our behavior or our choices are also the judgments of others. We are never intrinsically good or bad, innocent or guilty, but only to the extent that others think us so. If other people find me guilty or evil, then for all practical purposes I *am* guilty, I *am* evil. There is no other standard against which to measure my behavior, least of all my own account of myself, which has no meaning for others even (especially) if I assert it on my own behalf. Moreover, moral judgments cannot evolve over time; they cannot acquire greater force through practice nor greater truth-status through being widely held. In different places and at different times, people are judged by others and that judgment then *is* who they are. Like Richard Rorty today, Sartre held that values and moral judgments are incommensurable between societies and epochs. As a result, we have no basis from which to assess the claims of innocence or guilt made in other places or in the past.

Engagement and freedom, then, meant something very distinctive and morally neutral to Sartre. Since we have no grounds for seeking to bring about any particular social or political objective, for which we could offer no universally valid or acceptable argument, we act as we choose for reasons that are not intrinsically better or worse than those of people who act in opposite ways. We do what we can, not what we want, as Sartre put it. Engagement becomes not the means to some desirable end, but the end itself.[11] The difference between we who choose X and others who choose Y is simply the difference between winners and losers in the historical struggle. For us, X is right because we choose it, and X will be right in the eyes of history if we win. But the same might have been true of Y under other circumstances, and thus X is not better than Y in some other, stronger sense.

These were themes which in 1945 preoccupied Simone de Beauvoir even more than they did her companion. Most of her concerns echo those of the author of *Being and Nothingness:* the problem of responsibility in an absurd world, the arbitrary character of moral alternatives, the inherently unsatisfactory nature of engagement and choice. In the circumstances of wartime France, her major premise was unimpeachable: all choices with which individuals are presented may force them to be unfaithful to their profound desire to respect human life, yet choose we must. In the context of her refusal to sign the petition for clemency in the Brasillach case (de Beauvoir was writing in January 1945), this was an understandable position. Her minor premise is a little less secure, however. There exists, she asserted, no external reality by which such a choice can be evaluated (by this she meant that there are no universal criteria by which to assess a human action). Thus, she concluded, morality can only consist not in remaining faithful to some fixed (*figé*) image of ourselves, but in seeking to "base one's being" in some act or decision that will make our otherwise contingent existence *necessary.*[12]

The problem with Kant, according to de Beauvoir, is that there is no way in which we can deduce from supposedly universal maxims of justice, right, or truth what would be the correct action or choice at any given moment. Anyone faced with real choices in a particular situation "thus places himself from the outset beyond morality." Even if there were a proper, or "good," move to be made, we wouldn't know what it was. Thus, once we are engaged in history, once we take part in politics, we risk doing wrong. Ideas of justice or law have no purchase here, since their evaluation can only be undertaken in retrospect, and when we act we have no idea what the future will hold and thus how our decisions will be measured.[13] This is a curious line of reasoning, deducing as it does from the difficulty of knowing what is right the conclusion that we

11. See *Situations,* vol. 1 (Paris, 1947), 80. As Brunet put it to Mathieu, in *L'Âge de raison* (Paris, 1945), "À quoi sert-elle la liberté, si c'est pour ne pas s'engager?"

12. Simone de Beauvoir, "Idéalisme moral et réalisme politique," *Les Temps modernes* 2 (November 1945): 265, 268.

13. Ibid., 251.

should abandon the effort to discover it. And it is made even more opaque as an exercise in moral reasoning when we realize that what is being proposed here is not an account of the impossibility of ever being sure but the claim that truth (and with it justice, law, and so on) will be determined by outcome. This is not even utilitarianism, since it offers no criteria for measuring the advantages of alternative outcomes.

The political implications of such arguments are self-evident. For both Sartre and de Beauvoir, the Kantian reign of ends was only conceivable as the outcome not of morally informed choices but of revolution. This did not follow directly from their metaphysics but, rather, from a practical evaluation of the options open to the engaged thinker at that moment in history. Although engagement in public life was a compelling necessity if the writer wished to forge for himself or herself an authentic existence, the purpose of such engagement must be to contribute towards bringing about a world in which the hitherto inauthentic condition of all (writer included) would be overcome. For the time being, this required the intellectual to commit to opposing things as they are, not in the name of some hypothetically better state of affairs but in large part because the very act of opposing would not only release the intellectual from the discomforts of a contingent existence but would in itself change the rules of the existential game.

In the political configuration of postwar France, this pointed inevitably in the direction of Marxism, and thus communism. It should be clear that this was not because existentialism in its Sartrian guise was intrinsically sympathetic to Marxism; indeed, the two were logically incompatible. It was because they shared for the time being a common enemy, some overlapping language, and an affinity for denying the legitimacy of the present in the name of the claims of the future. The very real remaining philosophical differences help account for the continued unwillingness of nearly all the major philosophical figures in France to join the Communist party; even after 1949 and the increasing insistence of Sartre and others on the need to support the "workers' party" come what may, they could only ever do so for their own reasons and not for those of the Communists. But this was a sign of weakness, not strength. Sartre, de Beauvoir, and Merleau-Ponty could argue the case for commitment and a radical political attitude, but when it came to accounting for the programmatic and tactical substance of that attitude, they were helplessly dependent upon a quite different set of philosophical and ideological criteria.

These inadequacies exposed them from the start to damaging critiques, damaging, that is, in the purely formal sense—they did not prevent many readers, then and since, from finding such an approach persuasive and appealing. Sartre himself inadvertently pointed out one obvious weakness in his thinking as early as 1945: France should have fought on in 1940, he wrote; the future was unpredictable and who could know whether Germany would eventually win, whether the Russians would enter the war, and so on—the point is that one must do what is right on the basis of what one knows at the time.[14] Similarly, in his reflections on collaboration, Sartre made a strong case for the ideals of the Resistance— the values of freedom and the like are things that people can and do sincerely hold, while the collaborator's motives *must* be insincere. But this is in direct conflict with the whole tenor of existentialist reasoning— how, in Sartre's philosophy, could the French citizen of 1940 "know" what was right? Why is the collaborator's choice not as authentic as that of the resister, since the *goal* that each seeks to achieve is said to be irrelevant? And since Sartre's philosophy denies the existence of universal standards of moral measurement, how could we ever assert that one person's engagement is better or worse than another's?[15]

In their different ways, Raymond Aron and Albert Camus both identified the essence of this contradiction. Existentialism, Aron remarked, cannot invoke the Hegelian conception of History in defense of otherwise questionable actions; it offers no grounds for believing in the vision of historical rationality and necessity on which Hegel (and the early Marx) rested their arguments.[16] Three years later, Camus, in a famous letter, made the same basic point: how can you justify violence, or deny the application of universal criteria of justice and truth, if you don't believe in the certitude (or even, in principle, the likelihood) of History coming to your service and providing attainable goals that will make sense of past crimes?[17] Both Aron and Camus were responding to later and more overtly politicized versions of the thinking of Merleau-Ponty and Sartre, but their strictures also apply to the writings of the immediate postwar years. If Sartre had been able to share the extreme position of a Georges Bataille, who proposed a revolt against *all* rules, those of logic

14. Sartre, "La Nationalisation de la littérature," *Les Temps modernes* 2 (November 1945): 210.

15. See Paul Wilkinson, *The Intellectual Resistance in Europe* (Cambridge, Mass., 1981), 149.

16. Raymond Aron, "Messianisme et sagesse," *Liberté de l'esprit* 7 (December 1949): 16.

17. Camus, letter to *Les Temps modernes,* reprinted in *Actuelles,* vol. 2 (Paris, 1977), 116.

included, he might have been more consistent. But Bataille was consistent precisely because he had maintained his prewar stance, which consisted of a revolt against the constraints of history itself, a more thoroughgoing Nietzschean denial of *all* systems of value.[18] The existentialists' attempt to square the circle left them in a hopeless position.

The postwar school of French philosophy was also troubled by a further dilemma, one addressed but not resolved by Simone de Beauvoir. How do people whose ostensible commitment is to peace, freedom, and some sort of an idea of justice deal with the question of violence, constraint, and manifest injustice? Lacking an Archimedean point, they were compelled to ask of these things, do they serve History? Are they progressive? But not only is there never a clear answer to such questions, they also sound uncomfortably like the sorts of questions asked of fascism by intellectuals in the 1930s. Between Sartre's assertions of the virtue of "one-ness," of the "group-in-fusion" (to use a term deployed in later years), and the Fascists' idealization of unity and community, there was space for some confusion.[19] And when Merleau-Ponty defended "progressive" violence, how sure could he be that he was saying something fundamentally different from the early, radical Fascists and their "therapeutic violence"? Once you excluded intention and moral evaluation, these became murky matters. In the end, it all came down to a choice of sides, and after 1945 the intellectual supporters of violence and unity with the masses were on the Left. But this really only amounted to exchanging the aggressive catastrophism of the thirties for a sort of revolutionary lyricism. There was nothing stable about this shift—therefore, nothing to guarantee that the newfound "authenticity" of intellectuals meant much more than an availability for a different sort of change.

The frailty of their position, a sense that the membrane separating the authenticity of existentialists from the bad faith of Fascists was far too thin, was part of what drove postwar intellectuals into ever more radical postures, a sort of epistemological overkill. This accounts for their inability to commit themselves to compromise, or take the risk of engaging themselves in ethical or political issues that might bring them into

18. See especially Denis Hollier, ed., *Le Collège de sociologie* (Paris, 1979); see also Besnier, *La Politique de l'impossible*, 93ff.

19. On this, see Eric Werner, *De la violence au totalitarisme: Essai sur la pensée de Camus et de Sartre* (Paris, 1972), 209.

conflict with their only source of legitimacy, the force of history incarnated in the mass movements of the hard Left. A similar explanation may be helpful in understanding the correspondingly complicated stance of left-wing Catholics.

The circle of like-thinkers grouped around the review *Esprit* and the publishing house Le Seuil was marked by two salient intellectual characteristics. The first of these was a concern, mounting at times to an obsession, with renewal. In contrast to Sartre, Aron, and the *Temps modernes* team, these left-leaning Catholics were mostly outsiders, literally (Mounier was from Lyon), but also and perhaps more importantly, in their cultural resources, bringing to their community little of the confidence of the Parisian *normalien* elite. For them, renewal did indeed mean a sort of cultural housecleaning. Drawing on the language of the thirties but given additional force by the circumstances of 1944, they imagined, as Domenach put it, "the alliance of a cleansed spirituality with the concrete energy of the political revolution."[20] There was much emphasis on the "pédagogie de l'homme nouveau," an updated version of Mounier's emphasis in the early thirties on a "new middle age" (a concept borrowed from Nicholas Berdyayev, in whom most of the sources of "personalism" are to be found). Mounier's own first post-Liberation statement of his goals catches rather well both the style and the ambiance of the new Catholic mood:

Our task is not to remake a revolution already achieved, nor is it to save existing spiritual values, but progressively, with the clarity born of the passage of time, to suppress and surpass a stale spirituality and an anachronistic society and to help bring about, in due course, one of those periodic awakenings that are as salutary for the hearts of men as they are to their institutions.[21]

The second concern was with the need to be realistic, to avoid what was seen as the temptation to fall into a traditional Catholic style of abstraction, moralizing, and unworldliness. Like Sartre and his friends, Mounier and his colleagues had experienced History and did not wish to be left behind again. This desire to be in the front line at whatever cost to their spiritual comfort amounted on more than one occasion to an almost groveling approach in the face of history and the violence that attended its advance. In the same piece from which I have already quoted, Mounier conceded that one could not help being wounded at

20. Jean-Marie Domenach, "La Tâche de protestation," *Esprit*, January 1953, 28.
21. Emmanuel Mounier, "Suite française," *Esprit*, December 1944, 20.

the sight of violence, revenge, and rough justice, but "in his reaction to revolutionary brutalities the civilized man is too absorbed in looking at the bad guys [*les mauvais garçons*]."[22] In his editorial of March 1948, where he guardedly welcomed the Communist coup in Prague, Mounier again noted that one's sensibilities might be a trifle hurt by the apparently undemocratic tenor of the seizure of power. But progress has its price: "We are not here advocating some sort of ideal purity in politics. The first cement bridges that we now so admire also offended sensibilities when they first appeared."[23]

The reader will doubtless already have remarked a certain similarity between Mounier and the circle around Sartre when it comes to the handling of morally ambiguous political events, and this is no coincidence.[24] Like Merleau-Ponty and others, the writers at *Esprit* strove hard in the early postwar years to construct a bridge, in this case between their version of a Catholic ethics and the Communists' account of Marx. Indeed, after Maurice Thorez, Mounier was the nation's most visible advocate of a rapprochement between the two. Although a doctrinal union proved elusive, *Esprit* long harbored the illusion of a transformed communism, shorn of its totalitarian habits but resolutely revolutionary in spirit. Indeed, for a while in 1946, it accused the PCF of being insufficiently fervent in its daily practice. If the Communists had a weakness, in the view of most of the contributors to *Esprit,* it was only that their admirable political values were not sustained by that higher sense of the human vocation that only faith could bring.[25]

For the rest, however, Mounier and his colleagues were drawn to the PCF and its international movement in powerful ways. The antibourgeois, anticapitalist, antimaterialist discourse of the nonconformists of the early thirties appeared to find a comforting echo in the language of communism, and there is no doubt that the later admiration some Catholics would evince for Stalinism in the primitive East was an outgrowth of this desire to see in Lenin's Asiatic revolution a new beginning.[26] Moreover, Mounier (like other Catholics) could find in communism, if

22. Ibid., 21.

23. Mounier, "Prague," *Esprit,* March 1948, 357–58.

24. Except that Mounier was more concerned with the Christian condition than that of intellectuals.

25. See, for example, Jean Lacroix, "Y a-t-il deux démocraties? De la démocratie libérale à la démocratie massive," *Esprit,* March 1946, 357.

26. See Marc Simard, "Intellectuels, fascisme, et antimodernité dans la France des années trente," *Vingtième Siècle* 18 (April–June 1988): 62.

he sought it there, the Christian concern for the poor and the suffering—"Just as the Christian does not abandon the poor, so the
Socialist may not abandon the proletariat without forswearing his
name."[27] He could even tell himself, though this took a greater effort of
will and imagination, that communism had at least the potential to be a
more "personalist" community, where the individual-as-person mattered more than under capitalism, and where democracy was thus more
"authentic" (very much the key word of the decade) than in bourgeois
liberal societies.

The symbiotic relationship between communism and Catholicism in
France has been remarked upon by many people. Prominent Communist intellectuals had started life as active and practicing Catholics—
some of them, like Louis Althusser, at the Lyon khâgne,[28] as pupils of
Jean Lacroix, a major star in the *Esprit* galaxy.[29] Indeed, the move was a
natural one, at the epistemological level as much as at the sociological;
both represented world outlooks that were pessimistic about humanity
but optimistic with regard to history, and both were antagonistic to the
French republican tradition. Raymond Aron may have been right to
point out how morally confused was Mounier's "spiritual" opposition to
liberalism, his "anti-anticommunism,"[30] but there was one overriding
reason for this stance, and it carried weight at the time. Mounier and
some of his colleagues (in contrast, for example, to Jacques Maritain) had
placed their initial hopes in the Vichy "revolution" and were thus never
fully at home in the resistance spirit of the left Catholics who were to
form the MRP. Indeed, this hostility to the MRP, which endured
throughout the Fourth Republic (exhibited by persons further embittered by the colonialist practices of MRP ministers), was part of a wider
pattern of hostility to politics. Mounier and many of his co-contributors
to *Esprit* favored an aggressive, exhortatory style, demanding of themselves and their readers all sorts of public commitments, but at the same
time they were frequently suspicious of the compromises and shortcomings of party and parliamentary politics.[31] Only with the Communists

27. Mounier, "Fidelité," *Esprit*, February 1950.
28. The lycée class in which pupils prepare for the entrance examination to France's
Grandes Écoles.
29. Sirinelli, "Les Normaliens de la rue d'Ulm après 1945: Une Génération communiste?" *Revue d'histoire moderne et contemporaine* 33 (October–December 1986): 577.
30. Aron, "Politics and the French Intellectuals," *Partisan Review* 17 (1950): 599.
31. John Hellmann, *Emmanuel Mounier and the New Catholic Left* (Toronto, 1981),
201.

could they cast their moral lot, for the PCF (as it never failed to insist) was "un parti pas comme les autres."

Moreover, Mounier and many of his contemporaries had a bad conscience. Despite a sustained effort to whitewash the memory of 1940 in the January 1945 edition of the journal and again in a collective work published the same year,[32] the problem never quite went away. The desire to find some good in the Vichy regime had lasted well beyond the enactment of the first *Statut des Juifs,* which says something about *Esprit*'s moral priorities, and even though Mounier could point to a protest they published against the *Jud Suss* and to the republication of a piece by Péguy on Jews (both in 1941), the fact remained that it took this group a disturbingly long time to separate itself wholeheartedly and definitively from the Pétain regime. These strictures must be applied with care— some of *Esprit*'s postwar collaborators had passed the latter years of the Occupation in the Resistance or as deportees.[33] But it was Mounier who set the tone, and Mounier, like Sartre, did not have a "good war."

This did not prevent him and most of his contributors from displaying a remarkably confident and on occasion insufferably superior moral tone. Present from the outset, this became most marked towards 1950, just when the left Catholics were taking the greatest pains to remain anti-anti-Communist in the face of growing Communist atrocities in eastern Europe (see chapter 5). We, the argument would run, do not have to choose between communism and anticommunism, optimists and pessimists: "Against pessimism we have Faith. Against optimism, the harsh fact of injustice."[34] On controversial matters such as the attitude to adopt towards Tito, we take no stand, neither Titoist nor anti-Titoist. It is not our quarrel. This viewpoint might have been credible if it had been part of some larger moral vision in which internal Communist quarrels played no part. But it was applied, with Pilate-like disinterest, on almost every occasion. Even after David Rousset's revelations about the "concentration-camp universe" of the USSR, Jean-Marie Domenach could evince an air of effortless moral superiority. We, he announced, are neutral in such discussions: "We don't have to choose *our* camp."[35]

32. "Esprit 1940–41," *Esprit,* January 1945, 303–6. See also *Vers le style du vingtième siècle* (Paris, 1945).

33. Renée Bedarida, *Témoignage Chrétien: Les Années de l'esprit, 1941–1944* (Paris 1977). For her, resistance was a commitment made all the easier because it helped reconcile her personal conflicts and contradictions.

34. Mounier, "Fidelité," 181.

35. Domenach, "Une Révolution rencontre le mensonge," *Esprit,* February 1950, 195.

The refusal to "choose one's camp" is what truly marked the spiritu-
alists of the *Esprit* circle in these years, and it provoked predictable anger
within some parts of the Catholic intellectual community. François
Mauriac described Mounier (and Claude Bourdet) in 1947 as "ces mani-
aques de la pureté," which suggests something Savonarola-like about
them that is not wholly inappropriate.[36] Bernanos labeled *Esprit* "the
Catholic rear guard," which Mounier found especially wounding! What
was especially galling about the tone of *Esprit,* and the unquestionable
influence exercised by the journal within the intellectual community,
was that it managed to have things both ways, benefiting from impecca-
bly progressive credentials while claiming to be spiritually and politically
distinctive and with no responsibility for the practices of its political
allies. Mounier could never be accused of being, as Jean Paulhan
described Louis Martin-Chauffier, the Communists' "house Christian,"[37] but for that reason he was all the more influential and useful. To
be sure, Mounier's reiterated claim to be concerned above all with justice
and spirituality and the higher Christian virtues made particularly
damaging his failure to speak with a consistent voice at the time of the
postwar purge. But this was not something peculiar to Mounier—
others, including Protestants like André Philip and Denis de Rougement, also had little to say at the time. Resistance-era journals like
Témoignage Chrétien also made no secret of their wish to be associated
unambiguously with the Left, whatever difficulties this posed for the
more delicate consciences among them.

Mounier's importance lay in his capacity to present their situation to
the French in apparently simple black-and-white terms, employing rhetorical devices designed to emphasize the need for complete change and
wholehearted moral renewal. But, and this is the most compelling link
between the secular and the religious intelligentsia of the era, Mounier
also refused (or was unable) to construct any sort of ethical basis on
which fellow Catholics and intellectuals, not to speak of the rest of the
nation, might make their choices and explain, condone, or condemn the
actions of those around them. The outcome was an ethical vacuum filled
with noise. In this unpromising situation, post-Vichy France tried to

36. François Mauriac, *Journal,* vol. 5 (Paris, 1953), 10 June 1947. But note Mauriac's
encomium of praise to the same Mounier six years later—"J'aurai été le contemporain de
saints authentiques et me serai gardé d'eux parce que leur position politique prêtait à équi-
voque. Il faut que certains êtres meurent pour être rejoints." *Bloc-Notes, 1952–1957* (Paris,
1958), 11 March 1956.

37. Jean Paulhan, *Lettre aux directeurs de la Résistance* (Paris, 1952), 69.

produce some sort of debate about justice, evil, and political criminality. Not surprisingly, the results were less than edifying.

> *This, then, is the issue. We shall miss the point if we stick with an academic and idealized idea of the law. Positive law, like philosophies and civilizations, is born, lives, and dies.*
>
> Emmanuel Mounier

The *épuration*, as we have seen, raised troubling questions. Whom did one seek to punish? On what grounds? And to what end? The philosophical and ethical vocabulary of the engaged intelligentsia in postwar France offered little help, tending on the contrary to confuse and ultimately bury such dilemmas in global accounts of the human condition that left matters of moral and legal distinction to the tribunal of necessity or to the judgment of history. Nonetheless, the issue of justice could not be ignored, but on the contrary gave rise to heated discussions throughout the early Fourth Republic. The most intense disagreements, and finally the most radically historicist conclusions, emanated from within the community of Catholic intellectuals, and in what follows particular attention will therefore be paid to them. But the problem and the attendant ambivalence were universal.

During the last months of the Occupation, and into the initial period following the Liberation, the question of justice was still part of the larger struggle to defeat the enemy and secure freedom. In 1943, for example, it was self-evident that retribution, though it must be just, should above all be swift: "Where treason was public and admitted, the forms of Justice must be reduced to a strict minimum. Confirmation of identity followed by the death sentence is the only sort of Justice possible for those who were openly agents and recruiting sergeants for the enemy."[38] Even in March 1945 it was still reasonable for Julien Benda to warn the government of the risks it ran in delaying the punishment of collaborators:

As a government of patriots you should have punished the traitors as they deserved. If, as a result of your dereliction of duty, exasperated patriotic men lose patience and take things into their own hands, you will be responsible for whatever excesses such a people's justice produces.[39]

38. See the special number of the journal *Résistance* for 25 January 1943, quoted in Henri Michel and Boris Mirkine-Guetzévitch, *Les Idées politiques et sociales de la Résistance* (Paris 1954), 55.

39. Benda, in *L'Ordre*, March 1945, quoted in Jean Galtier-Boissière, *Mon journal depuis la Libération* (Paris, 1945), 183.

Although there was something overheated and a trifle dishonest about Benda's implied threat, it was not wholly implausible, and Benda was only pursuing a theme to which de Gaulle himself had given much thought a few months earlier. If the purge had been confined to such a policy of securing the necessary minimum of judicial retribution consistent with the need to restore the Republic, even its later critics would have been satisfied—or so they claimed.[40] But this was not to be.

In contrast to those like Paulhan or Mauriac who held that postwar justice should be applied with moderation and without rancor, some of the purge's most ardent defenders saw anger and revenge as positive, even laudable motives. It is an error, wrote Simone de Beauvoir, to suppose that one can punish without hate; only a response based in hate can achieve a "real transformation of the situation one rejects." In the act of punishing those who in our eyes have done evil, we recognize the importance of the freely chosen action: both that of the criminal, and our own act of retribution.[41] The argument was one she developed in the course of articles published within two years of the Liberation, and it is worthy of note that neither de Beauvoir nor her friends ever returned to the theme with the same attention in later years. It was as though the question of justice, for them, had been resolved once and for all. The occasional contributions to *Temps modernes* that dealt with the problem of justice in the coming years (and they were few and far between) served rather to reassure the reader than to provoke any reconsideration. It is true that in *Saint Genet* Sartre would confess that "moral Action" for us, today, is at one and the same time "inevitable and impossible," but this constituted a reiteration of the existentialist dilemma, not a reflection upon the ethical difficulties of passing moral judgments.[42]

If one was seeking to justify or excuse the punishment of one's political enemies on less rarefied grounds, the most obvious answer was to turn to the argument from revolutionary necessity. For this there were ample precedents in French history. When Jules Monnerot in 1947 set out to distinguish between the rigged show trials of Stalinist regimes and the postwar condemnation of Pétain and Laval, the centerpiece of his argument was the claim that the latter had indeed been condemned by revolutionary tribunals, but on the basis of facts and crimes, not forced confessions. In other words, a revolutionary tribunal was a source of judicial legitimacy, provided only that it passed its judgments in accor-

---

40. See Paulhan, *De la paille et du grain* (Paris, 1948), 113.
41. Simone de Beauvoir, "Oeil pour oeil," *Les Temps modernes* 5 (February 1946): 830.
42. Sartre is quoted in Anna Boschetti, *Sartre et "Les Temps modernes"* (Paris, 1985), 260.

dance with accepted rules of procedure and evidence.[43] But Monnerot's position, however well intentioned, was difficult to sustain. After all, if a revolutionary tribunal is engaged in the passing of judgment, at what must by definition be a moment when all is in flux and the previous political dispensations no longer apply, why should its hands be tied by legal formulas that are seen by the revolutionaries themselves as mere inherited excrescencies of the old regime? The experience of French history suggested that such limitations upon the range of methods open to "revolutionary justice" were hard to fix, and harder still to enforce.

Emmanuel Mounier grasped this, and his contributions to this discussion, together with those of others from the *Esprit* group, are among his most significant writings from the period. In 1944, *Esprit* took as hard and as realist a position on this subject as *Les Lettres françaises*. Like Benda, Mounier began from the claim that it would be impolitic to be too moderate. One might be a "lover of justice," an opponent of the abuse of power and much else, but such reactions risked isolating the well-intentioned intellectual from the "overall destiny of the era in which we find ourselves and from the community that, for good or ill, binds us to the participants in that destiny."[44] But unlike the secular intellectuals around Sartre, Mounier was not content to offer an apology for the excesses of the purge and then move on to other concerns. The problem of justice seems to have obsessed him, posing problems of conscience and duty to which he returned incessantly in the years 1946–50. In the course of 1947, on the occasion of the trial of Nikola Petkov in Bulgaria (the first postwar Communist show trial widely reported and discussed in France), Mounier wrote two influential articles in which he sought to reopen the debate around "political justice" and show how the eastern European context was comparable to that of the Liberation in France.[45]

In contrast with Monnerot and others, Mounier was critical of the conduct of the Liberation-era trials—those of Laval, Pétain, Maurras, and the rest. To prosecute these men under Article 75 of the existing Penal Code for crimes against the "external security" of the state was to diminish both the significance of their actions and the originality of the postwar circumstances.[46] The failure to initiate what he called "political tribunals" and to define new and openly political offenses was the reason

43. Jules Monnerot, "Liquidation et justification," *La Nef* 37 (1947): 8–20.

44. Mounier, "Suite française," *Esprit,* December 1944, 21.

45. Mounier, "Y a-t-il une justice politique?" *Esprit,* August 1947; "Petkov en nous," *Esprit,* October 1947.

46. For Article 75, cited in the Décret-loi of 29 July 1939, see Pierre Assouline, *L'Épuration des intellectuels* (Paris, 1985), Appendix 2, 158.

why the trials had been unsatisfactory and their outcome "badly suited to the purpose." Would it not have been honest as well as more useful to admit that there is a time for justice and a time for violence? Phases of violence, Mounier claimed, are necessary in order to recharge society with creative energy when it has lost its "élan" and retreated into formalism. As a model for this sort of revolutionary justice, Mounier again turned back to the 1790s and the arguments of the radical Jacobins.

Mounier began by quoting with approval the speeches by Robespierre and Saint-Just on the subject of the guilt of Louis XVI. Speaking on 13 November 1790, Saint-Just remarked of Louis, "We are here less to judge him than to fight him . . . one cannot reign in innocence: it is an evident absurdity. Every king is a rebel and a usurper. What relations of justice can there be between humanity and kings?" From Robespierre, he noted the speech of 2 December 1792 regarding the impending trial of the king: "There is no trial to be held. . . . A tyrant's trial is the insurrection; his judgment is the collapse of his power; his punishment, that demanded by the people's liberty." To drive home his point, Mounier concluded with Robespierre's famous summary of the source of revolutionary legitimacy, pronounced in February 1794—"The government of the Revolutionary is the despotism of liberty over tyranny."

Mounier's intention here is quite clear. In a revolutionary situation, the public interest (in Saint-Just's sense) overrides not only the interest of the individual but also any preexisting conception of justice or law. If the revolution is a movement in the pursuit of the universal good, and for Mounier this had become an axiom, then no prior constraint was imaginable: "If individual men are made to forge a living universality in the communities of mankind, collective justice trumps individual justice each time that this movement towards the universal requires it."[47] The defect of "individual justice" as defended by men like Mauriac, he wrote, is that it echoes the liberal obsession with the "isolated abstract individual." The task of those bearing public responsibility is to defend the justice of "the collectivity under threat."

In seeking to establish what he called the crime of "lèse-peuple," Mounier was building a significant bridge between recent domestic experience and contemporary challenges abroad. The analogy with 1793 pointed to two kinds of conclusions. In the first place, once a new social

47. "Si l'homme individuel est fait pour réaliser une universalité vivante dans les communautés des hommes, la justice générale peut primer la justice particulière chaque fois qu'il est nécessaire à ce mouvement vers l'universel."

order is established, the old order, the old regime, and its elites are by definition "guilty." Thus the "crimes" of Pétain and his fellow collaborators did not need to be proven according to existing law; collaboration was a crime by virtue of the outcome of the war—but *only* if the postwar order took seriously its responsibility for political and spiritual renewal. The French *épuration* had failed, Mounier concluded, because the French had missed their chance to transform society. Thus there had been no occasion for revolutionary justice, and the trials of the Liberation were a failure and a fraud.

But Mounier's second conclusion was therefore all the more important in his eyes. It is bad enough that we, the French, have "missed" an occasion; we must not fail to support others for whom the opportunity still exists. Thus he chose the occasion of the Petkov trial to expand his view of revolutionary justice into a prescription for contemporary politics. Our epoch, he conceded, seems to be one in which a diminished value is placed on human life, and this must be a source of regret. But there are times, he went on to insist, such as 1793, 1944, and the present (this was written in 1947), when "the death of someone condemned on political grounds seems sociologically inevitable." And if inevitable, then justifiable. Why? Because, Mounier concluded, "The political authority has a right of self-defense. The only discussion concerns the legitimacy of that authority, the seriousness of the threat, and the public character of the illicit activities in question."[48]

The conditional clauses here are not very helpful—for Mounier, legitimacy was a product of revolution; it was for the Bulgarian Communists to determine whether they were under threat, and *any* personal activity today could be construed as public. Petkov was as guilty as Laval, as Louis XVI, and for the same reasons. If such matters made Western intellectuals uncomfortable, if this seemed to them an odd sort of justice, that was to be expected: the violence of a revolutionary justice is "exercised in a prereflexive, uncertain terrain, in the service of a newborn order, against a used-up formalism and in search of a renewed sort of rationality." As to the wounded sensibilities of his fellow Catholics, Mounier summarized his position thus:

When Mauriac denounces the "attentat permanent" of a land without justice, he is encouraging his readers to believe that a chasm, that separating civilization from savagery, equity from sectarian fervor, has opened up between yesterday's justice, a justice of balances, ermine, and good men, and the political assassina-

48. Mounier, "Petkov en nous," *Esprit*, October 1947.

tions of today. But whatever support such a view may unfortunately find in those arbitrary and wild actions that disfigure the most legitimate of public anger, it is profoundly erroneous in its basic outlook.

In this view of things, it is hardly surprising that there was no place for charity. Charity, for Mounier and his colleagues, was a private matter and had nothing to do with justice. When Mauriac noted in April 1946 that there were people still in prison for "collaboration" who had committed no crime, and that this was a matter of injustice, not charity, his appeal was not heard, since the meanings attached to the term *justice* had by now moved far, far apart.[49] The position taken by *Esprit* in December 1944 was not to alter throughout these years: only mystics evoke "Christian charity," "the Christian pardon." To do so is to confuse "problems concerning internal attitudes of a spiritual nature, and political exigencies, which are autonomous."[50] Politique d'abord . . .

The historicized account of justice that Mounier was proposing entailed treating the postwar circumstances of France as radically new (or else claiming that they should have been new and would have been, had the revolution of 1944 not been aborted). This put many intellectuals into an inherently contradictory posture, since most of them were on record after 1945 as bemoaning the failure of France to change and criticizing the return of the Third Republic in the guise of the Fourth. But during the immediate post-Liberation months this contradiction was not yet apparent, as advocates of a revolutionary justice, a "new legality," pressed for the changes that would fulfill their demands and give plausibility to their claims. The concept of a "new legality" was treated as quite unproblematic, not only by writers in *Esprit* but also by Camus, who pressed for a new idea of justice in what he envisaged as a different, "collective" organization of society.[51] This new legality was to be the outcome (and guarantor) of what Simone de Beauvoir called "new values, created and imposed in the course of these years."[52] There is something breathtakingly naive about these lines (these values might be new to her, but most of them had quite a long ethical pedigree), but that should not lead us to underestimate the position they represent: they authorized a view of justice and the law that would play an important

49. François Mauriac, *Journal*, vol. 5, 30 April 1946.

50. Editorial, "L'Esprit du mois," *Esprit*, December 1944, 153.

51. Camus, *Combat*, 8 September 1944; and P. Fraisse, "Épurons l'épuration," *Esprit*, January 1945.

52. De Beauvoir, "Idéalisme moral et réalisme politique," 266–67.

role in postwar thought. References to "abstract justice" thus functioned in a manner similar to that of dismissals of "bourgeois society," as protective incantations against the overactive moral conscience.[53]

In the opinion of François Mauriac, France by 1947 was a society accustomed to injustice, inured to the defects of even the highest of its courts.[54] His opinion was perhaps not widely shared in quite that form, but disillusion with the jurisprudence of the purge was certainly widespread. The glaring contradiction between sentences meted out for apparently similar crimes had made people cynical, and even the most radical of Resistance intellectuals could not help but have doubts. Commenting at the end of the decade on the release of Georges Claude (imprisoned for life in 1945) and the reduction of Béraud's sentence, Claude Bourdet asked sourly why one had even bothered to condemn Brasillach, whose crimes were no worse than those of men like these. And if Béraud and others now deserved mercy, what did that make us, who just five years earlier had urged the execution of their colleagues?[55] To this rhetorical question there could be no comfortable answer, which is why few chose to pose it. Instead, the intellectual community preferred on the whole to turn its attention away from the unsatisfactory memory of the French *épuration* and towards fresh, foreign pastures, where the idea of a new justice could be applied without *arrières-pensées* and at minimum risk.

To be sure, the debate on justice, even the defense of "political justice," had always been hedged about with caveats. Of all people, it was Sartre who noted, correctly if inconsistently, "It is only the presentiment of Justice that permits us to be shocked by particular injustices." Even Mounier insisted that the most revolutionary of justices must conform to certain minimum truth criteria:

No situation in the world can justify those in power mounting nonexistent plots, pursuing the innocent, falsifying trials for terroristic effect, however salutary. A revolutionary justice is a rigorous and expeditious justice, but it must remain just.[56]

Yet in the absence of any clear sense of what such a concept of justice might mean, neither Sartre nor Mounier would have any defense to offer

53. See the acute observations of J-H Roy, "Les Deux Justices," *Les Temps modernes* 33 (June 1948).

54. See various entries in Mounier's *Journal*, vol. 5, for the spring of 1947.

55. Claude Bourdet, *Combat*, 3 January 1950.

56. Mounier, "Y a-t-il une justice politique?" 235–36.

against the blunt assertion of "revolutionary justice" in its crudest and most modern form. Like Jean Lacroix, they claimed to find in Vichy a set of circumstances that converted a "crime of opinion" into the "objective crime of treason."[57] From this to the idea of "objective treason" itself was but a small step, and one against which they had no recourse. The logical implications of such an elision were spelled out publicly and unambiguously by Karel Bacilek in another place and time. On 17 December 1952, in the wake of the Slánsky trial, he reported on the proceedings to the National Conference of the Communist Party of Czechoslovakia. Let us be clear, he declared: "The question as to who is guilty and who is innocent will in the end be decided upon by the Party with the help of the National Security organs."[58]

57. See Jean Lacroix, "Charité chrétienne et justice politique," *Esprit,* February 1945, 388.

58. Quoted in Pavel Korbel, *Sovietization of the Czechoslovak Judiciary* (1953, no place of publication), 22.

PART TWO

The Blood of Others

CHAPTER FIVE

Show Trials

Political Terror in the East European Mirror,
1947–1953

Ils commencent ici par faire pendre un
homme et puis ils lui font un procès.

Here they hang a man first and then
they try him.

Molière

By the late 1940s, information about life under Stalin and his system was
readily available to anyone. Indeed, ever since the mid-1930s there had
been a steady flow of news and revelations from the Soviet Union, followed after the war by an even fuller body of information about repression in the new European satellites. Personal memoirs, reportages, and
semiofficial acknowledgments had provided considerable detail concerning labor camps, mass deportations, and the reality behind the political
trials.[1] As early as 1935, talking to pro-Soviet writers in Paris, Denis de

1. See, for example, Victor Serge, *Seize Fusillés à Moscou* (Paris, 1936); and David Dallin
and Boris Nicolaevsky, *Forced Labor in the Soviet Union* (London, 1948). See also *Vers
l'union,* a pamphlet published in 1947 by the Mouvement fédéral de l'Europe centro-
oriental, which provided copious details of camps and deportations in the Soviet Union
for the years 1933–46.

Rougemont had been struck by their readiness to admit the presence of punishment camps in the Soviet Union, excused as part of the "dialectic of history" or else brushed aside as worthwhile sacrifices for such a "great and beautiful idea."[2] The revelations of the late forties, not to mention those of a later generation, were only news in the sense that some people were choosing to hear them for the first time.

Within this complex of troubling data, the Moscow trials of 1936–38 had long occupied the prominent place. Even before the publication of Arthur Koestler's best-selling *Darkness at Noon,* there had been something troubling, ghoulish about these judicial showpieces. For the most part they were treated by Western intellectuals as something exotic and mildly ridiculous, a sort of exercise in collective flagellation. The steady stream of absurd admissions of guilt (Krestinsky in 1937 was the only major Soviet victim who ever retracted even a part of the required confession) convinced only the most nakedly servile of Communist intellectuals, like Aragon, who wrote in *Commune* in 1937, "To claim innocence for these men is to adopt the Hitlerian thesis on all points."[3] The usual reaction was that of someone like Malraux, who did not try to claim for the trials any judicial or moral plausibility but insisted nonetheless, "Just as the Inquisition did not affect the fundamental dignity of Christianity, so the Moscow trials have not diminished the fundamental dignity of Communism."[4] Not everyone was so forgiving, however: André Breton publicly condemned the Moscow trials as a fraud, and Emmanuel Mounier, writing in *Vendredi,* distanced himself quite unambiguously from any political system that could condone such a shame.

The crimes being perpetrated in Moscow were veiled, in some measure, by the desire of intellectuals in the West to maintain unity of action against fascism during the middle years of the thirties. They were then forgotten in the maelstrom of war and occupation during the years that followed. By the time the Soviet Union emerged as an Allied victor in 1945, its past sins lay far away. What would later be seen as institutional characteristics of communism—terror, violence, injustice—were regarded with some benevolence as the growing pains of a new world. In any case, Stalin had now abolished the Comintern, had beaten Hitler, and could claim, through the intermediary of local Communist parties, to have

    2. Denis de Rougemont, *Journal d'une époque, 1926–1946* (Paris, 1968), 272–73; see also Jules Monnerot, "De l'autocritique," in *Preuves* 24 (February 1953).
    3. Aragon is quoted in David Caute, *The Fellow Travellers* (New York, 1973), 118.
    4. Malraux, quoted in Paul Hollander, *Political Pilgrims* (Oxford, 1981), 161.

played an active role in the domestic resistance. For many observers, the worst years of Stalinism seemed to be past.

Western intellectuals, the French especially, were thus psychologically unprepared for the onslaught of repression that hit Central and eastern Europe in the years 1947–54. Although the daily suffering of the population was largely hidden from Western eyes, a series of highly visible public accusations and persecutions made the headlines in the world press during these years. These came in three distinct stages. From 1944 until the trial of Nicola Petkov in Bulgaria (August 1947), the Communists were still engaged in a struggle for power, even if it was a struggle unequally weighted in their favor. They took reprisals against the non-Communist resistance in Poland,[5] played a deliberately prominent role in the purging of wartime collaborators, and harassed and undermined politicians of other political movements. Most of this activity passed without comment in the West, since it not only seemed to be part of an admirable process of postwar social change but also looked a lot like the purges and score-settling that, as we have seen, were taking place during these years in the West as well. Only with the trial and execution of Petkov (23 September 1947) did nonpartisan Western commentators begin to take notice. Petkov was the leader of the Agrarian Union in Bulgaria, and his general sympathies for the Left and social change were well known. To indict and condemn him for "criminal conspiracy" against the state was open cynicism and revealed a significant change in Communist strategy.[6]

The second stage in the Stalinizing of eastern Europe began shortly after the death of Petkov, with the formation in September 1947 of the Cominform, the split between Tito and Stalin a few months later, and a crescendo of political trials culminating in that of László Rajk in Budapest during September 1949. The emphasis was no longer on non-Communist politicians, most of whom had been driven from office and even from their country, but on dissident Communists themselves, or men and women whom it suited Stalin to treat as opponents. There was a bloody series of purges in the Albanian Communist Party, beginning with the arrest, trial, and execution of Koci Xoxe in May and June 1949. The Rajk trial in Hungary was also the first in a long line of lesser trials

---

5. At least four hundred people were shot and many more sentenced to prison in the *official* postwar reprisals in Poland, which served, as elsewhere, as a prelude and habituator for the show trials of coming years. See Marc Hillel, *Le Massacre des survivants* (Paris, 1985).

6. See *The Trial of Nikola Petkov* (Sofia, 1947).

in that country, thirty-one in all, every one of them secret (in contrast to that of Rajk, which had been well publicized and relayed direct to the Hungarian public). In addition, the regimes in Bulgaria and Hungary continued to prosecute church leaders, Catholic and Protestant alike, in an unbroken sequence of judicial persecutions of which the trial of Cardinal Mindszenty in February 1949 was only the best known.[7]

During this second stage the emphasis in eastern European terror was on those countries affected, or likely to be affected, by the Titoist heresy—Bulgaria, Albania, and Hungary. In the third stage, which lasted until about a year after the death of Stalin, the emphasis switched to Czechoslovakia and, to a lesser extent, Romania. Poland, although it suffered a steady series of domestic repressions, never underwent a major show trial, although plans to try Wladyslaw Gomulka were made but never put into effect. The Polish situation was unique in various ways, and the persecution there, although bad enough, never took the sort of shape it did elsewhere in the Soviet bloc. In Czechoslovakia, by contrast, it attained a degree of hysteria and horror unequaled anywhere in Soviet-occupied Europe.

The Czech Communists did not seize power until February 1948, making Czechoslovakia de facto the last country in the region to see its postwar institutions collapse into totalitarian dictatorship. Thereafter, the Czechs underwent the same experience as their Hungarian and other neighbors but in a belated, surreal form. Hundreds of priests and non-Communist politicians were tried, imprisoned, and in some cases executed; the most notorious case was that of Milada Horáková, the Socialist leader murdered in 1950 after her trial as one of the "leaders of a plot to sabotage the Republic." Making up for lost time and for their suspiciously Western and moderate image in Russian eyes, the Czechs then purged their own party of nearly two hundred thousand members during 1950–51 and followed this up with a steady series of arrests of prominent Communists during 1951 and 1952. In a final, sanguinary convulsion, the Czech Communist leadership and its Soviet advisors staged the trial of Rudolf Slánsky and thirteen others in November 1952. The trial was held *in camera* (though broadcast live), lasted just one week, and resulted in the execution of all but three of the accused. The originality of the Czech example consisted in the prominence of the accused (Slánsky had until recently been the secretary-general of the

7. See *László Rajk and His Accomplices before the People's Court* (Budapest, 1949); *The Trials of Jozef Mindszenty* (Budapest, 1949). For details of the Albanian purges see Lily Marcou, *Le Cominform* (Paris, 1977). See also François Fejtö, "L'Affaire Rajk est une affaire Dreyfus internationale," *Esprit*, November 1949.

party itself), the emphasis placed on the fact that eleven out of the four-teen were Jews, and the wholesale and enduring persecution of Czechs and Slovaks for years thereafter.

The Romanian experience ran parallel to that of the Czechs, with a series of trials of ousted Communist leaders reaching into 1954, with the prosecution in April that year of Lucretiu Patrascanu. In contrast with the Czechs, however, the Romanian victims (though many were Jews) were not persecuted for their ethnic origins or supposed Zionism, and some of the most prominent of them, like the former party leader Ana Pauker, were spared execution. Accordingly, the Romanian trials, de-spite the virulence of domestic score-settling that they revealed, and despite traditional French interest in Romania, lacked the news value of the Czech drama and played a lesser role in Parisian discussion.[8]

The politics and pathology of the East European show trials require a separate study.[9] A brief account of them is given here only in order to provide a point of reference for the discussion that follows and to illus-trate their importance at the time. Not merely were they contemporary with the high years of the postwar radical intelligentsia in Paris, but they also punctuated other news from the Soviet bloc, notably the further revelations about the "univers concentrationnaire" of Stalinism, as debated in the libel actions initiated by Viktor Kravchenko (January 1949) and David Rousset (November 1950–January 1951).[10] In order to understand their significance and the particular impact they would have on the Western consciousness, however, it is necessary to say a few words about the nature and purpose of these trials.

Two important distinctions have already been noted, between the persecution of Communists and non-Communists, and within the class of Communist victims, between those who were part of the anti-Titoist purges and those who fell victim to the last upsurge of Stalinist terror in the early fifties. A further distinction should also be drawn between those who were treated as ideologically deviationist and others, like the Slovaks Husák and Novomesky, who were accused of "nationalism."

8. For Romania, see Ghita Ionescu, *Communism in Romania, 1944–1962* (Oxford, 1964); Nicolas Baciu, *Des géôles d'Anna Pauker aux prisons de Tito* (Paris, 1951); and Matei Cazacu, "L'Expérience de Pitesti," *Nouvelle Alternative* 10 (June 1988): 51–53.

9. Among existing works see Annie Kriegel, *Les Grands Procès dans les systèmes com-munistes* (Paris, 1972); and George Hodos, *Show Trials* (New York, 1987).

10. See Viktor Kravchenko, *I Chose Freedom* (New York, 1946); Guillaume Malaurie, *L'Affaire Kravchenko* (Paris, 1982); David Rousset, "Au secours des déportés," *Le Figaro lit-téraire,* 12 November 1949; Théo Bernard and Gérard Rosenthal, *Le Procès de la déportation sans jugement* (Paris, 1954); and David Rousset, Théo Bernard, and Gérard Rosenthal, *Pour la vérité sur les camps concentrationnaires* (Paris, 1990).

This distinction was not always very clear in practice, but it mattered for the non-Communist left-wing observer in the West, who might be unsympathetic to "bourgeois nationalism" but was more likely to empathize with the Communist ideals of Rajk and his co-defendants. The Titoist defection confused these categories, which is one of the reasons it was targeted with such virulence by Stalin.

The reactions of the victims also varied significantly. With one exception, the East European Communist leaders placed on public trial all confessed their guilt, agreeing with the charges directed at them by the prosecutor. The exception was Traicho Kostov, the Bulgarian Communist tried in December 1949 who made a brief, desperate public retraction of his confession on the last day of his trial.[11] This near-universal acceptance of guilt, in a direct and perfected imitation of the Moscow confessions of the thirties, was integral to the purposes of these performances but was one of the chief hurdles for Western commentators who sought to make rational sense of the proceedings. The latter were quick to accept the guilt of those like Cardinal Mindszenty, the Protestant pastors of Bulgaria (tried in March 1949), or the Czech Socialists who either protested their innocence or else admitted the facts but rejected the Communists' twisted interpretations of them. From our present perspective, the destruction of civil and religious liberties and the brutal imprisonment and execution of hundreds of non-Communist leaders and thousands of their supporters in those years seem the greater crime. Rajk and Slánsky, after all, like Kostov and Pauker (or Bukharin and Zinoviev before them), had helped create and install these regimes and were themselves hardened Communist apparatchiks. Yet, for progressive intellectuals, it was the treatment of Communist victims that posed the greatest challenge to their own beliefs, and whose incrimination was most troubling.

It is also important to note the peculiarity and special circumstances of the *Czech* persecutions, which received the greatest prominence in the Western media. By the time of the Czech trials there was a long record of such affairs and their dynamic and structure were no longer a mystery. Whereas the Hungarian and other trials had taken place in the long aftermath of the war, the Czech ones came later and the memory of wartime affiliations had dimmed. Furthermore, the unambiguously anti-Semitic character of the Czech persecutions (all of East Europe's Communist parties had been dominated by Jews but only in Prague was this point

11. *The Trial of Traicho Kostov and His Group* (Sofia, 1949).

prominently reiterated by the prosecution)—albeit camouflaged as an attack on "Zionism"—and the fact that Czechoslovakia had been the region's only functioning democracy, before and after the war, made the news from that country especially disturbing. The sheer brutality and crudity of the Prague trials, the emphasis on the origins of the defendants, and the fact that they were orchestrated from Moscow in a manner not so self-evident in other, earlier instances made it harder to explain and account for them in the usual apologetic dialectic.[12]

Furthermore, the Czech experience highlights the distinction between political purges and show trials. After 1945, the Soviet Union was in a position to eliminate and terrorize anyone it wished. The Red Army had effective control of Poland, Bulgaria, Romania, and Hungary (not to speak of East Germany, where similar events took place). From 1948, the Communist party in every East European country had a monopoly of political power and was itself fully regulated by Moscow through the mechanism of the Cominform, as well as by direct links between the KGB and the local security apparatus. If it was just a matter of controlling the population, transforming the economic structure of the country, and eliminating opposition, trials were redundant. By the mid-1950s millions of people had passed through prison and labor camps in Romania or Czechoslovakia, for example; like their predecessors in the camps of Siberia, these people had never been formally tried, much less given a show trial. The trials were thus the tip of the iceberg, and they had a slightly different purpose.

In their format, they were merely more-or-less faithful imitations of the Moscow trials of the thirties. The Rajk trial of 1949 was perhaps the most perfect of the replicas—to the point that Gyula Alapi, the State Prosecutor, used in his speeches the very words and phrases first employed by Andrei Vyshinsky in 1937,[13] but even the Slánsky trial, despite its racist excesses and Grand Guignol atmosphere, was a carefully

---

12. For the Czech trials, see the various works of Karel Kaplan, *The Murder of the General Secretary* (London, 1990); *Dans les Archives du Comité Central* (Paris, 1978); *Die Politischen Prozesse in der Tschechoslowakei, 1948–1954* (Munich, 1986); "Zamyšlení nad politickými procesy" *Nová Mysl* 6–8 (June–August 1968). Also, *The Trial of the Leadership of the Anti-state Conspiracy Centre* (Prague, 1953).

13. Thus Alapie, the prosecutor in the Rajk trial: "Le seul moyen de se défendre contre ces chiens enragés, c'est de les abattre." Note the unmistakeable echo of the Soviet prosecutor Vyshinsky, in 1937: "Le seul moyen de se défendre contre les chiens enragés est de les fusiller." See François Fejtö, "L'Affaire Rajk quarante ans plus tard," in *Vingtième Siècle* (January–March 1990): 80; and Arkady Vaksberg, *The Prosecutor and the Prey: Vyshinsky and the 1930s Moscow Show-Trials* (London, 1990).

crafted and preplanned exercise on the Moscow model. These trials, like the Soviet originals, were strictly speaking not trials at all but, rather, "tribunals," set up and played out for the purpose of "mobilizing proletarian public opinion."[14] It was thus no accident that they caught the public eye, at home and abroad—they were designed for that purpose. Of the major trials, only that of Slánsky and his colleagues was closed to journalists and non-Communist foreign observers, though it was reported in full in the Czech press. Their object, then, was to mold and shape opinion. To what end?

In one sense, the show trials were straightforwardly functional. The major confessions of the forties and fifties, just like the little confessions of the Czech normalization of 1970, were intended to bring individuals into line with the policy of the regime, either by direct threat or by example. Thus the Bulgarian elections of 1949 were delayed until two days after the death of Kostov, to ensure a good result. The prosecution of Husák and his colleagues in Bratislava in April 1954 was a retroactive warning against Slovak nationalism, always a problem in the binational Czechoslovak state. As to the role of the confession, this had a long pedigree, even if we exclude the example of the medieval and inquisitorial techniques of earlier centuries. When German officers were tried at Kharkov in 1943 for war crimes they most certainly had committed, it was important to the Kremlin that they recite pre-scripted phrases describing their sins, even though the exaggerations and absurdities of their confessions made their actual crimes seem less likely.[15] The confession in its agreed form was aimed not at establishing guilt but at confirming the prosecution's account of the nature of the crime and the motives of the criminal. In this way the trial helped to sustain not the judicial but the ideological and historical legitimacy of the regime, by illustrating in a particularly acute way the nature of its opponents and thus the moral authority it could invoke in defense of its own actions.

There was, though, a more complex functional purpose behind the trials. In most attempts to extirpate heresy there is usually some truth behind the charge. That is to say, heresy and heretics exist, and from the point of view of orthodoxy their extermination is a reasonable, even an urgent goal. The difference in this instance was that the Soviet authorities could not openly accuse the heretics of their real deviation and thus

14. In *Cours d'instruction criminelle* (Moscow 1936), Vyshinsky explicitly justified tribunals in just these words. See Paul Barton, "Le Grand Guignol judiciaire de Prague," *Preuves* 23 (January 1953): 70.

15. See the discussion of the Kharkov trial in Arthur Koestler, *The Yogi and the Commissar* (New York, 1945), 143.

had to manufacture complex alternative charges. After the war European Communist parties were full of independent-minded men and women who had come to the movement during the war through the Resistance. This was as true in Czechoslovakia and Poland as it was in France and Italy. They could not be relied upon unquestioningly to obey central party authority in their own country, much less to accept dictates from Moscow. They were, in the context of Stalin's postwar strategy, much too inclined to advocate immediate radical social change, and they were primarily interested in revolution in their own national community. Worst of all, many of them had spent the war years (or longer, if they had fought in Spain) living in the West, and although they had returned voluntarily and enthusiastically to their Soviet or eastern European home after the defeat of Nazism, they were tainted by all manner of possible deviations—nationalism, cosmopolitanism, and above all autonomy of judgment.

These were, however, the same people who were now in charge of their local Communist parties and on whom the USSR must depend for control of its postwar imperial territories in Europe. Until the defection of Tito, the repression of such people was largely confined to the Soviet Union itself (and its Baltic acquisitions). Thereafter, the example of Tito became both a danger and an opportunity. Some of those who appeared in major show trials—Kostov, Rajk, and Clementis (the second figure in the Slánsky trial)—were genuinely vulnerable to the charge that they shared the goals of a Tito. In many cases, however, they had only been expressing views that in earlier years had been official Soviet policy. Thus Kostov's support for the idea of a Balkan Federation or Rajk's authoritarian but Hungaro-centered practices as interior minister were in line with Communist strategy—until the break with Yugoslavia, at which point they became (retroactive) treason. By placing such men on trial, the Soviet Union achieved a number of goals. It punished and removed locally prominent figures who might, like Tito, have become alternative poles of authority. It secured in power within the local party men like Rákosi or Gottwald, who depended on the Russians for their power and their position. It had a golden opportunity to include in the charges men and women who were suspect on other grounds but against whom there was no ideologically respectable case to be made. And, perhaps most important, the trials could serve as a warning to those who might have been tempted to follow the Tito line that they too were vulnerable.[16]

16. See Marcou, *Le Cominform;* Ivo Banac, *With Stalin against Tito* (Ithaca, 1988); Adam Ulam, *Titoism and the Cominform* (Cambridge, Mass., 1952); *Risoluzione e documenti dell'Ufficio d'informazione dei partiti comunisti e operai, 1947–1951* (Rome, 1951).

By 1952, the Soviet Union was no longer so worried about Tito. Its concerns had become more global and it was adjusting its military and strategic objectives in the light of the Korean experience and the apparent threat of war. As the wealthiest and the last of the European satellites, the one whose domestic party was still marked by memories of autonomy and self-interest,[17] Czechoslovakia was a natural target for Stalin's last thrust for control and monopoly, a move echoed in the attack on the Jewish doctors in Moscow at the same time. Thus, not only were all the old accusations rolled out—nationalism, Titoism, counterrevolutionary plotting—but the Czech Communists, already vulnerable to charges of having pursued their own line before and during the war, were now further accused of supporting (U.S.) capitalist interests via their assistance to Israel, an assistance ostensibly motivated by their Zionist fellow-feeling. As it happened, the Czechs had been used by the Russians to funnel weapons and assistance to Israel ever since the founding of that state, but the change in Soviet Middle-East policy required that someone take the blame for these past errors. Hence it was not enough to prosecute midlevel or even senior Czech and Slovak Communists—the leaders themselves had to go. The fact that Slánsky had been a faithful and brutal servant of Stalin was not only no defense, it was what made him both so vulnerable and such a perfect victim. If he was not safe, no one was.

The Czech example made clear what had been better hidden in earlier cases, the ultimately pathological nature of the show trials and their motivation. The crazy logic of the earlier persecutions could be applied in the Prague instance only by the truest of true believers, which is why Western reactions to it are so instructive. The cult of Stalin, which reached a peak with the celebration of his seventieth birthday in December 1949, did not seem directly to be at issue in the Czech case, in the way it had been in the early years of Tito's opposition to him, so that the terrible diabolization of the Slánsky trial seemed to have no anchoring premise. The usual arguments still applied—an error becomes a crime, from which it is then deduced that other crimes were intended, from which it is inferred that *all* the accused's motives were criminal, now and in the distant past—but the advantages of the procedure seemed unclear. In the era of very late Stalinism, the procedures and practices had outrun

17. The Czech Communists initially favored accepting the Marshall Plan and a "Czech route to Socialism," until brought to heel by Stalin. See Jacques Rupnik, *Histoire du Parti Communiste tchécoslovaque* (Paris, 1981), 191–94.

even their own peculiar rationale, and it was the misfortune of the Czechs to have been around to suffer the consequences.

These matters received considerable attention in France. They were also widely reported and discussed in Italy, the United Kingdom, the United States, and elsewhere. But in Paris the debates on this topic were unusually heated and agonized, and there were special reasons for the French interest. To begin with, France had the second-largest Communist party in the free world (after Italy), and one of the most Stalinized. Not only did the French Communist party play an active part in the international Communist movement, but its own domestic history intimately reflected events in Moscow, Prague, and elsewhere. Indeed, there was something almost ludicrously imitative about the PCF's practices in these years. Spanish war veterans, Resistance-era leaders, men known to harbor nostalgia for the comradeship of the Popular Front and the war were tolerated in the party until the onset of the Cold War; thereafter they were first marginalized, then expelled from the inner circles of power and eventually from the party itself. In nearly every case they were accused of deviations similar to those of the East European victims (Titoism, nationalism, indiscipline, and so on), and in at least one instance even subjected to a private "Moscow trial" in Paris.[18] Like the Czechs and Hungarians too, the PCF had a titular head, Thorez, who was protected from deviations (including his own) by the victimization of others.

Thus the French Left had a domestic as well as an international interest in the persecutions of the Stalinist era. Furthermore, many of the accused in the trials were personally known to French politicians and intellectuals. The Hungarian Rajk had been interned in the French camp at Gurs after the defeat of the Spanish Republicans, and indeed his time there was a prominent part of the case against him. Artur London, one of the defendants in the Slánsky trial, was known to many people in the French Resistance and among the Communist deportees and was the brother-in-law of one leading French Communist and future father-in-law of another.[19] André Simone, another defendant in the Prague trial, had been a prominent journalist in progressive Parisian circles during the thirties. Traicho Kostov had worked in Paris and also had a wide circle of French contacts; his dismissal from office on 6 April 1949 made the front

18. See Charles Tillon, *Un "Procès de Moscou" à Paris* (Paris, 1971).
19. Respectively Raymond Guyot and Pierre Daix. See Pierre Daix, *J'ai cru au matin* (Paris, 1976), 285ff; and Artur London, *L'Aveu* (Paris, 1968).

page of *Combat*.[20] And so on. In marked contrast to the Moscow trials, which concerned men with whom non-Communist Westerners had little contact or personal sympathy, the lists of accused persons in the postwar East European tribunals were full of people known to Western intellectuals, by name and often in person. Even Dominique Desanti, who at the time made something of a specialty of being "la Stalinienne de service," claims to have been shaken by the Prague trials of 1952 because of her personal knowledge of some of the accused.[21]

This closer personal acquaintance with the victims did not necessarily produce greater insight or even a marked increase in skepticism. But the sheer proximity of totalitarianism—the fact that it was now happening a few kilometers to the east of Vienna—made it so much more troubling even to those who sought to avoid drawing the obvious conclusions. Hence the reaction of Mounier, who doubtless spoke for many: "The system is moving West, its mystery is revealing itself with repetition. It is affecting men one knows better and concerning the plausibility of the charges against whom various people can judge from experience." Czechoslovakia especially seems to have rung warning bells in some quarters (though this may simply be a result of the fact that the Czech trials came so late in the period): Claude Bourdet thought that the Communists had made a serious error of judgment in applying their techniques in the Czech case. The West, he wrote, identifies with Czechoslovakia, which is "almost Western," more even than with Budapest or Sofia.[22]

There was one further local reason for the special French interest in the persecutions in East Europe. The Kravchenko and Rousset affairs, noted above, gave unusual prominence to the issue of Soviet camps, and more generally to the debate about communism, at the very moment when the persecutions in eastern Europe were at their height. This raised the stakes on both sides and made it harder for non-Communist defenders of the USSR to ignore even the smaller trials then taking place. The case of Kravchenko was easier to dismiss, for some at least. His book *I Chose Freedom* was published first in the United States, which already made it suspect in the eyes of many. Even Camus, as late as 1953, accused

20. See *Combat*, 6 April 1949. The trial of Cardinal Mindszenty was also prominently reported in this newspaper during February of the same year.

21. Dominique Desanti, "Tribulations d'une communicatrice," in *Contemporary French Civilisation* 13 (Summer–Fall 1989): 270. There was no evidence at the time of Mme Desanti's doubts. For another example of contemporary reportage, see Madeleine Jacob's reports from Hungary during the Rajk trial, in *Libération*, November–December 1949.

22. Emmanuel Mounier, "De l'esprit de vérité," *Esprit*, November 1949, 658; Claude Bourdet, "Les Aveux de Prague," *L'Observateur*, 27 November 1952.

him of having chosen to be a "profiteer" from capitalism.[23] His credentials as an exposer of corruption, terror, and waste in the Soviet Union seemed open to doubt—he had been a beneficiary of the system, his decision to escape had been belated, and there were minor errors in his account. But even those who believed his story claimed that it contained nothing new: Victor Serge had written about Russian camps in *Esprit* in 1937 and again in *Destin d'une révolution,* and anyone who had ignored Serge could certainly ignore Kravchenko.[24]

What gave Kravchenko prominence was the libel trial he brought against *Les Lettres françaises,* by then a journal fully and enthusiastically in the Communist camp. The paper had carried an article in November 1947 claiming that Kravchenko's autobiography was a pure fabrication manufactured by the Americans in Washington. At the trial, Kravchenko produced a steady supply of rather obscure witnesses in his support, but his opponents were defended by a series of depositions from significant figures among the fellow-traveling intelligentsia: Vercors, Jean Cassou, Albert Bayet, Joliot-Curie, and others. *Les Lettres françaises* lost and was fined a symbolic amount for damages, but in fact the impression left was of a Communist moral victory. Resistance intellectuals testified to the impeccable credentials of the French Communist party, which in turn stood for the Soviet party, which in its turn was thereby presumed incapable of acting as Kravchenko claimed.

The Rousset affair was significantly different. David Rousset was a left-wing activist, a survivor of the German camps, a friend of Sartre, and a Frenchman. Furthermore, his claim concerned not the general nature of Soviet society but one specific and ascertainable detail. Rousset published in the 12 November 1949 issue of *Le Figaro littéraire* an appeal to former deportees to help him set up an enquiry into Soviet labor camps. These, he argued, basing himself on the *Code du travail correctif* of the Soviet Union, were no mere passing defect of the system, much less the happy reeducation centers depicted by the Communists. They were instead, he wrote, integral to the structure and function of Soviet society and the Soviet economy. Within a week, Rousset received a reply in the form of an article by Pierre Daix, again in *Les Lettres françaises*. Daix, trading on his own moral authority as a former inmate of Mauthausen, accused Rousset of lying, of inventing his sources, and of caricaturing

23. Camus, *Actuelles,* vol. 2 (Paris, 1977), 167.
24. See Victor Serge, "Choses de Russie," *Esprit,* September 1936; and *Destin d'une révolution* (Paris, 1937).

the Soviet experience. Rousset then charged Daix and his paper with defamation and was able to produce at the subsequent trial not only an impressive stream of credible witnesses, including the remarkable Margareta Buber-Neumann, a former inmate of both Soviet and Nazi camps, but also some domestic support from Rémy Roure (a journalist with *Le Monde*), Jean Cayrol, and Louis Martin-Chauffier.[25]

Although Rousset also won his case, it has been suggested that he, like Kravchenko, did not score a moral victory and that his effort to publicize Soviet crimes had no impact on French intellectual consciousness.[26] This is no doubt partly true—since the *Code du travail correctif* existed and had been in print since 1936, no one who sought to be aware of its contents and their implications needed to remain ignorant. Moreover, even the argument between Rousset and Daix was not about facts but about faith. Daix and his supporters believed that the USSR had no concentration camps because to think otherwise was unimaginable; until this ceased to be the case, no amount of data would change their minds. But that was not true of everyone. Rousset's efforts forced *Les Temps modernes* to address the question of Soviet camps for the first time in January 1950 and elicited from Maurice Merleau-Ponty the confession that the facts "put altogether into question the meaning of the Russian system." The sheer numbers involved in the system of forced labor made of the Soviet system, he wrote, one that despite having nationalized the means of production and ended private exploitation leaves us asking "what reasons we still have for speaking of Socialism in respect to it."[27] Even Simone de Beauvoir, in *Les Mandarins*, was constrained to insert a series of anguished debates between Dubreuilh and Perron over the news of Soviet camps, though she managed to rearrange the chronology to make it appear that these debates had been taking place as early as 1946.

It is perfectly true that the impact on intellectuals was not always deep or enduring. *Les Temps modernes* broke with Rousset at the end of 1949 over what it saw as his anticommunism, or more precisely his willingness

25. See Rémy Roure, "Les Morts vivants," *Le Monde,* 11 November 1949. Pierre Daix's article appeared in *Les Lettres françaises,* 17 November 1949.

26. This is the view of Pascal Ory and Jean-François Sirinelli, *Les Intellectuels en France, de l'Affaire Dreyfus à nos jours* (Paris, 1986), 184–85.

27. See Merleau-Ponty and Sartre, "Les Jours de notre vie," *Les Temps modernes* 51 (January 1950): 1154–56. But as Raymond Aron noted, Merleau-Ponty still found the USSR to be, "grosso modo," on the side of the "antiexploitative forces." See Aron, "Messianisme et sagesse," *Liberté de l'esprit* 7 (December 1949): 29.

to work with anti-Communists in pursuit of his revelations about the USSR, proving that Sartre at least had learned little from the experience. By 1952 he could write, in "Réponse à Albert Camus," "We may be indignant or horrified at the existence of these camps; we may even be obsessed by them, but why should they embarrass us?"[28] and Claude Bourdet was already more interested in his crusade against France's colonial wars, expressly stating his intention to give the latter priority over any investigation into Soviet crimes. Camus's position was naturally very different, but then *he* had not waited until 1950 to declare himself. In a biting attack on Emmanuel d'Astier de la Vigerie written in October 1948, he called his opponent "a servant of the concentration-camp universe" and declared that concentration camps were, so far as he was concerned, an integral part of the state apparatus of the USSR.[29]

Even if there had been no direct echo within the intellectual community of the issues raised by these revelations, the news from the Soviet bloc would still have been a prominent matter in France. In the decade following the end of the war, Kravchenko's book rivaled that of Koestler on the best-seller lists.[30] One reason was that it was not just the Left that was mesmerized by events "over there." Right-wingers in France, as in Italy, saw the persecutions in East Europe as further ammunition in their battles against the Left at home. They were even happy, on occasion, to accept that Rajk and others might be guilty as charged—concluding from this that the system was vulnerable to internal divisions and would not long survive. During the Cold War, Left and Right alike shared in the view that the position one adopted towards Soviet camps or Hungarian trials was an important and integral part of one's stand on *the* major question of the day. For many fellow-traveling intellectuals, to defend the credibility of the charges being made in Prague or Budapest was to place oneself firmly on the good side of an insuperable barrier. To do anything less was to risk finding oneself in the other camp, alone and without friends. There was of course the "other side," which could boast a number of powerful and clear-headed thinkers—Raymond Aron's

28. Sartre, "Réponse à Albert Camus," *Les Temps modernes* 82 (August 1952). Note the earlier, ironic prediction of Jules Monnerot in 1947 that at its present rate of progress, *Les Temps modernes* would soon discover the existence of concentration camps in the USSR. What he did not predict was that after discovering their existence, the editors of the revue would promptly forget them. See Jules Monnerot, "Réponse aux *Temps modernes*," *La Nef* 37 (1947): 34.

29. Camus, *La Gauche,* October 1948.

30. In the years 1945–55, Kravchenko's book sold 503,000 copies in France; Koestler's *Le Zéro et l'infini* sold 420,000 copies. See *Le Débat* 50 (May–August 1988): 14.

writings on the subject of the Soviet camps remain impressive even today. But what characterized this period was precisely that Aron and his like *were* the "other side" for so many intellectuals, and as such their approval was not only not sought but actively avoided.

These were important considerations. When François Fejtö wrote a critical piece on the Rajk trial in 1949, he lost many friends—within the circles in which he moved, only Gilles Martinet, Edgar Morin, and the group at *Esprit* remained loyal to him.[31] The same was true for all those who broke with the Communists in these years; Morin was one of the first. We forget, if we are not careful, the charged atmosphere of these years and the complicated and multiple motives people had for choosing to remain on the Left—and thus, for many, on the side of the Communists, however uncomfortable the outcome. This alone was sufficient to promote an unhealthy self-censorship, blinding men and women to the evidence before their eyes. But because we are dealing here with people for whom simple denial was not sufficient, they sought to justify their allegiance and their continuing faith through a complex of arguments and explanations, addressed, one sometimes feels, less at their readers than to themselves. It is to these discussions that we must now turn.

31. See François Fejtö, *Mémoires, de Budapest à Paris* (Paris, 1986).

CHAPTER SIX

The Blind Force of History
The Philosophical Case for Terror

---

*Qu'on le veuille ou non, l'edification
socialiste est privilégié en ceci qu'on doit,
pour la comprendre, épouser son mouvement et adopter ses objectifs.*

Like it or not, the construction of
socialism is privileged in that to
understand it one must espouse its
movement and adopt its goals.

Jean-Paul Sartre

In the period 1944–56, there were four possible responses to Stalinism.
The first was simple rejection. This was the position of Raymond Aron
and a few others. It entailed denying that there was any credibility to the
claims of communism, whether as the embodiment and protector of the
interests of the working people or as the vehicle of progress and human
perfection in history. Within such rigorous terms it was possible to be
both intellectually consistent and morally coherent; but in the political
and cultural context of these years, it also placed one outside of the
mainstream of intellectual life. This does not mean that Aron could not
look to a community of like-minded thinkers; in the pages of *Preuves* or
Liberté de l'esprit, not to mention foreign journals, there were to be found

117

articles by Denis de Rougemont, Nicola Chiaromonte, Arthur Koestler, Claude Mauriac, Jules Monnerot, Ignazio Silone, Manès Sperber, Czeslaw Milosz, and many others. But however intellectually appealing this body of work, we should not suppose that its impact at the time was especially significant.[1]

The second response was simple acceptance. This, obviously, was the posture of Communist intellectuals like Aragon or Georges Cogniot. For them, at the time, the news from the Soviet Union and East Europe passed through a double filter. In the first place, rumors of concentration camps, torture, rigged trials, and so forth were simply denied. *Ex hypothesi* a Communist regime did not engage in such practices. But when denial was not possible—as in the case of the Soviet camps or the suppression of dissent in the new "people's democracies"—the events in question were simply redescribed in a language compatible with the self-description of communism. This whole process was so unproblematic once one adopted Leninist first principles that its mechanism need not detain us here. In any case, the category "Communist intellectual" is close to being an oxymoron, not because intelligent people could not be Communists (many were), but because their presence in the party qua intellectuals was not welcome. If they joined the Communist movement, they placed their cognitive skills at the service of the party and were required to believe, not analyze. The truly valuable intellectuals were not those who joined but those who remained outside the fold, providing the Stalinists with intellectual credibility by their support and their independent status as thinkers, scholars, or journalists.[2]

Third, there was a transient class of Communist intellectuals who did not really conform to the requirements of their menial status in the movement. People like Edgar Morin or Dionys Mascolo would initially follow the dictates of discipline, only to depart in the face of some intolerable demand. At this point they entered a limbo, peopled by Trotskyists, revolutionary syndicalists, and aging surrealists, who sought somehow to maintain a radical position compatible with opposition to communism. Their writings from the time, notably in the journal *Socialisme ou barbarie* or later in *Arguments,* are important signposts in the

1. Jean-Marie Domenach's attitude was probably typical. Commenting on Milosz's *Pensée captive,* he wrote: "On se référera [au livre de Milosz] avec bien des réserves, car la satire le déforme, et plus encore cette façon de décrire la condition des intellectuels de démocratie populaire, en l'isolant de la situation d'ensemble de la population." "Les Intellectuels et le communisme," *Esprit,* July 1955, 1213.
2. See Jeannine Verdès-Leroux, *Au service du parti* (Paris, 1983), passim.

history of late Marxism and in the private conflicts they reflect, but their impact too should not be exaggerated. It is true that they were often the target of virulent criticism from within the Communist and fellow-traveling press. But this represented less a concern with their impact or the threat they posed within the Left than a sectarian cast of mind, the same way of thinking that led Stalin to pursue and kill his defeated opponents long after they had ceased to matter. To exercise a monopoly of truth (as distinct from a mere monopoly of power) it is not enough to defeat the heretic; you must needs destroy him. Lacking the material capacity to do this in Republican France, the Communist Left placed its faith in reiterated ritual public condemnations.

The fourth response to Stalinism was the most complex and it is the one that concerns us here. Unable to join the Communists and unwilling to part company from them, a significant number of prominent French intellectuals devoted themselves not to condemning or defending the works of Stalin but to *explaining* them. What they sought was a plausible and convincing account of otherwise incomprehensible events, an account that could maintain the illusions of the postwar years and sustain the radical impetus supplied by the Resistance and its aftermath. Such an account could not, however, merely echo the defense offered by Communists. For a Mounier or a Sartre, a Bourdet or a Vercors, it was not sufficient to explain the failings of communism as the mere momentary defects of an inherently perfect system, nor, with certain exceptions, were they willing to deny the evidence placed before them. Theirs was the altogether more troubling task of acknowledging honestly (as they saw it) the realities of the Communist experience in all its horrors, and yet so explaining the latter as to be left with an experience and a project worthy of their dreams and defensible in their own philosophical and ethical language.

In what follows I have arranged these explanations in analytical rather than chronological order. One reason for this is that despite the fact that the major texts are spread over a decade of French history (1946–56), they not only address essentially unchanged issues but are in direct communication with one another. The various books and articles of Mounier, Merleau-Ponty, Camus, Sartre, and others constitute one long conversation, in which close attention was paid to the arguments of one's colleagues and opponents—more attention, in fact, than was ever paid to the events they were purportedly discussing. A second case for favoring the analytical over the chronological approach is that there was remarkably little internal development within these debates. When a person's point of view shifted significantly, he or she simply dropped out of this particular community of discussants. This is because, as noted above, the Parisian conversations of this decade were not evidence-dependent: news from Prague or Budapest or Sofia did not alter the terms of people's arguments—it simply offered a renewed occasion for entering the fray. When a political development did have a profound impact on someone, which was less common than might be supposed, at least until November 1956, it usually changed the very terms of the person's thinking, so that he or she lost interest in these ways of reason-ing, or joined the "other side." Sometimes there was an interim period, a sort of epistemological purgatory (there are hints of this in Merleau-Ponty's political essays of 1950, for example), but it was usually brief.

In *Humanisme et terreur*, which was published in 1947 but had already appeared the previous year as a series of articles in *Temps modernes*, Maurice Merleau-Ponty placed a bet upon history. Let us suppose, he wrote, that history has a meaning. Let us further suppose that this meaning is vouchsafed to us through change and struggle. Let us also accept that the proletariat is the force for revolution in our era. Finally, let us credit the Communists with their claim to embody the conscious-ness and interests of the proletariat. *If* these premises are correct, then the purges and show trials of the thirties in Moscow are shown to have been not only tactically and strategically wise but historically just. Although Merleau-Ponty did try to argue that the Soviet victory over Hitler justified some of Stalin's previous actions, he recognized that this did not constitute sufficient proof. We remain uncertain as to the out-come of all this, he acknowledged. The verdict of the future is not yet in. But we have no choice but to act as though it will be positive, because to renounce Marxism (i.e., to dismiss the Communists' claim) would be to dig the grave of Reason in history, after which there would be left only "dreams and adventures."[3]

This is the classic presentation of the argument from History. Like all influential arguments, it is really very simple. It took the central Marxist fantasy, of a human history simultaneously intelligible and manipulable, and inserted it firmly within Merleau-Ponty's own version of contem-porary French philosophy. Because it was written as a reply to Koestler's *Darkness at Noon,* it took as its subject the Moscow trials of the thirties, that of Bukharin in particular; but its application is universal. The ques-

3. Maurice Merleau-Ponty, *Humanisme et terreur* (Paris, 1947).

tion is not whether Bukharin and his associates were guilty, nor even whether or not their trials were rigged and the pretexts employed indefensible. What mattered was the overriding need to give our lives, our history, a meaning. Since such a meaning could not, in Merleau-Ponty's philosophy, be derived from any a priori postulates, it could be secured only after the fact. Human experience could be assigned a value, then, only in the light of possible outcomes. Not having any means of ascertaining these in advance, individuals must choose on the basis of a gamble.

In this light, it was perfectly possible that Bukharin might be proved right and his persecutors wrong. The distinction between truth and falsehood, right and wrong, just and unjust was not categorical but, rather, a product of process, even of chronology. Bukharin before his indictment was a leader of the workers' movement; after his condemnation he was a traitor to that same movement. Since the source of that distinction lay within the self-ascribed authority of the movement itself, the only relevant question was the legitimacy of that authority. Until history showed otherwise, this legitimacy came from one's understanding of the purpose of history and the role within that purpose of the Communist project. Here again, one was gambling on the future, in the name of human needs. Because it was not imaginable that history could be purposeless, the bet thus placed was not only the best available calculation but the only one compatible with a higher vision of humanity.

In Camus's summary and criticism of this argument, "the responsibility toward history dispenses one of responsibility towards human beings."[4] This is true, but it misses the essential ambiguity that Merleau-Ponty inserted into his argument. Merleau-Ponty took it for granted that reason-in-history is an enigma (this is one of the many significant ways in which he differed from even the most sophisticated of Marxists). We are adopting a posture in the face of the unknown, he admitted; but we *must* adopt *some* such posture, and this is the one most compatible with the aspirations of our era. Emmanuel Mounier put the same point slightly differently, at about the same time: "Political justice is only possible in an affirmation of a final goal of history."[5] The Moscow trials had been troubling, he admitted; assuredly, they may have helped defeat a Soviet Fifth Column and win the war, and were to that extent a good thing. But *if* they "definitively" circumscribed the meaning of justice in

4. Albert Camus, *Carnets,* vol. 2 (Paris, 1964), 249.
5. Emmanuel Mounier, "Y a-t-il une justice politique?" *Esprit,* August 1947, 231.

the Soviet Revolution, then they could not be excused. How then was one to decide?

The weaknesses of such an argument were clear from the outset.[6] Francis Jeanson, writing in *Esprit* in 1948, offered the following comment on Henri Lefebvre's claim that only the "dialectic" could give a view of the whole: fine, he replied, "but how can man envisage world history as a whole, situated as he always is at some point within it?"[7] Merleau-Ponty and Mounier were vulnerable to similar attacks—even if one agreed that a gamble on history was humanity's best hope, what grounds did one have, at any given moment, for gambling on one particular vision instead of another?

Jeanson is an odd candidate for the role of rational humanist critic of dialectical metaphysics. It was he, after all, who took it upon himself to respond to Camus following the publication of the latter's *L'Homme révolté* (or, rather, he was assigned the task by Sartre). In that review, written in 1952, he propounded the very argument he had condemned in the earlier article: since we cannot know whether a revolution is "authentic" or not, it is better to let it pass through its present phase and methods; however perverse they may be, these "in the present context, all things considered" are preferable to its destruction or disappearance.[8] As the only terror that contains within itself the possibility for its own overcoming, communism remains the best hope for a true humanism.

By 1952, however, Jeanson was little more than a mouthpiece for Sartre. The latter expressed his own version of the argument-from-History on many occasions, but at no time was he so articulate and precise as in the famous article written in the afterglow of the destruction of the Hungarian Revolution. This is a privileged position from which to see this argument in its final form, since it might be thought that the Soviet invasion of Hungary constituted sufficient evidence of history's verdict upon the Communist illusion, as indeed it did for many other people. But for Sartre, the Soviet actions had no bearing on the legitimacy of the Communist project: "Its analyses are just: the errors, ignorance, and weaknesses of the moment do not affect that." He disagreed with Merleau-Ponty (by then writing in *L'Express*), who claimed that the time had come to "déprivilégier" the Soviet Union. On the con-

---

6. For a classic dismantling of this position, see Raymond Aron, "Messianisme et sagesse," *Liberté de l'esprit* 7 (December 1949); and Aron, *L'Opium des intellectuels* (Paris, 1955).

7. Francis Jeanson, "La Morale de l'Histoire," *Esprit*, May–June 1948, 908.

8. Jeanson, "A. Camus ou l'âme révolté," *Les Temps modernes* 79 (May 1952).

trary, Sartre insisted, it is privileged by its goal (justice and liberty for all) and by the fact that it differs from all other systems and regimes in this respect.[9]

But then Sartre shifts gears. The West has nothing to offer in place of communism, he insisted. Thus, if it were to be the case that the USSR managed to make us see socialism in the light of the barbarities of Budapest, then all would indeed be lost, and no one would have anything to offer to humanity.[10] It seems, then, that for Sartre there was no conceivable circumstance under which we would abandon our faith in the Communist future, given our need to believe in *something*. No imaginable body of individual injustices could ever constitute, in itself, sufficient evidence of the general injustice of the system. As Sartre put it at the time in a private conversation with Stephen Spender, it would even be wrong to speak out against injustice in a Communist state—to do so would be to provide ammunition for use against a cause which is that of the proletariat and thus, in the long run, of justice itself. His conclusion? "Perhaps we live in a situation in which the injustice against one person no longer seems to apply."[11] Others no less tempted by History were, however, more susceptible to the evidence of their own eyes. In an editorial published in the same month as Sartre's own piece, *Esprit* confessed to having waited many years for an awakening of the soul, "which despite everything seemed more likely on the side where there was movement towards the future and a faith, however immanent." We bet on the Soviet Union, wrote the editorialist—and, he implies, we lost.[12]

To bet on history is to provide oneself with justifications for actions in the present which would, on other criteria, appear indefensible. Of these the most prominent was the Communists' use of violence to achieve their ends; it was no accident that Merleau-Ponty's seminal text was called *Humanisme et terreur*. The twentieth century was a violent century; but Communist violence was, or appeared to be, qualitatively different from the violence of reactionaries and Fascists. It turned its violence upon its own people—especially its own people—and it stood in direct apparent contradiction with the peaceful and humanist goals of the ideology on which it rested. In contrast with the random violence of

9. Sartre, "Le Fantôme de Staline," *Les Temps modernes* 129–31 (January–March 1957), especially 581–676.

10. Ibid., 678.

11. Stephen Spender, *The Thirties and After: Poetry, Politics, People, 1933–1975* (London, 1978), 181.

12. See "Les Flammes de Budapest," *Esprit*, December 1956.

Mediterranean fascism, or the racist frenzy of nazism, totalitarian socialism seemed to be distinguished by the organic quality of its violence—
terror as the very essence, the legal basis of the regime. In order to explain
away this aspect of communism, which had grown to terrifying dimensions in Stalin's later years,[13] a new distinction emerged: "Is violence
used to perpetuate a state of affairs in which violence is inevitable, or . . .
[is] it used in the interests of creating a truly human society from which
it will be possible at long last to banish violence altogether?"[14]

One response was to collapse Communist violence into some larger
category of human experience, within which it would lose its unique
flavor. This was the line of reasoning adopted by Merleau-Ponty, and
through his influence it can be found in much contemporary writing.
Violence, he suggested, is not merely that which we find morally or aesthetically offensive in brutal regimes. It pervades all aspects of life in all
regimes; it is everything and everywhere. All politics is necessarily a form
of terror, since politics requires the objectification of the other, a permanent denial of that intersubjectivity in which alone humanity might vest
its hopes. There is a violence of perception that takes many forms—
colonialism, wage-slavery, unemployment. Since all existing regimes are
thus based on violence, we cannot base our allegiances or judgments on
what these regimes do but only on what they are (or claim to be). This
claim, that all regimes are violent in their essence, derived considerable
emotional credibility from recent history, while the attendant suggestion, that there was something more inherently honest about a regime
that practiced its violence openly, appealed to existentialist sensibilities
—Communist violence was more *authentic*.[15]

This implied that there was thus something hypocritical about opposing Communist violence while one condoned or benefited from political
arrangements that practiced a violence of their own, and it was an idea
that appealed both to journalists like Claude Bourdet (an early activist
on behalf of victims of colonial violence in Madagascar and North
Africa) and to moralists like Mounier. So long as we have the poor and
the disadvantaged among us, the latter argued in his writings on "personalism," we are practicing "white" violence, participating at a distance

13. Even if one does not include the great terror of the early thirties, about which
there was still much ignorance. See Robert Conquest, *The Great Terror* (New York, 1968).

14. See Leo Huberman and Paul Sweezy, "On Trials and Purges," *Monthly Review*,
March 1953, 42–43.

15. See the discussion in Sonia Kruks, *The Political Philosophy of Merleau-Ponty* (New
York, 1981), passim.

in the diffused murder of mankind.[16] It does not seem to have occurred to Mounier to draw a clear distinction between killing and letting die, but then it is true that such fine analytical categories were not common in the French philosophical canon. But in this case it may also have been that Mounier's defense of violence was based on slightly different considerations. For him, unlike the Merleau-Ponty of *Humanisme et terreur,* there was a real difference between the violence of the Communists and the violence of the West, but it was a distinction that worked in favor of the former.

Writing in 1947, with half an eye on the French purges and the Moscow trials but moved to think about these matters by the developments in eastern Europe, Mounier contended that the criticisms addressed at the Communists were off target:

The political trials [in eastern Europe] are blamed for turning opposition into treason, for conflating regime and nation, for confusing the enemies of the regime with the enemies of the country. But the State and the nation are clearly distinct only in the normal structures that develop between crises. In the perspective of public safety, the whole nation is in the lifeboat; the State is everywhere because it must watch over everything.

In other words, the Moscow trials, like those of the French collaborators, were "crisis justice," a justice of public safety. Thus understood, they reveal their full "spiritual value":

The psychology of the accused, his personal destiny pale before the collective destiny, because at that moment the latter is facing life or death. Vyshinsky made the point brutally to the Moscow defendants: . . ."Here is the immediate, objective cause, the rest is psychology."

Buried somewhere deep inside this abdication of moral judgment there remains a nugget of dissent. For Mounier, violence is real, not just metaphorical; when things get out of hand, there is a "blind force that consumes blood and liberty. And circumstances [*sic*] know neither justice nor pity."[17]

Until 1952, this was also Sartre's position, when he chose to address the question. But thereafter, and beginning with "Les Communistes et la paix," he treated Communist violence not only as the necessary, objec-

---

16. Mounier, *Le Personnalisme* (Paris, 1950), quoted in John Hellmann, *Emmanuel Mounier and the New Catholic Left* (Toronto, 1981), 242–43.
17. Mounier, "Y a-t-il une justice politique?" 221, 223, 228.

tive expression of "proletarian humanism," the rough justice of history, but as something admirable.[18] By the end of the fifties he was describing it as the laudably efficacious "midwife of history," and throughout these years he, unlike most of his colleagues, never troubled to deny that the Soviet Union was terroristic in many respects. The gnawing admiration for retribution and terror, revealed in his attitude towards the purging of collaborators, found expression in his refusal to offer even the partial distinctions that marked the dialectical apologetics of his colleagues. For Sartre, violence, exercised at the expense of others over a suitable distance of time or space, was an end in itself.[19]

That he was not alone in this taste is something many foreign observers of French intellectual life have had occasion to notice. Writing in the London *New Statesman* in 1933, Peter Quennell remarked upon "that almost pathological worship of violence which seems to dominate so many modern French writers."[20] Forty years later this oddity was even more marked, with Foucault waxing lyrical at the thought of the September Massacres, Barthes and his colleagues singing the praises of the newly fashionable Marquis de Sade, and Sartre nearing the apogee of his career as an apologist for political terrorism. But there had been exceptions, in the postwar years as before: not everyone acceded to the apologist account of Soviet violence, and even some who did so maintained a discrete space for maneuver. Camus's critique of "progressive violence" in *L'Homme révolté* is too well known to require a summary, though it is noteworthy that of all Camus's many disagreements with him, it was this that provoked Sartre to break with his erstwhile friend. But in Sartre's own journal there appeared in 1953 a series of articles by Marcel Péju devoted to an analysis of the Slánsky trial in Czechoslovakia. Although he implicitly shared the general Sartrian line about revolutionary violence, Péju inserted an important note of warning: the very worst sin for a Communist regime would be for it to conduct traditional politics under the guise of "revolution." To use principles that *do* admit of violence to justify an unprincipled terror would be unacceptable: "If

18. Sartre, "Les Communistes et la paix," *Situations,* vol. 6 (Paris, 1964).
19. Sartre's writings from these years never quite descended to the level of his Maoist period. For an example of the latter, see an interview with *Actuel* 28 (February 1973), where Sartre asserts, "Un régime révolutionnaire doit se débarrasser d'un certain nombre d'individus qui le ménacent, et je ne vois pas d'autre moyen que la mort. On peut toujours sortir d'une prison. Les révolutionnaires de 1793 n'ont probablement pas assez tué." Quoted by M-A Burnier, *Le Testament de Sartre* (Paris, 1982); see also 182ff.
20. Peter Quennell, *New Statesman,* 26 August 1933, quoted by Samuel Hynes, *The Auden Generation: Literature and Politics in England in the Thirties* (London, 1976), 226.

they substitute, in other words, revolutionary mystification for liberal mystification, everything is put back into question."[21]

But how would you *know?* This was Camus's point, and it had been expressed earlier by Jean Paulhan in his debates with fellow resisters over the case for a violent postwar purge. Paulhan in turn invoked an earlier figure in his support, the Left's cultural hero Romain Rolland. Writing to Henri Barbusse in 1922, Rolland had sought to explain his refusal to line up with the nascent Communist movement: "I am not fighting one *raison d'état* only to serve another. And militarism, police terror, and brutal force are not sanctified for me because they are the instruments of a Communist dictatorship."[22] Autres temps, autres moeurs. What Rolland (and Paulhan) could not accept was the claim to apply different standards to apparently similar behavior. Indeed, despite his later career as a sort of progressive icon, Rolland would have been quite surprised to learn that one could only criticize a position if one first shared it. Yet this was the implication behind the defense of Communist violence offered in these years; unless you shared the Communists' account of themselves and their behavior, you could not evaluate their actions.

Thus in the very same article just quoted, in which he warned against a possible Communist abuse of the excuse of revolutionary terror, Marcel Péju also claimed that in order to enter the plea of mea culpa, intellectuals who now harbored serious doubts following the Czech show trials must first have been people who had judged communism by its own principles. In this case, they would not only have earned the right to criticize but would also truly understand what was at stake in Communist violence, the risks it posed for the legitimacy of revolution. Three years earlier, his colleague Louis Delmas, writing about Tito's rebellion and the death knell it rang for Stalinism, sounded a similar exclusionary warning: "Whoever cannot see that wherever Stalinism retreats without being replaced there has been a defeat of the whole workers' movement is nothing but an ally of the bourgeoisie"—and thus unfit to pass judgment on the actions of proletarian regimes.[23]

Unless one accepted the privileged status of the Soviet revolution, not only would one fail to grasp the meaning of its actions, but one would be condemned to *mis*understand them:

21. Marcel Péju, "Hier et aujourd'hui: Le Sens du procès Slánsky," *Les Temps modernes* 90, 91, 92 (May–July 1953). See part 1, 1777.

22. Rolland to Barbusse, in *L'Art libre,* January 1922, quoted by Jean Paulhan, *De la paille et du grain* (Paris, 1948), 145, n. 1.

23. Louis Delmas, "Réflexions sur le communisme yougoslave," part 3, *Les Temps modernes* 55 (May 1950): 1964.

Like it or not, the construction of socialism is privileged in that to understand it one must espouse its movement and adopt its goals; in a word, we judge what it does in the name of what it seeks and its means in the light of its ends; all other undertakings we assess in the light of what they refuse, neglect, or deny.[24]

This privileged position, this special epistemological status, was not to be accorded to any and all revolutionary regimes. It was very specifically reserved for the Soviet Union.[25] Thus the new regimes in East Europe were defended, not in their own right, but only as extensions of the privileged identity of the Russians' own revolution. Contemporaries treated the establishment of the Soviet empire in Central and East Europe as the logical extension of the Russian Revolution of 1917 in two distinct senses. In the first place, only the Russian Revolution could claim for itself an autonomous identity as a (*the*) Socialist revolution. Since Leninism not only explained the revolution of 1917 but also derived its legitimacy from it, the interpretation of the origins of Soviet society was as securely grounded as that of the bourgeois revolution in France. By contrast, the regimes in Europe were more ideologically vulnerable. They were (with the important exception of Tito's Yugoslavia) clearly the outcome of war and conquest and were tainted by the apparent absence of any internal dynamic—Communist power in Poland, Hungary, and elsewhere was all too obviously the product of external circumstances.

Second, the establishment of communism in the eastern half of Europe was from the start regarded by many observers as a device for protecting the revolutionary regime in Moscow itself. Far from being regarded as a weakness, this point received prominent attention in Western intellectual circles, especially during the Cold War. The virtue of communism in Romania or Czechoslovakia, therefore, was first and foremost that it was a further bulwark against any capitalist effort to turn back the historical clock and defeat the march of progress in its Soviet homeland. In the same way that the trials and purges of the thirties were contingently justifiable as an exercise in revolutionary self-defense, so the establishment of a defensive wall to Russia's West was seen as a normal and natural exercise of national self-interest. Even critics were willing to acknowledge this interest—for François Mauriac the Soviet invasion of

24. Sartre, "Le Fantôme de Staline," 677.
25. During these years. Later the privilege would be extended to Cuba, China, and others.

Hungary in 1956 was not a "Stalinist-style coup" but a normal political action by an empire on the defensive.[26] The actions of the Soviet Union after 1945 could thus be explained either as the legitimate defense of the heartland of revolution or as the imperial realpolitik of a superpower; in either case, the separate concerns of the local victims were secondary.

This, I believe, helps account for the ambivalence with which French writers responded to problematic developments in the Soviet bloc. Péju, in the article already noted, drew a clear distinction between the Moscow trials, which were "subtle" and "nuanced," and the later trials in East Europe, which lacked what he called the "heroic something" that he found in the Soviets' own experience of terror.[27] Mounier, a little earlier, insisted that what had happened in the Stalinist phase of Soviet history could have happened to any regime caught in the same trying historical circumstances.[28] But institutionalized and rationalized, this terror as now applied in Hungary or Czechoslovakia appeared indefensible. Hence the emphasis again and again on the Soviet revolution, which alone could provide the basis for one's continuing faith.

In these terms we can better understand why Sartre, in *Le Fantôme de Staline,* is so damningly dismissive of Hungarians, Communists and dissenting intellectuals alike. Socialism in Hungary under Rákosi, he insists, was "neither a Fascist dictatorship nor just any old tyranny: it did, despite everything, represent socialization." But it left in its wake (after 1953) a vacuum filled by violence and terror, which inevitably provoked a backlash of disintegration. De-Stalinization in East Europe had revealed a wasteland of deterioration and crimes. But in the USSR, by contrast, things were improving, de-Stalinization was popular, socialism advancing. Thus the Soviet invasion of Hungary, while bad in itself, was evidence of faults in the Hungarian copy, not the Soviet model. If the socialism in whose name Soviet soldiers were shooting people in the streets of Budapest was unrecognizable, this was the fault of the local Communist leadership alone.[29]

These fine distinctions infuriated Sartre's opponents. Communists like Michel Verret, writing in *Nouvelle Critique,* found Sartre's reasoning "paralogical": his explanation for events in Budapest was hyperidealist, blaming everything on the shortcomings of Communist leaders and the

26. François Mauriac, *Bloc-Notes* (Paris, 1958), 15 January 1957.
27. Péju, "Hier et aujourd'hui," part 1, 1787.
28. Mounier, "Y a-t-il une justice politique?" 228.
29. Sartre, "Le Fantôme de Staline," 616, 666, 673.

anarchist leanings of a few disoriented intellectuals.[30] But Sartre and his friends had not come on this explanation on the spur of the moment or by chance. When Merleau-Ponty finally acknowledged that one could not discuss the PCF without engaging the problem of the nature of the Soviet Union, he was roundly condemned by Simone de Beauvoir; why, she asked, did criticism of the French Communists entail any questioning of the revolutionary credentials of the original Leninist regime—"What has the Soviet Union to do with the matter?"[31]

This incredulous question from the "inénarrable Madame de Beauvoir" (Aron) is not as disingenuous as it now sounds. The link between the Soviet Union and its revolutionary origins and the various Communist movements of East Europe or France was treated as unidirectional. Lenin's seizure of power, Stalin's consolidation of power, and the proletarian interests in whose name they had purported to act served as the unimpeachable justification for the actions of Communists everywhere. But when the latter could no longer be defended by nonaffiliated sympathizers—in the wake of a particularly egregious show trial, the political inanities of the PCF, or the bloodshed in the streets of Budapest—this in no way reflected badly upon the living source itself. Individual Communists and their errors brought no dishonor to their parties; the crimes of these parties could never be attributed to the Soviet power on which they depended—and Soviet communism itself was both sustained by, and confirmation of, the self-evident truths of Marxism.

This reluctance to hold the Soviet Union responsible for the behavior of its dependents may seem curious coming from intellectuals who were nonetheless unwilling to throw in their lot with the party. But it responded to the logic of the period, for reasons to be discussed in part 3. It was also part of a further, complex dimension to Western responses to the events in postwar East Europe. For a certain class of Western intellectuals, the victim of the Rajk or Slánsky trials, of labor camps, anti-Semitic purges, and daily terror, was not some obscure local Communist politician, much less unknown thousands of workers, peasants, shopkeepers, and non-Communist writers and politicians. It was, or might become, Marxism

30. Michel Verret was commenting upon Sartre's interview in *L'Express*, on 9 November 1956. See Verret, "Sartre ou le compte des responsabilités," *Nouvelle Critique* 80 (December 1956).

31. Simone de Beauvoir is quoted by Raymond Aron in "Aventures et mésaventures de la dialectique," *Preuves* 59 (January 1956): 19, n. 11. See also Jean Co, "Staline, le fantôme de Sartre," *Esprit*, March 1957, 500–501 in particular.

itself. There was a widely articulated fear that the essential core of communism, the pure and timeless truth at the heart of the political system, would prove vulnerable to the inadequacies and faults of the contingent historical forms it had taken. "Le Communisme," one would frequently read at this time, "se dénature."[32] This line of argument has a long pedigree: it could still be found alive and well in the 1970s, and doubtless there are those today who still see in the collapse of communism in our own time the best hope for . . . communism.[33]

This, it could be argued, is a special failing of intellectuals—not only the idea that something called *communism* exists separate from and independent of the historical epiphenomenon itself, but also the astonishing belief that the defense of this ideal of communism (or Marxism) and the threats to its credibility transcend in importance all other, lesser issues. But whether or not it is a professional failing, it was widespread. It also reveals a remarkable political naiveté, not only about politics in general but about Marxist politics in particular. For what was missing in this community of thinkers fascinated—hypnotized—by the appeal of Lenin's revolution and its consequences was any acquaintance with the ideas of Lenin himself. In *Les Mandarins,* Simone de Beauvoir has one of her characters (Perron) argue at length that the moral pressure from enlightened Western Communists will lead the Soviet Union to modify its penitentiary regime, and indeed the whole book is a testament to the willful myopia of its author, who displays no grasp of the relationship of power and authority between Moscow and its satellite parties. But de Beauvoir was not alone. In one of his early postwar critiques of Soviet behavior, Emmanuel Mounier ends by insisting that his dissent from Soviet policy should in no way be seen as unfriendly. On the contrary; he hopes that his observations about the USSR's "over-enthusiastic" practices will be modified in the light of such friendly advice—"Are these remarks insulting to the Soviet Union? Not at all. The best sometimes attracts the worst, rather than the mediocre."[34]

In the eyes of many, the true crime of communism in these years was not its treatment of people, then, but the harm it was doing to its image and its own ideological foundations. For some the USSR under Stalin had long since ceased to be revolutionary, or at any rate sufficiently

32. On this, see Jules Monnerot, "Du mythe à l'obscurantisme," *La Nef* 39 (1948): 18.

33. For the Althusserian version of this "saving of the essence," see Tony Judt, *Marxism and the French Left* (Oxford, 1986), chapter 4; translated into French as *Le Marxisme et la Gauche française* (Paris, 1987).

34. Mounier, "Débat à haute voix," *Esprit,* February 1946, 181.

revolutionary to justify its own behavior. Boris Souvarine in the interwar years, Michel Collinet, Cornelius Castoriadis, and others in the forties, and a whole galaxy of *gauchistes* in the sixties all made this claim. It was also the view of a maverick like Georges Bataille, who saw in the Soviet Union's emphasis on patriotism, militarism, and national defense not a case for all and any political and ideological terror but rather a retreat from any sort of revolutionary credibility. On the other hand, writers who had never been a part of this particular radical community and who always prized themselves on their moral distance from the worst aspects of Communist behavior took rather longer to reach this conclusion and did so with palpable regret. As late as 1953, Jean-Marie Domenach could display a nostalgic sadness for the loss of revolutionary élan: "It is the misfortune of our society that no one any longer really opposes it. For the only ones who do so with efficacity, the Communists, do it in the name of a society that for all its just achievements itself has all the faults of an established order."[35]

Six years earlier, the editor of *Esprit* had expressed similar disappointment at the behavior of Communists. The regrettable feature of the Moscow trials, he observed, was not the charges themselves (and assuredly not the price paid by the victims, apparently) but the sheer dogmatism with which they had been presented. As a result, "even if the conspiracy was real, the impression of a forgery is inevitable." The punishments meted out to the victims may have been "necessary" (Mounier's word), but the way they were reached inflicts inexcusable wounds on "revolutionary humanism."[36] This degradation of Communist values was also remarked upon by Merleau-Ponty and Sartre in 1950, in their editorial commentary on the recent revelations concerning Soviet camps. Once again, the true crime was not the camps themselves, on which the two men had little to say, but the fact that the system was now so "degraded" that it could produce a Kravchenko. With such a person, they wrote, we can have no feelings of fraternity; he is the living proof of the inevitable decline "of Marxist values in Russia itself."[37]

The years 1949–50 were a turning point in this matter. Until then, and despite Mounier's musings on the disappointing appearance of the Moscow trials, the revolutionary probity of the Soviet Union had gone

35. Jean-Marie Domenach, "La Tâche de protestation," *Esprit,* January 1953, 21.
36. Mounier, "Y a-t-il une justice politique?" 233.
37. Merleau-Ponty and Sartre, "Les Jours de notre vie," *Les Temps modernes* 51 (January 1950): 1162

largely unquestioned, except, as noted above, from the non-Communist far Left. But in 1949 the impact of the Rajk trial in Budapest provoked a spate of articles questioning the meaning of such an elaborate exercise in judicial persecution. One such article, by Vercors, is of particular interest. This is in part because Vercors (Jean Bruller), the son of a Hungarian Jew, chose to publish his doubts in *Esprit*, a journal already remarkable for its sustained efforts to sit athwart an increasingly narrow fence. But the interest also arises from Vercors's role until then as a symbol of the intellectual resistance, a moral surety for the Communists with whom he had worked in close alliance since 1944. If Vercors was moved to express his doubts, then things must have reached a serious impasse for fellow-traveling intellectuals. But of what did his doubts consist?

His conscience, he wrote, was uneasy. But not so uneasy as to move him to sign a telegram to Budapest seeking clemency. Why? Because Vercors was not concerned with the verdict as such, with Rajk's guilt or innocence. One way or another, Rajk was a liar. Either his confession itself was a lie (Vercors did not stop to ask how it had been extracted), or else he had done some of the things he confessed to, in which case his whole life as a Communist was a lie. And even then he was not to be trusted, since the confession itself contained a number of contradictory and frankly incredible admissions:[38]

If I absolutely had to choose I would incline to think that Rajk and his fellow accused are guilty, guilty of some undertaking whose object is hidden behind disguised confessions. These are not innocent men whom I refuse to see critically judged.

What, then, was Vercors's objection? "The people are being misled. This I refuse to accept." The regime was hiding the truth, whatever that was, from the Hungarian people. The truth might be palatable or not, it might be "necessary for the victory of the cause we hold dear, I don't know." But to withhold the truth from the people was to treat them like children, and this *mépris* was unworthy of Marxists, especially of Marxists.[39]

38. For a full transcript of the Rajk proceedings, see *László Rajk and His Accomplices before the People's Court* (Budapest, 1949).

39. Vercors, "Réponses," *Esprit*, December 1949, 949–53. See also Jean Cassou, *Une Vie pour la liberté* (Paris, 1981): 254. He tells of being attacked at his section of the Mouvement des combattants de la liberté et de la paix on 31 January 1950 for his article in *Esprit*. When he left, he was accompanied only by Jean-Marie Domenach; they both subsequently resigned from the organization. For Cassou's article, see "La Révolution et la vérité," *Esprit*, December 1949, 943–48.

Thus, in addition to its failure to live up to its revolutionary origins and the damage it was doing to the credibility of Marxism, communism was spreading disillusion among the faithful, not through its actions but by the implausible and cynical explanations it offered for them. Within a few months of Vercors's article, this had become a widespread criticism among would-be sympathizers. Marcel Péju noted that Communist principles are threatened not when men die, however violently, but when "the ceremony that kills them is a caricature of what it could be if such violence was justifiable in a Communist perspective."[40] Louis Delmas, in *Temps modernes,* put the point succinctly: "Stalinism's greatest crime is perhaps its stifling of collective consciousness."[41] This was no isolated or casual comment. We have already seen that Sartre, six years later, could still maintain that history would show that the greatest sin of Rákosi and the Hungarian Stalinists was to have turned Hungarian intellectuals away from communism. "What is serious," wrote another contributor to *Temps modernes* in the months following the 1956 invasion of Budapest, "is that such a chasm has been dug between communism in power and the social classes whom it incarnates."[42]

But even this was fundamentally disingenuous. The real threat posed by Soviet terror in eastern Europe in the years 1944–56 was not to communism, nor even to its credibility among those it ruled, but to its place in the hearts of Western intellectuals themselves. The true pain was being experienced not in an obscure prison cell in Prague, or far away on some frozen quarry in Wallachia, but right here at home, in Paris. It was the sensibilities of French intellectuals that bore the brunt of the show trials. Thus Mounier commented on the judicial murder of Petkov in Bulgaria:

What anguishes us is not that a government acts rigorously and pursues its path firmly in the face of hostile forces. It is the sense of an inexorable mechanism that . . . risks consuming the Socialist revolution along with its adversaries.[43]

In the same piece, Mounier admitted that Petkov's corpse would haunt the European conscience (actually it was forgotten with remarkable alacrity). What he meant was not that a crime had been committed and that all men of justice must feel fear and shame; rather, he was suggesting that the damage that had been done to the reputation and image of Socialism might prove permanent.[44]

40. Péju, "Hier et aujourd'hui," part 1, 1773.
41. Delmas, "Réflexions sur le communisme yougoslave," 1973.
42. R. Borne, "La Fin du Stalinisme," *Les Temps modernes* 129 (January 1957): 1038.
43. Mounier, "Petkov en nous," *Esprit,* October 1947, 598.
44. He need not have worried.

In a similar vein, when Vercors and Jean Cassou wrote open letters in protest at the Rajk trial, they took enormous care to insist that not only did they not seek to join the camp of "anti-Communists," but that they were driven to protest by their very love of humanity and respect for the Communist party. Wounded in their sensibilities by the way in which the Communist movement was handling its internal opponents, they sought to condemn its mistakes the better to be able to work with it in the future. Thus it was not their fault that the PCF, intolerant of any dissent however well motivated, henceforward treated them as outcasts. Their intentions could not have been purer. As Mounier summarized it, commenting on the articles about Rajk that had been published in his journal, "Testimony of the sort we have published *is only of value for us to the extent that it can save socialism*."[45]

It was because of their overriding concern with "saving socialism," with the moral condition of communism, that French intellectuals displayed a distinctly selective sensitivity to developments in eastern Europe. Socialists, Agrarians, Populists, and other defeated echoes of eastern Europe's past were readily consigned to the dustbin of history. The trials of collaborators in Poland or Czechoslovakia were treated as unproblematic, comparable to similar postwar purges in France itself. With one exception, only the Communist victims of Communist terror aroused sympathy or attention in Paris. The exception was the trial and imprisonment of cardinals, bishops, priests, pastors, and nuns in eastern Europe in the years 1947–52. Similarly brutal treatment of religious leaders and their followers in the Soviet Union passed unremarked, just as it had been ignored before the war. For this there was one further explanation, in addition to the special credit accorded the Soviet Union in all such matters: most of the victims of religious persecution in the USSR were Orthodox Christians, Muslims, and Jews, none of whom was of much interest or concern to French sensibilities in these years. But the vast majority of the victims of Communist attacks on religion in eastern Europe were Catholics or Protestants: there were relatively few Jews remaining, and the Uniate and Orthodox faiths were significant only in Bulgaria and Romania, the two countries most remote from Western consciousness.

For this reason, considerable notice was taken of the persecution of faith in sovietized Europe, with Catholic commentators to the fore. Although François Mauriac was one of the few to devote space to the

45. Mounier, "Journal à haute voix," *Esprit*, January 1950, 133–34. The italics are mine.

condemnation of the archbishop of Zagreb in November 1946,[46] the trial of Cardinal Mindszenty in Hungary and subsequent indictments of pastors and bishops in Prague and elsewhere received prominent attention throughout the non-Communist press, with the notable exception of *Les Temps modernes*. In *Esprit*, which agonized over these attacks on the Church, a clear distinction was drawn. That Mindszenty and others were guilty as charged, in that they had admitted seeking to defend the Church against Communist propaganda and seizures of property, everyone could agree. It was normal and natural that the Church and a Communist revolution should find themselves in such conflict. But as to the accusation that Catholics or Protestant pastors had sought to spy for the West or overthrow the legitimate revolutionary government, this Mounier, Domenach, and others vigorously rejected. Where the regime had succeeded in extracting such confessions from a bishop or a priest, this was attributed to unknown pressure (Domenach suggested drugs).[47]

As a result, there is an insight and a moral clarity about the response to religious persecution that is altogether lacking in discussions of the trials of Communists. The proceedings against Mindszenty and his colleagues in the spring of 1949 provoked from the editors of *Esprit* a remarkably direct condemnation of Communist practices, one that was never invoked nor applied in any other instance:

Here is new proof that political justice in Communist lands is not satisfied with part of a man but wants him all, with his consent; for this it needs dishonored defendants, utterly guilty . . . of political and common crimes alike, for Esterhazy is charged with sexual perversion and Mindszenty with a further crime of currency dealing.[48]

Even the egregiously gullible *Quinzaine*, the epitome of fellow-traveling progressive Christian sentiment, could not swallow the arrest and banishment of Prague's Monsignor Beran, and it published a limp protest at the action, though without directly questioning the credibility of the charges.[49]

The protests at the persecution of churchmen constituted a special if revealing exception. Otherwise only the prosecution and punishment of

46. Mauriac, *Journal*, vol. 5 (Paris, 1953), 2 November 1946.

47. See Domenach, "Le Procès des évêques hongrois," *Esprit*, September 1951.

48. Mounier and Domenach, "Le Procès du Cardinal Mindszenty," *Esprit*, March–April 1949. But six months later, at the time of the trial of Rajk, no such strictures were applied, by Mounier or Domenach.

49. See *Quinzaine*, March 1951, and Yvon Tranvouez, "Guerre froide et progressivisme chrétien: La Quinzaine (1950–1953)," *Vingtième Siècle* 13 (January–March 1987): 83–95.

Communists aroused consistent debate in intellectual circles in Paris. Theirs seemed to be the special tragedy, precisely because it was the tragedy of communism itself. In our eyes, wrote one commentator, the least militant unjustly or inadvertently dispatched to Siberia counts more than all the cardinals in the world (this in *Temps modernes*). In the case of a Petkov, reasoned another writer, "The information available to us doesn't allow us to decide one way or the other."[50] His local support was questionable, his demeanor suspect, the accusations plausible. If Petkov and his fellow non-Communists *were* guilty as charged, then so much the better for the Communists. And if they were not guilty, they were nonetheless objectively the major obstacles to a revolutionary transformation of their society. For such persons, "The application of the (death) penalty is the business of the law (Hungarian, Bulgarian), not mine."[51] But similar circumstances, even less plausible demeanors, and identical accusations in the case of Communist leaders raised quite different issues. The implications of treason by erstwhile heroes of the revolutionary movement were of a qualitatively higher order.

There was thus an aura of romance surrounding the Communist adventure that gave to its failings and mistakes a truly heroic quality. This can be sensed even in the memoirs of the victims themselves, who shared with their French sympathizers and apologists a common feeling of tragic destiny. The books of Evzen Loebl, Bela Szász, and especially Artur London treat the terrible experiences they suffered and survived as somehow special and meaningful, significantly different from the tortures and deprivations undergone by others.[52] *Their* dilemmas, *their* struggle to sustain their belief in the face of the absurd, *their* special moral claims on the attention of the world, all these they present as something unique. It is curious that the memoirs and autobiographies of their wives and women friends tell a very different tale. From these there emerges a much more mundane story of naiveté, collusion, ignorance, and confusion. The women suffered their own tragedies but do not seek to elevate these to some metahistorical level of meaning. This, perhaps, explains why Artur London, upon his release from years of imprisonment, could melt readily into the community of like-minded Parisian radical intellectuals, while Jo Langer and Heda Kovaly were

50. André Rhimbaut, "Chroniques," *Esprit*, October 1947, 585.

51. Vercors, "Réponses," *Esprit*, December 1949, 953.

52. Eugen Loebl, *My Mind on Trial* (New York, 1976); Bela Szasz, *Volunteers for the Gallows* (London, 1971); Artur London, *L'Aveu* (Paris, 1968). On this subject see also Jeannine Verdès-Leroux, *Le Réveil des somnambules* (Paris, 1987), 164.

utterly mystified at the attitude of Western thinkers and found nothing to say to them. For these women, communism had demystified itself in the act of assuming power, whereas for writers in Paris its very assumption of power was sufficient proof of its transhistorical claim. Heda Kovaly, Rosemary Kavan, Marian Slingova, Edith Bone, and hundreds of others experienced communism as a daily lie; Mounier, Sartre, and their generation suffered it at a distance as a fascinating dilemma.[53]

53. Heda Kovaly, *Under a Cruel Star: A Life in Prague, 1941–1968* (New York, 1989); Rosemary Kavan, *Freedom at a Price* (London, 1985); Marian Slingova, *Truth Will Prevail* (London, 1968); Jo Langer, *Une Saison à Bratislava* (Paris, 1979); Edith Bone, *Seven Years Solitary* (London, 1957).

CHAPTER SEVEN

Today Things Are Clear
Doubts, Dissent, and Awakenings

Comment, en ton for intérieur, peux-tu supporter pareille dégradation de l'homme en la personne de celui qui se montra ton ami?

How, in your innermost feelings, can you bear such human degradation in the person of a man who was your friend?

André Breton

•

No one who reads the innumerable books, essays, articles, and polemical exchanges that studded French public life in the postwar years can fail to be impressed, in the midst of all that noise, by a certain silence. In the welter of verbal presences, there was, so to speak, one "great absence." This was a generation whose attention was incessantly directed at the responsibility of each person for his or her acts and their outcome, where humanism and the destinies of humanity were on every lip and where the untold suffering brought about by dictatorship and war was the measure of all political choices. Yet the human cost in deprivation, pain, injustice, and death that was the openly acknowledged price paid for the establishment of Communist regimes in half of Europe provoked hardly any expression of concern or protest. Even those who participated in this self-imposed moral anesthesia expressed occasional surprise at their own inability to respond. Jacques Madaule, writing in *Témoignage Chrétien* on the occasion of the publication of Kravchenko's notorious book, noted how "strangely unmoved" we are by such reports or by the "even worse dictatorship of Marshal Tito in Yugoslavia."[1] It was as though a long winter's night had fallen across the intellectual soul, shrouding in ambiguity all direct evidence of human suffering; through the murk, commentators could catch glimpses of the truth but only in the most abstract and ghostly form. From this selective and willfully partial data they then fashioned abstractions and images of the truth "over there" that conformed to their own spiritual requirements.

This exercise in collective moral anesthesia was not for the most part experienced as discomforting or difficult. On the contrary, it conformed to what we might now call a linguistic convention, in that the common language of political debate, both within political families and across ideological boundaries, excluded the deployment of the sort of moral categories that would have forced men and women to see their own actions and those of others in a different light. To deploy an alternative historiographical style, one might say that French intellectuals operated within a firmly circumscribed paradigm, whose attractions are now quite opaque. With a few notable exceptions, they simply would not, could not, see the meaning of the events they discussed. And when they did grasp tentatively at some insight into the reality of Stalinism and the significance of that reality for their own political universe, they normally let the uncomfortable and thorny truth slip from their minds again, once the moment had passed.

Thus, as we have already noted, one can occasionally find nourishing nuggets of moral revulsion buried within the steady diet of apologetic analytical oatmeal. But then the same author, or journal, will produce a few months later an argument or excuse for the latest horror that quite forgets the cautionary distance taken in an earlier piece of writing. Pierre de Boisdeffre, in his contemporary notes on the trials in 1947 of the Bulgarian Agrarian leader Petkov and his Romanian colleague Iuliu Maniu, was moved to protest at Emmanuel Mounier's response to these. Could not Mounier *see,* he asked, that after these trials any sincere collaboration with Communists was henceforth impossible?[2] To which the answer is

---

1. Jacques Madaule, "Faut-il croire Kravchenko?" *Témoignage Chrétien,* 3 October 1947.

2. Pierre de Boisdeffre, *Des vivants et des morts . . . témoignages, 1948–1953* (Paris, 1954), 14.

that Mounier, despite his own distaste for these same show trials, could not see because he would not. Within a few months of encouraging in his journal the publication of articles deeply critical of Communist judicial procedure, he would once again be asserting the need to have faith in the Communists' revolutionary purpose, whatever the bloody and embarrassing costs. Similarly, Claude Bourdet could in the same article criticize the Czech show trials of 1952 for their anti-Semitic and manifestly fraudulent character and then insist that we must continue to fight side-by-side with the Communists. We cannot trust the Communists, he concluded from his analysis of their behavior in Prague, but we must not abandon them.[3]

Only after 1956 do we find a certain linear continuity in political reasoning, a willingness to acknowledge the logic of experience, to draw sustained conclusions from the lessons of the moment. Until then it was as though there existed an unbreachable categorical gulf between one's immediate natural revulsion at the mistreatment of a fellow human being and the moral conclusions one should draw from that revulsion. This apparent inability to respond directly and simply to the sufferings of others was addressed by André Breton in September 1950, in an open letter to Paul Éluard published in *Combat:* following a by-then classic sequence of arrest and confession, Zavis Kalandra, a Czech historian who had befriended Breton and Éluard, was condemned and executed in Prague. Breton appealed to his former surrealist comrade to protest—"How, in your innermost feelings, can you bear such human degradation in the person of a man who was your friend?" Éluard's reply, published in *Action,* is symptomatic: signing petitions in defense of the victims of capitalist injustice, he wrote, "I'm too busy with the innocent who assert their innocence to worry about the guilty who proclaim their guilt."[4]

It was not so very long ago that things had been quite different. Within living memory of some of the postwar intelligentsia, and in the collective consciousness of all, there was the example of the Dreyfus Affair, in which the duties of the "intellectual" had been clear and the conflation of private emotions and public engagements uncomplicated and complete. The comparison of their own situation with that of the Dreyfusards was not lost on contemporaries. In his agonistic, Janus-like commentary on the trial and execution of Petkov, Mounier bemoaned

3. Claude Bourdet, "Les Aveux de Prague," *L'Observateur,* 27 November 1952.
4. Breton is quoted by Jean Galtier-Boissière, *Mon journal dans la Grande Pagaille* (Paris, 1950), 300. For Éluard's reply, see "L'Honneur des poètes," *Esprit,* September 1950, 378.

the condition of his generation. Petkov's corpse, he wrote, "shows nothing; no clear path, none of the fine confidence ["belles certitudes"] of our Dreyfusard parents."[5] In one sense Mounier was wrong—it was the very "certitudes" of the Dreyfus episode that directed the consciences of so many of his contemporaries and colleagues. For the generation that had come of age at the turn of the century (Langevin, Benda, Mauriac, and many others), the moral and political lessons of Dreyfus were clear. The difficult question was the use to which these lessons should be put. The younger generation, born in the years between Dreyfus and the coming of World War I, implicitly shared the values at stake in the Dreyfusard engagement but felt less comfortable invoking them. The experience of the interwar years and the Occupation had hedged moral absolutes and ethical confidence with doubt and skepticism. The choices with which they were now faced were perhaps analogous to those of 1898, and their engagement was still on the side of the good and the true, but a different vocabulary was adduced to give these choices and those norms a substance. It was thus rare to hear such people making direct reference to Dreyfus as the source of their own political positions. The case of Julien Benda, however, illustrates what happened when a man of the older generation did resort to the Affair in search of Mounier's "belles certitudes."

On a number of occasions after 1945, Benda turned to the Dreyfus experience to illustrate his present engagement. The unconditional alliance with the working class and its political leadership, he wrote in 1948, is the necessary basis for any defense against reaction, at home and abroad. What had been true of Waldeck-Rousseau was true for us today; a coalition of all progressive forces whatever their ideological or programmatic differences is the only sure barrier to the Right and the best route to the future.[6] In March 1948, this amounted to a blank check for Stalin (Benda's article was published a month after the Prague coup), for the belief in an imminent revival of fascism was sufficiently widespread in these years to give credibility to Benda's analogy. For him, the subtle dialectics of a Merleau-Ponty were thus redundant. One did not need to pretend that Stalinist regimes were good nor even deny the harm they wrought. One had only to claim for them membership in the open family of the Left and the banner of "republican defense" could be unfurled in good conscience. *Pas d'ennemis à gauche.*

5. Emmanuel Mounier, "Petkov en nous," *Esprit,* October 1947, 591.
6. Julien Benda, "Le Dialogue est-il possible?" *Europe,* March 1948, 7.

The second occasion on which Benda was to invoke the argument from Dreyfus was more complex. The Rajk trial drew from him an impassioned defense of the official Communist line. What, Benda asked, do those who harbor doubts really object to? The confessions of Rajk and his colleagues? And what do they find indigestible about these? Their use as evidence in the absence of any corroborating materials and in the face of grave doubts as to their credibility. But this is absurd, he protested. The anti-Dreyfusards also claimed that a confession is not a "proof"—in their case they were defending Major Esterhazy and asserting that his admission that he had written the famous "bordereau" (memo) was not conclusive evidence. We Dreyfusards, on the other hand, defended Dreyfus because he was innocent and refused to confess to the crime, and we correspondingly believed Esterhazy when he said he had done it.[7]

Once again, Benda insisted, it is all very simple. Not only does the Hungarian regime have the right to defend itself when under threat (republican defense again), but the criteria we applied in 1898 apply no less today. If a man confesses, we must suppose he is telling the truth and not apply a double standard. It is important to understand that Benda was writing this in good faith, in keeping, as he saw it, with a position of moral integrity and consistency, which he had presented in *La Trahison des clercs* and which he believed himself still to be upholding. As *Revue Socialiste* remarked, upon hearing Julien Benda invoke Dreyfus in defense of the alliance with Communists, "Are we dreaming?"[8] And yet Benda's confidence was the nearest thing to moral coherence within the fellow-traveling community. It required of him that he believe Communists in general and Stalin in particular to be operating under the same rules as Republicans, Socialists, and all other men of good will. But for someone of his generation, this was not only a reasonable belief but the only one compatible with the moral universe into which they had been born. It took greater intellectual courage than Benda or most others possessed to realize that not only had the rules changed, but the game was not remotely comparable to the one they had known.

It is for this reason that open moral condemnation of Communist practices was so uncommon from within the intellectual community, even (and perhaps especially) from those who had private misgivings.

7. Benda, "Esterhazy, l'affaire Rajk, et la démocratie," *Les Lettres françaises*, 13 October 1949.

8. Editorial, "Refus d'un dilemme," *Revue socialiste* 20 (April 1948): 339.

The sort of ethical vision consistent with such condemnation was not easy to sustain. More common was a public expression of simple despair—as in the case of Jean Baboulène, writing on the front page of *Témoignage Chrétien* following the execution of Petkov: "One can no longer, after this [crime], look East without despair."[9] A similar vein of moral anguish runs through some of the writings of François Mauriac on the occasion of the Petkov and Maniu trials and again in March 1951. Commenting on the four-power meeting being held in Paris about the time when the Slovak Clementis was first arrested (he would be hung along with ten others after the Slánsky trial), Mauriac imagined the ghost of Clementis present at the meeting; no world peace will be possible, he hears Clementis warning, that is "built upon the sacrifice of small nations."[10] In Mauriac's case, of course, there was never any moral ambiguity in these matters. In a mordant article on the Rajk trial and the way it had been reported in the French left-wing press, notably that of the Communists, he noted in particular the contrast between the stench of death that hung over Budapest and the upbeat style of one of the journalists: "Even over the succulent Hungarian breakfasts described by Madame Simone Téry one can see the shadow of a body, swinging." Others, like Marcel Péju, might be driven to concede that the show trials were "an immense edifice of bad faith," in which the charges were a "fake story, a distorted picture," but they fought shy, as we have seen, of drawing from this any larger conclusions about a system that could produce and stage-manage such monstrosities.[11]

Beyond Mauriac, the moral high ground remained sparsely occupied. Later on, the increased attention paid by some writers to the reports of torture in French colonies helped transform the discourse of radical politics by introducing into it, almost despite itself, a concern with human rights and normative ethical evaluations. Perhaps the best instance of this is in the writings of Claude Bourdet. Initially Bourdet's apologetics

9. Jean Baboulène, *Témoignage Chrétien*, 3 October 1947.

10. See François Mauriac, *Mémoires politiques* (Paris, 1967), 410; see also Mauriac's articles on Petkov's trial and Kanapa's commentary upon it, as well as on the Maniu trial in Romania, from October and November 1947, in *Journal*, vol. 5 (Paris, 1953). Camus, too, noted the international indifference to developments in the people's democracies: "Ce n'est pas nous qui avons livré les libéraux, les socialistes et les anarchistes des démocraties populaires de l'Est aux tribunaux soviétiques. Ce n'est pas nous qui avons pendu Petkov. Ce sont les signataires des pactes qui consacraient le partage du monde." Camus, interview, *Défense de l'homme*, July 1949; reprinted in *Actuelles*, vol. 1 (1950; reprint Paris, 1977), 233.

11. Mauriac, in *Figaro*, 31 October 1949; Marcel Péju, "Hier et aujourd'hui," part 2, *Les Temps modernes* 91 (May 1953): 2015, 2021.

for Stalinism conceded nothing in dialectical subtlety to those of Mounier or Sartre; from December 1951, however, he became ever more concerned with French practices in Algeria and elsewhere.[12] At first this produced a sort of moral bifocalism, but from the Slánsky trial and with increased emphasis thereafter Bourdet introduced into his commentaries on Stalinism some of the same criteria he was applying in the West. For Bourdet these issues were never truly comparable, and one must not exaggerate the infiltration of categories of assessment from one political debate to another. But with the increased discursive emphasis on illegality, cruelty, and exploitation, it was no longer quite so easy to condemn whole nations in the comforting name of necessity. Camus, too, took an early critical position on French racism,[13] but he had also rebelled somewhat sooner against the moral blackmail exercised by Communists; in 1948 he insisted that anyone who criticized repression of free speech under Franco, for example, both could and indeed must do likewise when speaking of the present condition of artists in the Soviet Union. Moral judgment was indivisible, whatever comfort it happened to provide for one's right-wing opponents. In this as much else, however, Camus was atypical.[14]

One reason for the relative absence of any consistent moral criticism from within the Left was the lack of an analytical framework in which to locate and ground such a critique. For a Catholic moralist like Mauriac this was less of a problem, especially once the acrimonious debates over the *épuration* had freed him from earlier loyalties to the coalitions of the intellectual Resistance. But for others, it was difficult to pronounce definitively upon the crimes of the Stalinists when, as we have seen, any very clear sense of justice was lacking. Hence, the paradox that among analytical critiques of Stalinism, some of the most consistent were to come from Marxists themselves. Of these, two of the sharpest pieces of writing were by Claude Lefort, written at either end of the worst years of Stalinist excesses and both published in *Temps modernes*. This is curious when one remembers that in the same journal there were being published throughout this period arguments and apologias diametrically opposed in style and content to everything Lefort sought to express. At one level this is a tribute to the ecumenical editorial policy pursued by

12. For Bourdet's denunciation of torture, see, for example, *L'Observateur,* 6 December 1951.

13. See, for example, Camus's article in *Combat,* 10 May 1947, condemning racism in Algeria and anti-Semitism in France itself.

14. See various articles by Camus in *Combat* during November 1948.

Sartre and his friends. On another, it might be taken to suggest that no one read—or in any case understood or cared—what anyone else was saying.

In his first article, on "Kravchenko et le problème de l'URSS," Lefort noted that the workers' movement was the victim of a myth, the idea that Stalin's USSR was in any sense a living revolutionary society. This was a belief also widespread among "bourgeois" commentators, who were happy to credit the Soviet Union with a "progressive" economy (reserving their criticisms for its repressive excesses). Among such bourgeois defenders of Stalinism Lefort included Merleau-Ponty, whose faith in the historically progressive character of the regime hinged on a positive reading of its productive forces and their revolutionary dynamic. The virtue of Kravchenko, Lefort claimed, was that he revealed this to be a lie. By providing further evidence of something "we already know," Kravchenko confirmed that in the perspective of class ("the only one that counts for us"), the Soviet Union was a bureaucratic exploitative society.[15] In his second article, written as an indirect response to Sartre's defense of the Communists' special claim to privilege, Lefort hammered home his conclusion: not only is the Soviet Union under Stalin not a workers' state, but it exists primarily for the purpose of exploiting those same workers; the purges and trials are a struggle to the death between competing interests within the ruling class. As to the rationalization and planning that so mesmerized Western commentators, this was bureaucratic exploitation of the proletariat. No more, no less.[16]

Lefort did not really differ from his opponents as much as he thought. He too believed that what determines the character of a social system is the level and nature of its production relations. He simply held, like Trotsky, that the Soviet Union *since* Lenin's death had ceased to develop and had frozen, under Stalin, into a despotic system of state capitalism. But even this position, leaving him as it did unable to explain why such a blockage had taken place, at least released him from any obligation to justify or explain away the crimes of what in his eyes was an illegitimate governing clique. A Marxist-like Lefort was thus quite well placed to situate and condemn the behavior of Communist governments; what he could not propose was any universalist platform of justice or ethics from which to criticize the specifics of Stalinist behavior. Like Jules Guesde at

15. Claude Lefort, "Kravchenko et le problème de l'URSS," *Les Temps modernes* 29 (February 1948), especially 1491–1509.

16. Lefort, "Le Marxisme et Sartre," *Les Temps modernes* 89 (April 1953): 1560.

the time of the first Dreyfus trials, he refused to take sides in an argument between equally unworthy antagonists. Not only did he condemn both the capitalist West and the Stalinist East, but he also treated the death struggles between Communist leaders as a matter of moral indifference.

In this respect, his task was simpler than that of his non-Marxist contemporaries, who sought to achieve similar analytical clarity about the Soviet system while maintaining a stance from which they could be morally engaged. Mauriac came perhaps the closest, comparing the Communists' treatment of their victims to the excesses of the French purges, a position from which he felt able to issue critical commentary, having been no less opposed to French domestic practices a few years before.[17] This was a comfortable position for Mauriac but not for most of his colleagues, whose attitude at the time of the *épuration* had been very different. Camus adopted a slightly different posture, standing outside of Marxism itself but treating the defects of Stalinism as part of the larger weakness of Marxism as a philosophy. Because Marxism is a procedural philosophy lacking in any jurisprudence, he wrote, it has no way of setting for itself a framework for justice or any other transcendent goal.[18] Thus there was no point expecting it to behave in accordance with any such norms, though this was no reason to abstain from judgment or condemnation. Others would reach similar conclusions, though it took them rather longer. Jean-Marie Domenach in 1955 finally conceded that if all it took to make Tito respectable again in Communist eyes was a visit from Khrushchev, then dialectics are mere magic—"the translation of essences." It was pointless to expect from such a belief system any coherent account of human behavior, but that did not excuse us from demanding it. To do as Merleau-Ponty had done, to make a pact with Marxism-Leninism for one's own ends, was cynical.[19]

Mauriac reached his conclusion in 1946, Camus acknowledged his own disillusion in 1948, Domenach waited until 1955. Countless others dropped away or rediscovered their innermost convictions at various points within these years. The manner in which doubt or disgust finally entered the soul varied widely. What was fairly universal was the external trigger, and this was frequently some news or event from eastern Europe or the Soviet Union itself. For writers like Claude Aveline, Jean Cassou,

17. Mauriac, *Mémoires politiques*, 365.
18. Camus, *Carnets*, vol. 2 (Paris, 1964), 286. This was written in 1949, following the Rajk trial.
19. Jean-Marie Domenach, "Les Intellectuels et le communisme," *Esprit*, July 1955, 1205, 1210.

and Pierre Emmanuel, the break between Stalin and Tito, and the subsequent attacks on Tito by the Communist movement, proved indigestible, not least because Tito's own regime—repressive, Stalinist, and a model of sovietization—had been much admired by Western intellectuals until that time.[20] For Merleau-Ponty, Vercors, and a few others, it was the Rajk trial, further abetted by the revelations about Soviet camps—although in Merleau-Ponty's case it took the outbreak of the Korean war to elicit from him an open statement of his position.[21] Curiously, the worst trial of all, that of Slánský and his associates in 1952, did not in fact produce many defections; most of those who could no longer find it in themselves to account for these things had already left the fold.

The Czech trial was particularly mysterious to many, in its timing, its obscure purpose, and its unprecedented racism. As a result, although much attention was paid to it in the French press, few could make any sense of it. What the Slánský trial seemed to show, in a way that the Moscow trials and the subsequent indictments of Kostov, Rajk, and the rest never could, was the essential impossibility of ascribing rational meaning or historical purpose to Communist terror. No Merleau-Ponty came forward in 1953 to offer a hypothetical para-Hegelian defense of the indictment of Slánský and his colleagues. No successor to Mounier appeared, offering an exculpation wrapped in a critique. There was no Cassou or Vercors to declare that this was too much, no Rémy Roure or Louis Martin-Chauffier to speak out against the suppression of evidence. All that remained was to protest or remain silent.

Protest was made easier by the fact that the Slánský trial was almost exactly contemporary with that of Ethel and Julius Rosenberg in the United States, and in the words of Jean-Marie Domenach, "There is more to this than coincidence and surface resemblances."[22] An appeal for clemency on Slánský's behalf was drawn up and then combined with an identical appeal for mercy on behalf of the Rosenbergs. The resulting petition was then sent to Presidents Truman and Gottwald. Among those who signed were Domenach and Albert Béguin of *Esprit,* erstwhile fellow-traveling intellectuals and artists from Louis Martin-Chauffier to Gérard Philippe, the Gaullist Claude Mauriac, Jean Cocteau, and others

20. See Claude Roy, *Nous* (Paris, 1972), 415; and Jean Cassou, "La Révolution et la vérité," *Esprit,* December 1949.

21. Maurice Merleau-Ponty, "Marxisme et superstition," *Les Temps modernes* 50 (December 1949).

22. Domenach, "L'Antisémitisme reste logique," *Esprit,* January 1953.

besides. The petitioning telegrams specifically disassociated themselves from any political affiliation and emphasized their common opposition to the death penalty for political offenses. Even so, there were those like Marc Beigbeder who preferred not to speak out against the Czech judgments (and some more famous names are absent from the list of signatories); but such heterogeneous and apolitical appeals would have been unimaginable a few short years before.[23] After the Slánsky trial (and the anti-Semitic hysteria that followed it, culminating in the "Doctors' Plot" in Moscow the following spring), support for communism was more tacit than open, more residual than deeply felt. The events of 1956—Khrushchev's "revelations," the Polish revolution, and Hungary—provided an exit from the dilemma of the left-wing intellectual; but the real break had already occurred. In this sense, 1956 was a delayed response; it represented a sort of time-lapse in sensibilities, a decent interval between the death of faith and departure from the church.[24]

Most fellow-travelers, as their later recollections and memoirs suggest, passed through these years in a sort of twilight zone, in which their thoughts and their words bore only a tangential relationship to one another. Many of them would doubtless have agreed with Mounier, in one of his last pieces of writing: "One day this notion of objective guilt will have to be addressed directly."[25] For Mounier that day of reckoning was mercifully avoided through his untimely death, but most others who were not thus spared still preferred to avoid the question. And yet Mounier had been right, for packed tightly within this phrase was the uneasy conscience and moral cowardice of an intellectual generation. The "objective guilt" of Pétain, Laval, and Brasillach had been extended to Bukharin, Tukhachevsky, Petkov, Kostov, Rajk, and Slánsky, together with millions of anonymous victims and capitalism itself. Behind this anodyne little error there lurked the spiritual cancer of modern thought.

Intellectuals are no better or worse than other people. They are not even very different. They live in communities; they seek the respect and fear the disapproval of others; they pursue careers, they desire to impress, and they revere power. In the years from World War II until 1956, in the intellectual community of Paris, the pressure to conform to a certain view of the world was tremendous, more perhaps than it had been before

23. For details of telegrams and signatories, see ibid., 147, n. 1; and L'Observateur, 4 December 1952. On Beigbeder's stance, see François Mauriac, Bloc-Notes (Paris, 1958), 27 December 1952.

24. For a further discussion of the significance of the events of 1956, see chapter 14.

25. Mounier, "Journal à plusieurs voix," Esprit, January 1950, 132.

or since. It is not surprising that we should find so few dissenting voices in the crowd, even on such deeply human issues as persecution, violence, and death. What is perhaps a little more surprising is that on these issues *above all,* there was remarkable harmony. The events in Soviet East Europe aroused much attention and heated discussion in France but generated remarkably little moral light. There was a fundamental conformism about the response to the show trials that remains curious even after one has exhaustively mapped out the context. On those unusual occasions on which someone said something different, or having said something different then remained faithful to his new position, the change of mood was dramatic. To pursue the earlier metaphor of the conversation, it was as though a guest had suddenly insulted the hostess, or pronounced the food inedible, or told a rude story. The exceptions to this rule were men like Mauriac or Bernanos, who resembled country pastors at a supper party, their dour clothes and grim pronouncements no longer a surprise and even half-expected. As to people like Raymond Aron, they would not have been welcome across the threshold in the first place.

Camus, who succeeded in making himself an unwelcome presence in just such a way after 1949, captured this aspect of the era in one of his notebooks. For many years, he like everyone else pretended not to know (or tried not to think) about the crimes of the Soviet Union and excused, also like everyone else, the repetition and perfection of these crimes in Stalin's European satellites. This was the more comfortable position and compatible with his former role as spokesman of the anti-Fascist Resistance and its revolutionary dreams. And then, almost as though it came as a sudden insight into the intolerable burden such a silence imposed, he ceased to censor himself and declared that he would forthwith speak his mind. Camus was no commonplace intellectual, neither in his insight nor in his honesty, and he managed to be about a quarter of a century ahead of his time. But in this case he spoke for the problem of the age:

One of my regrets is to have conceded too much to objectivity. Objectivity, at times, is an accommodation. Today things are clear and we must call something "concentrationnaire" if that is what it is, even if it is socialism. In one sense, I shall never again be polite.[26]

26. Camus, *Carnets,* vol. 2 (Paris, 1964), 267.

PART THREE

The Treason of the Intellectuals

CHAPTER EIGHT

The Sacrifices of the Russian People

A Phenomenology of Intellectual Russophilia

La foi consiste à croire ce que la raison ne croit pas.

Faith consists in believing what reason will not believe.

Voltaire

In order to appreciate the belief system of postwar intellectuals, we need to grasp that what is at issue here is not *understanding*, the cognitive activity usually associated with intellectuals, but faith. To react as people did to the impact of communism in the years following 1945, they had first to accept unquestioningly a certain number of the fundamental tenets of what amounted to a civic religion. But merely to say this is not enough; we have next to ask why a particular community should find one such belief system more plausible, more convincing, than any other. In the chapters to come I shall argue that the sources of intellectual behavior in these years, the reasons determining the peculiar sympathy shown towards Stalinism in all its excesses, are to be found in a network of French intellectual practices. These may be thought of as overlapping orbits, each reaching out a little further into national political and cultural traditions.

My hypothesis is thus as follows: at the center lay the will and the desire to believe in communism. Around this article of faith were wrapped various layers of argument deriving from specific Communist achievements in the recent past. In the next orbit was to be found a certain style of reasoning, a sort of epistemological double vision, which made it possible to explain Soviet behavior in terms not invoked for any other system or persons; this discourse, although especially applicable to the Communist case, did not derive from it and has older historical and philosophical origins and objectives. The same is true of the next layer, a long-standing habit of mind, hostile to various manifestations of modernity and individualism, which is sometimes referred to, in misleading shorthand, as "anti-Americanism." At a further remove, but still within the galaxy of established cultural practices, there was the peculiar combination of preeminence and self-hatred that has marked the intellectual as a public figure in modern France and contributed to ambivalence in the face of a proletarian politics. Finally, and providing all the above with their political and ideological anchor, there was the indigenous antiliberalism of the French republican intelligentsia. In what follows, I shall try to show how each of these conventions of French intellectual life played a part in the shaping of the postwar mind.

All faith entails denial as well as affirmation. The true believer, when faced with empirical or logical evidence in apparent contradiction with the demands of faith, has no reasonable choice but to deny what he or she sees, or hears, or thinks. How far this causes a problem will depend upon the strength of the individual's commitment—and the demands of his or her own intelligence. For Communist and non-Communist intellectuals alike, denial in this sense took two forms. In its simpler version, it meant refusing to believe that certain things had been done, that certain institutions existed, that certain people had suffered or died. For intellectuals who had thrown in their lot with the Communists and identified with them without reservation, this was obviously easier since the authority for such denial came from above. Autonomous intellectuals, however progressive and philo-Communist, could not look to the party as the source for their own opinions and were thus compelled to construct such denials for themselves. But in other respects the process was fundamentally similar. In its most acute form, it would find Sartre announcing in the early fifties, "I have looked, but I just cannot find any evidence of an aggressive impulse on the part of the Russians in the last three decades." A decade later his companion could still find nothing of truth or interest in the writings of Kravchenko (or Koestler)—"They are just telling stories."[1]

But by the sixties Sartre and de Beauvoir were no longer a reliable guide to general opinion. More typical, perhaps, was the earlier reaction of some to the Lysenko affair. Here the issues were prima facie clear-cut, in that even the most sympathetic of Western scientists were unwilling to give unconditional credence to the claims of a Soviet breakthrough to a new science of genetics. *Esprit,* like many other contemporary reviews, devoted considerable space to Lysenko in 1948. In the December issue, a number of its regular columnists each contributed a commentary on the affair. For modern readers, the curious aspect of these articles is their extraordinary willingness to give Lysenko's theory (or "Mitchourinisme," as it was sometimes called) the benefit of the doubt. Philippe Sabant, for example, asserted not only that it was a serious science from which Soviet agriculture was already benefiting (he offered instances of unprecedented increases in milk production, weather-resistant wheat, and so on) but that it was unthinkable that so august a body as the Central Committee of the Soviet Communist party would adopt it, were its scientific qualities not fully established. The whole economy was already benefiting:

Would Stalin have given doctrinal considerations precedence over the interests of the economy? And who believes that the Central Committee would have put at risk all existing agricultural institutions without serious evidence?[2]

Mounier, warier than his fellow contributor, confined himself to agreeing that Lysenko's views *seemed* perverse and unscientific but with this proviso: at some point in the future, they might be proved right. Who were we to say? And meanwhile, why should we unhesitatingly reject them, in the face of the claims now made on their behalf? "It could be that, in the face of precise discoveries in the USSR, Morgan's theories and classical genetics are now playing a dogmatic and delaying role."[3]

1. Sartre, quoted in Pierre de Boisdeffre, *Des vivants et des morts . . . témoignages, 1948–1953* (Paris, 1954), 241; Simone de Beauvoir, *La Force des choses* (Paris, 1963), 152: "Ils racontent des romans feuilletons." See also Pierre Debray, "Faut-il croire Kravchenko?" *Témoignage Chrétien,* 5 September 1947, where he dismisses Kravchenko's book on the basis of minor internal discrepancies and Kravchenko's refusal to accept the "exigencies" of revolutionary action as conceived by the Bolsheviks.

2. See Philippe Sabant, N. Grelet, and Emmanuel Mounier, "Trois Vues sur l'affaire Lyssenko," *Esprit,* December 1948, 891.

3. Sabant, Grelet, and Mounier, ibid., 899. See also Dominique Lecourt, *Lyssenko: Histoire réelle d'une science prolétarienne* (Paris, 1976).

The desire to give Stalin the benefit of all possible doubts, even (especially) in the face of the evidence, rested on complex abstract premises. In Communist hands, these took the collective form of "dialectical" reasoning. If Kostov admitted his guilt, he was guilty. If he denied it (as he attempted to do), this was proof that the trial was not rigged and that he was therefore guilty. Similarly, food rationing in France was a restriction, in Poland it was popular.[4] If communism ruled, then the people ruled. If the people ruled, they must perforce be happy—thus Paul Éluard, upon his return from a voyage to Hungary in 1949: "If the people are master in their own country this alone will ensure that in a few years happiness will be the supreme law, and joy the daily horizon."[5] Non-Communists could not usually aspire to the lyricism of an Éluard or the sheer cheek of a Desanti, but they argued outward from similar starting points. Merleau-Ponty and Sartre avoided the implications of the revelations about Soviet labor camps by turning the evidence against itself: the very fact that Communists have illusions about these camps is proof that they wish to believe well of humanity; they are therefore fundamentally different from Fascists (who also had camps), and we can continue to support them, albeit from afar. Jean Beaufret (according to Claude Roy) refused to "pronounce" upon the USSR, partly for "lack of evidence," but mostly because "we still lack a phenomenology of the Soviet Union."[6]

Beaufret is here somewhat unjust to his contemporaries. By the early fifties Sartre was well on his way to establishing just such a "phenomenology." The Soviet citizen, he asserted in 1954, enjoys complete freedom to criticize the system. Just because he doesn't seem to do it in ways we understand, it would be wrong to suppose that he is forced into silence. "This is not so. He criticizes more frequently and more effectively than us." In his desire to speak well of the Soviet Union, following his first visit there in 1954 (and to avoid the precedent of Gide), Sartre not only adopted the Communist claims for his own but gave them an exaggerated twist. The Soviet Union was peopled with individuals of a

4. See, for example, Pol Gaillard, "A propos des condamnations de Prague," *La Pensée* 46 (January–February 1953): 87. Marcel Péju, in "Hier et aujourd'hui," part 1, *Les Temps modernes* 90 (May 1953): 173, claimed that Kostov's brief retraction was proof that his confessions must have been voluntary. For an example of Communist lyricism, see Dominique Desanti, "Un Mois à travers la Pologne," *Democratie nouvelle* 6 (June 1958): 319: "Chez nous, les rations sont une limitation; ici elles constituent une faveur."

5. Éluard is quoted by Claude Roy, *Nous* (Paris, 1972), 162.

6. "Les Jours de notre vie," *Les Temps modernes* 51 (January 1950): 1160; Beaufret is quoted in Roy, *Nous,* 126.

"new kind"; even the few failings Sartre was willing to acknowledge (such as the execrable public architecture) were turned to advantage: the superfluous abundance of the Komsomol Metro station was understandable, he announced, because every passenger is the owner and seeks to show off and share his possession to the full. "It seemed to him," as Simone de Beauvoir put it approvingly, "that Soviet society had overcome in large measure the loneliness that eats at our own."[7] Like Jacques Armel, writing three years earlier in L'Observateur, he found the very absence of freedom of speech "as we understand it" evidence of the rise of the proletariat and of a true cultural liberation.[8]

Beaufret was thus wrong. He and his contemporaries had indeed constructed a "phenomenology of the Soviet Revolution," but it rested on an unusual premise: that of the self-annihilation of the observer. Before one could construct a case for the Communists, one had first to undermine one's own intellectual authority. The evidence, of camps, deportations, trials, and the like, had to be set aside, or placed in a sort of ethical parenthesis. As Mounier expressed it, "I want these stories to be untrue."[9] This is humiliating for an intellectual, and it explains the palpable sense of relief that overcame such people when they finally abandoned the effort. In retrospect we may find the condition of the French Communist party's own intellectuals more servile and pitiable, but it is not clear that this was the case at the time. The Communist intellectual might perform ridiculous rituals and say or write the most hilariously implausible things, but he or she was comforted by membership in a community. A formally unattached writer like Julien Benda, trailing a long reputation as a free-thinker, was forced into similar excesses without any of the comforts of camaraderie. Thus, when Benda sat on a platform in 1949 with Jacques Duclos while the Communist leader worked a crowd at the Mutualité into a frenzy of hatred for Rajk and his fellow criminals, he presented a sorry figure. Reduced to declaring, "A Republic must defend itself" (Dreyfus again), he was an "intellectuel de service." But so were Sartre, Vercors, Mounier, Bourdet, and many others, however assiduously they proclaimed their autonomy.[10]

7. Sartre, "La Liberté de critique est totale en URSS," interview in Libération, 15 July 1954. See also Simone de Beauvoir, La Force des choses, 329. In a letter to the president of the Foreign Commission of the Soviet Writers' Union, in July 1954, Sartre assured his correspondent that he would not behave like Gide. He was true to his word. See Ewa Berard-Zarzycka, "Sartre in Russia," Micro-Mega, March 1989, especially 79–85.

8. Jacques Armel, L'Observateur, 17 May 1951.

9. Mounier, "Débat à haute voix," Esprit, February 1946, 185.

10. See François Fejtö, Mémoires (Paris, 1986), 213.

It took a large dose of naiveté, of unworldliness, to swallow such a condition. In order to be able to write, like Jean-Marie Domenach, that we will always march with the Communists, that we have complete faith in their "sincere love of justice," one needed to have a powerful ethical digestive system, able to overcome the most painful of *crises de foi*. By 1953, Domenach, like his peers, had been exposed to a devastating array of evidence against the claim that Communists "sincerely loved" justice. We are all acquainted with the notion of a "will to power." What is harder to imagine but is perhaps required in order to appreciate the intellectual condition in these years is the "will to ignorance." But such a desire to believe well of a system that daily provided you with nothing but evidence against itself could only have been born of the most powerful and demanding of motives. Like a battered wife, the non-Communist intelligentsia of the Left kept returning to its tormentor, assuring the police force of its conscience that "he meant well," that he "has reasons," and that, in any case, "I love him." And like a violent husband, communism continued to benefit from the faith its victims placed in their initial infatuation. If it exercises such a fascination over us, wrote Mounier in 1946, "there must be something alive in it that appeals to our hearts." [11]

That "something" was certainly not Marxism. The latter, as Aron noted, played little direct part in French intellectual life. Most Marxists of the time were still, in Domenach's words, "hidebound materialists," and true believers were more commonly to be found among the "lumpen-intelligentsia" in the party itself. [12] The exceptions were outside the party, like the minority of Trotskyists, or else Communists within the fold like Henri Lefebvre, who exercised little influence in or out of the official circles. The distinction that became popular in the sixties, between historical Stalinism and theoretical Marxism, already existed in vitro in the earlier decades; but the difference was that few then paid consistent attention to this taxonomic subtlety. Historians, philosophers, and others who passed through communism attempted to practice their profession in some manner compatible with the general assertions of official dogma, but most of them made little serious effort to infuse their own work with Marxist theoretical principles. Marx was taken on credit rather than seriously studied; progressive intellectuals (and even some party members) told themselves that their reasons for

11. See Jean-Marie Domenach, "La Tâche de protestation," *Esprit,* January 1953, 18; Mounier, "Débat à haute voix," 185–86.

12. Raymond Aron, "Les Intellectuels français et l'utopie," *Preuves* 50 (April 1955): 11; and Domenach, "Les Intellectuels et le communisme," *Esprit,* July 1955, 1204.

aligning with the Soviet Union were truly their own, and the product of distinctive and autonomous motives—"Progressivism consists of presenting Communist propositions as though they arose spontaneously from independent reflection."[13] The strength of the Communist appeal derived from its ability to draw on other, more emotionally satisfying sources.

In the first place, there was the myth of the Communist Resistance. This was not only a myth, of course—Communists and the French Communist party really did play an important part in the anti-Nazi Resistance from 1941 on. But the fact that the Communists participated in the domestic Resistance in such an organized and prominent manner helped inflate their role into one of near-mythical status. Only the PCF had maintained a full-scale clandestine structure throughout the Occupation, with its own press (*L'Humanité*, *La Terre*, *L'Avant-garde*, *Cahiers du Bolchevisme*, *La Vie ouvrière*), militia, hierarchy of authority, and so forth. By 1945, and for years to come, the PCF was able to invoke the memory of this wartime Communist presence (and the accompanying sacrifices of its activists) as an argument against any temptation to side with the anti-Communists. This situation was by no means unique to France, but it was experienced with greater force in France than elsewhere.[14]

It seemed to many that communism in France would henceforth be something different from communism elsewhere (and from French communism in its earlier, bolshevized form). The identification of communism with the nation was assiduously cultivated by the PCF in the postwar years, and it was undoubtedly an affiliation with which most French Communists, from Thorez down, felt most comfortable. The situation of Communists before 1935 and between 1939 and 1941 (or indeed after 1947) had not been a comfortable one, and the insertion of the PCF at the heart of the Jacobin inheritance after 1944 seemed to make enduring sense. Thus the earnest desire on the part of non-Communist intellectuals to believe that the peculiarly alien aspects of the Bolshevik heritage had now been put aside seemed the more realistic for

13. Aron, "Aventures et mésaventures de la dialectique," *Preuves* 59 (January 1956): 5.
14. Thus Venerio Cattani, "Per almeno tre o quattro anni, non furamo communisti semplicemente per ragioni temperamentali e di sopravvivenza organizzativa" ("For at least three or four years it was only reasons of temperament and organizational survival that prevented us from becoming Communists"), quoted in Nello Ajello, *Intellettuali e PCI* (Rome, 1979), 178.

being shared by many Communists. Communism would transform France, and France would civilize communism:

This old civilization that it is assaulting will absorb and enrich it. This, indeed, could be France's essential contribution. Russia saw the Communist break-through; France could lead it into maturity.[15]

That was written in 1946. By 1949 the wish to see something unique, and uniquely French, in the PCF was a little battered by experience but all the more desperate for that reason. Reading Laurent Casanova's report on the party and the intellectuals (in which he introduced Zda-novism into the French vocabulary for the first time), Jean-Marie Do-menach still managed to find hope; at least Casanova and the party were interested in engaging with intellectuals, perhaps an "opening" was still possible.[16] The "extraordinary objective intelligence" that Sartre claimed to find in the PCF was not perhaps obvious to the naked eye, and few other observers located it there, but most of them continued to seek it. This was difficult after 1947, once the PCF had been dragged brutally back into line with the rest of the international Communist movement; the unique virtues of the wartime and immediate postwar French Com-munists were now once again lost in the monolithic language and prac-tices of Stalinism. The Communists could still claim a certain special status as the "party of the working-class" and would continue to benefit from "résistantialisme," but their appeal was now absorbed into some-thing else: the moral authority of the Soviet achievement.[17]

It may sound odd today to suggest that this distinction means any-thing. Communists always insisted that they were part of an interna-tional movement and that their special authority arose from their alignment with the heirs of Lenin. But when we are dealing with the appeal of communism to non-Communists the distinction *is* an impor-tant one. Stalin's abolition of the Comintern was taken very seriously, and the belief that postwar Europe would see a series of distinct national paths to socialism was widespread. This comfortable perspective had been reinforced by the wartime successes of the USSR. These, rather like the Resistance-era heroics of the local party, gave to communism a new meaning, divorced from that assigned to it by Marxists. This new mean-

---

15. Martin Brionne, "Ni zéro, ni infini," *Esprit,* May 1946, 701.

16. Domenach, "Le Parti Communiste français et les intellectuels," *Esprit,* May 1949, 729.

17. On the "extraordinary objective intelligence" of the PCF, see Sartre, "Le Réfor-misme et les fétiches," *Les Temps modernes* 122 (February 1956).

ing was captured in a single symbol, that of Stalingrad. Here was proof not only that communism was successful in Merleau-Ponty's sense, and which thus cast a seal of approval on the purges of the thirties, but that it was genuinely popular. How could one now doubt the broad proletarian base on which the regime in Moscow rested—if it had been the bureaucratic dictatorship depicted by its enemies, how could it have mobilized a continent, defeated the Nazis, and saved Europe from fascism? For once, Simone de Beauvoir probably speaks for a widespread sentiment when she writes, "Our friendship for the USSR was marked by no reticence whatsoever; the sacrifices of the Russian people had proved that the leadership incarnated their will." Stalingrad swept away all doubts, all criticisms, all memories of the Moscow trials and peasant famines. How could one not side with the victors?[18]

From this point of view, communism in Russia was simply a giant reflection of communism in wartime France, a movement dedicated to national liberation and social reform, supported by the masses, and commanded by truly popular (and thus legitimate) leaders. Simone de Beauvoir and others would argue that the Russians fought well because of the logic of their cause—they knew what they were fighting for. The Red Army was thus double proof of the truth of communism—it had defeated the forces of reaction and had been able to rely on the support of the masses in doing so.[19] The Red Army was also, literally and figuratively, the vehicle through which Russia returned to Europe, and as such it became the object of a cult all its own, venerated less as the harbinger of revolution than for its part in the recasting of the emotional geography of the continent. The old nineteenth-century left-wing sympathy for Poland and other aspirant nations had been steadily eroded in the course of the interwar years and was finally swept away after 1945 in a wave of Russophilia.[20] The "lands between" having proven vulnerable to fascism and impervious to social change, the hegemony that Stalin was about to exert over them was seen as a wholly good thing as well as a deserved reward for Russian sacrifices.

It was not surprising that French intellectuals should see Soviet victories in such terms, for they were not alone. Western politicians who

18. Simone de Beauvoir, *La Force des choses,* 17; see also Edgar Morin, *Autocritique* (Paris, 1958), 73.

19. Few people seem to have troubled to note that German soldiers also fought valiantly until the very moment of defeat. What did this, then, say about the claims of nazism?

20. See, for example, Jules Michelet, *Pologne et Russie* (Paris, 1852).

prided themselves on taking a cold, rational view of postwar geopolitics also saw certain advantages in the Soviet domination of eastern Europe, from the point of view of stability and a postwar settlement. Many of them, beginning with Roosevelt, attributed to Stalin limited, nationalist motives or else imagined in him a return to the diplomatic interests and maneuvers of the czars. Of especial interest was the postwar response of European socialists, however, for they were better placed than Roosevelt to know just what sort of threat communism could prove to their own existence. Furthermore, because most socialists at the time professed a continuing allegiance to Marxism in some modified form, they could not ignore or dismiss the revolutionary promises and program of the Communist movement, however much they questioned the good faith of those promises in Communist mouths. Yet the capacity of postwar European socialist leaders to place their faith in a reformed communism was very considerable and makes it easier to understand similar leaps of faith by others.

The Popular Front alliance had discouraged open criticism of Communists by their socialist allies, and until 1939 only fringe journals of the left like Souvarine's *Critique sociale* remained systematically antagonistic to Moscow. This was as true in Britain as in France—the difficulties Orwell had in publishing his essay on the Spanish Civil War are a well-known example.[21] The brief interlude from 1939 to 1941 did not really count, since for most of that period the opportunity for public criticism of the Communists on the part of the non-Communist Left was nonexistent. And after 1941, for good or ill, socialists and Communists were once again brought together in an anti-Fascist coalition. After 1945, however, socialists were among the first victims of Communist repression in eastern Europe, just as they had been in the USSR after the Bolsheviks' own revolution. There were trials of Bulgarian socialists in 1946, of Polish socialists in 1948. What was left of the prewar social democratic leadership in Hungary and elsewhere (many had been deported and were dead) lacked the experience to organize against the Communists and thus acceded, more or less willingly, to Communist pressure for unification of the Left. In a series of congresses these forced marriages were imposed on the indigenous socialist parties, already undermined by internal division provoked by pro-Communist minori-

---

21. George Orwell, *Homage to Catalonia* (London, 1938). See also Nicole Racine's contribution on Boris Souvarine and *Critique sociale* in *Des années trente: Groupes et ruptures* (Paris, 1985), especially 66ff.

ties within their leadership. The East German Socialist and Communist parties fused into the Socialist Unity Party in April 1946; the Romanians followed suit in November 1947. Between February and December of 1948 a similar process was conducted in Hungary, Czechoslovakia, Bulgaria, and Poland.

The reaction of Western socialists was symptomatic. Not only were there attempts to induce similar unifications in Italy and France, but even after they failed many socialists accepted the developments in eastern Europe as logical and necessary and refrained from open criticism. Ignazio Silone faced much abusive opposition for his efforts to prevent a united party being created in Italy from a fusion of the Partito Socialista Italiano di Unità Proletaria (PSIUP) and the PCI, and in France the SFIO (Socialist party) leadership was notable for its "pudeur" in refraining from criticism of the treatment of fellow socialists in the East.[22] As late as June 1947, the socialists' newspaper Le Populaire described François Mauriac as an ally of the "traitors' camp" for his attacks on communism. In the same year the West European socialists who dominated the Socialist International refused admission to the remaining independent socialist parties of East Europe (now in forced exile), treated the latter as pariahs, and publicly approved the legitimacy and propriety of the mergers with Communist parties then being planned.[23]

Only with the Prague coup were a few voices hesitantly raised in doubt. Characteristically it was Léon Blum (now as before a minority voice in his own party) who wondered aloud whether French socialists had done enough to support their eastern European comrades. By taking the pro-Communist socialist leadership over there at its word they had refused to listen to dissident socialists, exiled leaders, and other victims of Communist intolerance. For the sake of the socialists themselves, Blum concluded, we should have disagreed with them and opposed their desire to align themselves with Communists.[24] The socialist illusion crumbled rapidly thereafter (except in Italy, where the Nenni Socialists maintained a refusal to separate their fate from that of the Communists until well into the sixties), with the formation of political blocs and the increasingly virulent polemics of the Communists, at

22. See Paul Wilkinson, The Intellectual Resistance in Europe (Cambridge, Mass., 1981), 253; on socialists' "pudeur," see François Mauriac, Mémoires politiques (Paris, 1967), 365.

23. Le Populaire, 13 June 1947; see also Les Socialistes des pays opprimés réclament la liberté, la démocratie, et l'indépendance, report of the Conférence internationale des Partis Socialistes des pays du Centre et de l'Est européen, Paris, 13–15 March 1948.

24. Leon Blum, Le Populaire, 29 February 1948.

home and abroad. But the belief in a window of hope, from 1944 until early 1948, is a salutary reminder of the mood of the time.

Furthermore, socialist politicians (like intellectuals) were especially vulnerable to the pressure to choose, to identify with one side or another, in a divided postwar world. It was an essential trait of Stalinism, as well as a lesson derived from contemporary conflicts, that all experience was divisible and measurable according to a single criterion of choice. This choice was between "class blocs," represented on the one side by the Soviet Union and all it had come to stand for, and on the other side by its enemies, of whatever shape: "Between these two class blocs and their representation on our own territory, the French must choose."[25] Like socialists, left-wing intellectuals had good reasons for preferring not to choose, but they were increasingly left with little option. The Communists could invoke on behalf of their own cause all the best arguments and emotional appeals—devotion to the USSR, without limit or reserve, "is internationalism," announced Voroshilev in Bucharest in 1949, and the memory of war and anti-Fascist struggles was close enough for him to obtain a sympathetic answering response in non-Communist circles.[26]

Thus, many in 1945 would have found nothing from which to dissent in André Gide's explanation, given in October 1932, for his rapprochement with the then militantly sectarian Communist party:

Don't talk of conversion, I have not changed direction; I have always walked straight ahead, I continue to do so; the big difference is that for a long time I saw nothing ahead of me but space and the projection of my own enthusiasm. Now I advance towards something.[27]

Gide's own later disillusion did nothing to diminish the similar sentiments of a later generation. The only way out in an otherwise hopeless world was towards the socialist vision, argued an editorial in *Esprit* in the aftermath of the Soviet occupation of Budapest. We are tied by our hopes and by our past faith.[28] But by 1956 it was surely clear not only that the optimistic anticipation of a moderate "national" communism was misplaced but also that the larger commitment to the promise of

25. Julien Benda, "Le Dialogue est-il possible?" *Europe*, March 1948, 8.
26. Voroshilev is quoted by François Fejtö in "L'Affaire Rajk est une affaire Dreyfus internationale," *Esprit*, November 1949, 737.
27. Gide, "Pages de Journal," *Nouvelle Revue française*, October 1932, quoted in Evelyne Ritaine, *Les Stratèges de la culture* (Paris, 1983), 104–5.
28. Editorial, "Les Flammes de Budapest," *Esprit*, December 1956, 777.

Leninism, which had sustained various generations for three decades, was being ground into the dust by the Communists' own actions. In what, therefore, did this faith now consist?

The Soviet state, both in its reality and in the penumbra of half-truths that surrounded its image in the West, was the fulfillment of the dream of nineteenth-century thought. It was, in Carl Schmitt's phrase, "this extremist brother who took the European nineteenth century at its word." The sheer scale and ambition of Lenin's revolution, its very implausibility given the time and place of its occurrence, its combination of exotic context and familiar language, all gave it an appeal that transcended anything as mundane and petty as mere achievements or lack of them. From the very outset it had mesmerized the romantic imagination, while simultaneously asserting for itself roots in the classical, rationalist project of progress with which French thought and politics were so familiar. The impudence of the Stalinist claim to "transform human nature" not only placed the Soviet project firmly in the path of the European Enlightenment but attracted sympathy by its very absurd grandeur. Here, truly, was Prometheus-made-state.[29]

Thus even if the Soviet view of the future had not been the only game in town, at least in the view of the disenchanted intelligentsia of postwar western Europe, it would have seduced by its very ambition. Curiously, intellectuals instinctively understood that despite its claims to being a "workers' revolution," and despite their own enthusiastic support of that claim, the revolution of 1917 was in its essence a "revolution of the intellectuals," more even than had been true of 1848. The justifications offered by Lenin, Trotsky, or even Stalin for the seizure and maintenance of power, in Russia and elsewhere, appealed most strongly—indeed, only really made sense—to those steeped in the traditions of radical thought emanating from late eighteenth-century France. For workers (or peasants) a revolution is not made any more real or legitimate because its leaders and their heirs proclaim incessantly that it is a workers' or a peasants' revolution. But to the intelligentsia (whether Russian or French) this was sufficient. It was therefore not by chance that the postwar show trials emphasized *ad nauseam* the nonproletarian, nonpeasant origins of the accused. The prosecution, in speaking thus, was addressing itself not only to Hungarian or Czech workers or peasants but to a universal audience of the elect. As Camus came to realize, the USSR and its satel-

29. For Carl Schmitt, see *La Notion du politique* (Paris, 1972), 133, cited in Václav Belohradský, "La Modernité comme passion du neutre," *Le Messager européen* 2 (1988): 22.

lites were governed by *philosophes:* they were the fulfillment *ad absurdum* of the Western philosophical dream.[30]

At a distance, of course, these same Communist regimes appear to embody precisely the reverse of the Western ideal; they were crude in their methods, paid little attention to rights or justice, and depended on force for their inception and survival. Yet these defects of communism were, in the eyes of observers, its virtues If it was strong, victorious in war, and all-too-certain of its purposes, this came in pleasant contrast to the weaknesses and defeats of modern liberalism. If it was cruel and unjust and offended humanistic sensibilities, then all the worse for the humanist, victim of the very illusions that communism existed to overcome. Who, Henri Barbusse warned the 1935 Congress of Writers for the Defense of Culture, are we to doubt the actions of men of such stature as those who rule in Moscow? The intellectual who points criticisms at the leaders of world-historical revolutions not only is ineffectual but renders himself an object of ridicule. Among those who listened enthusiastically to this warning were not only André Malraux (of whom an empathetic response was to be expected) but also Mounier, André Chamson, Gide (still committed), and Heinrich Mann.[31]

For the mid-twentieth-century intellectual disenchanted with the failed promises of the nineteenth century communism offered the only remaining prospect for the reenchantment of the world. The fact that modern socialist thought derived its style and content from the early nineteenth-century struggle with liberalism for the heritage of the French Revolution was helpful; for here once again was socialism (in its modern form) engaged in battle with the lingering illusions of the liberal idea, a "frère ennemi," whose weaknesses it understood so well and addressed so unerringly. Even the Communist obsession with statistics was an asset in this struggle. It is sometimes suggested that postwar France, with its concern for productivism and output, offered especially ripe territory for the Communist appeal, since a community that measured its own recovery in such terms would be especially sympathetic to evidence of Communist achievement presented in figures for coal mined or wheat harvested.[32] As an explanation, this seems to me naive and culturally solipsistic. *All* West European nations were absorbed in

30. See Sandor Garay, *Volontaires pour la potence* (Paris, 1950), 177; Albert Camus, "Entretien sur la Révolte," in *Gazette des lettres,* 15 February 1952, reprinted in *Actuelles,* vol. 2 (Paris, 1977), 55.

31. Ilya Ehrenburg, *Memoirs* (New York, 1963), 306.

32. See, for example, Alain Besançon, *Une Génération* (Paris, 1987), especially 175–96.

"productivism" in these years, yet by no means all of them responded so enthusiastically to the charms of Gosplan. But to intellectuals, French or otherwise, this emphasis on socioeconomic data as the measure of Communist successes had the charm of reversing all the usual liberal criteria, while at the same time resting firmly on the "scientificity" associated with communism's special historical claim. It was, moreover, an emphasis peculiarly compatible with that tradition of positivist thought that had never quite died in France.

Postwar French thinkers, then, were particularly vulnerable to the charms and promises of the Soviet project. But the sacrifices of the Russian people, the heroism of the "Parti des fusillés," could account for only so much; some things even Stalingrad could not justify. Western intellectuals might yearn for the comforts and simplicities of oriental despotism, but they remained Western for all that, and their level of discomfort can be felt rising, palpably, in the writings of this period. The true believers of communism entered the church, but many remained outside, unable despite themselves to find solace in faith alone. Instead they would invoke a special standard of judgment, one that drew on earlier habits of argument but that was perfected in these years and allowed those whose souls rebelled at Communist practices to find at least some ease and comfort. This exercise in double-entry moral bookkeeping is perhaps the most representative of intellectual practices in these years, and it forms the subject matter of the next chapter.

CHAPTER NINE

About the East
We Can Do Nothing
Of Double Standards and Bad Faith

Nous n'avons pas à choisir entre le monde   We don't have to choose between a
de la terreur et celui du profit, même si ce   world based on terror and one based
dernier prétend défendre certaines valeurs   on profit, even if the latter claims to
spirituelles.   defend certain spiritual values.

                                             Jacques Madaule

Ever since the early thirties, intellectual life in France (as elsewhere at the time) had been permeated by moral bifocalism, the capacity to apply different criteria of truth and value to different phenomena. This should not be confused with moral relativism. The relativist holds that no absolute evaluations are possible. For the consistent relativist, it is not possible to say of an action or a statement or a political system that it is incontrovertibly good or evil, true or false, correct or in error. This does not preclude contingent judgments of value, nor does it exclude the possibility of simply choosing to believe a certain opinion or accept a certain course of action. What relativism does seem to exclude is any claim that your choice or action rests on absolute and timeless certainties.

Moral bifocalism is thus not relativist—or, more accurately, it is sometimes relativist, sometimes not. Its incoherence derives from the application of a double standard, the combination of an insistence upon certain normative values and the subsequent refusal to recognize their application in selected cases. Had the editors of *Temps modernes,* for example, consistently refused any "inquisitional tone" when commenting on political behavior East and West, they would have been quite entitled to assert, as they did when refusing to "encaisser Kravchenko," that "the inquisitorial tone seems to us out of place in a world where there is no innocence and which is apparently ruled by no immanent reason."[1] But this was not their consistent position—on the contrary, immanent reason (and thus innocence) were frequently invoked, but for the benefit of one side alone.

In its simplest form, the double standard was applied as a categorical proposition, a priori. One bloc or society or action was imperfect, flawed, even evil, whatever its apparent virtues; the other tended to the good and the desirable, however (contingently) imperfect or even unjustifiable its present condition. Capitalism and imperialism were wrong in principle and doomed by their past and present behavior; about them, therefore, one could be definitive and absolute in one's judgments. Socialism, by contrast, was in principle perfect, and its time was yet to come, so that *its* present circumstances and behavior were assessed in the light of a hypothetical future. Among other things, this meant treating capitalism (a historical and economic system) and socialism (a political and ethical idea) as comparable units of measurement, a mistake made by Camus no less than by others.[2] The point is well illustrated by attitudes towards racism. Racial or ethnic prejudice in the West was just that, prejudice, and to be condemned in the name of human rights, equality, and justice. In other words, on traditional, nonrelative grounds. But evidence of racial prejudice (such as anti-Semitism) in the East could not be what it seemed, because communism excludes the possibility of such prejudice *ex hypothesi*. Even if the evidence was incontrovertible, it could still be excused as the passing cost of History's forced march to a higher goal.

Both blocs, then, might appear to threaten liberty, but only one did so in the name and the interest of all and not merely in the service of the

---

1. See the editors' note following Claude Lefort's article "Kravchenko et le problème de l'URSS," *Les Temps modernes* 29 (February 1948): 1516, in which they distance themselves from Lefort's position.

2. See, for example, Camus in 1948, *Actuelles,* vol. 1 (Paris, 1950), 148.

needs of "wealthy exploiters."[3] When the Soviet Union intervened in eastern Europe, this was in order to create relations of a "new type" between sovereign states, whereas analogous activities by the United States (for example, via the Marshall Plan) constituted interference, or worse. For this reason, the apparent injustices of Communist governments fell under a special dispensation—"all political justice exercised in the name of the oppressed is legitimate to the precise extent that the authority exercising it is combating that oppression."[4] Thus the unimpeachable motives of communism were inscribed in its own self-definition, and there were no grounds on which to deny its good intentions. Capitalism, on the other hand, was not a transhistorical carrier of good intentions but an actual condition of experienced inequality and injustice, which must therefore be measured not by its intentions but by its acts. As Aron remarked, Sartre would insist that neither he nor the Communists desired oppression, whereas prison camps and their like were integral to capitalism. In this sense, the West "wanted" concentration camps, colonial repression, and police violence—they were essential to its nature and its survival. This meant that one's reaction to the existence of such things was very different in each case.[5] And in the very worst case, when Communists and capitalists alike seemed both to concede and accept the presence of the unacceptable, at least Communists admitted that this was the case, whereas the West sought to deny it:

What is certain is that the Communist leaders take responsibility for the regime, its strengths and defects alike. The liberal bourgeois pleads not guilty: he didn't make the world.[6]

The fact that capitalism was a product of history, and its bourgeois beneficiaries likewise, thus became incriminating evidence. The bourgeoisie's ignorance of its own crimes, even if genuine, constituted alienation and a kind of bad faith. Self-interested in their own behavior, "in the name of what kind of integrity, then, do they reproach others for the same realism?" This was a widely held view, its most articulate spokesman Emmanuel Mounier, who made something of a specialty of self-

---

3. Julien Benda was already taking this line in 1937. See David Schalk, *The Spectrum of Political Engagement* (Princeton, 1979), 43.

4. Emmanuel Mounier, "Y a-t-il une justice politique?" *Esprit,* August 1947, 231.

5. Raymond Aron, "Aventures et mésaventures de la dialectique," *Preuves* 59 (January 1956): 18.

6. Jean-Paul Sartre, "Le Fantôme de Staline," *Les Temps modernes* 129–31 (January 1957): 631.

laceration of this sort. By what authority, he would demand, does the West presume to pass judgment on the East? Who are we to judge?

We must remove this cancerous Western clear conscience, which has grown in the past two years to the point where it suppurates an anticommunism of social defense, this appalling clear conscience that suffocates even the inclination to form any healthy social awareness.[7]

A strange transference, a "transvaluation of values," was taking place. The argument ran thus: without a completely clear conscience of its own, the West should not presume to criticize the failings of others. Since the Western conscience is condemned never to be clear precisely because it rests on the inherent injustices of capitalism, all criticism of communism is for the time being precluded. Moreover, any such criticism from the West is further evidence of the West's own failings, since it points to an ignorance and irresponsibility that marks the bourgeois world for extinction. The worse things seem to get in the Communist world, the more we should ruthlessly investigate our own motives for being offended—the Prague coup of 1948, Mounier insisted, "does not entitle us to strut our good Western conscience."[8] For the editors of *Esprit*, capitalism was "this universe of the total lie," which offered no basis from which to pronounce definitively upon the defects of Stalinism, however troubling these might be. Under communism, the facts are neglected or even falsified, Domenach conceded; but in bourgeois society the facts "probably come to us deformed, refracted by class knowledge and an intrinsically mendacious climate." If capitalism and the liberties it proclaimed were a present and living lie, communism was a future truth, and this placed its current actions in a unique light and gave them special claims upon Western sympathy.[9]

Thus the task of the Western intellectual was not to defend some set of values hitherto associated with the bourgeoisie but, on the contrary, to reveal them as false, to have the courage to deny their universality. This

---

7. Mounier, "Fidélité," *Esprit*, February 1950, 181. ("Nous enlèverons à l'Occident cette tumeur de bonne conscience qu'il forme depuis deux ans au point ou il suppure l'anti-communisme de défense sociale, cette affreuse bonne conscience qui étouffe la disposition même à entreprendre les prises de conscience salutaires.") See also "Prague," *Esprit*, March 1948, 355.

8. "Quel bel exemple, de son côté, la France de la Libération a-t-elle à lui donner pour jouer la vertu offensée? De quelle autorité exiger d'elle [Czechoslovakia] une force d'autonomie que nous n'avons pas su preserver chez nous?" Mounier, "Prague," 354.

9. Jean-Marie Domenach, "Une Révolution rencontre le mensonge," *Esprit*, February 1950, 198.

did not imply adopting the arguments and defending the actions of Communists—that was the task of the Communist intellectuals. The latter, ironically, did not need to resort to a double standard since the single evaluative measure that they employed—the authority of the Communist party—was for them universally valid and applicable. The non-Communist intellectual, however, could not make this claim. The effort to retain some independence, to make the case for the Communists from outside their ideological frame of reference, was thus what created the difficulty and produced the complications. Conversely, there was nothing to prevent the independent intellectual from conceding that Stalinism was unattractive; all he or she sought to establish was that the immanent purpose it embodied exempted it from negative evaluations of the kind to which the contemporary West was so rigorously exposed. Moreover, the intellectuals themselves, products (however critical) of the bourgeois world, were not authorized to conduct such a moral investigation.

A second response to the dilemmas posed by contemporary developments was to place a curse upon both houses, to assert the essential comparability and identity of East and West. This was a trait especially marked in France up until 1948, but even after the onset of the Cold War the French intelligentsia showed a particular nostalgia for the ideal of a third way, a path between the two international and ideological blocs. In this respect there had been little advance since the first editorial of *Esprit* in October 1932, in which Mounier had announced, "We reject the evil of East and West alike."[10] Eighteen years later, in one of his last pieces of writing, the same Mounier could assert, with reference to the emergent McCarthyism in Washington, "The charge against Hopkins and Wallace is a Moscow trial in the making."[11] "Sanctimoniously astonished" in the face of Soviet and American examples alike, Mounier would insist throughout these years that both camps "share bad faith." The United States' protection of Franco paralleled and justified Soviet control in Czechoslovakia, American domination of Greenland had been achieved "by procedures identical to those of Soviet Russia in its zone of occupation"; accordingly, therefore, "the pages of *Esprit* are not for those who await History's truths from Tass, nor those who get them from the Associated Press."[12]

10. Mounier, "Refaire la Renaissance," *Esprit,* October 1932, 36.

11. Mounier, "Journal à haute voix," *Esprit,* January 1950, 127.

12. The description of Mounier's reaction is borrowed from Georges Duhamel's account of European reactions to the Soviet and American examples. See *Scènes de la vie future* (Paris, 1930), 240. See also Mounier, "Petkov en nous," *Esprit,* October 1947, 591 and 594; see also his editorial "De l'esprit de la vérité," *Esprit,* November 1949, 657.

On virtually every occasion when a French left-wing writer felt compelled to admit that there was something indefensible about a Soviet action, he would append to this admission a commentary noting the crimes of the Western allies. It was as though some gene had been inserted into the code of the intellectual, requiring him to seek out a counterexample every time he was moved to protest at something the Communists had done. Thus André Rhimbaut, commenting on the Petkov affair: "If Petkov has been unjustly charged, that doesn't entitle us to preach a crusade against the 'eastern democracies' (look at our own justice), nor to support the cause of the 'peasants' leaders of eastern Europe' now ensconced in New York." Similarly, Jean Cassou, even as he took his distance from the PCF after the Rajk trial, insisted that he remained an ally of the Communists, worried like them by the "appalling danger" of an American domination of France.[13] The editors of *Temps modernes* separated themselves from David Rousset not because he had revealed the existence of labor camps in the USSR, but because he had the bad taste to emphasize the existence of these camps above other causes. It was right and proper to criticize oppression everywhere, they wrote, but to address such criticism at the Soviet Union is to absolve capitalism of its crimes and failings— unemployment, colonialism, racism, and so on.[14]

This crude "distributive justice," which placed on an equal footing mass murder and wage labor, political trials and the contradictions of liberalism, was especially marked in the contemporary writings of Claude Bourdet. Bourdet brought with him the sensibilities of the disappointed survivors of resistance and deportation, sympathetic to communism despite their doubts, and profoundly disillusioned by postwar France. Here he is in October 1947, commenting on the growing anticommunism of the French middle class:

Behind talk of destroying communism, behind a cloud of vague words and honorable symbols can be seen the bitterness of the narrowest nationalisms, the most sordid appetites, the frightened cruelty of a bourgeoisie that failed technically and morally to fulfill its task. On the other side there is talk of expunging reaction, but in the name of a regime that has only been able to replace capitalist enslavement with that of the state.[15]

13. Rhimbaut, "Petkov," *Esprit,* October 1947, 584; and Jean Cassou, "La Révolution et la vérité," *Esprit,* December 1949, 946.

14. Merleau-Ponty and Sartre, "Les Jours de notre vie," *Les Temps modernes* 51 (January 1950), 1164.

15. Claude Bourdet, *Combat,* 18 October 1947.

What was here implied, that the French are in no position to criticize the Russians in view of their own failings, would be made explicit in later years, when even the description of Soviet communism as "state slavery" would be modified in the heat of Cold War polemic. By November 1949 Bourdet, like Louis Martin-Chauffier, was only willing to support Rousset's call for an enquiry into Soviet camps on condition that such an enquiry extend its terms of reference to include Spanish and Greek prisons, and social, political, and racial oppression in the Western democracies (France included). This would make it easier for Stalin to accept, he suggested, but was in any case a matter of fairness.[16]

By the time of the Slánsky trial, Bourdet had narrowed down his concerns and sharpened still further the analogy between Eastern and Western forms of exploitation and injustice. The French bourgeoisie, he wrote, would be better placed to criticize the conduct of the trials in Czechoslovakia if they would first release Henri Martin, a victim of France's own political justice for his protests at colonial practices.[17] It is true, he conceded, that here in France we do not force our political victims to confess to being former gestapo agents, but in other respects he asserted an essential comparability. There was some force in Bourdet's argument: these were the years of the repression and bloodshed in Madagascar, the hopeless and unnecessáry war in Indochina, the massacre in Constantine. Bourdet would soon be joined by Mauriac, Aron, and others in his crusade against French colonialist practices, and there are many who, then and now, would be tempted to agree with Sartre and Merleau-Ponty (writing in 1950), "You cannot deny (with the necessary nuances) that colonies are the labor camps of the democracies." Capitalism may show a less "convulsive" face than Stalinism, wrote Francis Jeanson in his review of Camus's *Homme révolté*, but what face does it show a tortured Malgache, a napalmed Viet, or a Tunisian beaten up by the Legion?[18] Left to itself, such a question carried force. More characteristic, however, was the assertion by Jean-Marie Domenach that those who had not protested at the treatment of the Malgaches were in no position to complain about the conduct of the Slánsky trial.[19] This was a politi-

16. Bourdet, *Combat*, 18 November 1949. See also Louis Martin-Chauffier, *Figaro*, 18 November 1949.

17. Bourdet, "Les Aveux de Prague," *L'Observateur*, 27 November 1952. Henri Martin, a sailor, was condemned to prison in 1950 and again in 1951 for his declarations of support for the Vietnamese insurgents and his campaigns against the war in Indochina.

18. See Merleau-Ponty and Sartre, "Les Jours de notre vie," 1164–65; Francis Jeanson, "Albert Camus ou l'âme révolté," *Les Temps modernes* 79 (May 1952): 2090.

19. Domenach, "La Tâche de protestation," *Esprit*, January 1953, 18.

cal equivalence designed not to elicit protest and moral engagement but to stifle it: unless you are willing to protest *all* evils, you have forfeited the right to speak about *any*. It does not seem ever to have occurred to Domenach and his colleagues that by the same logic their ambivalence in the face of earlier Communist crimes, not to mention his own youthful attraction to the radical Right, would have reduced them to silence throughout the Algerian war.

A similar argument from equivalence was occasionally invoked with reference not to the specific practices of capitalist states but to the very system itself. Why do we work ourselves up into such a fury over concentration camps in the Soviet Union, wondered Mounier in 1950? We should first look at our own domestic situation. Working-class Montreuil, he claimed, is

a spread-out concentration camp, whose inmates thought themselves liberated in 1936 . . . and who once again see the barbed wire closing in on them, the guardposts reoccupied, and behind them the invisible army of the powerful taking up again, silently, position after position.[20]

This is a classic example of the metaphor as obscenity. Mounier is so concerned with establishing the similarity between Communist and capitalist practices that he quite fails to notice the implications of his language. If Montreuil is a "concentration camp," what were Mauthausen or Belsen? If Billancourt becomes a "Gulag," what words will serve to describe the life of those who at the very time Mounier was writing were working and dying in Kolyma? The immodest and immoderate language of the intellectual Left, by collapsing all categories of the socially or politically undesirable into a single unit, deprived itself of any tool for genuine social criticism, any device with which to discriminate between the bad, the worse, and the evil. If Mounier (and others) truly believed that West and East were so interchangeable, and that Auschwitz was a serviceable metaphor with which to describe the daily lives of the working class in bourgeois society, then the tone of cultural despair that resonates in their writing and that of many of their contemporaries was well founded indeed.[21]

Of course they did not really believe anything of the sort. There was by the early fifties an inflation in the vocabulary of progressives, generating a political and moral discourse that seems to have carried people

20. Mounier, "Fidélité," 178.
21. Note the exculpatory metaphors of the time: "Un chantier plaît rarement à l'oeil, c'est d'abord un ventre ouvert, du sang, des tripes, pas joli," and so on. See Claude Roy, *Nous* (Paris, 1972), 406.

further than they intended. The very fact that Bourdet or Mounier thought it worth protesting the condition of the poor or the colonized illustrates, after all, their continuing faith in the power of reason and argument. And even if this seems too coldly logical, and we accept that people continue to protest and argue long after they have lost faith in the intelligence or goodwill of their audience, it should be noted that the language of moral equivalence that characterized these years was sometimes accompanied by an acknowledgment, however grudging, that not everything was identical, that Paris was not Prague, nor Washington, Moscow. "Of course," Mounier conceded in his notorious editorial of March 1948, "we are free and we can vote. But what is the substance and basis of this freedom?"[22] A few months earlier he had similarly admitted that although the United States is just as bad as the USSR in most respects, "the Western system of international feudalism is more flexible."[23] In short, as an editorial in *Temps modernes* agreed, in a reply to a letter from Gilles Martinet: we have always said it is nicer to live in the United States than under Stalin—but that is no reason to be critical of communism![24]

Thus, although many people tacitly invoked the Sartrian distinction between the apparently bad (but actually good) Communist world, and the genuinely evil (but superficially benign) capitalist one, this dialectical subtlety was hard to sustain in daily commentary. It was easier to condemn both sides and then retreat from the implications of one's criticism of the Communists by undermining one's own credibility as a critic. (We appear to be free, but are we really? As beneficiaries of bourgeois exploitation, who are we to condemn the Stalinist variety? And so forth.) Even the admission that life was better in the West did not imply any more far-reaching conclusions. In the first place it was generally assumed that it might be better for intellectuals but that for the proletariat, communism offered better prospects. Second, the fact that communism had come to power in historically underprivileged and backward parts of Europe gave it considerable moral credit, so that its social and military achievements were attributed to its own efforts, its economic and moral shortcomings to the accidents of geography and history. Third, the problems of communism were blamed on its opponents. Since Western intellectuals lived under capitalism, the best service they could render communism was to address their criticisms to its enemy—their own governments and their own social systems. On grounds both of responsibility and expediency,

22. Mounier, "Prague," 354. ("Mais quelle est la substance et l'assise de cette liberté?")
23. Mounier, "Petkov en nous," *Esprit*, October 1947, 594.
24. "L'Adversaire est complice," *Les Temps modernes* 57 (July 1950): 9.

they should worry less about the sins of Stalinism and more about those of their own leaders. In Mounier's words,

About the East we can do nothing. In time of plague, the healthy don't gather around to insult those afflicted, they inspect themselves instead for signs of the illness and take necessary prophylactic measures.[25]

This was Mounier's justification for refusing to support Rousset in his efforts, and once again his metaphor has led him badly astray. But the underlying sentiment was widely shared.

In the eyes of many French people at the time, by no means all of them sympathetic to communism, the West was responsible for the Cold War. From this it was but a short step to the idea that the most practical form of help that one could offer the victims of Stalinism in East Europe was to oppose Western "militarism" and American hegemony in Europe. This was the view of Bourdet's *Observateur,* which fed its readers a strong diet of attacks on U.S. aggression, charged with dividing and threatening Europe. "Capitalism," in Europe, became synonymous with "American imperialism," as though the indigenous European variant had never had an autonomous existence. Bourdet and his fellow contributors were echoing here the lingering dreams of the Liberation, the idyll of a neutral socialist France. If such a project had foundered, the blame could only lie with the United States and its West European collaborators. By extension and analogy, the failings and errors of the peoples' democracies were also treated as the direct consequence of imperialist pressures which had driven the Soviet Union and its allies into desperate measures.

In one of the most unintentionally comical texts of the era, Bourdet presented the Czech upheavals of 1951 and 1952 (the prelude to the Slánsky trial) as "hopeful" signs of growing Czech autonomy and re-sistance to Soviet control. If the West would only leave Austria and allow the emergence of a neutral Germany, he wrote, similarly positive developments could be expected there and in the rest of the Soviet bloc. Any attempt to rearm Germany, on the other hand, would frighten the Czechs "back" into Russian arms, aborting the current "efforts at liberation." But Bourdet doubted that "the masters of atomic destruc-tion" would have the sense to see the logic of such reasoning; the out-come would be a hardening once again of the geopolitical arteries, and it would be the fault of the West.[26] Bourdet was here shamelessly exploit-

25. Mounier, "Journal à haute voix," 127.
26. For Bourdet's explanation of the Slánsky arrests and trial, see *L'Observateur,* 27 November 1952, 24 January 1953, and 31 January 1953.

ing the terror in Czechoslovakia as a further opportunity to attack the United States, but he would not have been able to make such an implausible set of connections and misinterpretations had he not treated it as self-evident that all developments in eastern Europe were a direct product of Western policy and attitudes. In an intellectual community in which Simone de Beauvoir could be taken seriously when she described American films like *Shane* or *High Noon* as military propaganda designed to prepare Western audiences for a "preventive war," Bourdet's thesis seemed perfectly plausible.[27]

The context for such accounts of communism and its opponents, the circumstance in which intelligent people could be tone-deaf not just to cruelty and injustice but to incoherence and contradiction in political and moral argument is that of a fundamental *negativism*. It is for this reason that most significant intellectuals of the period were not in the Communist party. The overwhelming majority of writers, artists, teachers, and journalists were not for Stalin: they were against Truman. They were not for labor camps, they were against colonialism. They were not for show trials in Prague, they were against torture in Tunisia. They were not for Marxism (except in theory), they were against liberalism (especially in theory). And most of all, they were not for communism (except *sub specie aeternitatis*), they were against anticommunism.

The origins of French anti-anticommunism are to be found in the 1930s, in two distinct respects. The legacy of the Popular Front lived on still, dimmed but not forgotten. Moreover, Daladier's decree laws, and the banning of the party in the autumn of 1939, worked to the PCF's advantage in that they made of it a pariah movement, the one organization in French life clearly not responsible for any of the disasters of recent French history, an organization whose opponents included all those whom intellectuals despised: opportunist republican politicians, Catholic reactionaries, and Fascist demagogues. The fact that those within the SFIO who had taken overtly anti-Communist positions in the thirties— men like Paul Faure or Charles Spinasse—also went on to side with Vichy helped confirm this. In a political and cultural community increasingly polarized, one might not feel comfortable with the Communists, for all the obvious reasons, but one could not side with their opponents. Second, the political style of the thirties generation of intellectuals predisposed them to such a stance. The initial nonconform-

27. Simone de Beauvoir, *La Force des choses* (Paris, 1963), 344–45.

ism of this group took the form of a critique of liberalism that expressed itself as "ni fascisme, ni antifascisme." This was in the early thirties. With certain notable exceptions, this noncommittal attitude to fascism had been abandoned by the middle years of the decade but there remained an underlying ambivalence concerning authoritarian regimes in general. It was thus both psychologically and linguistically easy to assert in coming years that one's attitude to the politics of the far Left was "ni Communiste, ni anti-Communiste."

After the Liberation the fascist option was destroyed both militarily and ideologically. But the communist star shone all the brighter. Recalling the decree laws of 1939, Camus could reaffirm *Combat*'s Algiers declaration of March 1944: "Anticommunism is the beginning of dictatorship." Mounier, typically, was less cautious: "Anticommunism . . . is the necessary and sufficient force of crystallization for a return of fascism."[28] This postwar obsession with renascent fascism will be covered later; here it is enough to note that Mounier would feel able to say in 1946 that anticommunism *alone* would lead to a reemergence of fascism. From then until the late fifties, the French radical intelligentsia fed itself a steady diet of anti-anticommunism. All protestations of revulsion at Stalinist practices were muted by a sort of public self-censorship, the obsessive fear of providing aid and comfort to the enemy. This, too, was an Occupation-era legacy, a combination of the genuine desire to remain loyal to one's own side and the carefully cultivated belief that France was still a war zone, in which one had to "resist" the other side, avoid the temptation to "collaborate" with the American "occupiers" and their allies, and never give aid or comfort to those who had chosen the "easy" option. To this was added the comforting thought that the path one had chosen was complex, painful, and perhaps even hopeless. The Communists' behavior and the extremism of Stalin were a form of moral torture, but one must hold out and not give in to the temptations of class collaboration. What was more, it was precisely the sacrifices of those who rejected anticommunism that qualified them to criticize the Communists from a fraternal position.

Hence the increasingly shrill protestations of faith: "We retain . . . the right, the will and means to distinguish legitimate criticisms of communism from pharisaic anticommunism and war propaganda." "We have nothing in common with many opponents of communism." We will ally

---

28. Camus, *Combat,* 7 October 1944; Mounier, "Débat à haute voix," *Esprit,* February 1946, 185ff.

ourselves, Mounier announced in 1950, with *anyone* who defends human pride, civic and democratic courage, intellectual honesty, and spiritual freedom—but *not* with anti-Communists. From this, the reader could only infer, and was no doubt expected to infer, that anti-Communists did not, could not, defend intellectual honesty, civic courage, and so forth.[29] This was perfectly consistent with the general line of *Esprit:* a year earlier, Domenach quoted with approval Mounier's assertion that the mood of the frightened bourgeois of 1949—"Rather Truman than Thorez"—was comparable to that of 1939 ("Rather Hitler than Blum"). In this scenario, not only does Thorez (at the height of sectarian Stalinism) became the moral heir to Léon Blum, but, more significantly, Harry Truman and Adolf Hitler conflate into a single, all-purpose anti-Communist ogre.[30]

The absurdities of such a stance did not escape notice. From the Left, Pierre Monatte, whose credentials in this matter somewhat surpassed those of Mounier, Sartre, and others, warned against falling victim to Stalinist blackmail. One was not disqualified from the revolutionary heritage, he wrote in April 1947, nor did one forfeit the right to criticize Communists and conservatives alike just because one insisted that the true enemy of freedom and revolution in today's world was not Truman nor some ghost of Hitler but Stalin himself.[31] He might have added that those who were most vulnerable to such blackmail were the very people whose earlier political trajectories were vaguely doubtful, like Domenach, Claude Roy, or Claude Morgan. From the other side, René Tavernier made a similar observation two years later: in the terms being proposed by *Esprit,* those who saw in Stalin the force of evil were treated as though they were sympathetic to nazism.[32]

In this light, Sartre's later outburst ("An anti-Communist is a dog, I don't change my views on this, I never shall") seems immoderate only in its timing;[33] in the context of the late forties or early fifties it would have passed unnoticed. Only the a priori exclusion of any criticism of

29. Mounier, "Journal à haute voix," 131; also Merleau-Ponty and Sartre, "Les Jours de notre vie," 1161.

30. Domenach, "Le Parti Communiste français et les intellectuels," *Esprit,* May 1949, 737.

31. Pierre Monatte, writing in *Révolution prolétarienne* 1 (April 1947).

32. René Tavernier, "Les Illusionistes," *Liberté de l'esprit* 1 (February 1949).

33. In *Situations,* vol. 4 (Paris, 1961), 248–49. ("Un anti-communiste est un chien, je ne sors pas de là, je n'en sortirai plus jamais.")

communism from within the Left could account for the more extreme peculiarities and lacunae of intellectual politics in this period. Of these, one of the most striking to the modern reader is the ambivalence in the face of Stalinist anti-Semitism. Given the fresh memory of deportation and the extermination camps, why did the onset of virulent, overt anti-Semitism in the Peoples' Democracies not trigger a greater measure of criticism and reappraisal?

As part of the general repression of the Vichy memory that took place in Fourth Republic France, the record of indigenous anti-Semitism was choked off in these years. Or more accurately, and in keeping with the general treatment of France's own Fascists and collaborators, it was regarded as the work of a minority, a poison that had invaded the national body during the thirties and taken it over by force during the Occupation but which had now been expelled for good. This desire to put the unmastered past behind them was most marked among returning Jewish deportees, who sought above all to believe once again in France and in the egalitarian and humanist ideals of the Republic. There was thus a near-universal wish to see in racism and anti-Semitism nothing more than the extreme symptoms of reaction and fascism. This was further complicated by the attitude of Communists, many of them Jewish, who continued to see in racism a problem to be resolved by social revolution. Nations that had undergone such a revolution—the Soviet Union and now the countries of eastern Europe—were by definition freed forever from the scourge of racial hatred and persecution. Moreover, and this was no small matter, it was once again the Red Army that in its victorious progress into Europe had saved what remained of European Jewry from the death camps. With Stalin's defeat of Hitler, anti-Semitism had ceased to be an issue.

Thus in France as elsewhere, a strange silence fell over the Jewish question. The criminals had been defeated, the victims did not wish to talk of their experiences, the political class regarded the matter as closed. Deportation was discussed and remembered only in the context of the heroism of the Resistance; in Domenach's words, "After all, we weren't going to praise those deported on racial grounds: they were not among those whose deportation had a meaning in the struggle."[34] Certainly, there were occasional reports of anti-Semitic outbursts, and in their pri-

---

34. Quoted in Maurice Szafran, *Les Juifs dans la politique française* (Paris, 1990), 35.

vate writings some prominent figures continued to display towards Jews an ambivalence that dated from earlier decades.[35] But of serious attention to this subject, there was little. Once the Nuremberg trials had been completed, intellectual periodicals of the time turned their attention elsewhere. François Mauriac even suggested that attitudes towards Jews had in practice changed little since the thirties, though he was one of the very few to think the matter worthy of comment. As a consequence, the intellectual community in France was ill prepared for the onslaught of anti-Semitic prejudice that surfaced in the international Communist movement at the beginning of the 1950s.[36]

That French commentators should have been ignorant of the extent of popular anti-Semitism in Central and East Europe was perhaps understandable. Ignorance of this whole region was widespread in western Europe and would remain so for decades to come. The establishment of Communist regimes, however, led by Jews in many cases, had provoked a resurgence of local anti-Jewish sentiment, as had the return of deported and imprisoned Jews seeking the restoration of their land and property. Within Communist parties in Poland, Czechoslovakia, and Romania, intraparty disputes of an ideological or personal nature often highlighted the Jewish identity of some of the protagonists to the advantage of their opponents. But to Western observers, including most Western Communists, all of this was invisible. What they saw were Communist parties and states with Jews in prominent positions and whose official stance was resolutely against racial or ethnic prejudice or favor of any kind.

Thus, even after the reports of persecution of Yiddish-language artists in the USSR in the late forties, it was assumed in the West that the satellite states at least remained free of any taint of anti-Semitism; in Hungary, after all, it was the Jewish Stalinists Rákosi and Gerö who had tried and executed the non-Jewish Rajk. The violent language and openly anti-Jewish accusations that would culminate in the Slánsky trial and the "doctors' plot" in Moscow thus fell on wholly unprepared ground. What especially confused people in their response was the new anti-Zionist

35. There were some demonstrations during May 1945 protesting the restoration of their property to surviving Jewish deportees, now returned, notably in Belleville and along the Boulevard Saint-Martin. For an example of privately expressed ambivalence toward Jews, see André Gide, in his journal entry for 9 January 1948, commenting on anti-Semitism: "Psychologiquement et historiquement, il a sa raison d'être." Quoted by Jean Davray, *La Brûlure* (Paris, 1983), 185, n. 16.

36. Mauriac, *Journal*, vol. 5 (Paris, 1953), 12–13 May 1946; isolated instances of attention paid to the Jewish question at the time of the Nuremberg trials were articles in *Esprit* in September 1945 and in *Les Temps modernes* in December of the same year.

emphasis. Israel now replaced Yugoslavia as the model and headquarters of anti-Communist plotting, and Zionism emerged as a synonym for the nationalist deviation of which earlier victims had been accused. But whereas the earlier charges had reflected little if any popular sentiment, anti-Zionism resonated with real effect in the local audience to which it was addressed. No one in Czechoslovakia (or Romania, where Ana Pauker and others were victims of similar indictments in the course of 1953 and early 1954) was under any illusion as to the distinction between "Zionist" and Jew.

The invective and the accusations were ominously reminiscent of another sort of propaganda, still fresh in popular memory; thus wrote *Rudé Pravo* in a November 1952 editorial on the indicted men then being tried in Prague: "One trembles with disgust and repulsion at the sight of these cold, unfeeling beings," this "monstrous face of Zionist organizations." The "Judas Slánský" and other "elements alien to the nation" were nothing but "trash with a shady past," guided in their criminal activity by "Zionism, bourgeois Jewish nationalism, racial chauvinism," and an ideology "in the service of capital."[37] As Gottwald explained it at the Czech Party Congress in December of the same year, we let too many Jews into the party out of the goodness of our hearts, ignoring their class origins because of the past sufferings of the Jewish people.[38]

The trials were just the beginning. The humiliation of the survivors and their families, their treatment at the hands of the police, the prejudice and persecution they faced from fellow citizens are well documented, as is the common underlying theme of anti-Semitism that ran through eastern European politics and society in this period. There is little doubt that the era of the Slánský trial and its aftermath marked the turning point for many erstwhile true believers in eastern Europe itself. But this was not the case in the West. Certainly, there was no shortage of evidence had anyone sought it. Because the Western Communist parties were by then so slavishly tied to the Cominform line, the local Communist press echoed faithfully the sentiments being voiced in Prague or Warsaw. Pierre Hervé was by no means alone in his reiterated evocation of the "international Zionist plot," and the description in *France nouvelle* of the condemned prisoners in Prague is worthy of Julius Streicher: "trotskyists, titoists, Zionists, bourgeois nationalists, cosmopolites and

37. Editorial in *Rudé Pravo,* 24 November 1952.
38. Gottwald is quoted by Marcel Péju, "Hier et aujourd'hui: Le Sens du procès Slánský," part 3, *Les Temps modernes* 92 (July 1953): 159, n. 1.

war criminals . . . all united by the same golden chain, attached to the collar of the dollar."[39]

Even if they turned a deaf ear to *France nouvelle* and its hacks, progressive intellectuals ought to have been moved to caution by the enthusiasm with which events in Prague were greeted by the far *Right*; *Aspects de la France,* in December 1952, commented gleefully on the Slánsky trial: "The fate of those close to us interests us more than the misfortunes of Czech and Jewish vermin. Those people poisoned Europe; they are the source of our ills and of their own enslavement."[40] Jean-Marie Domenach, writing in *Esprit,* did remark upon the obscenities then surfacing in the French press. And yet, in the very same article, he refused to condemn the trial unconditionally, much less draw any general conclusions about the nature of Stalinism. "We must not imagine," he wrote, "that its repressive mechanism is so different from our own. We need more proof and know so little about the matter. . . . Let us not be so quick to throw stones. We must profit from the mirror of Prague." Further proof was needed, it seemed. Meanwhile Prague was a lesson, but a lesson about our own behavior, not that of the Communists.[41]

One notable silence in the face of Communist anti-Semitism was that of Jean-Paul Sartre. This is surprising for two reasons. In the first place, his own journal carried a lengthy, three-part analysis by Marcel Péju of the whole Slánsky affair. Péju took great care to distance himself from any anti-Communist interpretation of the Czech events, and some of his explanations of them were well off the mark (helped by his reliance on material provided by the Czech Embassy in Paris); but on one thing he was clear and unambiguous—the anti-Zionist emphasis might make sense in the light of Soviet foreign policy and the issue of nationalism, but in its form as in its substance, the Slánsky trial was anti-Semitic. Once we acknowledge this, he wrote, we are no longer mere spectators, but "vaguely complicitous, compromised and a little responsible." If Sartre was reading the work of his own contributors, it is hard to imagine how he could maintain his silence in the face of both the evidence thus presented and the conclusions to be drawn from it.[42]

39. Pierre Hervé's contributions to *Ce Soir* are cited by Pierre Daix, *J'ai cru au matin* (Paris, 1976), 313ff.; see also *France nouvelle,* 6 December 1952.

40. *Aspects de la France,* 5 December 1952.

41. Domenach, "L'Antisémitisme reste logique," *Esprit,* January 1953.

42. Marcel Péju, "Hier et aujourd'hui," part 1, *Les Temps modernes* 90 (May 1953): 1775.

The second oddity arises from the fact that Sartre had himself devoted some attention to the Jewish question in his well-known essay published in 1946. In that work he drew on his earlier philosophical speculations to present a picture of Jewish identity as deriving both from the opinions of others (the "gaze," once again) and the freedom of all people to choose and affirm their own attitude in the face of persecution. The Jew, in short, although "invented" by anti-Semites, was not doomed to be their victim, to have his or her existence shaped by the hatreds and prejudices of others. Freedom, for Jews as others, consisted in authenticity, in the free choice of one's own path. Here, then, was a special case of Sartre's general proposition about human existence but accompanied by unambiguous promises to speak out against anti-Semitism, *urbi et orbi*. After this, however, Sartre showed little further interest in the Jewish question. Nonetheless, he was associated with both the work itself (republished in 1954) and with his many public commitments to an unarticulated but endlessly reaffirmed ethics. It was thus reasonable to suppose that the growing evidence of anti-Semitism in the Communist movement at home and abroad would provoke a response from him.

Notoriously, he remained quite silent. François Mauriac, making direct reference to *Réflexions sur la question Juive,* demanded of Sartre a statement on the condition of Jews in the Soviet bloc, the persecution of Jewish Communists, the deportation and murder of Yiddish writers, and the growing rumors of an impending pogrom in Moscow itself.[43] But this demand for a moral commitment, for a significant intervention by Sartre, came just at the time of his enthusiastic adoption of the Communist cause and the publication of his strongest statement in defense of the open-ended legitimacy of Communist practice; the first part of "Les Communistes et la paix" was published in *Temps modernes* in July 1952, the second in November 1952. Not only did Sartre not comment on the Slánsky trial, he attended the Communists' "World Congress of Peace" in Vienna in the days immediately following the mass execution of eleven of those convicted. His only reply to Mauriac was to issue the following characteristic warning: "The problem of the condition of Jews in the Peoples' Democracies must not become a pretext for propaganda or polemic." He could not even claim to have needed time to prepare his response to these events, since no such response was ever to be forthcoming. As Étiemble reminded him, in an open letter published in *Arts* in July 1953, he had gone to Vienna, thereby giving his support to the

43. See François Mauriac, *Mémoires politiques* (Paris, 1967), 304–5.

Communists, *knowing* that he would say nothing about Jewish victims of Communist persecution.[44]

According to Simone de Beauvoir, all of this was a source of much agonizing for her partner, and we can probably believe her. Sartre, she reported, "never recovered from [n'encaissa pas]" the Prague trials, the Moscow "doctors' plot," the anti-Zionism of the PCF. He promised Mauriac that he would reply in his own time, a promise that he was able to abandon thanks to the death of Stalin. In other words, as de Beauvoir concludes, the departure of Stalin spared him the embarrassment of spoiling his relationship with his new-found Communist friends.[45] Sartre the existentialist might have argued that there are worse things in life than embarrassing one's friends or even oneself and that there are moments in history when an individual just must speak out, make a commitment to a position, and live the consequences. But Sartre the anti-anti-Communist thought otherwise. Once again, as in 1936, 1940, and throughout the Occupation years, he missed the opportunity to act decisively, to be consistent in his moral engagement. But that was his private tragedy. Anti-anticommunism, and everything it entailed, was the tragedy and dilemma of a generation.

44. Sartre, quoted by M-A Burnier, *Le Testament de Sartre* (Paris, 1982), 76; Étiemble, "Lettre ouverte à Jean-Paul Sartre," *Arts,* 24–30 July 1953, reprinted in *Littérature dégagée, 1942–1953* (Paris, 1955), 148. The third part of "Les Communistes et la paix" did not appear until April 1954.

45. De Beauvoir, *La Force des choses,* 312.

CHAPTER TEN

America Has Gone Mad
Anti-Americanism in Historical Perspective

L'Amérique, dans les années quarante-cinquante, n'était pas tellement bien vue par les Européens, et par les Français en particulier... les Européens détestaient l'Amérique parce qu'ils se détestaient.

In the forties and fifties, America was not very much *liked* by Europeans, and by the French in particular... Europeans detested America because they detested *themselves.*

Claude Roy

Ever since the first Spanish missionaries agonized over the status of the "noble savages" they encountered in the New World, European thinkers have had mixed feelings about the Americas.[1] Entranced by its emptiness, its riches, its tabula rasa on which the world could be written anew, they have been simultaneously repelled by its crude simplicity, its newness, its very modernity. And of all the Europeans, the French in particular have exhibited these mixed emotions in their most acute form. From the Marquis de Lafayette to Jean-Jacques Servan-Schreiber, they

1. Anthony Pagden, *The Fall of Natural Man* (Cambridge, 1982).

187

have found in America an energy, an openness, a protean possibility that they felt was lacking in the established habits and routines of their own society. But at the same time, others have turned away from it in distaste at its shallow culture and rapacious search for wealth and success. Very few French writers have taken the trouble, like Aléxis de Tocqueville, to study and analyze, with a critical sympathy, the underlying shape and drive of the United States; but many of his fellow citizens have succeeded and imitated him in his anxiety in face of the American model, harbinger of an ambiguous future.[2]

By the mid-nineteenth century, *America* was already a synonym in certain French circles for whatever was disturbing or unfamiliar about the present. The criticism of a Pierre Buchez was understandable in the context of the utopian vision of the Christian socialist tradition: "It is solidly organized egoism, it is evil made systematic and regular, in a word it is the materialism of human destiny";[3] but even here it is curious to catch the pessimistic, elegiac note, the sense that in one possible account of human history, the United States was a depressing warning of the future of Europe. More predictable in this respect was Edmond de Goncourt, commenting bleakly on the emerging Paris of the Baron Haussmann: "It makes me think of some American babylon of the future."[4] By the end of the century this point of view was already enshrined in school textbooks—in one such manual published in 1904, it was asserted that "America is becoming the material pole of the world; for how long will Europe remain its intellectual and moral pole?"[5]

The parameters of the modern French view of the United States of America were thus already set before World War I (and long before most French writers had any direct experience of the place itself). America had the wealth and might well soon enough acquire power. It was thus the most modern of worlds, the human enterprise stripped of tradition and inhibition, of complexity and sophistication. Europe, by contrast, was

2. General histories of this topic include René Remond, *Les États-Unis devant l'opinion française, 1815–1852,* 2 vols. (Paris, 1962); Jean-Baptiste Duroselle, *La France et les États-Unis des origines à nos jours* (Paris, 1976); Denis Lacorne, Jacques Rupnik, and Marie-France Toinet, *L'Amérique dans les têtes* (Paris, 1986).

3. Pierre Buchez, quoted by Michel Winock, *Nationalisme, antisémitisme, et fascisme en France* (Paris, 1990), 52.

4. Edmond de Goncourt in 1860, quoted by Deborah Silverman, *Art Nouveau in Fin-de-siècle France* (Berkeley, 1989), 20.

5. E. Jaliffier, *Cours complet d'histoire,* cited by Jacques Portès, "Les États-Unis dans les manuels d'histoire et de géographie de la Troisième République (1871–1914)," *Revue d'histoire moderne et contemporaine* 28 (January–March 1981): 204.

already "old Europe," rich in ideas, in heritage, in culture and under-standing. Either Europe's future lay in America (in which case all the worse for Europe), or else the struggle for the preservation of the values of the spirit would have to be undertaken against America. These senti-ments were reinforced and given new significance by the Great War, which, in revealing the terrifying destructive power of technical and eco-nomic resources, also made of modernity an exponentially more fright-ening and immediate vision. Moreover, there were now very good grounds for associating modernity and the monopoly of material resources with the United States; of all the great powers, it alone emerged unscathed—indeed, strengthened—from the experience of conflict. The resented beneficiary of the war, it was now the natural target of both radical ideol-ogy and cultural pessimism.

But in the years after World War I "America" as the symbol of moder-nity, materialism, and bourgeois self-satisfaction became synonymous with a larger and more abstract target of suspicion, "the West." Here, too, a background remark is necessary. This was by no means the first occasion on which European intellectuals had formed a suspicious, dis-missive dislike for their own world and looked longingly at some mysteri-ous other. The fascination for China and with things Chinese had swept some Western nations during the eighteenth century, and in the nine-teenth century many English, Germans, and French had been drawn into "Orientalism," the admiration for a half-understood mysterious world south and east of the Mediterranean.[6] Russia, too, had become a source of curiosity for some Western writers in these years. Although it did not follow axiomatically that an interest in Asia must be accompa-nied by dismissal of the Western heritage, there was a natural inclination to adopt for oneself the attitudes of non-Europeans towards the Euro-pean world. Thus the nineteenth-century czarist historians who culti-vated the Slavophile dismissal of "the rotten West" were echoed by Western admirers. Until 1917, however, the flow of Western self-hatred was damned by the unappealing and manifestly unsatisfactory forms of government and social order that held sway nearly everywhere else in the world. It was one thing to admire the Slav soul or prefer Chinese art or Islamic theology; it was quite something else to imagine that the politi-cal future of humanity lay in the Forbidden City or the Sultan's harem.

The Russian Revolution changed all that. Accompanied in short order by the secularization of Turkey, the rise of Arab and Indian nation-

6. Edward Said, *Orientalism* (New York, 1978).

alism, the emergence of Japan as a regional power, and the rumors of revolution in China, it seemed to suggest that if the East contained a mystery, it was the riddle of the future, not the enigma of the past. Young radicals of the twenties, even if not themselves Communists, saw in the upheavals to the East an energy and a promise altogether missing from an exhausted, static Europe. In his first significant work, the twenty-five-year-old André Malraux captured the mood of his generation perfectly, as he compared the West unfavorably to the promises of a once-exotic East. The Surrealists, too, were caught up in the enthusiastic vision of Western decline (in Spengler's sense) and the coming age of the East; this is Louis Aragon, speaking a year before the publication of Malraux's *La Tentation de l'Occident:* "Western world, you are condemned to die. We are Europe's defeatists. . . . May the East, your terror, at last respond to our pleas."[7]

During the twenties, in the period of nonpolitical, cultural radicalism that marked the immediate postwar generation, most intellectuals had little use for communism and their interest in the East was largely aesthetic and theoretical. Certainly the East was somehow fresher and more promising than the West, but the exact sociohistorical attributes of East and West remained elusive. The end of the decade and the first signs of the "nonconformists" of the thirties saw an increasingly precise formulation of the critique of Western civilization, with a growing use of the word *America* as a shorthand for all that was undesirable or disturbing about Western life. This critique took various distinct forms, each more political and extreme than the previous one.

In the first place there was America-the-modern, the crude outrider of history. In many novels, essays, and films from the late twenties and early thirties, the United States appears sometimes as metaphor, sometimes as example of everything that is amiss or foreboding about the present. In *Mort de la pensée bourgeoise* (a title that could stand for many in these years), Emmanuel Berl treated the rise of American power and influence as synonymous with the decline of all that was worth saving in Western culture—"America is multiplying its territory, where the values of the West risk finding their grave."[8] Two years earlier, André Siegfried had published a work devoted to the United States, in which he saw the

7. Aragon quoted by Pierre Astier, *Écrivains français engagés* (Paris, 1978), 89. See also André Malraux, *La Tentation de l'Occident* (Paris, 1926).

8. Emmanuel Berl, *Mort de la pensée bourgeoise* (1929; reprint Paris, 1970), 76–77.

country much as Chaplin would depict it in *Modern Times,* a land where people are reduced to automatons, a horrific depiction of the future of us all: "We Westerners must each firmly denounce whatever is American in his house, his clothes, his soul."[9]

At first reading, this sounds like simple anti-Americanism, and the same is true of Berl's writing as well. But the clue lies in Siegfried's suggestion that we inspect our own behavior first. "America" is us, or rather it is a part of us, everything that threatens the past, its values, its spirit. This may sound reactionary but clearly was intended to convey quite the opposite message. Berl was young and an outspoken radical. So were Robert Aron and Arnaud Dandieu, whose *Le Cancer américain,* published in 1931, was part of a critical diptych; the other half was *Décadence de la nation française,* also published in 1931. Taken together, these essays constitute not only a critique of productivism, anonymity, and modernity but also that demand for a moral, almost a sentimental revolution that gave this generation so much in common with its Fascist contemporaries abroad. Like Georges Duhamel's *Scènes de la vie future,* published in 1930, they saw in anything and everything American the evidence of a collapse of the specificities, the variety and depth, that had been the beauty and virtue of Western culture. Without them, it lost its redeeming features and was rotten, two-dimensional, ripe for revolution.

Some of these writers, Robert Aron and Arnaud Dandieu in particular, saw in "industrialism" the special sin of modernity and thus in American production techniques the epitome of the modern world in all its naked shame. This of course distinguished them from some Fascists and all Communists and connected them much more immediately to the sentimental fringe of reactionary politics. In France, as in Germany or Russia, there was an intimate relationship, forged in the Romantic era, between opposition to industrial society and nostalgia for earlier forms of authority and order. The counterpoint to this, utopian socialism and its various offspring in the anticapitalism of fin-de-siècle ruralists, was never as strong or popular, having been soundly defeated by urban socialist parties with their roots in an industrial labor movement. Thus those who saw in America the scourge of modern production and technology tended to be either implicitly conservative or else politically marginal. But this did not prevent them speaking for a significant intellectual

9. André Siegfried, *Les États-Unis d'aujourd'hui,* quoted in Winock, *Nationalisme, antisémitisme, et fascisme,* 57.

constituency. Even Raymond Aron in these years could quote with approval Bertrand Russell's assertion that the great task of the epoch was humanity's struggle against industrial civilization.[10]

In this context, the otherwise awkward figure of Antoine de Saint-Exupéry fits right in. Despite his own fascination with modern machinery, he looked upon industrial society as the generator of a profound spiritual emptiness, a universe in which human beings were lost, their individuality submerged in the totalizing tendencies evinced by *all* the major nations and systems of the era. German nazism, Soviet communism, and (especially) American capitalism were in this respect utterly alike for him, as for many others; Mounier's mysterious "personalism" operated from similar premises. France, he believed, was afflicted with the industrial disease, the American cancer, but still carried signs of hope and life. Hence Saint-Exupéry's willingness to fight for it still: "I shall thus oppose anyone seeking to impose one custom over others, one people over other peoples, one race over other races, one style of thought over all others."[11] Like the English, many French saw their country as struggling alone to preserve this individuality, this autonomy, in the face of the onslaught of the modern and the totalitarian.

During the thirties, however, there emerged a further and more distinctively ideological version of anti-Americanism, which associated the United States with capitalism and thus opposed it no longer in the name of anti-Western, much less anti-industrial sentiment but on behalf of an alternative modernity, the promise of Oriental redemption now associated with communism. Because communism was, as Saint-Exupéry and others noted, an ideology and a system as anti-individual and totalizing as "America," its appeal in these years was self-restricting; many progressive intellectuals found American and Soviet emphasis on production and material transformation similar and equally repulsive. But Soviet communism in the thirties was able to trade not so much perhaps on specifically anti-American sentiment as on anti-Western emotions of the kind already taking shape a decade before. Not only did it represent the future (for Marxists and many non-Marxists alike) but it was, from 1935, an active protagonist in defense of the present against the combined threat of fascism and reaction. Moreover, and after 1918 this was a strong

10. Raymond Aron, quoted by Jean-François Sirinelli, *Génération intellectuelle* (Paris, 1988), 592. The original source of the quotation was Henri de Man. Ernst Robert Curtius, in the twenties, described French nerves as "surtendus par l'américanisation de la vie moderne." See his *Essai sur la France* (1932; reprint Paris, 1990), 101.

11. Antoine de Saint-Exupéry, *Pilote de guerre* (Paris, 1942), 143.

point in its favor, the Soviet Union was part of the underprivileged of the international community, one of the many nations that had lost the First World War, whatever side they had been on.

For most French observers, the real winners in 1918 had been the "Anglo-Saxons." Perfidious diplomacy and raw financial power had made of the United States and Great Britain the only unambiguous beneficiaries of the postwar treaties. (Of course the British saw things differently and regarded the United States alone as having monopolized the economic benefits of victory.) Thus, for the first time in France there surfaced a vision of "Anglo-Saxon capitalism," a sort of international predator against whom France somehow metamorphosed into at best a fawning jackal, at worst a virtual proletarian nation. Hitherto the Left had treated all capitalism as international, all capitalists as equal in their interests and their crimes. But the tortured French psyche of the interwar years transposed the sins of capitalism onto foreigners in general and the Anglo-Saxons in particular. There would be many in the Resistance who vociferously asserted their intention of liberating France from the yoke of international Anglo-Saxon capital, even as they were engaged in a life-and-death struggle with collaborators who thought they were doing the same thing.

Finally, and in close if distorted relation to the forms already discussed, there was that variant of interwar anti-Americanism that made an implicit, or with growing frequency explicit, association between America and Jews. The roots of this prejudice also trace back to earlier decades: for very good reasons, Jews were associated with modernity in the European mind, in the sense that the free circulation of Jews in society, the opportunity for Jews to play an active and prominent role in public life, were the direct product of that Archimedean point of departure of the modern world, the great French Revolution. Whereas capitalism and industry might be metaphors for modernity, or three-dimensional symbols of it, the emancipation of the Jews of Europe was one of the defining acts of the modern era, emblematic of the rationality of enlightened thought and its incarnation in modern government and law. It was thus both logical and quite astute of those for whom modernity was the problem to treat the presence of Jews as its most telling and troubling symptom. Jews (like Americans) were rootless, connected only to their means of livelihood and to the present. Because taste and appreciation were the work of centuries of national and popular culture, Jews (like Americans) necessarily lacked taste and refinement; their access to wealth, however, broke the natural bond between material power and

cultural authority so that (like Americans) they could now pollute Western culture with their purchasing power and their preferences.

This was no extremist, fringe prejudice. Edouard Drumont's commentary on the Eiffel Tower, "this stupid witness to modern life . . . that
will prove such a boon to the Jewish industrialist,"[12] could have been
made by any number of people, and probably was. Anti-Semitism was
respectable on both sides of the political divide right up until 1944, and
many of those writers who expressed distaste at Jews and what they stood
for would have been horrified to be accused of prejudice, much less
racism or incitement to genocide. Gide was no philo-Semite for all his
Dreyfusard engagement, and Georges Bernanos, who wrote with such
acerbity of Catholic atrocities in civil-war Spain, had published an
influential book only a few years earlier in which he not only praised the
heritage and influence of Drumont but explicitly associated anti-
Semitism with its respectable twin, anti-Americanism.[13] Paul Faure and
the large minority within the SFIO who opposed Léon Blum after 1937
never made any secret of their latent anti-Semitic feelings and could
indulge them precisely because there was a long tradition, dating at least
to Proudhon, of conflating anti-Semitism with anticapitalism. Now that
capitalism was increasingly treated as distinctively and primarily American, the circle was complete. For Blum to favor standing up to Hitler, at
the risk of war, suggested his willingness as a Jew to sympathize with the
interests of Anglo-Saxon economic imperialism. By 1940 very little distinguished the extreme fringe of such Munichois socialists in France
from the thinking of a Robert Brasillach. What separates us from
America? Brasillach asked in an essay written early in the war. The answer
is threefold: its hypocrisy (a frequent charge), its dollars, and international Jewry. As the last bastion of Jewish power in the world, the
United States was the enemy of revolutionaries and reactionaries, anti-
modernists and socialists alike.[14]

Although the war and the occupation changed the terms of politics
for the Left, the intelligentsia of Vichy continued to operate in the same
vein. Thus the initial appeal of Vichy to many antirepublican intellectuals cannot readily be dissociated from both the anti-American and
anti-Semitic language that permeated the regime.[15] It was one of de

---

12. On Drumont, see Michel Winock, *Edouard Drumont et Cie* (Paris, 1982), passim.
13. Georges Bernanos, *La Grande Peur des Bien-Pensants* (Paris, 1931).
14. See Robert Brasillach, *Journal d'un homme occupé* (Paris, 1955), 438, 445.
15. For example, see P-A Cousteau, *L'Amérique juive* (Paris, 1942).

Gaulle's weaknesses in his struggle against Pétain that he was so dependent on the "Anglo-Saxons"; resisters and collaborators alike had little good to say about these. The British had let the French down in 1940, bombed their fleet, and now sat secure behind their maritime barrier. Continuing the struggle could only serve the interests of the Americans and the British, and in the eyes of the left wing of the Resistance itself it made little sense to liberate France from fascism if it was only to be handed back to the incompetent bourgeoisie who had brought about its collapse, now even more beholden to foreign capital.

Thus the war was less of a break and a divide than might be supposed. Anti-Semitism lost its respectability, but in a complicated paradox, anti-Americanism was exacerbated. There were many reasons for this: in simple terms there was resentment at the United States for its wartime bombing of French cities (Royan, Le Havre), for its de facto occupation of France during the months of liberation, for what was seen as American plenty in the midst of French penury, for its postwar monopoly of wealth and power, and for its hegemony within a Western alliance that many French would rather not have joined.[16]

In a more complex syndrome of frustration and impotence (which the British shared, but to a much smaller extent), the French, intellectuals especially, resented the very fact that they had been liberated by the Americans, resented their humiliated postwar status and more particularly the need to go cap in hand to Washington for assistance with French reconstruction. The Russians, by contrast, could be admired and appreciated from afar. The diplomatic nadir would be reached in 1948, but long before then the decline in French international standing was evident to all. In the winter of 1946 Léon Blum went to Washington to secure emergency American help and a reduction or liquidation of French war debts. The price he paid for this, in the Blum-Byrnes accords of May 1946, was a lowering of tariffs and other economic barriers, as a result of which France was to be exposed to more American products, material and cultural, than ever before. Coming on the heels of generalized disillusion with the Fourth Republic and disappointment at the failed aspirations of the Resistance, this American "invasion" made the United States the natural target for all those—and they were many—who needed to hate someone in the grim postwar years.

16. In the spring of 1945, 59 percent of those polled thought the availability of food was worse than before the Liberation; 79 percent said they were worse off than six months earlier. See Hilary Footitt and John Simmonds, *France, 1943–1945* (London, 1988), 213.

To these new considerations must be added elements of continuity. Although an aversion to the modern was not revived in its earlier shape, it persisted in a new form. The enthusiasm for modern German thought that had so characterized younger writers during the thirties was now thoroughly incorporated into the indigenous French variant; among its central props was the Heideggerian distaste for "technical civilization." Although French existential philosophy did not pay to this side of Heidegger the same attention he would receive from his Central European readers, the subterranean presence of this dimension of his thought is unmistakable.[17] In many of the expressions of distaste for American culture and its dehumanizing impact, in much of the sympathy expressed for Communist campaigns against modern production and products there is the distinct echo of the discourse of the thirties. Alexandre Kojève, in his declining years, mused that humankind, if tormented by the desire to act when there was nothing left to do, could always in the last resort "live like Americans." Even some anti-Communists shared this sentiment; Georges Bernanos devoted many of his last writings in the forties to warnings against the despotism of technology, the robotic civilizations looming over the horizon from West and East alike.[18] The true enemy was the "productivist spirit" itself.

In this sense, Claude Roy was quite correct to see in French dislike for the Americans a sublimated self-hatred. The productivist obsessions of the postwar years, which characterized Communists no less than others, at least until 1948, seemed to many to be turning France away, for good or ill, from its traditions, its habits, its true self. The "personalist" revolution of Mounier's dreams was threatened, he wrote in 1946, more by the United States than by anything else, the Soviet Union included.[19] Ten years later, his editorial successors at *Esprit* remained firmly fixed in this opinion:

We reproach Socialist ideology with idealizing man and being blind to his fallibility, but the average American is blinder still. What can one expect from this civilization that mocks and caricatures Western spiritual traditions and is propelling mankind into a horizontal existence, shorn of transcendence and depth?[20]

17. For an example of the Central European reading of Heidegger, with an emphasis on his debt to Husserl, see the work of Jan Patocka, for example, *Philosophy and Selected Writings,* ed. Erazim Kohák (Chicago, 1989).

18. See the various writings collected in Georges Bernanos, *Français si vous saviez, 1945–1948* (Paris, 1961).

19. Emmanuel Mounier, "L'Homme américain," *Esprit,* November 1946.

20. Editorial, "Les Flammes de Budapest," *Esprit,* December 1956, 773.

This was no isolated commentary. Throughout this period, *Esprit* in particular would spice its columns with disparaging remarks about American culture and almost as a matter of form would temper any criticism of
Communist society with a patronizing or dismissive reminder of the
greater spiritual threat across the Atlantic. Thus, an editorial in 1952
reminded its readers, "From the outset we have denounced in these
pages the risk posed to our country by an American culture that attacks
at their roots the originality, the mental and moral cohesion of Europe."[21] By comparison, the Soviet threat was puny indeed.

From such quarters, however, views of this sort were perhaps to be
expected—the slightly suffocating air of moral superiority that wafted
across the pages of *Esprit* (or of *Le Monde,* whose editor disliked the
Communists but despised the United States) was always likely to make it
unreceptive to the charms of "the American way of life." Similarly, it
comes as no surprise to find Maurice Merleau-Ponty discovering that he
had more in common with the Communists, in theory and despite
everything, than with the Americans—"All in all, man's appreciation of
man and a classless society are less vague, as the principles of a global policy, than American prosperity."[22] Of more enduring interest, perhaps,
are the opinions of François Mauriac, who could not be accused of even
the mildest of philo-Soviet motives. Mauriac, like Thierry Maulnier
before him, felt no need to go to the United States in order to decide
what he thought of it—by the end of the fifties "the American way of
life" was simultaneously alien and familiar: "This nation . . . is more foreign to me than any other. I've never been there . . . what is the point? It
has done more than just visit us; it has transformed us."[23]

Mauriac did not come by his views in a hurry. Like de Gaulle, his distaste for things American was rooted in his culture, his religion, and his
sense of the importance (and the decline) of his country. Although he
was too intelligent not to appreciate the strategic inevitability of American presence in postwar Europe and never gave himself to the more
extreme forms of resentment evinced by his colleagues, he was on more
than one occasion sympathetic to their mood. In September 1950 he
noted with some empathy an outburst from Claude Bourdet in *L'Obser-*

21. Editorial, *Esprit,* June 1952.
22. Merleau-Ponty, quoted by Olivier Mongin, "Les Conditions d'une interpréta-
tion: Merleau-Ponty et Claude Lefort," in Evelyne Pisier-Kouchner, ed., *Les Interprétations
du Stalinisme* (Paris, 1983), 315.
23. François Mauriac, *L'Express,* 29 August 1959.

vateur (one of many such): "France is getting ever more committed to the unstable, impulsive, sometimes hysterical American camp. . . . " "Hysterical, unstable, impulsive"—there is an advance echo here of Sartre's suggestion that "America has gone mad," although Bourdet was writing long before the dénouement of the Rosenberg affair. Mauriac's language was more moderate, but the idea that there was something uncontrolled, shallow, and unreliable about America was one he shared.[24]

One reason for this was that, like Bourdet, he was growing more preoccupied with the looming colonial crisis. This made him progressively more critical of France's own governments but also very sensitive to the moral standing of France's critics from abroad. The issue festered throughout the Vietnam years but came to a head at the time of Suez. Who on earth are the Americans, Mauriac wrote in October 1956, to criticize French colonialist behavior? Not only have they practiced a colonialism of their own to good effect, but in order to do so they were not above resorting to genocide: "Are we reduced to taking lessons from this great exterminating nation?"[25] Some of those who, unlike Mauriac, remained committed to France's colonial destiny would invoke the risks of handing the former colonies over to others—Jacques Soustelle feared that an independent Algeria would fall into Arab nationalist, Communist, or American hands, probably all three in quick succession. This idea, that decolonization was a zero-sum game among great powers, in which France's loss would be the Americans' gain, was widespread at the time.[26]

Thus the shift in intellectuals' attention after 1956, from communism to anticolonialism, entailed no abandoning of anti-Western and anti-American sentiment. But whereas anti-American feeling in earlier years turned on more abstract and metaphysical conceptions of high culture or the human condition, the West was now charged with the much more concrete and demonstrable failings of imperialism and racism. On these issues, French intellectuals shared a broad measure of agreement. Étiemble, a critic who was otherwise pitiless in his attacks on the confused thinking of his progressive colleagues, not only agreed with them that America was a worthless civilization whose highest achievement was the *Reader's Digest* but also warned Americans against presuming to offer advice to the French on how to live. Writing at the time of widely held

24. Claude Bourdet is quoted by François Mauriac, *Mémoires politiques* (Paris, 1967), 400.
25. Mauriac, *Bloc-Notes, 1952–1957* (Paris, 1958), 12 October 1956.
26. See Paul Sorum, *Intellectuals and Decolonization in France* (Chapel Hill, N.C., 1977), 79.

anxiety about impending atomic war, he suggested, "Rather than promising what might be an all-too-perfect, even eternal repose," Americans should look to their own sins. The treatment of Negroes was alone sufficient to disqualify the United States from proffering lessons in morality or *savoir-vivre*.[27] He did not go as far as Mounier, or the Abbé Boulier, who warned against condemning communism for fear of bringing comfort to the "imperialists," but he did espouse their claim that only those with "clean hands" could speak out.[28]

This question of the clean conscience troubled many in this decade. In the immediate postwar years, America seemed annoyingly guilt-free, untroubled by Europe's complicated and ambivalent past. It was this combination of a clean conscience and technological resources that would, Mounier thought, be the Americans' strongest suit in their drive to world domination, and thus not surprisingly it was with some glee that he, Sartre, and others devoted their time and their journals to demonstrating just how dirty the Americans' hands really were. Arthur Koestler protested that one did not have to be pure and without sin in order to see and denounce the greater sins of others, but his was a lonely voice in these years.[29] The injustices perpetrated within the United States and exported abroad in the baggage train of the Marshall Plan were invoked to excuse its critics from turning their attention to injustice elsewhere. One further reason for this was that its postwar domination of western Europe gave a perverted plausibility to the suggestion that the United States had somehow become the heir to the Nazis. In this light, not only was it incumbent on all progressive thinkers to direct their fire at the Americans, but even the latter's would-be allies found themselves in a delicate position.

The French Communists were adept at exploiting this situation. Like their comrades in Italy, Czechoslovakia, and Yugoslavia, among others, they proposed themselves as the heirs to a national bourgeoisie that had failed in its task and surrendered to foreign and Fascist domination. They conflated the hitherto distinctive political languages of party, class, and nation into a single vocabulary, initially deployed against Germans but available for exploitation, with virtually no change, against the new occupiers and their local collaborators.[30] Intellectuals and non-Communist politicians whose own Resistance-era credentials were thin

27. See Étiemble's contributions to *Les Temps modernes* during 1948 and 1949, reprinted in *Littérature dégagée, 1942–1953* (Paris, 1955), 76ff.

28. The Abbé Boulier is cited by François Fejtö, *Mémoires* (Paris, 1986), 213.

29. See, for example, Arthur Koestler, *The Trail of the Dinosaur* (New York, 1955), 51.

30. See Lily Marcou, *Le Cominform* (Paris, 1977), 51, n. 16.

thus took comfort in such terminology. At first sight, the analogy that was drawn with Nazi Germany may seem incredible, but it secreted a certain logic. For a man like Julien Benda, who had espoused a lifelong antipathy to Germany, even the defeat of Hitler was no guarantee of success. German ideas might yet triumph in other hands. In the postwar years there was no longer a Germany across the Rhine to hate and fear; but there was an American government that was consciously and deliberately reviving its half of the old German empire, the better to oppose and block the revolutionary ambitions of the Soviet Union.[31]

Until 1948 these sentiments were muted. The postwar settlement was still in flux, many French politicians of the center as well as the Left were seeking to obtain American and British support for a thorough dismantling of the German state, and Russians and Americans were still engaged in negotiations, however unfriendly and unproductive. But once the divisions hardened, the Marshall Plan was approved, the American plan for a revived German republic presented, and French dreams of neutrality shattered, the interchangeability of Americans and Germans became common currency in many circles. The Communists now bluntly asserted the common identity of old and new occupiers. France was again an "occupied country"; the influence of American culture and capital was as pervasive and pernicious as had been that of the Nazis in the thirties and forties, and the task of all true Frenchmen was to "resist."[32] Such analogies fell on fertile soil. *Esprit, Observateur,* and especially *Témoignage Chrétien* displayed steady hostility to anything and everything American in the years 1948–53; economic aid, the Berlin airlift, Nato, the Korean War, the proposals for a European defense force, and the rearming of Germany were treated not merely as political or military errors, nor even as evidence of an American desire to extend and secure its economic influence. More than this, they were written and spoken about as confirmation of the Americans' drive to occupy and humiliate Europe, and France especially.

By an interesting transposition, the very modernization of France came to be seen by some as a trick; if the most modern society of all, the United States, was now the occupier, any indigenous French efforts to transform the economy or reconstruct economic and political life could

31. Julien Benda, in *Les Lettres françaises,* 23 December 1944.
32. Thus Pierre Daix drew an analogy between American cinema and its influence and that of the Nazi propaganda films of Leni Riefenstahl. See *Les Lettres françaises,* 28 October 1948.

only be to the advantage of the Americans. Thus, according to Simone de Beauvoir, Mendès-France and "le mendésisme" sought merely to "improve" capitalism and colonialism from a technocratic perspective. They were but puppets. Looking back in her memoirs, she was still asserting from the vantage point of the early sixties, "It was in fact nothing but a spruced-up Right."[33] As to France's participation in a reconstructed Europe, "the European myth" was dismissed as nothing more than an American ploy to restore German power as a counterweight to the legitimate authority and influence of the Soviet Union in the East. The failure of the Liberation was now firmly if anachronistically placed on Washington's doorstep. Hardly had a humiliated and exhausted France fought its way out of one occupation than it was subjected to another, more complete, more damaging, and against which a spiritual resistance was thus morally incumbent upon all.

It is perhaps worth noting that such anti-American sentiment was most frequent in the intellectual milieu. One opinion poll of 1953 found that the highly educated segment of the French population was also the one most likely to be critical of the United States, which is perhaps to be expected but merits reflection. After all, economic problems and political uncertainty were universal, and the power and privileges of the United States were as obvious to the least-informed worker as they were to the most sophisticated scholar or journalist. The shadow of America was everywhere in these years. Nowhere was this more abundantly obvious than in the film industry, commonly cited by critics as evidence of the American invasion. During the Vichy years, French films had dominated the domestic market for the first time since World War I, American and other foreign entertainment being largely banned. But from 1946 the importation of American films (including many third-rate productions, which had accumulated during the war years) grew apace: in the first six months of that year just 36 American films were distributed in France; for the equivalent period in 1947 the number had reached 338. For most of the decade to come, American-made films constituted over 50 percent of the total number in distribution and secured around 43 percent of the viewing public. Most of these films had no redeeming value (the American cinema of the thirties had been distinctly better), and many of them were extraordinarily banal and simple-minded. Where they were not straightforwardly nationalistic or anti-Communist,

33. Simone de Beauvoir, *La Force des choses* (Paris, 1963), 340.

they were little more than unsubtle advertisements for the least interesting aspects of modern American life.[34]

Nonetheless, a steady diet of Rita Hayworth, Coca-Cola, and overpaid American soldiers does not seem to have had unduly distorting effects upon the common French perception of the United States and its relationship with France. The same public that had resented being liberated and "occupied" by the Americans was quite clear by 1948 that U.S. aid was vital to French national recovery. This did not make the United States universally popular: despite the fact that in 1950 it was the foreign country that most people *liked* more than any other, it was also the one with the highest negative coefficient: more people also actively *disliked* it than disliked any other country, Germany included. But except for the young and the highly educated, the French were overwhelmingly sympathetic to the United States in general even as they feared and resented its economic power and were opposed to some of its foreign policies, including support for a renascent Federal Republic in Germany. In 1953, 61 percent of those asked were "sympathetic" to the United States, only 8 percent expressing "antipathy," 5 percent "distrust," and 1 percent "hate." It is thus worth noting that a sizable percentage of the Communist electorate had no apparent dislike for Washington—only 10 percent of all persons questioned would have favored a Franco-Soviet alliance.[35]

On this issue more than any other, then, the intellectual community was isolated from the rest of the country. There is a certain logic to this. One of the distinctive and enduring differences between France and the United States has been the insignificance of the intelligentsia in the public life of the latter. In marked contrast to their French homologues, American intellectuals are marginal to their own culture. For a multitude of reasons, the intellectual in America has no purchase upon the public mind, not to mention public policy. Thus there was (and remains) about the United States something profoundly inimical and alien to the European and French conception of the intellectual and his or her role. If "America" represented the future, then it pointed to a society in which the role of the intellectual, real as well as self-ascribed, would be dramati-

34. Patricia Hubert-Lacombe, "L'Acceuil des films américains en France pendant la guerre froide (1946–1953)," *Revue d'histoire moderne et contemporaine* 36 (April–June 1986). One result of this wave of American films was to generate some quiet nostalgia for the cultural protectionism of the Vichy years.

35. "Enquête sur les sentiments et attitudes des Français à l'égard des Américains," *Sondages* 2 (January–February 1953): 6–7, 30–32, 52–56.

cally reduced. The contrast with the Soviet Union, which presented itself as a society in which the intellectual, the artist, the scientist played a respected and vital role, was thus particularly marked in this respect. In this as in other ways, the USSR seemed profoundly *European*. To oppose America and its way of life was thus among many other things an act of enlightened self-interest on the part of the European intellectual, a defensive move on behalf of an idealized *European* West in the face of the alien version held out from across the ocean. If *that* was the future of the West, then better the East, which offered values instead of technique, commitment instead of isolation, hope and struggle instead of satisfaction and prosperity. That some of the East European show trials made a point of emphasizing just these themes was, therefore, a further argument in their favor.[36]

The apparently marginal position of French intellectuals with respect to America was not a problem at the time. Most intellectuals were astonishingly unfamiliar with opinion (and indeed life) outside of their own rather restricted cultural and social world. When they looked for workers, they found Communists. When they sought an echo of their views and the impact of their views, they found it in a plethora of journals directed primarily to them and them alone. Although they did not normally realize this, the intellectual community of Paris was almost as hermetic and as divorced from the nation as that of London or even New York. But most important of all, French intellectuals wore their very marginality as a badge of honor. Sometimes, with the early Sartre, they made a sort of self-lacerating virtue of their own isolation; later, and also with Sartre, some of them would seek to lose their identity in engagement. But even in the latter case the engagement itself was an action intended to overcome the existential condition of intellectual life and thus made of that lonely, marginal condition the central theme of the intellectual's experience.

These characteristics had marked the intelligentsia ever since it first became conscious of its own existence. What distinguished modern intellectuals from their Romantic, bohemian, Dreyfusard, or nonconformist predecessors was this: whereas the latter had nearly always made a virtue of their condition, postwar intellectuals, in their anti-Americanism as in so much else, no longer trusted to their own judgment. It was not sufficient now that the "modern" was aesthetically

36. See, for example, the indictment in the *Trial of the American Spies in Bulgaria* (Sofia, 1950), 116, where the victims are accused of a "servile undervaluation of the East."

unpleasing or spiritually unworthy. It had also to be in some demonstrable, "objective" sense false, wrong. The formal measure of this was the good or ill it brought or would bring to the masses, but it did not follow from this that the general enthusiasm of the masses for things American therefore constituted a hurdle. In place of the mass of the population, with its unreliable and contradictory opinions, there was substituted instead a hypostasized and coherent Working People, in whose name the otherwise self-abnegating intellectual could pass judgments. For *these* people, America was a threat. To *this* mass of working persons, Western values were a hypocrisy. In the implicit name of *their* interests, progress and the progressive position could be identified and followed. To this Elysian Billancourt of the mind we must now direct our attention.

CHAPTER ELEVEN

We Must Not Disillusion the Workers
On the Self-Abnegation and Elective Affinities of the Intellectual

Un homme peut adhérer au Parti Communiste sans accord ni sur la doctrine, ni sur les moyens, par simple désir de rompre, de couper les ponts avec la bourgeoisie, de se sentir lié à une classe.

A man may join the Communist party without agreeing with either its doctrine or its methods, from a simple desire to break away, to burn bridges with the bourgeoisie, to feel himself linked to a class.

Roger Stéphane

The petite bourgeoisie, it is said, is the class everyone loves to hate. Of the intellectuals it might be said that they are the class that loves to hate itself. Ever since the category *intellectual* came into common usage, one part of the identity of the intellectual has been the aspiration (like that of the working class, according to Flaubert) to disappear. The sense of being peripheral, of being a commentator on the margins of society, has haunted the European intelligentsia for nearly two centuries. Once the idea took root, beginning with the Saint-Simonians, that society was divided into useful and useless classes, there has been an unbroken tradition of intellectual self-abnegation, a desire to merge with or work for the useful class, to be at one with progress and History, to change the world and not merely understand it. For obvious reasons, this sentiment has been most forcefully expressed on the progressive wing of politics: long before Stalin imposed on intellectuals the duty to abase themselves before the party line, the engaged and affiliated intelligentsia of the European Left saw in their alliance with the labor movement an opportunity to submerge their own cumbersome identity in that of the masses. The apparent paradox, that the European socialist and labor movement was conceived and led by middle-class intellectuals, is thus no paradox at all.

Indeed, the belief that intellectuals should cast their lot with the workers was from the beginning part of a larger conception of the proletariat as in some sense the "true" intelligentsia. It was Jaurès, not Gramsci, who first mooted the idea that the intellectual in capitalist society must identify with the concerns of the working classes not on self-denying, altruistic grounds but because it was the instinctive idealism, the necessarily transcendent interests and vision of the proletariat that made it the true intellectual class.[1] The Gramscian conception of the "organic intellectual" was a logical corollary to this argument, deriving its strength from the specific circumstances of Italy, but by the early twentieth century the line of reasoning thus implied was universally acknowledged within the European Left, from Saint Petersburg to Paris. There remained, however, an unresolved ambivalence as to the precise function of bourgeois intellectuals in these circumstances: should they continue to operate qua intellectual or should they deny altogether any claim to superior knowledge and moral authority and submit instead to the will of the organic and collective intelligence of the revolutionary movement?

Within the French context, this tension between the intellectual-as-revolutionary and the intellectual as ally or ancillary to the true revolutionary movement became more acute between the wars. On the one hand the indigenous *ouvriérisme* (workerism) of the French and the markedly popular (or at least populist) nature of the local Communist leadership meant that the PCF and international communism generally were simultaneously attractive and repulsive to progressive intellectuals. The dominant trends within the radical, or dissenting, intelligentsia were aesthetic and apolitical. Surrealism, and artistic and literary innovation in general, were the major forms of radical and countercultural

---

1. Jaurès is quoted in Pascal Ory and Jean-François Sirinelli, *Les Intellectuels en France, de l'affaire Dreyfus à nos jours* (Paris, 1986), 26.

expression for the post–World War I generation. On the other hand, especially after 1932, the isolated oppositional intellectual was an ambiguous figure, as likely to be sympathetic to fascism as to Marxism or communism. The sarcastic antibourgeois anger of Nizan might draw him to the PCF, but similar sentiments in many of his contemporaries led them to look longingly at the "proletarian fascism" of Mussolini.

Fascism and communism both played on the guilt and vulnerability of intellectuals, challenging them to follow through on their antibourgeois sentiments and cast their lot with the movement of action, of change, of rejection. Paul Vaillant-Couturier appealed, on behalf of the Association des écrivains et artistes révolutionnaires, for support and participation from writers and others who wished to "struggle alongside the proletariat"; but similar appeals to artists and intellectuals went out from Fascist movements and regimes, which organized congresses and festivals at which intellectuals could share the energy and optimism of the masses, in contrast with their own sense of cultural pessimism and social isolation. There was, however, an important difference. The intellectuals who were drawn to the extremist movements and regimes of the radical Right may have sought to give to their life and times a purpose and a meaning but did not usually desire to lose their identity in the common struggle. On the contrary, the Fascist intellectual was more like a mercenary, an outrider, at the service of people and movements with whom he or she had little or nothing in common. There was a distinctive masochist aspect to this, a desire to see derided and destroyed the very world of which one was also a product and beneficiary. But this was frequently accompanied by a nostalgia for a different world of authority and values and hierarchy, which the Fascist masses and their thuggish leaders might help bring about but which would not be theirs to inherit. The Fascist intellectual, in other words, continued to believe in the role of the intellectual.[2]

Here, then, communism and fascism parted company. Although there is some justice in the view that Louis Aragon and Lucien Rebatet, for example, had more in common than they might have cared to admit—in their scorn for the bourgeoisie, its bland moralism, and its material achievements—the distinctions remain important.[3] Fascist

2. See Alastair Hamilton, *The Appeal of Fascism* (London, 1971); and Stephen Spender, *The Thirties and After* (London, 1978), 197.
3. See the comparison proposed by Étiemble, *Littérature dégagée, 1942–1953* (Paris, 1955), 202.

intellectuals like Rebatet, Drieu, or Brasillach maintained, so they insisted, an aesthetic and political autonomy. They *chose* to be Fascists, and in making this choice, they were, as they thought, consistent with their vocation as intellectuals. Progressive intellectuals, however, including those in the thirties who chose to support but not join the Communist party, were forced to see themselves as breaking with their vocation, swept by history and necessity rather than by choice into a movement whose goals they shared but which asked of them that they abandon their autonomous intellectual identity. In certain cases the contrast is illustrated in their subsequent work. The would-be Fascist intellectual might draw on Fascist themes, but his political affiliation imposed no aesthetic straitjacket.[4] Progressive intellectuals, by contrast, strove to write or speak, to practice their art, if not from the point of view of the proletariat then at least in harmony with its presumed interests and needs. Where they could not do this, where they found it impossible to derive an aesthetic from the yet-to-be-established values of a classless society, they were in an uncomfortable, alienated, and divided condition.

The self-abnegation of the progressive intellectual took various forms. Common to all of these was the admiration for strength, "purity," and the simple verities, missing in the traditionally complex and ambivalent stance of the intellectual but found by many in the proletariat and its party. Some of this was an inheritance from the ambiguous extremism of the thirties (notice the similarities between Sartre and Drieu in their dislike of weakness and softness—the latter's scorn for modern man with his "feeble muscles and fat belly" echoed by Sartre's yearning for violence and action), but much, too, was owed to the image of the Communist Resistance. Even in their criticisms of the PCF, sympathetic commentators yearned for its former firmness—"One would have liked the party of the working class to show itself in the electoral battle what it was during the Occupation: the party of purity and firmness [le Parti de la dureté et de la pureté]." Thus Jean Foresta in 1947 bemoaned the Communists' apparent compromises with bourgeois society.[5] Communist intellectuals themselves would also look to the simple strengths of Communist (working) man; casting around for an illustration of André Marty's utter

---

4. An exception is architects, who were obliged to conform to the grandiose self-image of the regime, at least in their public commissions.

5. See Jean Foresta, "La Crise du communisme en France," *Esprit,* October 1947, 603.

isolation and an incontrovertible proof of his sins, Annie Besse described a section meeting that followed the party's criticism of its erstwhile hero: after the report from the Central Committee, she assured her readers, a simple worker stood up and announced that he no longer loved the name Marty, "and speaking thus, the Communist worker clenched his fists."[6]

The ridiculous bathos of this scene and the transparent seriousness with which it is recorded and presented capture well the two-pronged thrust of progressive *ouvriérisme:* an unabashed admiration for the worker in all his simple strength and an utter abdication of critical perspective on the part of the intellectual. "Pur et dur," the worker and the worker's party exercised a magnetic and unimpeachable appeal. Even at his most critical, Sartre was willing to defend the achievements of *Hungarian* Social Democrats, in contrast with the petit-bourgeois underachievers of the SFIO—the Hungarians, he wrote in 1956, were at least "hard Socialists."[7] Here the instinctive preference for the exotic over the domestic combines with the self-despising admiration of the weak for the strong. Éluard, too, was not immune to such sentiments. Visiting Romania in 1948 (a country impoverished and divided by decades of dictatorship and war), he claimed to find that "sunshine of happiness" missing in the miserable, mirthless, gray world of his native France. In Romania he found certainty, energy, strength. In France, an ambivalent lassitude.[8]

There were two ways in which the intellectual could be at one with the workers. The first was to treat the working class as an elite community, a "chosen people," from whom one would not be separated, no matter how strong the temptation nor how difficult the path. This had been Mounier's position even before the war ended; commenting on the prospects for a revolution in postwar France, he recalled the earlier failure of the Girondins and blamed it on their "lack of contact" with the masses. It was not that the latter were politically infallible, he wrote, nor that they conferred infallibility on all who allied with them but that they, the working people, bore and nourished that political instinct without which ideas and good intentions were vain and impotent.[9] From this

---

6. Annie Besse, "Sur l'humanisme socialiste," *Nouvelle Critique* 45 (April–May 1953): 44.

7. Jean-Paul Sartre, "Le Fantôme de Staline," *Les Temps modernes* 129–31 (January–March 1957): 610.

8. "Je viens d'un pays ou l'on ne rit plus, ou l'on ne chante pas. La France est dans l'ombre. Mais vous avez découvert le soleil du bonheur." Éluard is quoted in Jean Rounault, "Aragon, Elsa, Éluard à Bucarest," *Preuves* 14 (April 1952): 38.

9. Mounier, "Suite française," *Esprit,* December 1944, 24.

position he never deviated; two years later, in 1946, he warned against cutting oneself off from the proletariat (that "elite of action"), which would be a criminal move, destructive of everything in which we believe. Just as we need the workers, so they need us. "Builders of cities" were essential to the coming revolution, but so were "forgers of men." True, the Communist party might appear to constitute a barrier, preventing communication between progressive thinkers and the working people, but this must not be allowed to impede progress; we must not "allow ourselves to be cut off from the proletariat because some administration refuses us a visa." Accordingly, two new columns were promised for the pages of *Esprit* in 1950: "News of the Downtrodden" (Chronique des écrasés), reporting on cases of injustice towards the poor and defenseless; and a page devoted to "Proletarian reality," in which any readers who were in contact with the "real world of the worker" were invited to communicate their insights to the journal.[10]

This earnest determination to align with the proletariat under all circumstances did not die with Mounier. His successors were no less committed. In January 1953, and in the teeth of the Slánsky trial and the accompanying signs of Communist intransigence and worse, Jean-Marie Domenach reaffirmed his position and that of his journal and its readers: "Theoretically and in practice, we seek to share in the rise of the masses, in the coming of a civilization of labor."[11] This is the authentic voice of early nineteenth-century Christian Socialism and its Saint-Simonist sources. It differed from the stance of the party intellectual only in this significant respect: for the affiliated Communist the idea that the party might constitute a barrier to communication with the proletariat was unthinkable. In other ways, however, the progressive intellectual and his or her *soeur-ennemie* in the party shared a similar outlook. Writing shortly after Domenach and commenting like him on the Czech trials, Annie Besse affirmed that "our humanism" is on the side of the poor and oppressed, not of those whose crimes have brought them to their present condition; unlike Slánsky and company, "the workers are innocent . . . they are at the heart of the just struggle that contains the future of the world."[12]

An alternative form of affiliation was one that maintained a stronger

10. See Emmanuel Mounier, "Débat à haute voix," *Esprit*, February 1946, 175; and "Fidélité," *Esprit*, February 1950, 180, 182.

11. Jean-Marie Domenach, "La Tâche de protestation," *Esprit*, January 1953, 28.

12. Annie Besse is quoted in Jeannine Verdès-Leroux, *Au service du parti* (Paris, 1983), 78.

implicit sense of the importance of the intellectuals and spoke not in terms of allying with the proletariat but of keeping up their spirits in the face of adversity, of not "abandoning" them. In this language, the intellectual had the responsibility of protecting and nourishing the vulnerable working masses, rather than merely falling prostrate at their feet. The two approaches bespeak different sensibilities, even though they occasionally emanate from the same pen (an illustration of the ambivalent and confused thinking that marked much writing on this subject). In its best-known form, this second approach consisted of the famous warning, "Il ne faut pas désespérer Billancourt" (We must not let down Billancourt [the site of the giant Renault works near Paris]), but Sartre was not the first to express the view. In a letter to *Action* in January 1946, Mounier disassociated himself from any attempts to "go beyond Marxism," because any questioning of Marxism at this point would weaken the position and the resolve of the workers. On those occasions when he did tentatively question Communist acts (as in the trial and execution of Petkov, in Bulgaria), he took care to advise his readers that he only did so because the moral risks to which communism was exposed by its actions risked undermining the faith and prospects of the workers. All political positions were to be judged in the light of the needs of the workers (as determined by the intellectual making the judgment), and no abstract or morally "neutral" points of view were to be entertained. As Mounier summarized it in 1950, "We reject the abstraction that omits the point of view of Montreuil" (a workers' suburb of Paris). The geography of the metaphor is different, but the thrust of its message is the same.[13]

There is something distinctly condescending about this line of reasoning, an aspect of intellectual "slumming" that did not go unremarked even at the time. Intellectuals in these years demonstrated a remarkable capacity to be both humble and patronizing at the same time, combining a complex of inferiority with a sure sense of noblesse oblige. Simple explanations, or even simple untruths, were to be the fare of simple people, whose illusions could not stand the test of harsh verities and bad news. This was not a new idea—in the thirties Romain Rolland had kept his opinions on the Soviet Union to himself, "stifling" the need to speak out, and he was one of many.[14] But in the thirties this

13. Mounier, letter to *Action,* 15 January 1946; "Petkov en nous," *Esprit,* October 1947, 599; "Fidélité," 178.

14. Thus Romain Rolland on his *real* view concerning Stalin and the USSR in 1937: "I stifle the need to say it and to write it," quoted by David Caute, *The Fellow Travellers* (rev. ed. New Haven, Conn., 1988), 130.

self-censorship had been part of a genuine desire to hold the line against the Fascist foe, to maintain the united front of the Left against a very real enemy on the Right. Morally misconceived, it made some political sense. In the forties and fifties, the enemy existed for the most part in the imagination of the intellectual, and the refusal to speak out was justified not in the name of anti-Fascist unity but on behalf of a childlike working population who would not understand. Paul Éluard, who could be obtuse enough when circumstances required it, was nevertheless perfectly lucid on the absurdities of Zdanov and his "Socialist Realism." But he refused to breathe a word of his doubts, or his disdain, in front of fellow Communists in his working-class district. "The poor things, it would discourage them," he explained to Claude Roy. "We mustn't upset those who are struggling. They wouldn't understand."[15] On those rare occasions when this line of reasoning seemed insufficient, it was suggested that perhaps workers had different standards, that what would shock a mere intellectual would have a quite different meaning for a worker:

That which might seem intolerable to a bourgeois or an intellectual attached to an individualist form of civilization can be liberating to a worker used to union discipline and a collective existence.[16]

In this last image, the worker becomes something more than a child, an ideal, a well-muscled, simple-minded "other"; he is credited with wholly alien sensibilities. What the intellectual finds intolerable, the worker (in Paris or Prague, Lille or Lodz) not only finds inoffensive but may actually like and appreciate. One person's chains are another's liberation. The proletariat is patronized and protected not just because it might become dispirited and abandon the struggle but because in its world there has been a transvaluation of values. But how, then, is the intellectual to communicate with these aliens, with whose sensibilities and needs he or she seeks alignment? How is the gap between worker and thinker to be bridged? The answer for many was self-evident: by the intermediary of the Communist party, however rebarbative and unprepossessing it might appear and however uncooperative. It was not that Communists and workers were one and the same; as Sartre pointed out in *Qu'est-ce que la littérature?* the workers' cause is not axiomatically

15. See Claude Roy, *Nous* (Paris, 1972), 166.

16. Guy Clairbois in *La Quinzaine* 13 (15 May 1951), quoted by Yvan Tranvouez, "Guerre froide et progressisme chrétien," *Vingtième Siècle* 13 (January–March 1987): 89.

identical with that of the PCF, but only through the latter can we reach them. Later on, though, he would alter his views considerably, claiming that the Communist party *was* the working class—it embodied their true and essential interests:

In Stalinism, as in the old reformist socialism, the working class recognizes its own image, its work, the provisional repository of its sovereignty. You claim that this minority is harming the working class. But how could it? It draws its power from the proletariat, which could not turn its own activity against itself.[17]

Somewhere between the Sartre of 1947 and that of 1953 are to be found the sentiments of most of his progressive contemporaries. Some, like Jean Lacroix, were extreme Sartriens *avant l'heure:* "Communism does not claim to add anything essential to the profound will of the masses—it is but the proletariat made conscious."[18] Others would have felt more comfortable with the opinion of Claude Jamet, writing in 1935: however disillusioning the reality of Communism, even if the Soviet revolution were to prove an "extinct volcano," "it would be necessary, in the limits of the possible, to continue pretending otherwise . . . yes, to lie, heroically."[19] To reject the Communists and their claims would be to abandon all hope of communicating with the proletariat. What made this position difficult was not its apparent absurdity, its denial of any autonomy of judgment, but the willfully disagreeable actions of the Communists themselves. Had it not been for Stalinism, many felt, the path to a common sensibility and unity of spirit between workers and thinkers would have been much smoother. But however awful the PCF might become, loyalty was unconditional: "Do what you may, say what you will, *we* shall never Koestlerize . . . because one does not abandon the proletariat."[20]

It required an extraordinary faith and a consistently high incidence of self-denial in order to maintain such a point of view. Certainly the Communists provided ample opportunity for a change of heart. Not only

---

17. See Sartre, *Qu'est-ce que la littérature?* in *Situations,* vol. 2 (Paris, 1948); "Réponse à Claude Lefort," *Les Temps modernes* 89 (April 1953): 617; "Les Communistes et la paix," *Situations,* vol. 6 (Paris, 1964).

18. Jean Lacroix, "Y a-t-il deux démocraties? De la démocratie libérale à la démocratie massive," *Esprit,* March 1946, 354–55.

19. Jamet quoted in Jean-François Sirinelli, *Génération intellectuelle* (Paris, 1988), 618.

20. Mounier, "Journal à haute voix," *Esprit,* January 1950, 130. Contrast Arthur Koestler, writing in March 1948: "Fear of finding yourself in bad company is not an expression of political purity; it is an expression of lack of self-confidence." See Koestler, *The Trail of the Dinosaur* (New York, 1955), 50.

were these the years of Stalinism in its most reductive, Manichaean, and paranoid form but even those progressive intellectuals who wound themselves in to the most tortured and contradictory postures were rarely rewarded with even a nod of approval from the PCF itself. On the contrary, Sartre, Mounier, Bourdet, and their friends were more often the target of abuse and insult from the Communists, their contradictions and hypocrisies ruthlessly revealed and documented in the Communist press, for the edification of a readership who can only rarely have read them in the original.[21] Communists had little use for independent intellectuals who felt obliged to discuss the crimes and errors of Stalin and his followers, even if these discussions nearly always ended in an offer of unconditional absolution. If the Communist party was indeed the vehicle alongside which the bourgeois intelligentsia were to ride into battle with the working masses, then it was a decidedly uncomfortable journey. But the more the driver sought to throw off these enthusiastic fellow-passengers, as the vehicle lurched and reeled along its dialectical path, the more they clung on and swore that they would never abandon the journey. For there could be no going back.

Like the Communists, intellectual fellow-travelers despised not only the rotten world of the bourgeoisie but also and especially their own role within it. Their vaulted, exaggerated sense of the importance of the intellectual within that world is precisely what generated their remarkable association of radicalism and abusive self-hatred. Nothing so became the Communist party, in the eyes of many intellectuals, as its justified mistrust of "the isolated intellectual," of people like them.[22] The Communists might have some way to go in resolving their own dilemmas, but they had already helped resolve those of the intelligentsia; in his commentary on the 1948 Prague coup, Mounier concluded by warmly urging the Communists to "exorcise their own demons, as they have exorcised ours."[23] As a "collective intellectual," the Communist movement could do no wrong (which opinion constituted, in its ironic way, an exaltation of the claims of the intellectual but transposed onto a higher plane), even if its actions, and especially the opinions of its own in-house spokesmen, were often indefensible. Indeed, writers like Sartre had nothing but scorn for the party's *own* intellectuals; neither they nor

21. See, for example, the attacks on Bourdet, Mounier, and Cassou by Alfred Boscarlet, in *Cahiers du communisme* 2 (1950): 69–70.

22. "Le Parti Communiste se méfie justement de l'intellectuel isolé." Jean Lacroix, "Y a-t-il deux démocraties?" 354–55.

23. Mounier, "Prague," *Esprit*, March 1948, 364.

the Marxism they espoused was very intelligent, he wrote, and certainly not remotely as intelligent as the party itself. It was a source of regret to him that with their privileged access to the proletariat and its collective intelligence, they were unable to make a better job of humiliating and overcoming mere isolated thinkers like himself: "This marvelous tool that they possess—how one longs for it to give them a crushing superiority over those who just think at random."[24]

This self-abnegation of the intellectual in the face of history and its horsemen was rooted in the view, articulated by a few and held by many, that the intellectual was by nature a "traitor." He or she was either a traitor to the causes believed in, always standing a little aside from them and therefore never wholly "authentic"; or else intellectuals were traitors to their class by virtue of this very engagement in such causes. The condition of the intellectual, that is to say, is treasonable by definition. This sentiment has resurfaced most recently in the works of Pierre Bourdieu and his colleagues, for whom the beneficiaries of higher education in bourgeois society are by definition led to betray, even as they are themselves betrayed by the illusions of their condition.[25] As a characteristic trope of the French intelligentsia it thus has a fine pedigree, this curious expression of an oversophisticated conscience never at ease with itself unless engaged in unremitting self-condemnation.[26] Its omnipresence at this time, however, suggests the need for some explanation that goes beyond the accidental or the biographical. Certainly the latter accounts for much. Sartre's famous sense of his own worthlessness—of the unremitting absence of meaning and value in his origins, his career, his output—is only the extreme pole of a sentiment shared by many, as their memoirs reveal. Adherence (literal or merely emotional) to the Communist party or the proletariat conferred a sense of identity and community on those who, by their own account, lacked either. Men like Roy, Morgan, Domenach, and others had swung from Right to Left since the late thirties, and the long crisis of schizophrenia that some of them claim to have experienced during the period 1948–56, especially if they had joined the party and remained in it, was probably less painful than the

24. Sartre, "Le Réformisme et les fétiches," *Les Temps modernes* 122 (February 1956): 1158.

25. Pierre Bourdieu and Jean-Claude Passeron, *Les Héritiers* (Paris, 1964); Bourdieu, *La Noblesse d'état* (Paris, 1989).

26. "La mauvaise conscience de nombreux maîtres de la pensée occidentale les empêche de reconnaître le crime dès qu'il ne s'agit plus de condamner vaillamment 'un monde pourri.'" Mircea Eliade, "Examen leprosum," *Preuves* 14 (April 1952): 26.

sense of isolation and exclusion that preceded this commitment and was to follow it.

If intellectuals signed away their critical faculties to give some meaning to their "little private histories,"[27] they nonetheless retained in nearly every case a degree of real autonomy in their own professional sphere. Very few artists, playwrights, scientists, historians, or philosophers of this era who paid lip service to the Communist project and scorned its critics ever let it invade the sanctuary of their work. In the case of those who were still young, like the sociologist Edgar Morin or the historians Emmanuel Le Roy Ladurie, Maurice Agulhon, or François Furet, it might be argued that they were saved by their youth. But older scholars like Georges Lefebvre also managed to maintain academic integrity even as they put their conclusions at the service of the revolution. Picasso and Fernand Léger, Joliot-Curie and Jean-Pierre Vernant remained faithful to their artistic and scientific callings while striving resolutely to defend the most absurd official positions of their Communist colleagues and allies. This points to a curious neutral region in intellectual sympathy for Stalinism and may offer a further clue to the nature of that sympathy.

In order to develop this argument it is necessary to establish certain distinctions. Leading, successful, influential figures in the intellectual community were rarely to be found in the Communist party. Aragon is an exception, and the prominent use made of him by the party is symptomatic of his unusual standing. Most older party intellectuals were either second-rate performers in their field or else intellectuals only in the broadest, generic sense—schoolteachers, journalists, provincial professors, librarians, and the like. Thus when the party demanded conformity in the intellectual sphere—whether in the interpretation of events, adherence to aesthetic "principles," or the selection of fictional subject matter, it was not placing too great a burden on most of its own intellectual membership. Conversely, it was in no position to enforce such standards on outsiders and conspicuously failed to do so. Second, most intellectuals who joined the PCF, including those who would later make prominent careers in their field, were very young at the time. The typical Communist intellectual in 1950 was a man or woman in his or her twenties. Vulnerable to party pressure, these people were nonetheless not yet established figures, and they were on the periphery of the Communist movement. If their work did not always conform to the mandated

27. Claude Roy, *Moi, Je* (Paris, 1969), 464.

norms, it did not matter very much. The older generation of established writers, scholars, and artists did not join the party, on the whole. Like Mounier, Camus, Sartre, Merleau-Ponty, and their colleagues, they initially maintained a friendly distance, supporting communism for their own reasons. Their work as novelists, playwrights, philosophers, or historians had begun well before the Liberation, and their aesthetic, as distinct from their political, identity was in no way dependent on or related to the workers' movement. Even when, as with Sartre, this was a source of regret, they did not and could not change it. At most they ceased producing artistic or scholarly work and confined themselves to political activism. More commonly, they did both, in a tense and contradictory juxtaposition.

In this book I am concerned chiefly with these well-established people and much less with their younger colleagues. The latter, together with the lesser intelligentsia of the party rank and file, form the subject of Jeannine Verdès-Leroux's important work, and their history is a different one.[28] The Communist party itself had an interest in exaggerating the support it received from intellectuals, for a number of reasons: like Czechoslovakia, Poland, or Russia itself, France is a country in which the political and cultural role of the intelligentsia is a prominent and recognized fact of public life. As the putative heir to the best traditions of the nation, the PCF laid claim to this inheritance as to others. Furthermore, the prominence of the Parisian intellectual community in postwar France was indisputable, and the Communists had every reason to seek to extend their influence into such circles. But the party's interest in, and pressure on, intellectuals varied somewhat according to their activity. Those whose work related directly to the subject matter of Communist discourse (historians, sociologists, economists) were of curiously little concern, despite the fact that historians especially thronged to the party in considerable numbers. Novelists, painters, and sculptors, on the other hand, were of much greater value to the party, as pure intellectuals whose symbolic presence at public meetings and in front organizations was especially highly valued.

None of this was wholly new. In the thirties it had been common for people like Gide, Rolland, or Malraux to act in a similar capacity as cultural guarantors for the Communist line, and the Spanish civil war had shown that intellectuals could be both engaged and retain their creative

---

28. See Jeannine Verdès-Leroux, *Au service du parti* (Paris, 1983); and *Le Réveil des somnambules* (Paris, 1987).

autonomy—no one accused Picasso, Malraux, or Bernanos of having abandoned his artistic soul. What brought about a significant change was the pronounced emphasis after 1948 on artistic conformity, on "socialist realism" and the "two cultures." "Proletarian" art was not a new idea—the Russian debates of the twenties were quite well known and the Association des écrivains et artistes révolutionnaires had pressed hard for "committed" art in its propaganda of the early thirties. But Communists and non-Communists alike had felt free to ignore such pressures, which had been muted in the Popular Front years, especially during the Resistance and the Liberation. Following the establishment of the Cominform, however, and the "two camps" theory, which Zdanov and Stalin invoked to justify the increased rigidity of Communist practice after 1947, artistic (and scientific) conformity became a serious issue. We have already seen the ambivalence and inadequacy of progressive intellectuals' responses to symptoms of Zdanovism in the Lysenko affair and even in the show trials, which are in some sense best thought of as the bloody practice of which socialist realism is the theory. When Laurent Casanova formally imported Zdanov's aesthetics into the French milieu, he aroused the same wary, mealy-mouthed response:

One cannot deny in all this a real effort at coherence and also humility, a submission to the concrete realities contained in the proletariat's historic struggle, which gives to the intellectual elements of an authentic greatness.[29]

This is not some Communist functionary but Jean-Marie Domenach, writing in *Esprit*. He goes on to say that the utter submission of literature, art, and science does place the *Communist* intellectual in a "contradictory situation"; what he does not appreciate is just how contradictory was his *own* situation, as an intellectual content to praise the forced submission of his fellow intellectuals to "concrete realities." In France, Casanova had no weapon of enforcement beyond expulsion from the party, but in the East, "concrete reality" meant something altogether more specific, as Domenach well knew. The response of André Breton was much more to the point. Under present circumstances, he wrote, with direct reference to his former friend Aragon, "the shameful word 'engagement,' which has become popular since the war, stinks of a servility which art and poetry abhor."[30]

29. Domenach, "Le Parti Communiste français et les intellectuels," *Esprit*, May 1949, 736.
30. André Breton, March 1948, quoted by Jean Galtier-Boissière, *Mon journal dans la Grande Pagaille* (Paris, 1950), 212.

In practice, Communist and non-Communist intellectuals alike devoted little real attention to the aesthetic or epistemological implications of the "two camps" theory. Those who took Lysenko half seriously were never professional scientists, much less biologists. André Stil provoked nothing but silence in the community of painters. Picasso was so unconcerned as to provide a decidedly inappropriate portrait of Stalin for a Communist journal, and his "caricature" was officially rejected and reproved. *Les Temps modernes*, characteristically, responded to things it found embarrassing by ignoring them. From 1948 until 1956 there is astonishingly little space in its pages devoted to events in the Peoples' Democracies, and even less to the cultural policies of communism. Simone de Beauvoir, in her memoirs, does reprove her earlier self for excess of "idealism" in her essays of the forties and regrets her failure to be more down-to-earth and "realist" in her language.[31] But she is indulging this mild and rare self-criticism in the name of *ouvriérisme*, not socialist realism, an important distinction. On the whole, the cultural dimension of Stalinism was something with which French intellectuals were least at ease, just because it came closest to things they knew and cared about: "We were more intolerant of idiocy in areas we knew well than of crimes in those of which we knew little."[32]

In contrast with contemporary Italian intellectuals of the Left, the French did not openly insist that the axis of progress/reaction in culture is not the same as in politics; they merely kept their thoughts to themselves.[33] This moral dishonesty may not reflect well upon them in retrospect—and it should hardly be accounted a matter of pride to have dissented from totalitarianism over bad art but not over mass murder— but it did allow practicing artists, novelists, and the like to maintain their professional integrity while adhering to the progressive line in public affairs. This seemed all the more important in that many in the postwar generation were drawn together and to the side of the Communists by a further consideration, a theme of surpassing urgency, a grid through which all contemporary politics were viewed and which lent a distorted image to everything it touched—the issue of "peace."

From one point of view it is odd to find the theme of "peace" at the heart of contemporary debate. This is because the memory of 1938 was

31. Simone de Beauvoir, *La Force des choses* (Paris, 1963), 80–81.
32. Claude Roy, *Nous*, 445.
33. For Italian debates on similar themes, see Elio Vittorini, "Rivoluzione e attività morale," *Il Politecnico* 38 (November 1947); and Vittorini, *Gli anni del "Politecnico": Lettere, 1945–1951* (Turin, 1977).

still fresh, and the emphasis on peace at any price—Chamberlain's famous "peace for our time," Blum's "cowardly relief"—was not forgotten. *Appeasement* was a dirty word and *Munichois* a profound insult. But all the same, intellectuals of the postwar decade had abiding memories of the pacifist mood of the thirties and their own earlier opposition to war and bloodshed. Many of them were old enough to remember the First World War or even to have fought in it, and the conflict with Hitler had not completely obliterated the earlier one and the impact it had left. The war of 1940 had been fought under ambiguous circumstances: not only had it been declared on behalf of a Poland that was then left to bleed dry, but it was fought in the name of a residual antifascism even as Daladier strove to retain some semblance of a friendship with Mussolini. Until the Germans crossed the Meuse, the French had no territorial ambitions in the conflict, and from the outset the far Left and the radical Right were opposed to pursuing the fight. Assuredly, Vichy, the Occupation, and the emergence of a Resistance had altered the terms of engagement, but the uncertainties of World War II and its meaning had by no means obliterated the much more deeply implanted lessons of the Great War and its aftermath.

Thus the conflict with Hitler that had so perturbed interwar pacifist sentiment did not ultimately douse it. On the contrary, it confirmed it. The pacifists of the earlier decade had been repelled not only by the prospect of another round of Sommes and Verduns but also by the apparent irrationality of fighting to uphold a settlement, that of Versailles, in which few believed. Hitler, Mussolini, and their French friends had played very effectively on the theme of international injustice, the suggestion that the Great War had not only been an unnecessary and futile massacre of the innocents but that it had ended in a massive social and diplomatic injustice. Neither the Soviet Union nor Germany was pleased with the outcome, and even among those who would oppose them there was an unease, an awareness that the international dispositions of the interwar years rested on indefensible foundations. But when the next war finally came, as everyone anticipated it would, these doubts were temporarily laid to rest, at least among those who took up the struggle against nazism. The antifascism of the resisters was the one sure and unimpeachable motive that all could share. With the defeat of Hitler it would again be possible to look to peace but this time on morally defensible premises.

In one sense, then, the de facto peace settlement of 1945 was regarded as altogether more satisfactory than that of 1918. The ambiguity of the

German situation was cleared up, since the loser was no longer a struggling democratic republic but a defeated totalitarian dictatorship. The
Russians had emerged as victorious and had seen their lost territories and
imperial frontiers restored, and the war had been fought and won not for
the interests of nations (or capitalists) but in the name of peoples and
ideals. The case for preserving the peace of 1945 seemed altogether
stronger than that for its predecessor, the more so in that the postwar
revolutions of the forties had apparently succeeded in the very countries
where they had been defeated by local reaction and foreign arms in the
years 1918–23. The only muted complaints came from Poles and their
fellows in the Soviet zone of Europe; but the idea of opposing the Soviet
hegemony in that region was anathema to a broad swathe of opinion in
the West. After six years of war, no one in France, in the years after 1945
any more than in 1939, wanted to "die for Danzig" (or Gdańsk).

An important constituent of this postwar obsession with peace was,
paradoxically, that same antifascism that had finally drawn prewar
pacifists into war. Now that Nazism and its friends were defeated and the
Soviet Union and its allies victorious, the only possible beneficiary of a
weakening of that alliance, of divisions among the wartime victors, or a
conflict between them, would be fascism itself. This may sound curious
to the modern ear, but it made some sense at the time. The years
1938–44 had been a profound shock, an awakening to political realities
of which many had previously had little idea. For the best of them the
experience had taught them something of the shocking specificity of fascism; more violent, more extreme, more total in its hatred and its convictions than anything they had previously encountered, it was the true
and ultimate force of evil. To the struggle against fascism, now and for
the future, all else must be subsumed. For others whose awakening to
the evils of fascism had been slow and who were all too well aware of this
as they contemplated their own record, there was a lot of ground to be
made up. Above all else, one must not again be found wanting, left
behind in the struggle.

"Fighting the last war," then? Perhaps, although we should recall that
in 1945 and for a few years to come, the threat of a revival of fascism
seemed plausible, if only by analogy with the aftermath of World War I.
If the Americans once again left Europe (as most expected and many
wished), and with Britain weakened perhaps beyond repair, a revival of
the German threat was a plausible hypothesis. In any case, anti-Fascist
feeling and the fear of being once again caught unawares were widespread
and real. For this reason postwar intellectuals continued to maintain, as

Klaus Mann had done at the Paris Congress of anti-Fascist intellectuals in 1935, that their position was defined by whatever fascism was not. This was worthy as far as it went, but it left them with a negative, reactive attitude towards politics, with their affiliation and engagement defined by the behavior, real or imagined, of others. If a renascent fascism was the danger, then it did indeed make sense to line up with the only continental force capable of blocking it, the Communist movement and the Red Army.

These feelings were exacerbated and given point by the collapse of the postwar alliance and the onset of the Cold War. Beginning in the summer of 1947, it really did seem for a while as though the West and the Soviet Union might come to blows over the German question, the plans for U.S. economic aid, and the Soviet Union's increasingly rigid grip over its zone of influence in East-Central Europe.[34] The expectation of war was widespread (especially in France) and was directly responsible for the increasing sympathy for the Soviet Union in the writings of contemporary intellectuals. Claude Bourdet was all the more inclined to accept the prosecution and execution of Nikola Petkov in that he was convinced by the Communists' claim that Petkov had sought a "Western intervention" in Bulgaria's affairs, an intervention that would have sparked regional, perhaps continent-wide conflict. Within France, intellectuals detected a "war psychosis" and identified the anti-Communist rhetoric of the authorities as its primary source; in the end it was very simple—"Anticommunism is a force for death . . . a force for war."[35]

In such circumstances, the struggle for peace came to subsume and replace all other issues. Because fascism would be the beneficiary of war and because it was the United States that was accused of provoking the conflicts and divisions that seemed to be on the brink of open warfare, the drive for peace and the defense of communism merged into a single theme. From 1946 until the death of Stalin, no other topic so dominated public discussion, directly or subliminally. The defense of democracy and the preservation of peace merged into a single goal, the prime duty of the writer in the view of one prominent figure.[36] The progressive Christian intelligentsia was especially obsessed with this theme, allowing

34. See, for example, François Mauriac, *Journal*, vol. 5 (Paris, 1953), 20–21 July 1947.

35. Claude Bourdet, in *Combat*, 21 September 1947; Mounier, "Débat à haute voix," *Esprit*, February 1946, 145.

36. On the artists' duty to "defend peace," see Jean-Richard Bloch, "Responsabilité du talent," *Europe*, August 1946, 88.

itself to be blinded by it into the most incredulous and indefensible positions, much as its successors in the 1970s and 1980s would make of peace and disarmament a demand transcending any concern for justice or rights in eastern Europe.[37] Zdanov might be stupid, and Stalin cruel. But armaments were the ultimate stupidity, war the final cruelty. By 1950, the progressive intelligentsia was beginning to sound remarkably like the pacifist writers of the thirties, unconsciously echoing the latter in its apologias for totalitarianism and dictators. Even Camus, who could by no stretch of the imagination be described by 1953 as sympathetic to Communist practices, nonetheless prefaced a collection of his writings published in that year with the claim that the preservation of peace, the rejection of warlike attitudes from whichever side they came, was the main task of those who took part in public life.[38]

The Communists played on these sensibilities to remarkable effect, proving even more adept at such exploitation than the Fascist journalists of the late thirties. The credibility of the Communists in this matter derived not merely from their anti-Fascist credentials but also from the fact that Stalin was indeed content with the postwar dispensations. Although it is arguable that after the change of direction in 1947 the Soviet Union was more actively interested in disrupting the West, until then the division of Europe had been to the Communists' advantage. Thus, from 1945 until 1948, Stalin had acquired considerable credit among Western sympathizers as a "man of peace"; the division consecrated at Yalta, the subordination of the coalition governments of the East European states, the trials of their erstwhile leaders were all viewed through the twin spectrum of "Soviet security" and "popular revolution." To this should be added the widespread sympathy for the Soviet Union arising from the Americans' monopoly (until 1949) of the atomic weapon. Sartre spoke for many in his generation when he wrote in *Le Fantôme de Staline* that Stalin had only established "satellite" states as a response to the Marshall Plan, *"cette manoeuvre de guerre."* Until then the Soviet Union had sought merely to guarantee and preserve its own external security. By its defensive moves in 1948 and afterwards it had preserved the peace and saved Europe for socialism.

This was written at the end of 1956. By then the Soviet Union had also benefited from its vigorous opposition to the rearmament of Germany and Stalin's emphasis from 1951 on "peaceful coexistence." But

37. See Václav Havel, "Politika a svědomí," *Svědectví* 18, no. 72 (1984).
38. Albert Camus, "Avant-propos," *Actuelles*, vol. 2 (Paris, 1953).

even in the period 1948–51, when communism was at its most aggressive and sectarian, it had retained the identification with "peace" in the eyes of its admirers. Indeed, it was precisely in these years that this identification was most forcefully asserted. In Wroclaw in August 1948, the Movement for Peace held its founding congress, at the same time as a parallel Congress of Partisans of Peace was held simultaneously in Prague and Paris. This meeting was followed in April 1949 by a national conference of the newly formed Mouvement des intellectuels français pour la défense de la paix, held in Paris and attended by, among others, Louis Aragon, Jean Cassou, Pierre Debray (for *Témoignage Chrétien*), Paul Éluard, the Joliot-Curies, Picasso, Fernand Léger, Paul Rivet, Seghers, Vercors, Jean Wahl, Jean-Louis Barrault, and Madeleine Renaud—a veritable *Almanach de Gotha* of the progressive artistic elite of postwar France. Seghers took the opportunity to press the claims, the "intellectual presence," of France through books and other writings—"through its books, France must show its desire for peace."[39]

The World Peace Congress met for a second time in November 1950 and again in Vienna in December 1952, a few days after the end of the Slánsky trial. For most of this period its activities were dominated by the so-called Stockholm Appeal, issued in March 1950 by the permanent committee of the World Congress of Partisans of Peace. Like the Cominform in these years, from which they took their cue, the appeal and the various congresses were devoted to gathering support from the widest possible international constituency in opposition to war and to any modification of the postwar settlement. All the various peace movements and their meetings were ostensibly directed by committees composed of influential and well-known figures from the artistic and scientific communities but were in practice controlled, much like their forebears of the thirties, by hard-working Communist functionaries, many of them based in Prague. They succeeded in gathering many millions of signatures (though much of the bulk was made up of "voluntary" adhesions from the Communist bloc or from members of various Communist parties around the globe), and there is no doubt that the peace initiatives of the Communists added considerably to their appeal and their legitimacy in the eyes of non-Communist intellectuals.

The French intelligentsia played a disproportionate role in these

39. See *Mouvement des intellectuels français pour la défense de la paix*, proceedings of the Conférence nationale, Paris, 23 April 1949, 19.

organizations. Frédéric Joliot-Curie and Jean Lafitte were the nominal heads of various international movements, while Pierre Cot was a prominent figurehead at the International Association of Democratic Jurists, a comparable institution whose prime function was to deflect attention away from Soviet crimes by focussing international concern on injustice and inhumanity in the non-Communist world. More than elsewhere, prominent local figures were active in the French branches of these movements; when they left them, it was not normally through any disillusion with the "peace movement" as such but usually because the Communists had found fault with their behavior, as when Cassou and Domenach were condemned by their local peace movement branch in 1950 for Cassou's criticism of the Rajk trial and Domenach's support of him. As the guests of peace organizations, French journalists and artists visited East European countries and wrote enthusiastically about their experiences, seemingly unaware that they were regarded, by their hosts and their hosts' victims alike, as "pigeons," the happy successors to the "useful idiots" of the thirties.[40] Their naiveté apparently knew few limits; writing in praise of Yugoslavia in 1950, Domenach criticized the Soviet Union for arrogating to itself the right to define who was and who was not a "peace-loving" regime—our Communist friends in the peace movement claim no such monopoly, he insisted.[41]

Their vision blurred and tinted rose by the maneuvers and alignments of the Communists and their own longings and doubts, French intellectuals were thus exposed and vulnerable after World War II in a way they were not before or since. Of someone who could seriously believe in 1950 that there was a distinction to be drawn between the policies of Stalin and the attitudes of "our Communist friends in the peace movement," it can well be said that he would believe anything. But Jean-Marie Domenach was not alone—Simone de Beauvoir had drawn similar distinctions, and analogous hair-splitting arguments were the staple fare of progressive intellectuals. In the context of this period, one can see how otherwise intelligent and sophisticated people came to such positions; indeed, given the various factors already noted, it may even appear as though the postwar condition of the French intelligentsia was

40. Jo Langer, *Une Saison à Bratislava* (Paris, 1979), 246. Langer notes that most of the "pigeons" were French, Italian, or Indian. See also Paul Hollander, *Political Pilgrims* (Oxford, 1981); and Fred Kupferman, *Au pays des Soviets* (Paris, 1979).

41. Domenach, "Une Révolution rencontre le mensonge," *Esprit*, February 1950, 195.

the natural product of a history and circumstances that gave them no alternative exit. This is certainly not so; moral conditions, unlike economic ones, are always elective. Nevertheless, it did seem to many as though there was indeed no other political or moral option for the *bienpensant* intellectual of these years. In order to understand the circumstances in which such could appear to be the case, we must now turn our attention to an empty space at the center of French political thought.

PART FOUR

The Middle Kingdom

CHAPTER TWELVE

Liberalism, There Is the Enemy
On Some Peculiarities of French Political Thought

Nous sommes parfaitement capables de faire un culte national de l'horreur et de jouir sous le spasme des guillotines. Nous l'avons toujours su, n'est-il pas vrai? Nous n'en parlons jamais, nous jurerions même du contraire: mais les prophètes du fanatisme, c'est chez nous qu'ils se sont levés les premiers.

We [French] are perfectly capable of making a national cult of the horrific and writhing in pleasure at the thud of the guillotine. Haven't we always known this? We never speak of it, indeed we swear the contrary: but it was among us that the prophets of fanaticism first surfaced.

Pierre Emmanuel

At the heart of the engagement of the 1940s and 1950s there lay an unwillingness to think seriously about public ethics, an unwillingness amounting to an incapacity. An important source of this shortcoming in the French intelligentsia was the widely held belief that morally binding judgments of a normative sort were undermined by their historical and logical association with the politics and economics of liberalism. It was a widely held view that liberalism, with its political language based on individuals

229

and their rights and liberties, had utterly failed to protect people against fascism and its consequences, in large measure because it provided them with no alternative account of humanity and its purposes—or at any rate, no alternative account sufficiently consistent and attractive to fight off the charms and dangers of the radical Right. Faced with nazism and the Occupation, intellectuals had been forced, so it was argued, to find their guidelines and their political community elsewhere. The liberal hour had passed.

At first sight, this is a strange position to associate with the *postwar* intellectual. It is one more frequently encountered in studies of the mood *between* the wars, when liberalism and democracy were unfashionable, as much the enemy as fascism (or communism) itself. It might have been expected that the experience of war and occupation, of individual and collective resistance, would place a premium upon rights and freedoms. Superficially, this was indeed the case. But once political and moral theorists were again faced with circumstances in which liberties and justice were threatened, they responded in ways that suggest little had changed. Fascism had been defeated and communism was now the ally, albeit an uncomfortable one. Liberalism, however, remained the enemy. To understand why this was the case we have to make a brief detour through the history of modern French political thought.

At this point it might be objected that most French intellectuals were not political theorists and historical debates about liberalism were for the most part alien to their experience and concerns. This is correct; very few postwar writers took a direct interest in political ideas as such. Their concerns were primarily literary, philosophical, or artistic. Yet everything they said and wrote was either politically charged or else open to political exploitation, and this was universally acknowledged. Indeed, it is precisely in these years that the claim was widely advanced that all intellectual and artistic life just *is* political, and that to deny this is bad faith. Moreover, the distinction between the political and the nonpolitical collapses at this point: political thought, political argument, is not some rarefied and exotic species of cogitation that attends to a circumscribed subset of human activity, of interest only to its practitioners. It is the very language in which all public activity is described, criticized, or proposed, and the terms of political discourse thus establish the vocabulary for all interventions in the public sphere. This is especially the case in France, where the identity of intellectuals has long been shaped by the place they occupy in the public life of the nation and where the distinction between the political and the nonpolitical is both arbitrary and artificial.

Matters are further complicated by the peculiar weakness of the liberal tradition in French life, which means that to discuss it entails addressing oneself to an absence. The public space in modern France has been occupied by many contending actors and ideas, but liberals and liberalism have not been prominent among them. Thus we may say of Merleau-Ponty or Mounier, as of Mauriac or Benda, that their nonpolitical concerns, whether metaphysical, literary, or moralist, are deeply rooted in generations of debate over the place of Catholicism in human affairs; in a century of radical political speculation; and in many decades of argument over the desirability or necessity of terror, violence, and revolution. Few would deny that on this terrain, moral speculation and political dispute in France are, or had become, inseparable. But the traditional issues of liberal political life that informed the concerns of intellectuals in some other cultures have been curiously absent in France. This makes all discussions of rights, autonomy, or the limitations of power peculiarly abstract in the modern French context and can convey the impression that the trajectory of liberal thought in France has little or nothing to do with the thoughts and actions of intellectuals. This is not the case, but to understand why, we need to address a set of issues rather different from those treated so far.

Liberalism is not a tidy and definable political concept. It is as much a historical construct as socialism or any other complex account of social arrangements. Like socialism, it had its intellectual roots in the social thought of the eighteenth century and derived its modern shape from the social and political configurations of early nineteenth-century Europe, in the aftermath of the French Revolution. Although not inherently concerned with or dependent upon ideas of rights (natural or otherwise), it became from early on closely bound up with a certain conception of those rights, what Isaiah Berlin, following John Stuart Mill, was to call "negative liberties." These are rights or freedoms that individuals hold *against* the community, in the sense that they are rights inhering in persons not because they have a certain place in society, nor because society has accorded them these rights by virtue of their membership of the citizenry, but just because they are autonomous human beings, whose claim is superior to that of positive law or the preferences of others. However such rights were defined, they could only be invaded or traduced on very specific grounds pertaining to the identical rights of other persons or to the overriding and urgent interests of all. The object of laws and constitutions in such a situation is to enshrine and protect these rights. Government is constituted to no other end, certainly none that may override the rights of those whom it exists to defend.[1]

1. For the classic statement of this position, see John Stuart Mill, *On Liberty* (London, 1859); also Isaiah Berlin, *Two Concepts of Liberty* (Oxford, 1958).

This is an idealized account of liberalism. No such system has ever existed, even at the most noninterventionist epochs in the nineteenth-century history of Britain or the United States. But as a vision of the relationship between government and citizen, between community and individual, between state and society, it played a powerful part in forming the political and moral sensibilities of those who lived in "liberal" societies. Even when they were in radical opposition to their government, dissenting from it in the name of class or other sectional interest, they were nearly always constrained to employ the language of liberalism and of rights *against* their opponents. Hence, for example, the easy adoption of rights language by radicals in nineteenth-century Britain, invoking against the aristocracy or the middle classes the very vocabulary the latter deployed in defense of their advantages and privileges.

In France, as in much of continental Europe, liberalism came to mean something rather different. As in the Anglo-American tradition, it connoted a social arrangement in which existing privileges were protected if they could be defended on universal principles, and where a new secular ruling class availed itself of the former language of opposition to secure its own status against the claims of a revolutionary class below. But in contrast with developments in Britain or the United States, liberalism in France was rooted in its moment of origin, virtually impermeable to new claims and new interests. Accordingly, therefore, those whose rights went unprotected or whose interests were not covered by existing arrangements looked to alternative devices with which to advance their claims, rejecting liberal society and its rights as inadequate and hypocritical. Echoes of this divergence between the two conceptions of liberalism may still be found today in the very different meanings attaching to liberalism in the United States (where it denotes the far, permeable left of mainstream politics) and Italy or Germany, where it refers to the political organization and ideas of the industrial and commercial elites. But it was above all in France that the term *liberalism* disappeared from the political canon of the left—without attaching itself with much success to the center or right. This is a curious development, on the face of it a paradoxical one. Nowhere more than in France was modern politics born into a debate about society in which rights were on everyone's lips. France, it has been proclaimed *ad nauseam,* was the country of the Rights of Man, the nation whose many constitutions have paid manifest attention to the rights of men and citizens, the country whose revolution is the founding moment for modern politics throughout Europe and much of the world. But the problem in France was that from an early point in the development of modern political traditions, rights lost their extrapoliti-cal status and became an object of suspicion. They ceased, as it were, to be taken seriously.

The reasons for this are complex. Recent studies have paid close atten-tion to significant changes in the meaning and use of rights language during the Revolution, and they have drawn our attention to the impor-tance of the Revolution as the moment at which France both embodied and formalized a certain tradition of enlightened political thought and also began to diverge from it.[2] This attention to the presence of "rights-talk" in the French Revolution is to be welcomed as a departure from the more static account of French political thought that treats it as structur-ally determined by the omnipresence of the centralized state in all public theory (a rare instance in which Tocqueville's account of things was taken altogether too seriously). Certainly the state played a major role in French political life and thought before as after 1789, in contrast with its lesser place in comparable speculation in Scotland, Italy, and elsewhere. It was axiomatic for many in the French Enlightenment that individual interests and needs were *not* likely to find harmony in the immanent pro-cess of competition and self-advancement; it would always take an authority of some sort to define and assure the development of society to the advantage of all. Even those individuals and groups who typically benefit from the controlled anarchy of the market had, in France, a long-standing habit of looking to the state for assistance and protection, and the state, since the advent of the Bourbons, had been all too pleased to respond.[3]

Nonetheless, it was not the all-pervading presence of the centralized interventionist state, transforming itself from monarchy to republic with minimal inconvenience, that vitiated the liberal project in France. It was the internal contradictions of that project itself, in the form in which it emerged in revolutionary France, and in the special circumstances of such a revolution. The initial value of rights, the reason why they were so aggressively asserted by the makers of the Revolution, was their use as a language with which to justify and legitimize the creation of a new sover-eign power (in France as in the contemporary United States). But in assuming this enabling role, rights lost their other, older meaning of a limit upon power. In the United States, by contrast, the same rights of

2. Marcel Gauchet, *La Révolution des droits de l'homme* (Paris, 1989).

3. This is Raymond Aron's argument in "Les Intellectuels français et l'utopie," *Preuves* 50 (April 1955), especially 10.

the "people" that were asserted against the British as a basis for independence were then deployed in the first ten amendments to the Constitution as protections for that same people against their newly established
government. There was something of this in the first French constitution, but whereas in the United States all residual rights (those not specifically named in the Constitution itself) were left with the citizenry, in
France it was the law that took up the slack.[4]

All this would have mattered less had the framers of successive French
republican constitutions not felt obliged to maintain the emphasis upon
rights. This emphasis was understandable, of course. Unlike their American counterparts, the French could not assert the "self-evidence" of
popular authority, nor the "natural" authority of those who claimed to
speak for rights on behalf of the "people." Burdened by centuries of
monarchical and clerical authority, theirs was an insecure and truly radical departure from the "natural" arrangements of society, and the continued emphasis on the rights of the "people" was an incantation in
defense of a claim to authority that was otherwise extremely unsteady
and fragile. If the Revolution did not govern in the name of and on
behalf of the nation, on what else did its power rest? But at the same time
the constitution-makers of the Revolution, moderate and radical alike,
were not only asserting their authority to rule, they were also seeking to
govern, and to do this meant that they had somehow to restrict the very
rights that they had just invoked. Thus in the course of the Revolution,
the language of rights underwent a rapid if subtle change; from a device
with which to defend the individual person against the overpowerful
ruler, it emerged as the basis for advancing the claims of the whole
against the interests of its parts. Far from protecting the citizen against
the caprice of authority, rights became enshrined as the basis for
legitimizing the actions and caprices of that authority against the very
citizens for whom and in whose name it exercised power.

The specific shift entailed here was that from the rights of man to that
of the rights (and duties) of citizens.[5] Abstract or natural rights were
displaced in favor of positive and concrete rights that depended upon
membership of a formal community and that could be forfeited in the
event of a citizen's failure to perform the tasks assigned him in that community. Such rights became contingent. They were at the mercy of the

4. See "La Constitution de 1791," *Les Constitutions de la France depuis 1789* (Paris,
1970).

5. Compare the *Déclaration des Droits de l'Homme et du Citoyen* in the Constitution of
1793 with the *Déclaration des Droits de l'Homme et du Citoyen du 26 aôut 1789*.

interpretation of the law. But because the only legitimate source of law was the government, the idea of rights in France became dependent upon the superior claims of the all-powerful authority of the Assembly. In a closed circle of constitutional theory that was common to moderates, Jacobins, and Thermidoreans, whatever their other differences, the very rights of the people that gave the revolutionary governments their legitimacy also gave them the authority to restrict the practice of rights and liberties by that same people. "Men" might have no self-evident duties, but citizens did. Since their first duty was now to obey the law, their right to noninterference in any given sphere of human activity was always to be contingent on the larger interests of the community, as defined by the authorities and enshrined in the constitution.

The practical implications of these developments were of course felt immediately. The theoretical and ideological lessons would only emerge later. It was during the early years of the nineteenth century that critics of the Revolution drew from its invocation of the language of rights radical and contradictory lessons. The first socialists treated their revolutionary predecessors' emphasis upon individual rights as an intellectual error, as well as political hypocrisy. It was an error in that it attempted to derive from the claims of individuals a form of society and government that could only be grounded in interests shared by whole classes of persons, defined by their part in the social order. The influence of the Saint-Simonian conception of a society divided into the productive and the unproductive, developed by Saint-Simon's heirs (notably Comte) into a vision of history classified by stages on the ladder of progress, nullified any such concern with the isolated individual. Within society, separate persons acquired claims, rights, and duties only by virtue of their place in the productive system. To speak of isolated rights, much less rights *against* society, made no "scientific" sense.[6]

In such an account, those who did persist in asserting such notions could only be seeking to advance their own interests. This argument gained support from a curious quarter. Liberals themselves during the years 1820–48 were coming to see the Revolution as bicephalic; the achievements of 1789, defined as they had been at the time in terms of rights and limitations upon authority, were desirable and should be

6. For a fuller development of this argument, see Tony Judt, "La Révolution française et l'idée socialiste à la lumière de 1848," in François Furet, ed., *L'Héritage de la Révolution française* (Paris, 1989); and Tony Judt, "Rights in France: Reflections on the Etiolation of a Political Language," *Revue Tocqueville*, January 1993, forthcoming.

secured, whereas the promise of the radical moment of 1793, also grounded in rights but of a more ambitious kind, was to be closed.[7] The distinction between limited "negative" rights and the "positive" rights entailed in the Jacobin project of a goal-oriented authority was thus clearly articulated for the first time. Liberals themselves saw the deployment of rights in the Revolution as problematic, acceptable only if restricted to a vision of rights that limited the activities and reach of government. But for socialists, such a restriction was precisely what made the category suspect to those, like themselves, who sought to place government at the service of social transformation.

With the growing historicist perspective of socialists and liberals alike, the rights language of the Revolution was thus situated at a particular moment, fixed in time, and associated for better or worse with the projects and limitations of the revolutionary era. To move beyond the Revolution of 1789 was thus to move beyond its language. Like Marx, the French socialists of the early nineteenth century treated "rights talk" as the ideology of the bourgeoisie, whose revolution it had helped secure.[8] Tending to equilibrium, and socially divisive in their emphasis upon the protection of the isolated individual, such rights *against* interference were at best an anachronism, at worst a sham, and in either case superfluous in a socialist future. In their place, the Left turned instead to a new language derived from a new question. No longer asking "For whom and under what restrictions may we govern?" (an issue that had been resolved by the enabling discourse of the Revolution itself), they sought instead to answer the question "To what end should we govern?" Such a question, which was common to all the competing strands of socialist thought in the early part of the last century, entailed certain important assumptions: society has goals towards which it is striving, these are ascertainable in advance, and it is the duty of government to identify and achieve them.

Here, the historicist critique of the liberal, individual rights of 1789 fused with the social criticism of early industrial society to produce a new rights language, superficially in the tradition of its predecessor but in fact decisively at variance. This development can be seen in the Constitution

7. On French liberal thought in these years, see Stephen Holmes, *Benjamin Constant and the Rise of Modern Liberalism* (New Haven, Conn., 1984); Pierre Rosanvallon, *Le Moment Guizot* (Paris, 1985); and André Jardin, *Histoire du libéralisme politique* (Paris, 1985).

8. Karl Marx, "On the Jewish Question," in Robert Tucker, ed., *The Marx-Engels Reader* (New York, 1978); and François Furet, *Marx et la Révolution française* (Paris, 1986).

of 1848.[9] Rights were now not only enshrined in citizens alone (no reference to "the rights of man") but referred above all to collective rights of socially determined units of people (citizens, workers, children, families, and so on). Moreover, the rights that citizens were now assumed to possess were uniquely "claim rights," the right to education, to public assistance, and other rights—charges upon the community in return for the performance of social and political duties. Rights, in other words, had become the language in which to describe a social project. Buried within this language was a twofold belief. For the reformers (radical and otherwise) of this period, politics was to be replaced by a science of society. The function of government was to reduce the space between what should be and what is; that space—its complexity, its injustice, and its inadequacy—was seen not as something inherent in any society but as the historical (and thus transcendable) product of the Revolution itself. The claims that could be pressed by constituent subgroups within society thus arose from the very divisions and imperfections in the social order that government existed to reduce and, ultimately, abolish.

The second assumption entailed in the political language of this period was that this drive to create a "transparent" society, to overcome the heritage of the "bourgeois" revolution, must of necessity be at the expense of the claims of the individual. Individual rights were no longer the solution; they were, in effect, the problem. They described, reflected, and perpetuated that very division of society into competing, contentious, isolated units that the Revolution of 1789 had created and which it would be the task of a subsequent revolution to resolve. There had thus emerged an elision between historicity and morality that would augur badly for French thought. The "rights of Man," vitiated and circumscribed by the moment of their success, were *past rights and therefore false*. Because they could not be part of any creative project, any *telos*, they were not so much indefensible as irrelevant to radical discourse. It was not merely reactionary to assert the claims of the individual against those of the community; it was irrational to do so.

In a curious way, the political Left had thus by 1848 come to share with the far Right a common critique of the Revolution. Both sides, though for diametrically opposed reasons, saw the ambitions of the *liberal* moment of the Revolution as indefensible and unsustainable. The most clearheaded of the conservative theorists of the postrevolutionary

---

9. See "Droits des citoyens garantis par la Constitution," chapter 2 of the Constitution of 1848, in *Les Constitutions de la France depuis 1789*.

generation, notably Joseph De Maistre, dismissed as absurd and dangerous *any* attempt to remake society according to some anterior conception of the rational or the desirable. The social order not only was complex and opaque but must remain so. The fragile fabric of human community was only sustained by order and tradition, and attempts to render it transparent or rational would not only fail but produce self-defeating disorder and conflict.[10] "Rights" were an absurd illusion, and the primacy that they accorded to the self-determining individual a dangerous and divisive hubris. From Saint-Simon to Marx, the Left critique echoed much of this opinion; the attempt to remake society along lines laid down by abstract prescriptions was for them, too, an illusion. The difference is that for the newly emergent postrevolutionary Left, the project of imagining society anew had been irrational only in the circumstances and moment of its undertaking. Redescribed and properly set in a "science" of society, it was not only rational but necessary. But in that redescription, in that science, the space for a liberal conception of society and the rights of its members disappears.

But what, then, of republicanism? Between Maistre and Saint-Simon there was much political and conceptual space, filled during these years by the activities and aspirations of the republican heirs to the Revolution itself. But of all the enemies of liberalism and rights, it was the republicans who were to prove the most conclusive and deadly. If for no other reason, this is because in contrast to the reactionaries and the revolutionary socialists, the republicans of nineteenth-century France succeeded in coming to power and staying there, and the manner of their success placed the final nail in the coffin of liberal thought in French public life. Despite the fact that the Third Republic was to become, of all French regimes, the one most respecting of personal and political liberties, its written constitution subordinated all individual claims and interests to the absolute authority of the parliament. Neither the citizen nor, after 1877, the executive power had any recourse against the authority of the Assembly. Insofar as this regime can be said to have had any goal, it was that of stability, coming as it did after a series of republics, monarchies, and empires, none of which had succeeded in binding the French into a unified political nation. The legitimacy of the Third Republic would thus derive initially from its ability to minimize division and eventually from the mere fact of its capacity to endure. Republicans and monarchists in the 1870s, therefore, had a common interest in reducing to the

10. Joseph de Maistre, *Considérations sur la France* (1796; reprint Geneva, 1980); and Massimo Boffa, "Maistre," *Dictionnaire critique de la Révolution française*.

minimum any reference to social or historical projects; the Republicans especially needed to distinguish themselves from the failures of the past and, more recently, from the experience and objectives of extreme social republicanism as displayed and defeated in the Paris Commune.

Republicanism, then, came to consist chiefly in the creation of a citizenry capable of living in and sustaining the Republic: hence, the marked emphasis upon civic education in the years 1879–1905. Here statesmen like Ferry or Gambetta were indeed reaching back to the political ideas of their revolutionary predecessors, but for a very particular purpose. For a republic to work, its citizens and their representatives must be "one and indivisible" (Sieyes); the body of the king was to be replaced by that of the Assembly. Universal manhood suffrage would ensure that all active (meaning adult male) citizens were a part of this collective sovereignty, while the education and enlightenment of this citizenry would guarantee that reason alone sufficed to bridge whatever gap remained between private and public interest. The experience of 1793 remained a warning against too vigorous a pursuit of the logic of power implied by such a theory, but this was no reason to exclude the Jacobins from the republican pantheon—a point explicitly made by the first generation of republican historians who, starting with Aulard, treated Danton and (later) Robespierre with due respect.

The Third Republic would in time accord rights to its citizens in a number of ways—the right to a free press, to an elementary education, to their own property (for married women, hitherto excluded from this privilege), to strike and to form unions. But the Rights of Man (or citizens) were nowhere enshrined in the Constitution, nor did they form any part of the politics or language of republicanism. They were, instead, collapsed into the long-established and now unstated premise of republican thought, that the virtuous Republic simply *was* the final embodiment of interests and rights within a society. To establish a separate set of articles in which to list the distinct rights and prerogatives of the individual would thus have been, in such a conception, redundant.

This conclusion was reached, in part, through a form of verbal substitution. With growing frequency as the century drew to a close, writers and politicians ceased describing France as a political space within which distinct and conflicting interests might compete for power and spoke instead of the political nation as a single being, compounded into a unique and morally unimpeachable whole. France, as Michelet had put it, was "a great political principle." Already, under the Second Empire, Victor Duruy, Louis Napoleon's education minister, had written to his employer, "France is the moral center of the world." It was the late nineteenth-century republicans who first deployed to the full the idea that France *stood* for something, proselytizing an ideal of civic virtue and implicitly denying any potential or actual differences or divergences within the nation itself. If there was a goal to which fin-de-siècle republicanism strived, it was thus the creation of "Frenchness," an identity whose self-ascribed moral superiority would compensate for the gloomier aspects of recent history.

The republicans' success in securing their regime and the manner in which this success was achieved altered the French political landscape. A universal and undifferentiated democracy replaced the ideal of liberty as the subtext of mainstream republican language. This unconcern for rights and liberty had no significant impact until the crisis of the 1930s, when the central weakness of the republican consensus was tragically revealed. But it did mark the final decline of the liberal tradition of the early nineteenth century. The latter never recovered from its association with the reign of Louis-Philippe and the conflict with socialists and republicans into which this link had embroiled it. But even before 1848, liberal thought in France had been undermined by its explicit rejection of the Jacobin era; it had thereby rendered itself incompatible with the republican institutional vision of later years, whose own legitimacy derived from the Revolution of 1792 and after. Furthermore, the major political question facing nineteenth-century France concerned institutions—what sort of political or constitutional regime to establish and how to make it stick. Once their dream of an English-style constitutional monarchy foundered on the rocks of social division in the mid-1830s, liberals had nothing to offer in this discussion.

What is more, fears of social turbulence had pushed liberals of the Guizot generation towards an ambivalent sympathy for a strong executive power. As a result, French liberals of the Restoration generation and after were unable to commit themselves to the utilitarian or ethical individualism of their British contemporaries. The French polity seemed to them to have inherited such a fragile and divided nation that social stability rather than individual rights took first claim on their attentions. This was not unreasonable from their perspective, but it led them to a series of political positions and alliances that isolated them from the sort of popular support that would have been necessary to translate liberal instincts into political influence. Following the collapse of "their" regime in 1848, French liberals were pushed aside first by republicans and then by the Empire: in both cases the renewed emphasis on institutional solutions to social problems placed the spotlight on a debate to which liberals could no longer usefully contribute. After 1871, the one contribution that liberalism might still have made to constitutional debates, through a defense of the rights and liberties of the individual in the face of the assault of republican universalism, was precisely the one that their social conservatism and political marginality inhibited them from making. In these circumstances, the spotlight placed by the Dreyfus Affair upon the defense of rights proved brief and atypical. Despite the legacy of a renewed if temporary interest in rights among politicians of the Left, and the birth of the Ligue pour la défense des droits de l'homme, the central concerns of French political language soldiered on unaltered. It was not until 1946 that the language of rights was once again inserted into a French constitutional document, and only in 1971 did a constitutional court for the first time declare that rights thus enshrined in a constitution should have the status of positive law rather than be regarded as statements of benevolent and general intent.[11]

What was missing, then, in the political language of contemporary France were the central premises, the building blocks of a liberal political vision. The French radical tradition of reflection about the relationship between state and society was dominated by a combination of republican premises and Marxist projections, conflating the capacities of the state and the interests of the individual. Quite absent was the liberal assumption of a necessary and desirable space between the two, between the individual and the collective, the private and the public, society and state. To the extent that political thought in France did treat of this space, it was seen as an undesirable incoherence, a messy and contingent inheritance to be resolved away. The conception of politics as the sphere of activity within which people negotiated their differences without any expectation of fully resolving or ultimately abolishing them, though central to early nineteenth-century liberalism, was missing from mainstream republican and socialist thought. In these circumstances the unconcern for rights made perfect sense—rights being precisely those concepts that persons in society claim in their protection, to fill the gap between the desirable and the real in public affairs.

Between this etiolated quality of modern French political thought and the moral condition of politicized intellectuals there was a close and influential link. When Marcel Péju published his lengthy analysis of the

11. See Jean Rivero, *Les Libertés publiques* (Paris, 1974), vol. 1, *Les Droits de l'homme*, 96–141.

Slánsky trial he took care to claim that "liberal thought," in contrast to that of the Marxists, was inherently mendacious and mystificatory, unable to confess to the gap between its principles and its practices and thus in no position to criticize such gaps in others. Like Louis Dalmas a few years before, he was willing to find offense in Communist actions but *not* on liberal grounds, vitiated by the hypocrisy of Western behavior.[12] This obsession with "unmasking" the "false" morality of liberalism runs like a thread through the writings of the postwar years.[13] Péju and his contemporaries took it for granted that if there was a gap between the proclaimed intentions and actions of a Western thinker or politician, this could only be because the person in question was either the victim of an illusion or else just lying. That the human condition might simply entail such imperfections, that the "hypocrisy" in question was the homage of vice to virtue rather than evidence of a pathological social condition, was not an explanation many found appealing.

What was thus effectively excluded from the progressive intellectual's epistemological universe was the category of "liberal intellectual," occupying the political and social space between a utopian future and a nostalgically reclaimed past. Such a space did not exist in France. For this the Left was not wholly to blame.[14] Ever since Dreyfus, and following Maurice Barrès, the nationalist Right had treated the term *intellectual* with contempt, reserving it for their opponents on the Left, who in turn were happy to adopt it for their own. Moreover, Left and Right alike shared a vision of the intellectual as someone defined by a search for truth in abstractions; distaste for the confusions and realities of public life; and fascination with the exotic, the aesthetic, and the absolute. It was precisely such a view of the intellectual that would lead Sartre and his generation to seek to merge and lose their identity as intellectuals in the great flow of History. What neither Left nor Right could readily imagine was the notion of an intellectual attracted to the untidiness and the compromise of liberalism or the defense of the individual and individual rights for their own sake. From the point of view of Sartre, for whom pluralism was the very source of alienation, the problem and not the solution, this was absurd and could only describe a hack, a servant of the

12. Marcel Péju, "Hier et aujourd'hui: Le Sens du procès Slánsky," part 1, *Les Temps modernes* 90 (May 1953): 1777; and Louis Dalmas, "Réflexions sur le communisme yougoslave," part 3, *Les Temps modernes* 55 (May 1950): 1970.

13. See, for example, Jean-Paul Sartre, *Plaidoyer pour les intellectuels* (Paris, 1972).

14. Although it was Jaurès who was perhaps the first to treat of "right-wing intellectual" as an oxymoron.

dominant ideology. And in that case the person in question was not liberal but conservative, reactionary. Or, more precisely, conservative *because* liberal.

Absurd or not, liberal intellectuals nonetheless existed. But they subsisted in a variety of ways on the fringes of French intellectual life—as Catholic novelists and theologians like Mauriac or Maritain, as heirs to the French moralist tradition of Montaigne and La Bruyère (Paulhan being perhaps the best-known example), or as outsiders like Raymond Aron and his circle. On the face of it, the suggestion that Mauriac, Paulhan, and Aron were outsiders or marginal may sound foolish. But I do not wish to suggest that they were unknown or unread. By marginal I mean something different; they were not in a position to form or shape intellectual practices and opinion in these years but were instead forced to respond to them. A substantial part of the journalistic output of Mauriac and Paulhan, of the essays and books of Aron in the years 1946–56, was devoted not to presenting their own opinions but to refuting the opinions and behavior of others. Indeed, some of their most interesting and influential writings from this period were composed in response to the ideas of their opponents.[15] It is well known that whereas Aron read Sartre with care, the latter strenuously ignored his former friend for the best part of three decades. Within the intellectual community, genuine liberal thinkers like Aron devoted a disproportionate amount of their enormous talent to pointing out, again and again, the errors and failings of others. This is a worthy undertaking, but it is almost by definition a secondary, subservient condition.

Indeed, the liberal intelligentsia in postwar France was exotic in a very precise sense. Among the contributors to liberal journals and revues like *Preuves* or *Liberté de l'esprit* there was in these years a disproportionate presence of foreigners. Sharing space with Aron or Claude Mauriac were Denis de Rougemont, Ignazio Silone, Nicola Chiaromonte, Manès Sperber, Czeslaw Milosz, Mircea Eliade, Stephen Spender, Karl Jaspers, Bertrand Russell, Sidney Hook, Arthur Koestler, E. M. Cioran, Konstanty Jelenski, and many others.[16] Paris was still the natural magnet for

---

15. See, among others, Raymond Aron, *L'Opium des intellectuels* (Paris, 1955); and Jean Paulhan, *Lettre aux directeurs de la Résistance* (Paris, 1952).

16. See Pierre Grémion, "*Preuves* dans le Paris de la guerre froide," *Vingtième Siècle* 13 (January–March 1987): 63ff.; Arthur Koestler, *The Trail of the Dinosaur* (New York, 1955); and Sidney Hook, *Out of Step* (New York, 1987). Of notable interest are the works of Manès Sperber. See, in particular, *Et le buisson devint cendre* (Paris, 1949); *Porteur d'eau* (Paris, 1976); *Le Pont inachevé* (Paris, 1977); and *Au delà de l'oubli* (Paris, 1979).

exiles of all sorts, from McCarthyite America, Communist Central Europe, or authoritarian hispanic dictatorships. Many of these people were former Communists, and they would be joined by others in the course of the 1950s. This made them especially well informed and clear-sighted about Marxism and its political consequences, but it did not assure them an audience. On the contrary, in the atmosphere of the time (everywhere in the West, but especially in Paris), their views and arguments were polluted by their origins, by their experience, and by their present political affiliations. The fact that Milosz, for example, could undertake a devastating psychological analysis of the Communist mind from within did not make him more authoritative in the eyes of those he sought to convince; on the contrary, his very insight and knowledge rendered him suspect.

More than their anticommunism, it was the very cosmopolitanism of their origins and interests (including their frequent advocacy of the idea of a federal Europe) that made of these liberals something especially alien. The obsession with "Frenchness"—French problems, French values, French debates—that had marked the Uriage circle of 1940 continued unabated into the postwar years, so that liberalism and *its* language and concerns, which were anyway peripheral to the dominant local traditions, became something even more distant and inaudible. It is no accident that the major French liberal thinkers of these years published and taught abroad as much if not more than in Paris and were better known to an international audience than they were at home.

Furthermore, the postwar obsession with History, with the need to align oneself with the forces of progress and action, the premium placed on success and on victory (in battles real and imaginary alike), gave to liberalism an inevitably woebegone air. An emphasis on rights or freedom for its own sake has a necessarily defensive character, and for the many different reasons discussed in earlier chapters, most postwar intellectuals sought to identify with change and the offensive. Modern intellectuals of the Right, from Drieu to Roger Nimier, were losers, aesthetic anarchists at war with themselves and the world, out of step even with their political allies. Those like Raymond Aron who sought to stake out the middle ground were thus vulnerable and isolated, sharing much of the cultural and philosophical formation of their opponents on the Left and very little of the asocial solipsism of their allies on the Right. Under different circumstances, their natural interlocutors would have been people like Merleau-Ponty, just as François Mauriac might at other times have had more common ground with Mounier. As it was, despite being engaged in their own way, they lacked firm footing in an intellectual community for whom, as Rougemont noted in his *Journal,* engagement implied "enrollment."[17] Their emphasis on the need to treat critically of *both* sides in the Cold War while still choosing the lesser evil, on the importance of defending simple principles and accepting the complexity and inadequacy of a society based on the balance of competing interests, was too thin a gruel for the nutritional needs of most progressives. Most of the latter, once the initial aura of postwar hopes had disappeared, were more concerned to denounce the world than to change it, so that the practical and programmatic aspect of liberal thought was yet a further factor separating the two sides.

The later influence of Raymond Aron in particular should therefore be set aside, if we wish to understand the situation in these years. There was more to intellectual life in postwar France than the self-regarding progressive community discussed in this book, but theirs was the dominant voice, theirs the terms of reference and debate. Just as Aron's liberalism would finally flower in his own land after a delay of nearly three decades, so Sartre and his contemporaries were themselves the beneficiaries of a *décalage,* a time-lapse that brought to the forefront of French intellectual life a set of concerns, including the distaste for liberalism and all its works, that were shaped and nurtured in the interwar years. Even Aron and his circle had been influenced by that experience to the point that independent thinkers like himself or Ignazio Silone were sometimes reluctant to think of themselves as "liberals," with all that implied of empiricism, philosophical naiveté, positivist optimism, and political failure. As early as 1947 Silone was to speak of his regret at having been too willing to place on the shelf certain principles of liberty and human dignity, conceding terrain to the claims of history and realism, a confession later echoed by a small army of conscience-ridden intellectuals—Albert Camus, Edgar Morin, Maurice Merleau-Ponty, Pierre Emmanuel, and many others.[18] But at the time, even for individuals whose whole public identity would later be shaped by a commitment to the most liberal of moral stances, liberalism was at best a troublesome friend.

17. Denis de Rougemont, *Journal d'une époque, 1926–1946* (Paris, 1968), 370–71.

18. Ignazio Silone, "Sur la dignité de l'intelligence et l'indignité des intellectuels" (speech given at International Pen Club conference, 5 June 1947), *Les Temps modernes* 23–24 (August–September 1947): 409.

CHAPTER THIRTEEN

Gesta Dei per Francos
The Frenchness of French Intellectuals

<table>
<tr>
<td>Ce n'est pas qu'il y ait chez nous beau-
coup moins de sots qu'ailleurs. Mais
même nos imbéciles sont, je crois, mieux
avertis que ceux des autres pays. L'air
qu'on respire en France, l'atmosphère, est,
si j'ose dire, une atmosphère critique.</td>
<td>It isn't that we have fewer fools than
anyone else. But even our fools are, I
believe, better informed than those
of other countries. The atmosphere
in which we breathe in France is,
dare I say it, a critical one.</td>
</tr>
</table>

François Mauriac

The circumstances and attitudes described in this book are peculiarly French. The history of Parisian intellectuals in the postwar years, their collective myopia in the face of Stalinism, is distinctively and unmistakably a French history. But to what extent, in what respects, is it *uniquely* French? In the terms in which I have discussed the intellectual community after 1945, the historical, circumstantial, and personal issues that helped define postwar political engagement were all rooted in the local experience; but some of that experience was common to other countries and other cultures. The impact of World War I on liberal society, the appeals of fascism and communism, the illusions and disillusions of the thirties, World War II, Occupation, Resistance, purges, and the Cold War are part of the history of modern Europe and marked the memory and behavior of men and women everywhere. The moral and political dilemma posed by Stalinism in postwar Europe affected intellectuals in every land.

Furthermore, the capacity to respond to this dilemma in strange and ethically incoherent ways was by no means confined to the French. Such respected denizens of a liberal culture as Bernard Shaw or the English historian G. D. H. Cole wrote the most awful drivel in defense of the Soviet Union. It was Shaw who announced that workers in the Soviet Union *loved* their Stakhanovite, shock-working comrades, whereas the English proletariat would quite properly oppose any such practices in *their* factories; Cole, in a pamphlet published as early as 1941, maintained that sovereign states that proved unable to defend themselves in war had no right to exist. It would be better, he said, to let Hitler keep all of Central and East Europe than to reestablish the little nation-states there; but best of all would be to allow a victorious postwar Soviet Union simply to absorb Poland, Hungary, and the Balkans.[1] Among the successors to these interwar fellow-travelers was another Englishman, Arnold Kettle, who wrote in the *Manchester Guardian* in 1958 with reference to Soviet control of cultural life, "One of the essential differences between a socialist and a capitalist society is that in the former the burden of full responsibility is accepted by its leaders. . . . Responsibility involves error and abuse; but it is nonetheless a higher, more humane attitude than irresponsibility."[2] Sartre said it better, but the argument is identical.

Things were no different among the radical intelligentsia across the Atlantic, where a non-Communist Marxist economist like Paul Sweezy had gone to enormous lengths to explain and justify the show trials in Prague, describing the "violent anti-Zionism" of the Soviet bloc as tragic but inevitable and justified by U.S. actions; Sweezy and a colleague even attempted a quantitative comparison of socialist and capitalist violence, from which they concluded that the USSR and the Peoples' Democracies

---

1. See Paul Hollander, *Political Pilgrims* (Oxford, 1981), 139. G. D. H. Cole, *Europe, Russia, and the Future* (London, 1941), quoted in Serban Voinea, "Satéllisation et libération," *Revue socialiste* 105 (March 1957): 226.

2. Kettle quoted by Hollander, *Political Pilgrims*, 733.

emerged far superior.[3] Also widespread among Anglo-American intellectuals was the belief that their distaste for Communist practices was a result of their own privileged position. They might not wish to live under communism, but they wanted to believe that this was evidence of their own weakness, not of communism's defects. This was a widespread point of view in the thirties, but it can be found as late as 1977. Thus Mary McCarthy mused on the charms of post-Stalinist Communist life:

Socialism with a human face is still my ideal. Living under such a system would require quite an adjustment, but it would be so exciting I hope one would be willing to sacrifice the comforts of a life that one has become extremely used to. I think that the excitement would make all the difference.[4]

Whatever else may be unique to the French, we may thus conclude, idiocy is universal. But this does not resolve the question. As important as the opinions themselves is the way in which they are expressed, the numbers of people expressing them, and the status and influence of those people within their community. Here the French circumstances are rather special, for reasons that have to do both with the general condition of postwar France and with some inherited characteristics of the French intelligentsia.

Ever since the eighteenth century, the French intellectual (to employ a convenient anachronism) has displayed certain distinctive traits. This is not the place to discuss in detail the plausibility of traditional and modern accounts of those characteristics; for our purposes it is enough that they were widely believed to exist. Foreign observers, notably the English, took a special delight in mocking the French; Dr. Johnson in 1780 wrote of his contemporaries south of Calais, "A Frenchman must be always talking, whether he knows anything of the matter or not; an Englishman is content to say nothing, when he has nothing to say." Johnson, like so many eighteenth-century Englishmen, is a hostile witness, but had he known of the opinions of M. Béat-Louis de Muralt, writing a half-century earlier, he might have been comforted in his prejudices. Reflecting, like Johnson, on the differences between the French and the British, Muralt suggests that one feature in particular distinguished his own countrymen: "Style, whatever it expresses, is an impor-

3. Leo Huberman and Paul Sweezy, "On Trials and Purges," *Monthly Review*, March 1953.

4. Mary McCarthy, quoted in Paul Hollander, *Political Pilgrims*, ix. There are echoes here of Norman Cameron, writing in *New Verse*, 11 October 1934: "I believe that Communism is necessary and good, but I'm not eager for it." Quoted in Hynes, *The Auden Generation* (London, 1976), 154.

tant thing in France. Elsewhere, expressions are born of thoughts . . . , here it is the reverse; often it is expressions that give birth to thoughts."[5]

This is more than just a witty aphorism; the importance of rhetoric and style in France are incontestable, shaping thoughts and ideas under an unquestioned discursive authority, in contrast with England, for example, where the vernacular and the literary had merged into a rich but open, almost anarchic language. With rhetorical primacy there came abstraction, a power attaching to language and concept independently of the thing they sought to express or describe. Some such process affected other languages—German, perhaps Italian; but France, French ideas, and the French language were exponentially more important (in the eighteenth century especially), and the power of discourse and those who practiced it was further reinforced by the presence of a strong central authority of an altogether more mundane sort.

The relationship between the intellectuals and the powers in France was shaped by the pervasive role of the state in national life, before the Revolution no less than after it. The intellectual Enlightenment in France can be thought of as a mostly one-sided conversation between philosophers, journalists, and others on the one part and the royal power on the other. Replacing the Church as the counterweight to the secular authority, writers and others discovered their public identity in the act of criticism, representing the interests of the people, of humanity, or simply of reason to a government reluctant to listen or understand. From early on, therefore, French thinkers were accustomed to address themselves to the state and to see themselves as intermediaries between the latter and the rest of humanity. In most of the rest of Europe, with the partial exception of Vienna under Joseph II and Berlin under Frederick the Great, there did not exist a sovereign power both strong enough to act and willing to listen (or at least to allow the expression of opinion). In Britain, once again the natural point of comparison, the question of power, institutions, and forms of government and the law had been resolved at an earlier date. "Intellectuals" in Britain addressed themselves to one another, to an emerging social audience, or to specific issues on which they were critical of the performance of the authorities. They never coalesced into a common body defined negatively by its critical stance towards the status quo.

5. "Le Stile, indépendamment de ce qu'il exprime, est une affaire importante en France. . . . Ailleurs, les pensées font naître les expressions . . . , ici il arrive le contraire; souvent les Expressions font naître les Pensées." Béat-Louis de Muralt, *Lettres sur les Anglois et sur les François* . . . (1728; reprint Paris, 1933), 261.

The French, by contrast, were squeezed into an uncomfortable corner. Addressing themselves to the state in their desire for reform or change, they were of no direct concern to it, posing no immediate social or political threat. It was therefore during this period, in the generations before the Revolution, that French thinkers acquired the habit of proud marginality, of seeing themselves as a counterestablishment of the mind, organized into sociétés de pensée, académies, and cercles—ever more radical in their dissent as their impotence and ineffectuality became more marked.[6] The true comparison is thus not between French thinkers and their homologues elsewhere in Western or Central Europe, but between the intelligentsia in France and that which would form in nineteenth-century Russia, *mutatis mutandis*. The difference in France was that the intelligentsia was concentrated in a capital city of international importance and benefited from the accident of a major political upheaval, the Revolution of 1789, which preserved the centralized state but made of it an interlocutor much better adapted to the theoretical and political concerns of the intellectual community. In post-Revolutionary France, that is to say, the intellectual-as-critic could now be both in opposition to authority and a vital part of the political system itself. Even more than in the Ancien Régime, those who were the most critical of the state and its acts now looked to that same state to transform itself and the society it ruled, and in doing so they inevitably became ideological collaborators in the struggle for power, "state intellectuals" even in their opposition. Under the old monarchy, writers could occasionally aspire to align themselves with the state, to lose their isolated and marginal position through some form of intellectual employment or service, resulting, as Bourricaud puts it, in "all sorts of coy flirting with an authority empowered to dispense favors."[7] Now those same *"coquetteries"* were elevated from professional service into ideological and party-political identification, a relationship offering less pecuniary reward but much greater psychic satisfaction.[8]

6. On public opinion in the eighteenth century, see Keith Michael Baker, "Public Opinion as Political Convention," in Baker, *Inventing the French Revolution* (Cambridge, Eng., 1990); on prerevolutionary "political societies," see Reinhart Koselleck, *Critique and Crisis* (Cambridge, Mass., 1988), and more generally Ran Halévi, "L'Idée et l'évènement: Sur les origines intellectuelles de la Révolution française," in *Le Débat* 38 (January–March 1986).

7. François Bourricaud, *Le Bricolage idéologique: Essai sur les intellectuels et les passions démocratiques* (Paris, 1980), 45.

8. See the interesting summary of Augustin Cochin's account of the eighteenth century's "surinvestissement idéologique" in sociétés de pensées, académies, and so on, by Blandine Barret-Kriegel, "L'Écologie française du Stalinisme ou l'homme idéologique," in Evelyne Pisier-Kouchner, *Les Interprétations du Stalinisme* (Paris, 1983), 335. For Cochin, see François Furet, *Penser la Révolution française* (Paris, 1978), part 2, section 3.

The implications of this steady politicization of intellectual life in France and its tendency to absorption in the imagining of projects and counterprojects for the state were obscured and postponed by the institutional instability of the first two-thirds of the nineteenth century. But in the Third Republic, and with the growing security of the professional and commercial classes from which the intelligentsia was mostly drawn, the self-conscious and self-ascribed role of intellectuals reemerged in its recognizably modern shape, located for the first time within certain parts of the university and producing the "dissident state employee," natural heir to the eighteenth-century *pensionnaire*.[9] In this respect the Dreyfus Affair is a truly telling moment, not so much in the well-known sense in which it helped create the modern idea of the engaged intellectual, but rather in the ways in which intellectuals chose to understand that engagement. There were many who agreed with Émile Durkheim that while scholars and writers had a "strict duty to participate in public life," they should participate *qua* intellectuals rather than suborn their actions and writings to the needs of the moment or party politics. What they had to offer, in other words, was not merely assistance to the cause of justice or support for the defenders of the Republic but a vision of society, of the ways in which the inadequate present might be rendered into a better future. Even for those who did not share Durkheim's critique of modern society, with his dream of seeing contemporary anomie overcome in a fully "integrated," conflict-free world, the image of the engaged intellectual bringing to the community a wholly articulated moral countervision was very attractive. Like Durkheim, many intellectuals (and not just those in socialist circles, such as Jaurès or Lucien Herr) treated the tensions and conflicts and defects of contemporary France as contingent, pathological deviations from something better and possible that it was their special task to articulate. Their disillusion and redirection in the political aftermath of the Affair is well known (the case of Péguy was only the most famous), but the style of intellectual engagement was firmly established.[10]

The most remarkable feature of this style is the *confidence* with which intellectuals in France inherited and adapted their self-ascribed role as the moral arbiters of the nation, a sort of parallel state inscribed with the same authority and responsibility as the real one. From Jules Simon and his

9. On this and the more literary counterculture of conservative intellectuals, see Christophe Charle, *Les Élites de la République* (Paris, 1987).

10. Steven Lukes, *Émile Durkheim: His Life and Work* (Stanford, 1985), 331.

notion of the "secular preacher" to Jean-Paul Sartre and literature as the "subjectivity" of a society in permanent revolution, the heirs to Voltaire were remarkably consistent in their emphasis on the task, the mission of the intellectual.[11] France, of course, could only constitute a partial arena for such aspirations, and most intellectuals, however much they claimed to be engaged in local issues, were in practice concerned above all with thinking for "humanity." (In later years François Mauriac would profess astonishment at the "ministry that our 'thinkers' attribute to themselves; I am impressed at how the occupation of writer confers on its practitioners the right to speak out for humanity as though they incarnated it.")[12] This was a claim made the more plausible because by the time of the emergence of the modern intellectual community, France, thanks to the Revolution, had become a universal model, her experience part of the collective European memory. Being French gave Parisian writers a uniquely dual identity and thus authorized them to bear a special burden. Henceforth, their marginality, their opposition, their elective condition of revolt and protestation within France itself was precisely what elevated and integrated them into a superior, transnational community and defined their cultural significance (in France and abroad); from Dreyfus on, this special confidence of *French* intellectuals would distinguish them from their peers in other cultures. During the 1930s, when English writers experienced for a fleeting moment a similar sense of involvement, of revolt, of importance, they would quite reasonably think of themselves as having somehow become "honorary French intellectuals."[13]

With this confidence in their importance and their right to speak for more than merely parochial interests, the modern French intelligentsia accentuated still further the local cultural habit of rhetoric and abstraction. Émile Durkheim, who did so much to help define the shape of intellectual practice in republican France, was also one of the most astute commentators upon it, noting in *L'Évolution pédagogique de la France* the tendency to the impersonal and the abstract in French thought and seeing in it a distinctively Gallic trait, dating at least to the seventeenth century and attributable in part to Jesuit pedagogical habits.[14] He might well have invoked his own Dreyfusard colleagues as further evidence, since (in contrast with

11. Jules Simon is quoted in Jean-Louis Fabiani, *Les Philosophes de la République* (Paris, 1988), 149.

12. François Mauriac, *Mémoires politiques* (Paris, 1967), 284.

13. See Emmanuel Berl, *Mort de la pensée bourgeoise* (Paris, 1929), 106; Stephen Spender, *The Thirties and After* (London, 1978), 158.

14. Émile Durkheim, *L'Évolution pédagogique en France* (Paris, 1938).

the conservative, literary, and anti-Dreyfusard "intellectuals" around Barrès, Brunetière, and the Académie française) they showed a common temperamental aversion to the concrete, the individual, and the given, preferring to identify their commitment with ideas and social values rather than the disruptive, divisive, and empirical claims of isolated persons, however unjustly persecuted. Like Mounier in later years, Durkheim and his friends had something of a horror of the "individual," preferring instead to think in terms of the more abstract "person."

This genius for abstracting, reifying, and generalizing is what made it possible for perfectly peaceable and gentle men to advocate violence, for persons of moderate personality to see nothing amiss in an admiration for excess, and for clearheaded and gifted thinkers to ignore (or "overcome") simple rules of coherence and logic. Similarly, an accompanying tendency to reason by analogy rather than according to principles of identity and contradiction offered greater opportunities for expansive and imaginative reasoning but at the price of an occasional loss of contact with reality. Thus, to take a single example, Georges Bataille, whose fascination with violence had a strong influence over two generations of writers, would claim of "violence" that it was a moment of excess that called our conventional perceptions, our daily lives, into question; it opened our eyes to the limitations of reason. In his words, "Against the absolute of reason, violence is the other of language."[15] Those who are condemned to silence, whose voice is not or cannot be heard in the usual discourses, must thus use violence to express themselves. Violence, in this understanding, is thus doubly revolutionary: it is the dialectical counterpoint to the imperialism of language, and it is the means of expression of those who are victims of actual imperialism. In the passage from Bataille to Sartre, a witty analogy would become a political slogan.

Closely related to this common skill at manipulating and extrapolating from abstract concepts was the widespread uninterest among French intellectuals during the first half of this century in knowledge of a more concrete or empirical sort. With the important exception of history, the social sciences in France suffered from chronic underdevelopment. The ease with which people would write and speak upon subjects of which they were all but ignorant relieved them of any obligation to acquire detailed information or set it in any disciplinary context.[16] Claude Lévi-Strauss remarked upon this at the end of the thirties, but it was a trait

15. Bataille, quoted in J-M Besnier, *La Politique de l'impossible* (Paris, 1988), 155.
16. See the somewhat disingenuous observations of Régis Debray, *Le Pouvoir intellectuel en France* (1979; reprint Paris, 1986), 104.

even more marked in later decades; anthropology and sociology lacked institutional roots in French academic life and often operated, until the fifties, as little more than aspects of applied philosophy. Economics was another discipline of which most intellectuals were astoundingly ignorant. This was crucial, because it allowed them to take on faith the claims of Marxists and Communists, while they confined their critical attentions to political and philosophical questions with which they felt more comfortable. It might be argued that economics is in principle no less abstract and given to generalization than the older disciplines from which it descends. But economics is about the first-order workings of social systems, the goods they generate, and the ways in which the latter are distributed, rather than about the general principles governing our preferences for one system of authority over another, which was what traditionally interested French thinkers who occupied themselves with such matters.

The study of history was another matter. Indeed, in one respect at least, the French intellectual community was altogether *too* well acquainted with the past, or at least that part of it pertaining to contemporary France. The nineteenth-century interpretations of the Revolution, which had hardened into dogma by the middle of the Third Republic, provided tidy reference points for those who sought, reasoning once again by analogy, to locate their own positions and roles and condemn those of others. In no other European culture were intellectuals so absorbed by the desire to position themselves in relation to a foundation myth, a myth that provided both political and moral coordinates with which to evaluate one's actions and alliances (the fact that the Russian Bolsheviks were similarly obsessed with the French Revolution and its significant turning points is one of the features of Soviet discourse that made it so very palatable to its French admirers). One cannot readily conceive of British writers classifying those who disagreed with them according to political battles dating from the rule of King George III, nor even of Spanish or Italian intellectuals invoking the Peninsular War or the debates of the Risorgimento in defense of their own ethical preferences. But in excoriating Albert Camus for his publication of *L'Homme révolté*, Sartre resorted quite naturally to the charge that his former colleague had "made his Thermidor."[17]

Thermidor, in the French historiographical lexicon, had put an end to the Jacobin terror, and it was the myth of the latter that truly dominated

17. Jean-Paul Sartre, *Situations,* vol. 4 (Paris, 1961), 91.

and distorted intellectual exchange. Terror as an ideal, terror as a method, terror as a regrettable necessity, terror as metaphor, terror in every shape and form permeated intellectual consciousness.[18] Terror, too, was integral to the larger picture of social processes that the Revolution had bequeathed to modern French thought, the idea that all *real* change comes and can only come as the result of a single, clean break. Anything short of such a break was inadequate and thus fraudulent. This obsession with the Revolution disfigured French intellectual life in two ways. It introduced a permissive attitude towards extremist positions of all sorts, just because of their extremism, and it gave hostages to the most radical forms of historicism, especially those that absolved individuals of any private moral responsibility for the era in which history had placed them. It is perhaps for this reason that the French were so vulnerable to the charms of *German* thought. After all, as Elio Vittorini noted in 1957, the French intelligentsia was on the whole utterly impermeable to any foreign influences or ideas and had been so since 1815.[19] The one exception was the often-noted willingness to import and adopt the more radical forms of post-Kantian German Romantic thought. Vittorini offers no explanation for this, but it may not be so very mysterious. The French lacked (and still lack) a theory of their own historicist practices. The general drift of French philosophy since the early eighteenth century has been in directions distinctly at variance with the trajectory of French social thought, not to speak of French history itself. In these circumstances, German thought, from Hegel to Heidegger, has proved extremely serviceable. After all, as Heine noted as early as 1831, "our German philosophy is but the dream of the French Revolution."

The rhetoric of "terror" might have been thought to have exhausted its value after 1945, now that the national community had experienced a real and recent terror of its own. Certainly, the violent language and the aggressive admiration for action and death that so distorted the intellectual exchanges of the 1930s did not recover in quite their old form. But the historical metaphors and analogies were revived and renewed by the postwar vision of revolution and social transformation and reinforced by the Communists' claim to the Jacobin inheritance. Moreover terror, after 1945, was something that one could all the more enthusiastically support because it was now being perpetrated by and at the expense of other

18. See, for example, Maurice Blanchot, "Le Terrorisme méthode de salut publique," in *Revue française,* July 1936.
19. See Elio Vittorini, in *France-Observateur,* 3 October 1957.

people, in far-away countries of which one knew little. The insistence that the Occupation had taught the importance of history made the latter even more central, so that, if anything, the French Revolution as a sort of moral spirit level, a measuring device for choice and judgment, acquired fresh importance. In a political culture sorely lacking in unity or common points of reference, the Great Upheaval of 1789–93 substituted for the social and ideological cohesion to be found in more stable lands, with the result that what united the French was precisely their agreement over what it was that divided them. It was, of all people, Emmanuel Mounier, in one of his lucid moments, who captured perfectly the implications of this heritage for French intellectual life: we French, he wrote in 1944, are well endowed with "private customs" (*des moeurs privés*), but (in contrast with the English) we lack any comparable political ones. As a result we oscillate endlessly between pusillanimity, hesitation—and overexcited fanatical extremism.[20]

So much for the *longue durée*. Of equal importance in shaping modern attitudes was the condition in which the French found themselves in the aftermath of the Liberation. The nation was in a collective depression, divided by remorse and resentment at the memory of 1940. France's own national "retreat from history"[21] during the four years of occupation produced not only an urgently felt need to be once again part of history and at the center of affairs but a special vulnerability in the face of those whose wartime successes and achievements had truly put them in the moral and political vanguard. Thus it was the same syndrome that produced resentment at the all-conquering Americans and assured a nearly unconditional admiration of the Russians and their local Communist comrades. The only active role now open for France, it appeared, was to resist the temptation to become anti-Communist and to refuse the benefits of collaboration with the Anglo-Americans.

At the root of it all was a deep collective sentiment of inferiority, all too easily shaped into an aggressive "nationalism of humiliation," in Alfred Grosser's words. Here there was a curious and unbroken continuity of sentiment between Vichy and the early Fourth Republic, with widespread resentment at the "Anglo-Americans" for once again leaving France to bear the burden of a continental war, while they stepped in to

20. Emmanuel Mounier, "Suite française aux maladies infantiles des révolutions," *Esprit,* December 1944, 30.

21. The phrase is that of Paul Thibaud, "La tragedia dell'Est come terapia democratica," in *Micro-Mega,* April 1989, 67.

reap the benefits. The Anglo-Americans, François Mauriac felt, could be counted on to leave the French in the lurch, just as they had done in 1919. This was his view in 1946, and he returned to it in 1951, noting that during and after the Liberation the Americans and the British treated his country like a "poor relative," taking advantage of its ailing condition to strip it of its few remaining assets (he had in mind the British treatment of the French in Syria). No wonder, he concluded, that some of us dreamt of a rapprochement with Moscow.[22] Mauriac was echoing a widespread sentiment; once the extent of French economic and strategic dependence became clear, after 1946, various opinion polls illustrate clearly the emotions this generated: despite their overall admiration for the Americans in particular as "young, rich, and powerful," the French were increasingly uncomfortable with what they felt was the domineering attitude of those same Americans towards their European partners.[23] In Mounier's words, French freedom and independence were now truly fragile, dependent on "parliamentary relics and American parcels."[24]

This bitterness was universal, so great was the fall. What does it mean now to be French? asked Étiemble in August of 1946: "Seen from a distance, we are just forty million losers."[25] The fact that it was the Western allies who had rescued the French from the grip of nazism made things worse, not better. Despite the heroism of the Resistance and the best efforts of General Leclerc, the French felt doubly humiliated, by 1944 no less than 1940. Sartre was among the first to notice this, describing in the very months of France's liberation how "in the space of five years we have acquired a formidable inferiority complex." Indeed, the rise of Sartre coincided precisely with the eclipse of France, and there is some elegance in this, since Sartre was nothing if not the philosopher of his own inferiority, as an intellectual and as a man, truly the thinker best suited to speak for a nation whose emotional condition he came closest to representing in his own troubled person.[26]

This condition found expression in a number of distinctive and interrelated forms. Of these the most important was the frequently articu-

22. Mauriac, *Journal*, vol. 5 (Paris, 1953), 13 September 1946; *Mémoires politiques*, 288.

23. "Enquête sur les sentiments et attitudes des Français à l'égard des Américains," *Sondages* 2 (January–February 1953): 17–25.

24. Mounier, "Prague," *Esprit*, March 1948, 355.

25. Étiemble, in *Combat*, 18–19 August 1946.

26. Sartre, "La Nationalisation de la littérature," *Les Temps modernes* 2 (November 1945), notably 207–8.

lated fear of declining into the status of a third-class nation. As in the aftermath of World War I, the French were torn by conflicting sentiments: on the one hand the desire to get back to normal, to pretend that things were somehow as before; on the other the silent appreciation that things would never, could never, be the same again. For a few years after 1918 the French could take comfort from their illusory hegemony on the European continent and their apparent immunity to the economic crises affecting their neighbors. No such fantasy was possible in the 1940s. In the words of François Mitterrand, "My sense of belonging to a great nation . . . had been wounded. I lived through 1940: no need to say more."[27] In contrast with the mood of the interwar years, the French were under no illusion as to their condition—while in the heady weeks of liberation, in September 1944, 64 percent of those polled thought France had recovered its place as a "great power," by 1949 less than 37 percent believed this to be so. The military and political elite were just as realistic (in marked contrast to their culpable delusions of a decade earlier), which is why they were willing, after 1947, to commit France to various strategic and economic alliances in which it would not play a dominant role.[28]

The alternatives seemed truly depressing. Writers, generals, politicians, and economists fell over one another during the 1940s to offer grim scenarios for France's diminished future, each choosing a geographical metaphor according to his or her prejudice. François Mauriac agonized over a France reduced to insignificance, "a France sitting quietly between Honduras and the Republic of San Marino";[29] Edmond Michelet, the army minister in December 1945, pressed his case for a larger military budget by warning his colleagues of the implications of inadequate spending on arms and matériel: "We must be careful not to become Montenegro." Two years later, Jean Monnet pressed the case for rapid economic modernization: without it, he advised René Mayer, "we shall become Spain."[30] But modernization was almost as frightening as decline. The very people who most vociferously announced France's impending demise were often to be found rejecting all proposals

27. See François Mitterrand, *L'Abeille et l'architecte* (Paris, 1978).

28. Robert Frank, "Le Dilemme français: La Modernisation sous influence ou l'indépendance dans la décadence," in René Girault and Robert Frank, eds., *La Puissance française en question, 1945–1949* (Paris, 1988), 137–38.

29. Mauriac, *Journal,* vol. 4 (Paris, 1950), 9 March 1945.

30. Michelet and Monnet are both cited in Girault and Frank, *La Puissance française en question,* 139–40. As so often, Monnet's was the more realistic (and more Euro-centered) perspective.

for practical change. What Julien Gracq called "the mood of 'no'" was once again an aspect of Jean-Paul Sartre that faithfully reflected a wider collective refusal to envisage the future. The problem with any project to remake France along lines dictated by efficiency or restructuring was partly that such projects smacked of Vichy (at least in its early, technocratic incarnation), but more that they necessarily implied a certain sympathy for the modern, the foreign, the American way of doing things: an admission of the bankruptcy, in every sense, of the French way. In a culture already deeply insecure, already battered by changes over which it had no control at home and abroad, such proposals were instinctively repelled. Simone de Beauvoir's suspicion of Mendès-France, Roger Vailland's famous outburst against the iniquities of refrigeration, were thus symptoms of a deeper unease.

Hence the reiterated incantations in praise of neutrality. Although political arguments for remaining neutral in the Cold War were mostly left-wing in inspiration, the general national desire to be beholden to neither camp was at least initially common to Left and Right alike (de Gaulle was only the most famous example from the conservative side). The Right disliked the Americans at least as much as did the Left, and the desire to find a basis from which to reassert French independence, to give France an international identity, was by no means uniquely a progressive sentiment. At first, from 1944 until 1948, the French worked hard to create for themselves a space between the United States and the Soviet Union, hoping to be some sort of a bridge holding together the wartime allies while keeping a safe distance from both; writers such as Mauriac could not come to terms with the idea that, trapped between empires, "France would no longer be the nation whose choice defined the spiritual significance of a conflict."[31] Politicians like Bidault and de Gaulle on the one hand, Mollet and Blum on the other, were united in this desire to give France back some such space for choice and influence, which was the primary objective of French diplomatic efforts in these years. Economic constraints, military realities, and disagreements between the superpowers after the unsuccessful conferences of 1947 meant that neutrality for France was hopelessly unrealistic, as Schumann and Bidault came to appreciate. But for the longest possible time men such as Blum tried to prevent the inevitable; witness his speech in the Vélodrome d'Hiver in October 1947, where he argued that the

31. Mauriac, *Journal*, vol. 5, 15 March 1946. See also Anton De Porte, *De Gaulle's Foreign Policy, 1944–1946* (Cambridge, Mass., 1968), 70–72.

French sought instinctively and naturally to avoid association with either camp: "The French people wish to remain themselves." The Communists naturally played on this desire for national autonomy, emphasizing that the USSR's main postwar interest was in sustaining the independence and security of *all* European nations, but in this case they were not necessarily being cynical; Thorez, at the 11th Congress of his party in June 1947, strenuously asserted the need to avoid being forced to choose between two camps, and like many French Communists he was most at ease when pressing the case for French national independence.[32]

More than anyone else, it was the nonaligned intellectuals who yearned for neutrality. Long after Communists on the one hand and Socialists, members of the Mouvement républicain populaire (MRP), and most Gaullists on the other had abandoned the search for a neutral, independent France, and when many were thinking instead of securing France's future through intra-European cooperation, progressive journalists continued to press the case for neutrality. Claude Bourdet, as we have already seen, was in the vanguard of such efforts, closely followed by Mounier and his colleagues at *Esprit*. As late as 1950, Mounier was still denying the need to choose between the United States and the Soviet Union. Both were warlike and dangerous, he insisted—the United States by its very nature, the USSR by its present actions, though he remained optimistic about its future. A third way was not only possible for France, it was the only acceptable way for France and for the Europe whose interests France shared and represented.[33] This yearning for a third way had a distinctive source: in their heart of hearts, French thinkers sought to avoid choosing a camp not merely because they found something unsatisfactory in both alternatives, but because they had already identified and elected to stay with their own camp: France.

But if France was so reduced, if its new-found inferiority was at the heart of the postwar condition, how could "France" be an object of veneration, the measure of intellectual purpose? As Raymond Aron pointed out at the time, "France in its abasement no longer satisfies their appetite for greatness."[34] And yet there was an almost desperate emphasis upon the special

32. Blum is quoted by Lily Marcou, *Le Cominform* (Paris, 1977), 69. For the Communists, see for example Duclos, in *L'Humanité*, 1 July 1948. Thorez's ambivalence is cited in Jeannine Verdès-Leroux, *Le Réveil des somnambules* (Paris, 1987), 233. The French Communists were soon to be brought sharply into line by the Russians at the founding meeting of the Cominform. See Eugenio Reale, *Avec Jacques Duclos au banc des accusés* (Paris, 1958).

33. Mounier, "Journal à haute voix," *Esprit*, January 1950, 131.

34. Raymond Aron, "Politics and the French Intellectuals," *Partisan Review* 17 (1950): 600.

role France and her culture had now to play, and this emphasis makes a curious sort of sense: France's reduced place in the real world in no way inhibited the claim that there was something universal about the nation, its experience, and its role. Echoing the nineteenth-century confidence of a Duruy or a Lavisse, France's cultural elite asserted the special place of their nation, reiterating the special mission of France, the moral center of the world, even as the country itself struggled to catch up sufficiently to remain at best a second-class power. Thus François Mauriac again:

At no time in its history has this great Nation, now so small, been so clearly aware of its vocation; whatever human still remains in the relations between peoples, France incarnates this and knows it.

This was written in December 1945. Three years later Mauriac had not changed his tune; in contrast with Britain, he wrote, France has "a disinterested outlook on the world."[35]

In a similar vein André Siegfried, writing for an American audience, informed his readers that the Frenchman is naturally and instinctively universal in his outlook, he "oversteps the narrow limits of racial or nationalistic prejudices and attains effortlessly [*sic*] a humanist, international concept of man." To the reader of 1991 (American or French) this is mildly amusing, evidence of that "wretched self-delusion" in which some of the French excelled. It speaks to the magnificent confidence of the educated French person, the sense that we *are* "civilization," which was beginning to fracture in the 1930s but whose decline was yet to come. It is what enabled contemporaries to make quite startling claims on behalf of France and Frenchness at the very moment of greatest national self-doubt.[36] Of these claims, four stand out. The first was that France was and remained the natural capital of humanity; the second, that French civilization was "naturally" superior to others; the third, that as a consequence of the first two claims France was an example and a model for all, and the fourth that France's history and role marked it out as a "chosen" nation in an almost mystical sense.

In his classic *Histoire de la France (cours moyen)* Lavisse ends thus: "France is the freest, the most just, the most human of fatherlands."[37]

35. Mauriac, *Journal*, vol. 4, 13 December 1945; *Mémoires politiques*, 272–73.

36. André Siegfried, in Edward M. Earle, *Modern France* (Princeton, 1951), 6. The phrase "assez piètre auto-mystification" is from Michel Crozier, "Les Intellectuels et la stagnation française," *Esprit*, December 1953, 772.

37. Quoted in Paul Beneton, *Histoire des mots: Culture et civilisation* (Paris, 1975), 51–52.

Two generations later, and in the wake of a national disaster even worse than the one that had so shaped Lavisse's own generation, François Mauriac echoed these sentiments almost to the word: "Our country is the most humanist par excellence . . . our moralists carried to perfection that science of man which is valid for all, Christians and unbelievers alike." Mauriac, however, is a troubling witness, since he was given to occasional self-criticism and doubt—one week after writing the lines just quoted, he warned himself and others against ceding too readily to the "dangerous happiness" of indulging in a timeless vision of France. Siegfried, by contrast, had no such doubts; in the work cited above, he announced without shame that "any thought whatever, filtered through the French spirit, thereby receives clarity and order." He would no doubt have agreed with the editorialist in Le Monde who declared, in February 1945, that France is always in the avant-garde of human progress.[38]

If France was the capital of humanity, the repository of values that all could share, then it followed that France was in some sense culturally superior to other nations, its values more than merely parochial, its experience special. This was the second claim that sounded through much postwar writing. This emphasis on the nation's special virtues of taste and intellectual refinement helped compensate for the loss of power and the visible hegemony of the Americans. In Crozier's ironic commentary of 1953, "We may be in a malaise, yes, but other nations are so ridiculously unsophisticated, they know so little about living well, that one can always reflect that it is we who are the lucky ones." As Mauriac was to write a few years later (but with absolutely no irony intended), the United States suffers from "excess in all matters, which is the thing most alien to our own spirit." Like Malraux, he scorned the mere "mercantile" culture of the Americans; at issue here, however, was not just American inferiority but the naturally privileged status of the French. Likewise Julien Benda, proposing a common European language, took it for granted that this language would be French. After all, according to Jacques Chardonne, "only the French know what prose style is."[39]

Third, France, in this perspective, was more than simply a special and

38. Mauriac, Journal, vol. 4, 21, 27 March 1945; Siegfried, quoted in Earle, Modern France, 15. For the editorial in Le Monde for 1 February 1945, see Paul Sorum, Intellectuals and Decolonization in France (Chapel Hill, N.C., 1977), 32.

39. Mauriac, in L'Express, 29 August 1959, quoted by Michel Winock, in Nationalisme, antisémitisme, et fascisme (Paris, 1990), 70; Julien Benda, "Une Conscience européene est une chose à créer," La Nef 24 (1946): 12; Jacques Chardonne, Lettres à Roger Nimier (1954; reprint Paris, 1985), 8.

privileged case of humanity; it was the very exemplar from which others could yet derive hope. France, Mauriac believed, would save what remained of Europe from the infernal circle of technology and destruction (Heidegger, of course, had briefly held out similar hopes of Nazi Germany). Should France fall short in this task, should it ("the most human of lands") fail, "on that day humanity will truly have entered the age of the termite." This curious projection onto France of all manner of apocalyptic hopes suggests a distinctive echo in Mauriac of the Gallicanism that so shaped the thinking of his ancestors: a nation somehow transubstantiated, an object of faith and veneration in its own right. Camus was thinking along similar lines in 1947, though for different reasons and in less apocalyptic terms: "France, today, lacks the resources of its capacities . . . this is an opportunity . . . our country can still be an example." On all sides there was a common agreement that France (and therefore French thinkers) had a unique historical vocation, a special duty towards other, lesser nations: to teach them how to live. For these reasons France must never, wrote Albert Bayet, be satisfied with mere survival: "Let us understand that a France that was merely cautious, however prosperous in a bourgeois manner, would cease, in its own eyes and those of others, to be France."[40]

Other nations, it might be thought, had more to worry about in 1945 than whether or not France would still be around to set them an example, though French intellectuals were certainly correct to believe in the special place France occupied in Western culture. But Mauriac, Bayet, Camus, and even Siegfried were not really addressing humanity in general: they were speaking to other Frenchmen, via humanity as a whole. This can be seen most clearly in the fourth claim that one finds in these years, the suggestion that France was the chosen nation in one very particular sense. This was the idea that France was somehow a sacrificial victim whose suffering made sense as the price paid for the regeneration of Europe. Again, the outsider may find this wholly inappropriate—if we are to go in search of "sacrificed nations," then Poland, Yugoslavia, the Baltics, even Spain, have a stronger claim than France and are all, along with Jews and Gypsies, ahead of her in the queue for privileged victim status. But none of these, not even Spain, can claim to be a "great" or

40. Mauriac, *Journal*, vol. 4, 15 April 1945; *Journal*, vol. 5, 25 December 1946; Albert Camus, *Actuelles*, vol. 1 (Paris, 1950), 125–26. For Albert Bayet, see his editorial in *Action*, May 1945, quoted in Louis Bodin and Jean-Michel Royer, "Vocabulaire de la France," *Esprit*, December 1957, 673.

"historical" nation, and it was just this fact, the combination of France's importance in the past and her sad condition in the present that made the image of sacrifice and suffering so appealing. Saint-Exupéry had caught the mood as early as 1941, noting, "France has played her role. It consisted in presenting herself for destruction, and then in being shrouded, for a time, in silence."[41] The idea that France was to be redeemed through suffering was widespread among members of the Uriage community, who shared these mystical fantasies with many in Pétain's own entourage. Even after the war, and again with half a nod to the defeatist xenophobia of the Occupation years, the diarist and gossip Jean Galtier-Boissière spoke for many when he fancifully compared France to a human bait dangled before the German crocodile by her allies: "But this time we really almost got eaten, and the hunters took their time in pulling us from the monster's jaws."[42]

France, then, was special, privileged, superior, an example, a victim. But at the same time, as Aron reminds us, France after 1945 was a decidedly inadequate stage for the ambitious intellectual. And so the chauvinist instincts of the national intelligentsia migrated, half unaware, to the side of another, different nation, whose state seemed a worthy vehicle for their own aspirations to universal significance and whose ideology made of it the heir to the erstwhile transcendent standing of France. By championing the Soviet Union, the French bourgeois intellectual overcame his or her provincial irrelevance and once again spoke with and for history, without having to make more than the most superficial adjustments to one's language and assumptions. Once again the universal thinker, the intellectual was freed from the constraints of real French history, even as it was that same history (*dixit* Sartre) that had brought this new consciousness in the first place. The hyperrationalism of the Soviet system, the alliance of philosophy and the state in its highest form, thus exercised a magnetic fascination upon an intellectual community familiar with such relationships in its own culture. The very same cultural superiority and parochial chauvinism that sound so anachronistic and provincial in the writings of Mauriac at this time could be made to sound fresh, radical, and internationalist in the pages of *Esprit* or *Temps modernes* when applied to the claims of the USSR. In short, the complex of motives that led intellectuals in postwar France to reiterate and reemphasize the spe-

41. Antoine de Saint-Exupéry, quoted in Beynon John, "Saint-Exupéry's *Pilote de guerre*: Testimony, Art, and Ideology," in R. Kedward and R. Austin, eds., *Vichy France and the Resistance* (London, 1985), 103.

42. Jean Galtier-Boissière, *Mon journal depuis la Libération* (Paris, 1945), 217.

cial place of their nation not only illustrates the sensitive and insecure mood of the times but also offers a clue to the ease with which, in these years in particular, French intellectuals could look so benevolently upon similar language employed on behalf of the Soviet Union.

What of the rest of Europe? Were the French unique? And if so, in what particular respects? In one sense, the attitudes and "positions" of the French intellectuals *were* shared by intellectuals elsewhere precisely because of the continued importance of Paris as a cultural reference point. Existentialism and its political accoutrements were popular in Latin America, for example, just because they were fashionable in Paris, much as Lacan and Derrida are lionized among American scholars today largely on account of the mistaken assumption that they are important in France.[43] Everyone knew that the debates among Parisian intellectuals were mere matters of fashion. Like Jacob Burckhardt a century earlier, they understood that "after a couple of weeks even the wittiest of books gets abandoned in Paris."[44] But then the New Look was mere fashion too. This was no reason not to adopt such things for oneself. What in Paris was to some extent the product of pure chance was attributed great significance abroad just because of its Parisian provenance. Thus, seen from within, the role of the various new and revived periodicals and the prominence of their young directors and contributors were simply a product of the war and the unusually rapid transfer of intellectual authority to a new generation. Even Simone de Beauvoir, not given to modesty, admits in her memoirs that what looked from a distance like high intellectual polemics were often family squabbles among intimates, blown out of all proportion by outsiders.[45]

Moreover, some of the foregoing observations concerning postwar France apply *mutatis mutandis* to Europe in general. The growing awareness that Europe was no longer the only power nor even the major one in world affairs was a common theme in European political writings of the thirties and was naturally reinforced by the experience and outcome of the world war. Remarks about France and French attitudes in this respect therefore apply to European sensibilities as a whole. Similarly, the

43. See Julian Gorkin, "La Crise des intellectuels et le masochisme communiste de Sartre," *Revue socialiste* 66 (April 1953): 425.

44. Quoted in Marie-Jeanne Heger-Etienvre, "Jakub Burckhardt et la vie intellectuelle française sous la Monarchie de Juillet," in *Paris et le phénomène des capitales littéraires* (Paris, 1984), 166.

45. Simone de Beauvoir, *La Force des choses* (Paris, 1963), 45–46.

specific postwar experience of France was partially replicated in a number of places. Retribution and even *résistantialisme* feature in the postwar experience of Czechoslovakia, Belgium, and Norway, among other places, and Norway (like the Netherlands and Denmark) passed retroactive laws against collaboration remarkably similar to those enacted by the French. Communist parties everywhere played on local sentiments analogous to those displayed by French progressives, and ignorant, hypocritical, or downright idiotic pronouncements were made everywhere, as we have already noted. Closer inspection, however, reveals subtle variations. Whereas British intellectuals in the thirties had often mimicked their French counterparts, and a significant minority of the interwar Oxbridge elite lined up with the Communist party, after 1945 those writers and artists who offered to support or defend Stalinist practices were in fact very few and marginal; in contrast with France, there was nothing about the experience of World War II in Britain that would revive the great cause of the thirties. It is true that in Britain (as in Italy) the caliber of those intellectuals who actually joined the party was superior to that of the French, but their numbers were insignificant, as was the Communist party in Britain, never more than a tiny minority among the political Left. Within the non-Communist Left, apologists for communism like Konnie Zilliacus or John Platts-Mills were expelled from the Labor party and found little support from the progressive intelligentsia. Anti-Americanism in Britain was strong, certainly,[46] but it was balanced by an enthusiasm for things British, especially after 1950, rather than by support for the Soviet bloc. In short, the British intelligentsia, lacking the recent experience and troubled conscience of the French, had less reason to turn away from their local concerns. To be fair, they had never been very cosmopolitan in the first place, so nothing much had changed.

Curiously, the intellectuals of eastern Europe make a better comparison. Like their French counterparts, though for different reasons, they had long assumed the mantle of the nation, spokesmen for the culture, the identity, the soul of their land. Indeed the Czech intelligentsia especially embodied on a reduced scale many of the historical traits associated with the French. Havlíček, Palacký, Masaryk, Patočka, and, most recently, Havel were invested by their compatriots with a very special function: they were the source of the young nation's knowledge of itself;

---

46. In the words of one wartime joke: "What's wrong with the Americans? They are overpaid, oversexed, and over here!"

they were its representatives, its "meaning" on a larger, European stage. The same is true, *grosso modo,* of the intelligentsia of most of modern Europe's smaller, newer nations, where the roles of Montaigne, Racine, Descartes, Voltaire, Hugo, Jules Ferry, Jaurès, Péguy, and even Maurras often had to be performed by one person, in sequence or sometimes all at once. What makes the Czechs different, and more interesting for our purposes, is their postwar ambivalence, their sense before and especially after 1948 of the moral ambiguities of their country's recent past and their own place in that past. Munich, the wartime collaboration with the occupying Germans (with certain infamous exceptions the Germans treated industrial Bohemia and Moravia rather well, certainly in comparison with their behavior in neighboring Poland or Russia), the ambivalent attitudes towards communism of the postwar progressive politicians and intellectuals, the retributive purging and expulsion of the Sudeten Germans in 1946, the initial enthusiasm for the Communist coup all make of Czech recent memory something problematic in much the same way that Vichy and the Resistance are troubling to the French. For the "Vichy syndrome" the Czechs can offer "the Munich syndrome"; for overblown *résistantialisme* and overenthusiastic purges, the Czechs can offer the same thing. And more than any other nation except the French and the Italians, Czechs of all classes but intellectuals especially welcomed the Russians, the Communists, and the promise of revolution.[47]

This said, the analogy, though revealing, has its limitations. Certainly, Czech thinkers too were disillusioned with "bourgeois democracy" and the memory of its prewar failure. Like Milan Šimečka, many of them could have said that they knew it chiefly through literature and thought of it as stupid, barbaric, and finished.[48] But the Czech intelligentsia were to experience liberalism's totalitarian heir in their own land; resistance, compromise, collaboration, violence, moral cowardice, and so forth were lived categories, experienced in relation to communism. In France, the war once over, these were abstractions or metaphors to justify support of actions and ideas being practiced at the expense of others far away. Thus, although we may say that the history of recent Czech literary and intellectual life does indeed suggest that there was nothing

47. See Bernard Michel, *La Mémoire de Prague* (Paris, 1986); Jaroslav Seifert, "Writers as the 'Conscience of the Nation,'" comments delivered at the Second Writers' Congress, Prague, April 1956, in *Kosmas* 4, no. 2 (1984); Viktor Mamatey and Radomir Luza, eds., *A History of the Czechoslovak Republic, 1918–1948* (Princeton, 1973).

48. See Milan Simecka, *The Restoration of Order* (London, 1984; orig. *Obnoveni poradku,* Bratislava, 1984).

intrinsically unique about the range of behavior associated with French intellectuals, in practice the different postwar circumstances of the two cultures make the reference opaque. Finally, although it is true that the very insignificance of their national base and the provinciality of their language and history made Czech intellectuals notably cosmopolitan and universalist in their aspirations, the sheer world-historical significance and cultural centrality of France distorts all comparisons. From a sidelong glance at Czech history we learn that many of the attitudes and failings attributed to the French were indeed widespread in Europe. But in order to go beyond this we need to look elsewhere. A closer and perhaps more telling comparison is that with Italy.

It is the similarities between French and Italian postwar cultural and political history that are initially most striking. All the debates and problems, the hypocrisies and dishonesty associated with France's recent past and the official treatment of that past have their almost exact equivalent in the Italian experience, from the incomplete postwar purges to the recent debate over the extent and nature of resistance during the liberation of Italy from fascism. The same exaggerations and distortions on both sides of the debate, and the same motives, personal and political, lie at the heart of these national dilemmas in both countries. The Italian intellectuals too underwent a retreat from Marxism in the later 1970s, generating for the first time in more than three decades open and honest discussions about the meaning and value of freedom and human rights. For the first time in thirty years, according to one scholar, these things could be discussed in Italy "without illusion or demagogy" (senza mistificazione e demagogie).[49]

But it is not simply that the memory (and mismemory) of the recent past is a problem common to both sides of the Alps. The history itself, the thing remembered, is remarkably similar. The Italians too were living down an era of authoritarian rule, as a result of which there was a premium placed on antifascism and on a language that emphasized notions of resistance, commitment, radicalism, revolution, and the like. The Italian Communists, like the French ones, could legitimately claim to have played a central role in the anti-Fascist struggle, and this gave them a unique moral authority for many—especially in view of the starkly clerical element in the major party of the center-right. The short-lived Parri government of 1945 proposed a thoroughgoing purge of Fas-

---

49. A. Bruno, *Marxismo e idealismo Italiano* (Florence, 1979), 99–100.

cists and their supporters as a prelude to Italy's postwar moral and material reconstruction, but the Christian Democratic government of the following year suspended the trials of Fascists and collaborators. Partly as a result of this many intellectuals formerly attached to Parri's Action party switched their affiliation to the Communists in disgust at the emerging postwar compromise. In short, the Communists in Italy, perhaps even more than in France, were the residual legatees of anti-Fascist sentiment and were able to play on this theme so as to imply (again, as in France) that anticommunism was tantamount to philofascism.[50]

Moreover, Italy was also liberated by foreign (Anglo-American) armies, and anti-Fascist sentiment there too would be transformed into anti-Americanism with remarkable ease, at least among intellectuals. The Communists—Italian, revolutionary, and proletarian—exercised a fascination similar to that of their French comrades, trading on the "need for certainty" that so characterized the intellectual mood of the postwar years.[51] Their very dogmatism was seen by some as a virtue— Alberto Moravia in 1944 described communism as the natural and proper heir to Catholicism—although the rigidity of the anti-Communist coalition and the presence in it of former Fascists inhibited many (including even men like Ignazio Silone and his group around *La critica sociale*) from openly attacking the Partito Communista Italiano and its Soviet allies. If anything, the ignominious collapse of liberal Italy twenty years before, the collaboration of monarchy and church in Mussolini's regime, the fact that Fascism had lasted a generation in office, and that the Communist party claimed plausibly to be its only continuous organized opponent all gave to the PCI a special cachet that even the PCF could never attain.[52]

The Italian postwar intelligentsia was thus under considerable pressure to identify with the history, the aims, and the program of the Communist movement, and the PCI was quite successful in securing real intellectual support, more than in France and of a distinctly higher

50. See Nello Ajello, *Intellettuali e PCI, 1944–1958* (Rome, 1979), 79ff. See also, but from a prejudiced perspective, Paolo Spriano, *Le passioni di un decenno, 1946–1956* (Rome, 1986); and Gian Carlo Pajetta, *Le crisi che ho vissuto: Budapest, Praga, Varsavia* (Rome, 1982).

51. Giorgio Petracchi, "Russofilia e russofobia: mito e anti-mito dell'URSS in Italia, 1943–1948," *Storia contemporanea* 19, no. 2 (April 1988): 241.

52. Alberto Moravia, *La Speranza, ossia cristianesimo e communismo* (Rome, 1944). Contrast this with Moravia's later writings, such as "Il cucolo communista," *Il mondo*, 4 February 1950; and *L'uomo come fine e altri saggi* (Milan, 1964).

caliber, in and out of the party. One reason for this was the very different nature of the Communist leadership in Italy. In contrast with France (or Britain and elsewhere) Italian communism was founded and led by educated, cultivated people who could address themselves to the concerns of the national intelligentsia in its own language. Italian intellectuals were thus not forced to apologize quite so insistently to themselves or the world for the behavior and writings of their local Communists. But one should not exaggerate this difference. Like the PCF, the PCI was obliged to follow the Moscow line, especially from the autumn of 1947, and communism was as ideologically monolithic in Italy as anywhere else. Whatever compromises were entailed in identifying with the Communist movement were in principle the same in Rome as in Paris.

This said, the Italian context was different in certain subtle but important ways. Whatever ambivalence Italian intellectuals might have felt about liberalism had been diluted by a long experience of fascism, the longest in Europe; whereas in 1925 the progressive intelligentsia had little nostalgia for the defeated political system of Giollitian Italy, by 1944 the terms of reference had altered. A new generation had emerged for whom, even if liberalism was not the solution, it was fascism and fascism alone that was the enemy, together with its craven allies in the old institutions of monarchy, church, and aristocracy. Second, the Italian intelligentsia, although it undoubtedly told self-serving stories about the Risorgimento and even about its own significance within the anti-Fascist coalition, never had, concerning its own identity and importance, the sorts of illusions and expectations vested in French intellectuals and *their* past. It lacked a single gathering point: Turin, Milan, Florence, Rome, and Naples all competed at one time or another for the role of national cultural capital. It lacked a single institutional base: the Italian university was geographically and structurally diverse, with no undisputed hierarchy of status or function. And it lacked a common audience. Many of its most important figures were from the geographical periphery—the South, Venetia/Friuli, the Islands—so that intellectual life in Italy never acquired that hermetic, self-referential, introverted air which so distinguishes that of the French.

What all of this meant, in brief, was that the national intelligentsia of Italy did not set itself tasks and burdens in the manner of the French (or the Russians, Czechs, and Poles). Furthermore, its concerns were distinctly at variance with those of the French. Most Italian intellectuals at midcentury were ex- or neo-Croceans, marked by a tradition of idealist philosophy and historicist thought dating back to Vico. Benedetto

Croce was no liberal, but he eschewed the sort of solipsistic metaphysics that shaped French thinking in the same years.[53] From Croce, through Gramsci, and on to the postwar generation of Della Volpe and his peers, Italian philosophy, Marxism included, was dominated by a search for the Archimedean point from which it would be possible both to have knowledge of the human condition and to have grounds for acting so as to change it. The early Sartrian option ("on s'engage et puis on regarde") and the waffly personalism of Mounier and company were no solution to this sort of question, which is why Italian intellectuals took Marxism much more seriously, even from outside the Communist party.[54]

In addition, Italian intellectuals were far more open to foreign influence of various kinds (in this as in other respects, the intellectual histories of Italy and France faithfully echo general characteristics of the story of both peoples). The interest in other cultures and their products is reflected in the special Italian enthusiasm for reading material in translation, which meant that much more was available to Italian readers, especially in the initial postwar decades, than was placed at the disposal of French ones. Cut off by twenty years of fascism, young Italians were hungry for news and views from the outside, whereas the French at precisely this time were turning in on themselves and reasserting their own cultural primacy. The Italians, never having been able to claim an equivalent universal status, had no such sense of loss. Even the dominant Crocean tradition worked against provincialism, since not only was it parasitic upon other traditions in other countries, but it provoked in reaction a desire among young Italian scholars to learn of different approaches and interests, so as to escape the constrictions of their local cultural monopoly. All in all, the Italian intelligentsia, fearing provincialism, looked abroad and beyond its own inherited concerns. In this it was also assisted by certain peculiarities of the Communist party itself.

53. See Norberto Bobbio, "Benedetto Croce e il liberalismo," in *Politica e cultura*, ed. Norberto Bobbio (Turin, 1955), 211–68.

54. See Sergio Bucchi, "I filosofi italiani negli anni 1945–1970," in *Lettera dall'Italia* 11 (1988); and Richard Bellamy, *Modern Italian Social Theory* (Stanford, 1987). Writing in 1956, Carlo Cassola declared, "Gli intellettuali della mia generazione che sono diventati communisti nel corso della Resistenza . . . provenivano tutti da una esperienza crociana. Ora a mio modo di vedere nel comunismo essi hanni portato non l'esigenza liberale . . . ma piuttosto lo storicismo assoluto, e conseguemente una forma di totalitarismo mentale." ("The intellectuals of my generation who became Communists during the Resistance . . . all came from a Crocean background. Now as I see it they brought to communism not liberal expectations but rather an absolute historicism, and consequently a form of mental totalitarianism.") See Ajello, *Intellettuali e PCI*, 9.

The most important consequence of the higher general level of the PCI leadership was a wider latitude allowed intellectuals who came within the orbit of communism in Italy. Thus, the doctrinal journal *Rinascita*, although it faithfully followed the Soviet line, would allow the occasional piece by a nonconforming author, something unthinkable in these years in any French party publications. When François Fejtö published his study of the Peoples' Democracies, it was ignored or angrily condemned in the French Communist press, whereas the Italian Communist reviewers were more nuanced, never resorting to accusations that Fejtö had joined the club of Koestler, Rousset, and Kravchenko, and so on.[55] *Il Politecnico*, the periodical directed by Elio Vittorini, which in some respects performed functions comparable to those of *Temps modernes* during the late forties but addressed a wider audience, engaged in a number of open debates with Togliatti and other Communists on issues ranging from socialist realism to the "two cultures" and beyond. Even if the PCF leadership had been capable of debating with someone like Merleau-Ponty, it is unthinkable that they would have agreed to do so, especially in the Cominform era.[56]

These differences were illustrated at the time of the trial of Traicho Kostov in December 1949. The French Communist and fellow-traveling press either ignored Kostov's brief, courageous retraction or else exploited it to show how free and spontaneous the trial really was. The correspondent of *Unità* (the PCI daily), Carmine de Lipsis, not only reported the incident in full but was one of those present who raised the issue at the post-trial press conference in Sofia and sought "clarification."[57] The point is not that the Italian Communists ever openly dissented from Moscow; they did not (nor could they) and within the party, Togliatti ran an organization as centralized and rigid as that of Thorez. But on issues likely to touch the sensibilities of his progressive intellectual allies, Togliatti ensured that his party presented a consistently more palatable image. One factor was his decision (the "svolta di Salerno") to give the postwar PCI the task of resisting fascism and constructing a stable democracy in Italy, rather than preparing the way to revolution. In practice this had been the postwar strategy of the French Communists as

55. François Fejtö, *Mémoires, de Budapest à Paris* (Paris, 1986), 230.
56. See *Il Politecnico* 16 (January 1946), which reproduced articles by de Beauvoir and Mounier. For *Il Politecnico*, see Franco Fortini, "Che cosa e stato *Il Politecnico*," in *Dieci inverni, 1947–1957* (Bari, 1973).
57. See *The Trial of Traicho Kostov and His Group* (Sofia, 1949).

well, but it had never been as clearly articulated in their pronouncements, so that to be associated with the PCF was always to be aligned in
some way with revolution and against "bourgeois democracy." The Italian Communists, by contrast, could plausibly be seen as the advance
guard of democratic parliamentarianism, so that to be an intellectual ally
of the PCI in postwar Italy carried distinctly more moderate connota-
tions. As a result, fellow-traveling intellectuals in Italy did not feel constrained to offer up the same absurdities as their French colleagues, their
"workerism" was muted (though still audible), and their sense of self-
abnegation altogether less acute. For these reasons, among others, the
PCI did not suddenly fall from grace in the eyes of the intelligentsia at
the news of the 1956 Soviet invasion of Hungary, and Italian intellectuals had less to live down in later years.[58]

Comparison with the contemporary situation elsewhere helps isolate
and illustrate the special circumstances of France. French intellectuals
said and did much the same things as intellectuals in other places, but
their pronouncements carried extra weight. Whatever they said, they
tended to say it more confidently and more often than was the case elsewhere; the ambitious and all-embracing form in which French thinkers
pronounced upon the world gave to their writings a force that was lacking in the more provincially self-conscious work of intellectuals in other
lands. In part this was because the traditional status of intellectuals inside
France conferred upon their pronouncements more domestic prominence, but mostly it was a result of the unique situation of France within
Europe. The already privileged standing of the French in European cultural history was temporarily exaggerated after 1945 by the utter absence
of any countervailing intellectual or artistic authority elsewhere. Germany was in eclipse, Russian and East European cultural life was dev-
astated, Spain was isolated by the regime of General Franco. Britain
was as marginal as ever to European intellectual debates and Italy was
absorbed in its own struggle to recover from a generation of fascism.
Despite France's own decline, it was paradoxically more important, in
proportion to the surrounding nations of old Europe, than it had been
at any time since 1815. Its intelligentsia was thus correspondingly dominant in the life of the European mind and would remain so for twenty
years. In this sense, Mauriac and others were correct to claim for France

58. For the Italian Communists' reaction to the events of 1956, see *Il PCI e la svolta del 1956,* reprinted from *Rinascita* 14 (April 1986).

a special place and unusual privileges, though they were wrong to suppose that this situation would endure.

France thus remained, in Koestler's words, the "burning lens" of Western civilization, giving to the thoughts and deeds of its postwar intellectual elite a disproportionate importance and resonance.[59] The local obsessions of the French thus expanded to fill the European void, transforming peculiarly Parisian debates into universal pronouncements. The circumstances of the time thus worked like an alchemy, converting quantity into quality, making of Parisian intellectual exchanges and opinions something truly significant. The irony is that despite their universalist aspirations—and the cosmopolitan audience for their writings—French intellectuals were peculiarly unsuited for this role. Their distaste for pluralism, for variety and indeterminacy in their *own* community, made them unable to recognize or sympathize with similarly pluralist and contradictory values in the political culture of others, or understand what was at stake in efforts to defend such values. At a time when circumstances favored the claims of French thinkers to speak out on behalf of the human condition, they offered not moral leadership but ideological ambivalence. The natural spokespersons for Western culture at a crucial juncture, they were uniquely ill suited to the task.

59. See Arthur Koestler, "Land of Bread and Wine," in *The Trail of the Dinosaur* (New York, 1955), p. 40 in particular. This essay is a condensed version of two articles that appeared in the *Observer* (London) in February 1948.

CHAPTER FOURTEEN

Europe and the French Intellectuals

The Responsibilities of Power

Dans les années où la peinture était systématiquement détruite en URSS et dans les démocraties populaires, vous prêtiez votre nom aux manifestes qui glorifiaient le régime de Staline. . . . Votre poids pesait dans la balance et ôtait l'espoir à ceux qui, à l'Est, ne voulaient pas se soumettre à l'absurde. Personne ne peut dire quelles conséquences aurait pu avoir votre protestation catégorique à tous . . . contre le procès de Rajk, par exemple. Si votre appui donné à la terreur comptait, votre indignation aurait compté aussi.	During the years when painting was systematically destroyed in the USSR and the peoples' democracies, you lent your name to statements glorifying Stalin's regime. . . . Your weight counted in the balance, and took away hope from those in the East who wanted not to submit to the absurd. No one knows what consequences a categorical protest from you might have had . . . against the Rajk trial, for example. If your support helped the terror, your indignation would also have mattered.

Czeslaw Milosz (Open letter to Pablo Picasso, 1956)

The special status enjoyed by French intellectuals after World War II carried with it peculiar responsibilities. This privilege (or burden) was recognized by French and foreigners alike, although in slightly differing terms. For Parisian writers, it consisted of the duty and the right to speak in the name of humanity, to pronounce upon the human condition and to be understood in this sense even when engaging in apparently local debates. For outsiders, it meant that choices made or refused in Paris would have an impact and receive an echo in far-away places and be read, quoted, and misquoted by an audience far greater than that accorded any other intellectual community. The asymmetry of these perspectives produced a curious incongruity: unrestrained either by political repression or cultural modesty, the French forged a community of words distinguished by its unique mix of political urgency and moral airiness. Risking few consequences for their actions, French intellectuals in the postwar decade suggest a community marked by a shortage of historical gravity. But for their audience, especially the unusually attentive one east of Vienna, every word weighed heavily in the balance.

For the dissident intelligentsia of Europe, France had long exercised a very special attraction; although England was the safest country of exile during the nineteenth century, the secure shelter for defeated rebels from Marx to Kossuth, France was the natural home of the disinherited intellectual. By living in France and addressing themselves to the French in their own language, writers like Heine, Mickiewicz, Mazzini, and Herzen could make their cause known to a wider audience and, through the medium of Europe's common language, make of that cause something universal. The special significance of the French Revolution had given the centrality of France—already an established feature of *ancien régime* Europe—an extra dimension, to which the glittering urbanity of nineteenth-century Paris added a further gloss.

This unique French status might have been expected to diminish with the rise of Germany, the relative eclipse of France (before and after 1914) and the establishment of nation-states in the old imperial heartlands of the continent. The intellectuals of Germany, Poland, Czechoslovakia, Hungary, Romania, and Yugoslavia now had their own concerns, which they did not need to project onto the international stage by way of Paris, and their linguistic and cultural horizons were increasingly bounded more by Berlin and Vienna than by Paris. But the rise of fascism, the extinguishing of democracy through most of central and southern Europe, focused attention once more on France, which in the thirties was again swollen with intellectual and political exiles and émigrés from much of Europe. France too figured prominently in the cultural life even of those Europeans not yet constrained to leave their homeland: with the Nazi seizure of power in 1933 and the Catholic coup d'état in Vienna a year later, Czech structuralists, Austrian logicians, and German aestheticians turned naturally to Paris, which became a sort of clearing house for modern thought.[1]

What was true for professors was no less true for politicians, especially those of the far Left. Thousands of young Central European Communists ended up in France, either by going there directly or else after a stint in the International Brigades fighting in Spain. Anna Losonczy's father (a future victim of the post-1956 repression in Hungary) studied for a year in Besançon before returning to Hungary upon the outbreak of war. Vlado Clementis was active as a militant in the Confédération générale du travail (CGT) at Noyelle (near Lens) on the eve of the war; and Artur London, his fellow victim in the Slánsky trial of 1952, was one of many hundreds of Czech, German, and Hungarian Communists who came to the French Resistance via service in Spain. Laco Holdos went from Franco's prisons to internment in France, thence to Buchenwald as a deported resister, after which he returned to his native Czechoslovakia where he spent years in prison during the fifties as a victim of Communist terror. His trajectory is emblematic but not atypical.[2]

Even after the reestablishment of democracy in Western Europe and the imposition of communism in the East, the special place of France was not lost. Exiles, voluntary or otherwise, found their way to Paris and chose the medium of French and the French intellectual press to tell their story and argue their case. Indeed, in the 1970s and 1980s, the dissident and exiled intelligentsia of eastern Europe would play the role of catalyst in galvanizing and shaping French reactions to events in the Soviet zone.[3] In the forties and fifties, however, their influence was distinctly dimmed, confined to the margins, and ostentatiously ignored by the dominant circles of the time.[4] This raises a curious question. If writers like Milosz, Eliade, and their peers were so unable to convince or influence their French contemporaries of the malevolent significance of the Communist experiment, why did they persist in the effort? In Britain

1. On the emigration of Central-European intellectuals, initially to France and then to the United States or in some cases directly to America, see H. Stuart Hughes, *The Sea Change* (New York, 1975); Martin Jay, *The Dialectical Imagination* (Boston, 1973); and Jay, *Permanent Exiles* (New York, 1985).

2. See Anna Losonczy, interview, *Nouvelle Alternative* 11 (September 1988); Artur London, *L'Aveu* (Paris, 1968); Karol Bartosek, René Galissot, and Denis Peschanski, eds., *De l'exil à la Résistance* (Paris, 1989), 231, n. 5.

3. Jean-Marie Domenach, *Enquête sur les idées contemporaines* (Paris, 1981), 59.

4. "Parlons de tout, sauf de ces choses qui concernent les petits peuples et au sujet desquelles nous avons reçu la consigne de nous taire." François Mauriac, *Journal*, vol. 5 (Paris, 1953), 17 January 1946.

or the United States, the potential audience for such people was always greater, and more sympathetic, just as it was for the liberal intelligentsia of France itself. Considering how few of them took seriously the voices from the East, why were the intellectuals of France always the favored object of attention?

To answer this question is to grasp something essential in the sociology of European intellectual history. When the intellectuals from Poland or Hungary sought to explain to the West why the survival of culture is so crucial in their country, why poetry or music matters so, and why the intellectual is at once vital and vulnerable in the national culture, it was only in France that they found or expected to find immediate empathy and understanding. The magnetic appeal of France for East European intellectuals thus went beyond the accident of exile, resistance, or Latin brotherhood (as in the Romanian case); in Paris, the dissident thinker was in familiar surroundings. It was thus natural for the intelligentsia of half of Europe to appeal to the luminaries of Parisian cultural life—and to take very seriously the response or silence that met their words.

The widespread indifference of French intellectuals to the sufferings of their contemporaries in Prague, Budapest, or Warsaw was a source of special pain not only because of the sense of neglect and isolation that ensued but because here too the French were playing out on a universal register a local drama in which the intellectuals (Communist and non-Communist) of Central and East Europe had themselves only recently engaged. The intelligentsia of this part of Europe had emerged from the war with some of the same sense of urgency and enthusiasm that marked the French themselves. The ambiguities of occupation, resistance, and liberation were not so very different in Czechoslovakia or Poland, and the initial concessions, moral and political, accorded to the Communists mirrored those made (albeit at no comparable cost) in Paris or Rome. Milosz's "Ketman" is Polish, after all.[5] The capacity to excuse the inexcusable, to rationalize the inexplicable, to turn away from the intolerable, was already well practiced in this part of Europe thanks to the German occupation, and there were those in Prague or Budapest who salved their conscience at the sight of Stalin's victims with arguments that would have been familiar to Sartre, Mounier, or Bourdet.[6] But in the Communist states there was the real and present threat of arrest, imprisonment, and worse, a balming thought with which those of

---

5. Czeslaw Milosz, *The Captive Mind* (New York, 1953), chapter 3, "Ketman."
6. See Karel Kaplan, *Dans les Archives du Comité central* (Paris, 1978), 65.

uneasy conscience would later salve their memories. No such excuse could be offered for those in Paris who made the same mistakes.

Here, once again, there entered the problem of asymmetry. Eastern European intellectuals had long known all about France, as they knew all about Germany, England, or Italy.[7] Western European culture was *European* culture; Western European political history was the spinal column of the continent's past, whereas the cultural and political monuments of the other half of Europe lay hidden from view. East European intellectuals treated Voltaire, Diderot, Balzac, Hugo, and Anatole France (not to speak of Robespierre, Blanqui, and Clemenceau) as part of their *own* cultural baggage; but the converse was never the case, and they knew it.[8] The secondary, marginal status of the cultures and peoples of East Europe was a painful truth but an accepted one. So long as the poets, musicians, novelists, and philosophers from Vilna, Lvov, Prague, Budapest, and Bucharest could enter into the universe of the French, they forgave the intellectuals of Paris for their failure to make equivalent gestures in response. But what characterized the situation after 1945 was precisely this, that the French closed the intellectual frontiers. The community of the universal intellectual was redefined to exclude those who were victims of Stalinism, consenting or otherwise. Eastern European writers understood this too—as noted above, they had themselves at first been tempted to make similar distinctions. What seemed unforgivable and inexplicable was the failure of the French to see what they—Poles, Czechs, and others—now saw. For the intelligentsia of Europe's eastern half was now doubly excluded: deprived of its own national culture by the Communists and forbidden entry into Europe's universal culture by the latter's own accredited guardians.

Hence the embittered, resentful, saddened tone with which East Europe's intellectuals spoke of and to the French, even as they persisted in the effort to capture their attention. Some of this tone can be attributed to political memories of prewar political betrayal—it was Edouard Benes who announced in October 1938, "In the eyes of history my great error will have been my loyalty to France."[9] But for the most part, the phenomenon is essentially that captured by Milosz as early as

7. See Milosz, "L'Occident," in *Preuves* 33 (November 1955).

8. As Jeannine Verdès-Leroux remarks, *Les Lettres françaises* was more widely read in East Europe than it was in France, and more influential. See *Le Réveil des somnambules* (Paris, 1987), 330–31.

9. Benes quoted by Jean-Baptiste Duroselle, *La Décadence, 1932–1939* (Paris, 1979), 364.

1951 in *The Captive Mind*: the syndrome of "disappointed love." It is the sense of injury, of pained surprise at Western Europe's blissful indifference to the fate of its eastern neighbor. Does Europe not realize, wrote Mircea Eliade in 1952, that she has been amputated of a part of her very flesh? "For, . . . all these countries *are in* Europe, all these peoples belong to the European community." The appeal is addressed to "Europe," but the intended audience is unmistakably French. Many years later Milan Kundera made an almost identical point:

Having for a long time been the nerve-center of Europe, Paris is still today the capital of something more than France. Unfortunately, I think it is the disappearing capital of a disappearing world.

No less than Milosz a third of a century before, Kundera's appeal is marked by "a great sum of disappointments and a remnant of hope."[10]

The curious similarity of mood and language that unites Czeslaw Milosz's complaint of 1951 with Milan Kundera's lament published in 1984 points to a remarkable continuity in the relations between French intellectuals and their homologues to the East. If anything, the situation deteriorated after 1956. Until then, French and other Western intellectuals were speaking essentially the same language as the dissidents and exiles from the people's democracies, even though they were using it to say diametrically opposite things. Both sides (indeed *all* sides) were obsessed with the problem of communism and debated the future of humanity in terms of that problem. Even the anti-Communist community took seriously the claims of Marxism, paying it the compliment of constant critical analysis. And eastern Europe was on everyone's agenda, even if, once again, for rather varied reasons. In the debate over Stalinism, labor camps, and show trials, history was the common medium of exchange that linked French intellectuals with intellectuals elsewhere, even as it divided them.[11] If their moral message was not understood by the West, the intellectuals of East-Central Europe could at least take some comfort in being at the center of their opponents' attention.

After 1956, however, following the discrediting of Stalin and the occupation of Hungary, communism, and with it the credibility of Marxist language and categories, lost its grip on the imagination of the Central European intelligentsia. At first heroic, then destructive, it had

10. Eliade, "Examen leprosum," *Preuves* 14 (April 1952): 29 (emphasis in original); Milan Kundera, *Lire* 101 (February 1984): 36; Milosz, "L'Occident," 9.

11. Pierre Grémion, *Paris-Prague* (Paris, 1985), 65.

now become simply repressive, the ordinary form of inefficient, corrupt, sterile totalitarian power. Revisionist intellectuals like Kolakowski gave up the effort to speak to the regime in its own voice and left its ideologues to their own Orwellian devices. This process unfolded at varying rates, most rapidly in Poland, slowly in Czechoslovakia, for reasons having to do with the initial degree of enthusiasm and terror in each country. With the Warsaw Pact invasion of Czechoslovakia in August 1968, communism, and with it the socialist dream itself, lost its final foothold in the erstwhile leftist intelligentsia of eastern Europe, leaving behind a wasteland of cynicism that would eventually and slowly be replaced by a new generation of opponents whose arguments were grounded not in a humanist socialism but in human rights and the demand for a state of law.[12]

In the West, however, and especially in France, events took a different turn. There, too, communism began to loosen its control on the utopian imagination, its appeal polluted by Khrushchev's revelations and the sight of tanks in the streets of Budapest. But the declining charms of Muscovite communism in the West were not accompanied by any diminution in the status of Marxism, nor in any loss of affection for the radical vocabulary that had carried the hopes of the postwar Left. East and West thus began to diverge abruptly, to the point that the Dubček reforms of 1968, the "Prague Spring," met uncomprehending, even hostile reactions from some sections of the French Left.[13] Nor did the French or other Western intellectuals pay very much attention to the "normalization" that followed Dubček's fall; only after 1974, and then for reasons of their own that had little to do with the course of events in the Soviet bloc, did the Parisian intellectual community once again begin to look eastward, this time with a modicum of sympathy if not understanding.[14]

The years 1956–74 thus represented a lost opportunity for French intellectuals. Starting from a shared premise—that November 1956 marked the end of an era in which communism had dominated the radical imagination—they moved not closer to their eastern European

12. See Tony Judt, "Dilemmas of Dissidence: The Politics of Opposition in East-Central Europe," *Eastern European Politics and Societies* 2 (Spring 1988).

13. Thus certain members of the Parti Socialiste unifié, on the Prague reformers: "Victimes consentantes des idéologies petites-bourgeoises (humanisme, liberté, justice, progrès, suffrage universel secret)"; see A. Badiou et al., *Contribution au problème de la construction d'un Parti marxiste-léniniste du type nouveau* (Paris, 1969), quoted in Grémion, *Paris-Prague*, 79.

14. See Tony Judt, "The Rediscovery of Central Europe," in Stephen Graubard, ed., *Eastern Europe . . . Central Europe . . . Europe* (Boulder, Co., 1991).

audience but further away, to the point of losing all contact with a large part of their international constituency. In 1956, French intellectuals thus parted company from much of the rest of the European intellectual community at just the moment when they could still have reasserted their leadership, in East and West alike. By the time Sartre went to Prague in 1963 and sang the praises of socialist realism to an amazed audience of Czech students and intellectuals, themselves about to embark on the movement leading to the reforms of 1968, the rupture was complete.

To understand why the years 1956–74 represented a lost opportunity, we must take a closer look at the *way* in which French progressives broke with the promise of communism and the reasons for their move towards the non-European world, towards *tiers-mondisme,* instead. It is not easy to be precise about the moment at which communism lost its appeal. At the level of individual choice such disillusion can be dated variously from 1918 to 1989. But there is little doubt that between the death of Stalin, the uprising in Berlin, the rehabilitation of Tito, the Secret Speech, and finally the invasion of Hungary, a qualitative shift took place within the collective consciousness of the European intelligentsia in general, the French in particular. In 1955, Raymond Aron, always a shrewd observer, noted totalitarianism's declining charms—it could retain its hold on those already seduced but found fewer neophytes.[15] Since seduction, political or otherwise, depends for its success on confidence as much as on charm, the significant factor was probably communism's *own* loss of confidence, which can be dated to the years between Stalin's death and the fall of Imre Nagy. In France, this coincided almost exactly with the growing prominence of a new and largely unrelated issue, that of decolonization.

We have already had occasion to note that a concern for developments in the Maghreb and elsewhere was being expressed in the *Combat* of Camus and Bourdet as early as 1947. *Les Temps modernes* began to take up the issue after 1950, and there were sporadic articles in *Esprit* throughout this period. But for most people it was the bloodshed in Morocco in 1953, followed by the catastrophe of Dien Bien Phu, which brought the problem of France's colonies to the fore. François Mauriac, for example, blamed his initial failure to take note of the conflict in Madagascar and developments in Africa upon his earlier obsession with the Communists

15. Raymond Aron, "Les Intellectuels français et l'utopie," *Preuves* 50 (1955): 13.

and his support for the MRP. But the coup in Morocco changed all that—"from then on I was committed."[16] In this case the growing problem in North Africa abruptly redirected Mauriac's attention away from the Communist threat, which had dominated his political writings for the previous seven years. For others the process came about in the reverse order: released in 1956 from the need to define all their engagements in relation to the PCF and Moscow, they could give their full attention to the emerging nationalist movement in Algeria, the about-turn in Guy Mollet's policy, the humiliation of Suez, and the moral dilemma posed by the actions of the French army.

Whatever the sequence, the outcome of this shift in concerns was to turn the attention of the French intellectual community away from the Soviet Union and its eastern satellites and towards the colonial crisis. It does not minimize the significance of the Algerian problem, nor the moral crisis arising from the use of torture on captured Algerian nationalists, to note that this newfound interest in the colonial condition had the advantage of directing interest away from communism at a convenient moment. Any serious debate over the meaning of communism after 1956 not only would necessarily have entailed some difficult soul-searching for those who had defended or justified Stalin's practices, but would have placed on the agenda both the status of Marxism itself as a political theory and language and the legitimacy of the French Communist party, still the dominant force within French Left politics. In the declining months of the Fourth Republic, however, the theory and practice of communism (past and present) were set aside, their place taken by the more pressing and transparent issue of an incipient civil war.

Part of the appeal of the colonial question was that it posed seemingly straightforward moral choices, in contrast to the complex, opaque ones associated with communism. Radical politics, public engagement, and a clear conscience all seemed to dictate firm opposition to the practices of the colonial state, although the special status of Algeria made the extreme solution—independence—unpalatable to otherwise well-intentioned spirits like Camus. Ambiguities that would surface in retrospect (the internecine squabbles of the nationalists, the doubtful wisdom of openly advocating military disobedience, and others), were ignored by many at the time, giving to the struggles and alliances of the years 1954–62 a simple and unilateral meaning they never really had. Moreover, Algeria's peculiar symbolic place, at once a crisis of domestic

16. François Mauriac, *Bloc-Notes, 1952–1957* (Paris, 1958), 13 October 1955.

politics and a harbinger of the coming conflicts of decolonization, made of it for engaged intellectuals an ideal exit from the Communist imbroglio. Involvement in the heated discussions over France's North African policy served at once as a retreat to national concerns and a bridge to a renewed internationalism, distinctive and satisfying.

The insertion of the Algerian episode between the philocommunism of the years 1945–56 and the *tiers-mondisme* that marked the sixties places a question mark over François Furet's otherwise elegant encapsulation of this matter: "The mystery of life was no longer buried in Billancourt, it would have to be sought in the *Tristes Tropiques*."[17] Between the quiet abandonment of the "party of the working class" and the uncritical championing of peasant radicalism in the Third World there was a space, filled by the passage of time and the failure of the PCF to keep abreast of its intellectual constituency. For one of the important side-effects of the Algerian episode was that it revealed the inadequacy of the PCF when faced with the challenge of mobilizing and leading dissent on this issue. The Communists' unwillingness to take a clear and radical stand over Algeria forced previously sympathetic intellectuals to find alternative criteria for engagement, displacing the PCF and its claim to speak for a constituency of workers, and substituting the indigenous and colored peoples of the world for whom intellectuals could speak without having to pass through the party. This process can be seen at work in the pages of *Les Temps modernes* during the course of 1960–61, coinciding with the visit of Sartre and de Beauvoir to Cuba in spring of 1960 and preceding by a few months Sartre's famous preface to Fanon's *Les Damnés de la terre*,[18] and is confirmed in numerous accounts from the time. The interest in China developed by Claude Roy is to be explained, he wrote, by his desire to escape the "stench" of Stalinism. In various sequences, Roy and his younger contemporaries moved from Algeria to Cuba, thence to China, Vietnam, Cambodia, and, in some instances, the Palestinians.[19]

The unifying theme here is the escape from Europe, sometimes literally. Whether expressed as a simple desire to associate with the rising nations of the non-European world, or more radically manifested in the denial of European values and the conscious adoption (at a distance) of the goals and practices of anti-intellectual terror in China or Cambodia, this *tiers-mondisme* also reflected a refusal to confront the continuing

17. François Furet, in *Le Débat* 50 (1988): 13.
18. Jean-Paul Sartre, preface to Fanon, *Les Damnés de la terre* (Paris, 1961).
19. Claude Roy, *Nous* (Paris, 1972), 488.

story of European communism, in France or elsewhere. Whether it also constituted a change of direction within the French intellectual community is another matter. To the extent that *tiers-mondisme* required of intellectuals that they turn a blind eye to terror or persecution, it hardly differed from the price extracted from fellow-travelers in the forties and fifties; there had been a "cultural revolution" in Czechoslovakia in the early fifties, when intellectuals and "bourgeois" had been expelled from their homes in the cities and forcibly deported to the countryside, and there was to be another in 1970.[20] If there was a difference it was this: in order to live with the turbulent news from eastern Europe it had been necessary to deny it, to manipulate and launder it. In the case of the Third World, however, many French and other European intellectuals positively gloried in the news of violence, persecution, and poverty coming from Latin America, Africa, and Asia; it took altogether less dissimulation and self-delusion to justify the sufferings of non-Europeans.[21]

In 1956, then, there began not so much a major shift in mood as a transfer of allegiances. The Communist question was not engaged, much less resolved: it was abandoned. Only in the mid-1970s, when the revolutionary appeal of the non-European world had itself run into the ground, did the attention of the intellectuals return to Europe. In doing so it was inevitably brought face to face with the enduring Communist legacy in the other half of the continent; only then, and only in part, was the agenda of 1956 taken up and addressed. The close association between disillusion with the utopia of peasant revolution and the first stirrings of anti-Marxism in formerly radical circles illustrates the point.

It is sometimes suggested that the Algerian crisis was indeed a turning point (and the years 1956–58 thus of enduring significance) because it brought to the arena a new generation unaffected by the trauma of the Occupation and the succeeding years and thus able to effect a true shift in French intellectual concerns.[22] Like much else in the recent prosopography of French cultural life based on the category of generations, this is either self-evident—each succeeding cohort naturally brings a new set of concerns and experiences to the fore—or else it is made to

20. For a personal account of the so-called "Operation Seventy Thousand must be productive," see Jo Langer, *Une Saison à Bratislava* (Paris, 1981).

21. For a rather overstated account of this syndrome, see Pascal Bruckner, *Le Sanglot de l'homme blanc* (Paris, 1983).

22. See, in particular, the work of Jean-François Sirinelli, "Générations intellectuelles," *Les Cahiers de l'IHTP* 6 (November 1987); and Jean-Pierre Rioux, "La Guerre d'Algérie et les intellectuels français," *Les Cahiers de l'IHTP* 10 (November 1988).

carry too great a burden of explanation. After all, there had been new generations before the Algerian one; the "Hussards" around Roger Nimier in the early fifties reacted against the then-dominant *résistantialisme* by resorting to an apolitical nihilism, skeptical of all authority and commitment. Why was *theirs* not the moment of change, the point at which postwar concerns gave way to newer, less ideologically charged ones?[23] The "Algerian generation" was perhaps fortunate, both in the moment of its appearance and the moral clarity of its cause, but to see it as a major turning point is to concede rather too much. Like the Communists and ex-Communists of the preceding generation, those who came to political awareness with the onset of the colonial crisis had an interest in claiming that something definitive happened in 1956, but the evidence of subsequent years suggests otherwise. At most, we may say that when intellectuals of this period would come to reflect upon their own trajectory, they would find good reasons for dating their own illusions or disillusions from this year. But good reasons are not always good history.

To understand the meaning of 1956 in French political culture and in relations between French and other European intellectuals, it is thus perhaps more helpful to ask not what changed but what remained the same. In the first place, the intransigent self-confidence of the postwar intelligentsia survived largely unscathed the experience of the Stalinist years. Were this not the case, the wilder shores of *tiers-mondisme* and Althusserian Marxism of the mid-sixties could never have been reached. The remarkable moral self-assurance behind the idea that *they* were the conscience of humanity continued to inhabit not only Sartre and his friends but even transmitted itself to some of the younger intellectuals of the Algerian generation, for whom an anti-French position at this time could be articulated as a variant and continuation of the anti-Western vocabulary of the postwar decade; in taking a stand over torture, the rights of Arabs, or the claims of colonial peoples in general it was possible to be unabashedly anti-French in the name of a cause over which one need feel no qualms of moral conscience.

Such was not the position of Raymond Aron, François Mauriac, or their successors, who stopped well short of advocating mutiny or seeking a French defeat. But among the signatories of the "Pétition des 121"

23. For the "mood" of the Hussards generation and their attitude towards the engagement of their elders, see "Paul et Jean-Paul," in Jacques Laurent, *Les Années 50* (Paris, 1989), 13–65.

in 1960, encouraging soldiers to refuse to bear arms against Algerian nationalists, were to be found not only the predictable names of Sartre, de Beauvoir, Lanzmann, Claude Roy, Marguerite Duras, and Vercors, but also Pierre Vidal-Nacquet and Jean-François Revel, not to speak of Dionys Mascolo and André Breton.[24] For the Algerian imbroglio also raised new questions. If France was now the aggressor, repressing the legitimate rights and claims of indigenous peoples in the name of higher French interests, what remained of the universal values hitherto associated with the nation? To be a patriot for France in 1958 risked bringing one into conflict with the very goals of human emancipation for which postrevolutionary France was said to stand.

In a curious way, Algeria, far from constituting an insuperable hurdle, thus helped ease the transition away from the previous attachment to universalist projections of a "certain idea of France." The language of liberation, of revolution, was now released from its national shackles and could travel freely, attaching itself to the most exotic of foreign visions. After the adventure of Algeria, which for all its drama was very much an intellectual success, French intellectuals could reenter the international arena, with a renewed sense of the global meaning of their concerns and purged of their earlier sins without having ever had to acknowledge them. The "concessions" (Camus) shown towards foreign lands claiming to realize the intellectuals' own dream were now so far forgotten as to be subject to renewal and rebirth.[25]

The Algerian episode and the domestic constitutional crisis that accompanied it also helped accentuate another long-standing feature of the French intellectual landscape. This was the utter alienation of the intelligentsia not only from the political culture of France but also from the social changes the country was undergoing in these very years. 1956 may be best known for its emblematic status in the history of communism, but it also fell right in the middle of the most complete and rapid socioeconomic transformation France had ever experienced. The modernization of the economy begun a few years earlier was gathering pace; the move from countryside to town was in full flow; the astonishing population boom was working its way through the institutions of education, soon to reach the universities where it would explode; the

24. For details, see Sirinelli, *Intellectuels et passions françaises* (Paris, 1990), 193–224.
25. See Camus's 1955 reply to Domenach's self-satisfied account of his own "liberation" from the thrall of communism, quoted in Eric Werner, *De la violence au totalitarisme* (Paris, 1972), 41.

French economy, and with it French foreign relations, were about to become intimately and irrevocably intertwined with those of the rest of western Europe. Meanwhile the intellectual Left not only failed to account or allow for these developments, it largely ignored their very existence. The hermetic, self-imposed isolation of many intellectuals in these years is quite remarkable, allowing them to proceed on into the sixties and even beyond as though nothing had altered, at home or abroad. François Bourricaud has described this rather well. Writing of Simone de Beauvoir and her recollections of the years 1956–62, he comments:

One is struck by the sort of alienation in which the existential-Marxist mandarins lived these years. France repelled them, and unable to be real rebels, they felt like outsiders.[26]

It is thus not really surprising that the "liberation" from communism associated with 1956 in popular memory was followed by few serious attempts to come to grips with the meaning of the Stalinist episode. Quite the contrary—most of those who took the opportunity to part company with communism, either by leaving the party, or in the case of nonmembers by loosening the bonds of their support for it, simply breathed a sigh of relief and moved on to other matters. If the editorial in the December 1956 number of *Esprit* announced that "we should go back and seek out the root of the evil in the very origins and principles of Communist society," the recommendation was not taken up. As the same writer went on to remark, the revolts in Poland and Hungary have freed *us* [*sic*] from a stifling embrace: "Our common captivity is at an end"; whereat the Poles and Hungarians were left to their own devices and the newly liberated readers of *Esprit* looked to fresh pastures.[27]

Such insight as was forthcoming in the months following Budapest was mostly kept private. Jorge Semprun, who could legitimately claim to have placed his life on the line, and not merely his conscience, acknowledged the point many years later:

What was intolerable was to have lived in the frozen light of that schizophrenic faith, in an aberrant and emasculating division of one's moral and intellectual conscience. The secret report released us, it at least gave us the chance to be freed from that lunacy, from that sleep of reason.[28]

26. François Bourricaud, *Le Bricolage idéologique* (Paris, 1980), 191.
27. Editorial, *Esprit*, December 1956, 775.
28. Jorge Semprun, *Quel beau dimanche* (Paris, 1980), 318.

Even so, there were those who might well have chosen to remain in the fold had the French Communist party not been so obtusely determined to refuse all debate, to deny all the evidence, including that released by the Russians themselves. The Italian example undermines the comforting fiction that all men and women of goodwill broke with the faith in these years; by acknowledging and openly discussing the revelations of Khrushchev, the Partito Communista Italiano managed to preserve some of its domestic credibility and a good portion of its intellectual support. It would have taken but little effort by the PCF to restore or retain the allegiance of at least some of its flock. That it was incapable of such an effort says much about the nature of communism in France but is of little credit to its former followers and friends.

The break with communism, which for many simply amounted to the recognition of a state of divorce that they had internalized and stifled for some time, also had little or no impact on the attachment to Marxism, which remained, in Sartre's words, "the ultimate philosophy of our time." French intellectuals continued to take Marxist analysis, especially Marxist economics, on credit; whether the defects and crimes of the Stalinist era were attributable to the pathology of the man or the avoidable errors of the party line, few questioned socialism's claim to promise higher production and a more just and efficient distribution of goods. This too was a brake on critical commentary, since it posited a continuing faith in the evidence of the future and inhibited a full and final departure from the utopian perspective. New journals like *Arguments,* as well as older ones such as *Socialisme ou barbarie,* thus restricted themselves to criticism of the Soviet Union cast either in decaying Trotskyist terms or else shaped by an uneasy moral distaste, logically incompatible with the analytical and historicist language of the critics themselves.

Pierre Emmanuel was therefore mistaken when he wrote, in the heat of events, that the year 1956 was seeing the end of "ideal man," the lifting of the "burden of a Golden Age."[29] What was lifted was one cloud of political illusions; but the assumptions that had shaped them, the intoxicating vision of collective betterment, the benefit of the doubt given to all utopian projects, were hardly dented. The confidence with which such projects would soon be reengaged not only illustrates the limited impact of the events of 1956 but enabled many to turn away from their previous commitments not only without qualms but with the very

29. Pierre Emmanuel, "Les Oreilles du roi Midas," *Esprit,* December 1956, 787.

cleanest of consciences. To have been deluded in the decade 1946–56 was to have made what could now seem to have been a brave choice: those who had buried their doubts and misgivings in order to take the Soviet side in the Cold War could now cast themselves as the reluctant heroes of an impossible situation. Their very responsibility for the crimes of the epoch now became a badge of courage, endurance in the face of a Stalinist challenge revealed in all its magnificent horror. There were many in the years 1957–74 who could console themselves with Pierre Courtade's dismissal of Edgar Morin: "I was right to be wrong, while you and your kind were wrong to be right."[30]

The apparently insouciant ease with which the French intellectual Left thus put the Communist moment behind it was bought at the cost of its credibility and prestige in the rest of Europe. Ex-Communists turned to their academic and professional careers, the intellectual journals found other arenas in which to display their concerns, and the theory and practice of Marxism were diverted into ever narrower and more esoteric paths, finally collapsing into the black hole of Althusserian silences. The French Communist party, its membership and votes steadily declining, lost a generation of young radicals in the years 1957–66 and never recovered. Sartre continued to pour forth a string of absurdities (notably following his visit to Vilna in August 1965), finally breaking with the Communists in 1968, when he could do so on their left and with the support and adulation of a new constituency.[31] The special claims to attention of the French intelligentsia were now channeled through more abstruse media, with Lévi-Strauss, Barthes, Lacan, Foucault, and their heirs replacing the generation of Camus and Sartre. The audience for French thought shifted quite noticeably from eastern and southern Europe to Britain and the United States, where the earlier, self-consciously political engagements of the postwar intellectuals had met less sympathy but which now found in the structuralist and poststructuralist discourse of a new generation a language no less exotically and ambitiously Parisian but easier to assimilate to the apolitical traditions of Anglo-American high culture.

What was lost was the special meaning of the term *French intellectual* in continental Europe itself. It is perhaps true that the uniquely privi-

---

30. Courtade is quoted by François Fejtö, *Mémoires* (Paris, 1986), 216. ("J'ai eu raison d'avoir tort, tandis que toi et tes semblables avez eu tort d'avoir raison.")

31. Sartre is quoted in *Le Monde*, 3 December 1968; see also "Sartre in Russia," *Micro-Mega*, March 1989, 88.

leged place of the postwar French thinker in a ravaged Europe could not in any case be sustained, once the cultural life of Germany or Italy had begun to recover. It might also be added that the dramatic migration to the United States of Central-European intellectuals before 1940 was now bearing fruit in the form of the reexport to their native land of ideas and reputations newly forged in New York and elsewhere. But the failure of the French intellectual community to respond fully and honestly to the events of 1956, the refusal—at least until the later 1970s—to engage in a rigorous self-examination, and above all the ease and speed with which attention was diverted away from the embarrassing legacy of communism within Europe itself all conspired to shake and weaken the affection for France and the faith in French thought that had been the leitmotif of intellectual dissent in Europe until that time.

More than their past errors or their occasional air of overbearing superiority, it was the ineffable solipsism of so many French intellectuals that finally broke their hold on the European imagination. Uniquely, they seemed unable to grasp the course of events. Despite their best intentions, Sartre, Mounier, Merleau-Ponty, and their spiritual heirs did not see themselves projected onto the stage of history but rather saw history reduced to the categories and dimensions of their own intellectual trajectories. Because of their neglectful uninterest in Europe's eastern half from 1957 until the later seventies, French intellectuals in recent years have found themselves discovering truths that had already been self-evident to others for three decades; similarly, Merleau-Ponty's acute self-criticism in *Les Aventures de la dialectique* loses some of its force when we recall that he was revealing weaknesses in his earlier arguments that had long since been obvious to outsiders. In Aron's words:

Merleau-Ponty would like his immediate postwar *attentisme* [vis-à-vis Moscow] to have had its "objective conditions" and wants his present attitude to be seen as a response to altered circumstances. I believe he is mistaken and is confusing the time it took him to understand the situation with a change in conditions.[32]

This chronic inability to distinguish between autobiography and the history of the world afflicts intellectuals everywhere. And it was the very conflation of the parochial and the universal that constituted the special charm of French culture for its foreign admirers. But from 1945 until 1956, the European audience for French ideas and writers could comfort

---

32. Maurice Merleau-Ponty, *Les Aventures de la dialectique* (Paris, 1955); Aron, "Aventures et mésaventures de la dialectique," *Preuves* 59 (January 1956): 5.

itself with the thought that because Paris was concerned with the same dilemmas and choices as everyone else, the peculiar rhetoric and rhetorical form of French self-interrogation was important, and one must listen to, and seek a hearing from, these people. But disappointed love is one thing, heartless abandon quite another. The fantasies and errors of the decade after World War II were common to all, but the trajectory of many of the French in later years was unique, leaving a trail of bitterness and lost illusions whose cost in French intellectual prestige has yet to be fully calculated.

Conclusion: Goodbye to All That?

Longtemps nous n'avons point compris la révolution dont nous sommes les témoins; longtemps nous l'avons prise pour un évenement. Nous étions dans l'erreur: c'est une époque; et malheur aux générations qui assistent aux époques du monde!

For a long time we did not understand the revolution we are witnessing; for a long time we took it for a mere event. We were wrong: it is an epoch, and woe to those generations present at the epochs of the world!

Joseph de Maistre

Time is a distorting mirror. The 1940s and 1950s seem a very long way away, part of another world. The intellectuals of those decades came from a different France. For all their sophistication, they grew up in and responded to a provincial, introverted culture shaped by the Great War and its aftermath. The little world of Left Bank Paris was symptomatic in its way of the France of la Madelon and Clochemerle, a France that was about to transform itself almost beyond recognition and at a pace and in directions beyond the comprehension of most of its own educated elite.

The "Trente Glorieuses" of the French intellectuals,[1] the decades during which they basked in the glow of national and global admiration and emulation, span the years 1945 to 1975; but the leading figures of this generation were all born in the period running from the end of the Dreyfus Affair to the outbreak of World War I, and the culture they represented, the concerns and assumptions that informed their lives, were already waning even as they emerged into the spotlight of their public careers. Sartre, Mounier, and their cohort appear in retrospect as the Indian summer of an older French civilization, their heirs and epigones mere glowing embers in a banked fire.

Furthermore, the revolutions in eastern Europe and the collapse of the Soviet Union have removed and obliterated whatever had remained of one of the main political and ideological pillars of postwar European life. During the seventies and eighties it was still possible to engage polemically with the fellow-travelers of the forties and fifties, calling back across the decades to remind them of their ill-judged commitments and marshaling in evidence the continuing repression of dissidence and opposition within the Soviet bloc. Since the events of 1989 such polemics seem redundant, even ill judged. Who, now, takes seriously the promises of Marxism, the assurances of even modest utopian futures? Yet here, too, the acceleration of history contributes to the hazards of intellectual time-travel: for in France more than elsewhere, it is only very recently indeed that such promises and assurances began to lose their interest. The myth of revolution, the moral leverage of 1917, were alive and well and living in Paris not only in 1956 and 1968, but also in 1981.

It is thus very tempting to treat of the events and people in this book as history, not only in the obvious and respectable sense that they form part of our past but also as something well and truly behind us. The context of the postwar years was distinctive. The intellectual monopoly exercised by *Les Temps modernes* was unique, as its competitors (*La Nef, L'Arche, Terre des hommes,* and many others) fell by the wayside; the special standing of *Esprit* within the Catholic intelligentsia and beyond, with sales in the tens of thousands, was not to be sustained. The intellectual-as-hero is a dying genre and nothing is easier today than to dismiss the experience of postwar French intellectuals, buried under a heap of hindsight, piled high with moral indignation. Few would now dissent from Elio Vittorini (writing in 1958) in his assertion that from 1944 to 1956, all French intellectuals had at least one lie by which they lived and

1. The phrase is that of Jean-François Sirinelli, *Génération intellectuelle* (Paris, 1988), 638.

wrote.[2] But that was then, it is said, and this is now. Taking our cue from Václav Havel, we "live in truth." Things have changed, it is said; we were blind and now we see. The past is another country, and *they* did things differently there.

Things have assuredly changed. Not only is France no longer the center of the world, but claims to that effect are no longer part of the cultural baggage of French thought. Within France the state continues to play an extraordinarily important role in public and private life, but it is now commonplace to hear doubts expressed on the practical wisdom and propriety of allowing it to do so.[3] Accompanying this has been a decline in habits of political thought associated with a strong state, themselves weakened by the collapse of the political party and tradition most closely associated with the concept of the state-as-provider. The tragicomic fall of the French Communist party has had serious and by no means uniquely positive electoral consequences, but among intellectuals it has helped undermine the attraction of appeals to authority (political or ideological), further reinforcing contemporary distaste for grand theories in general and Marxism in particular.

Even if intellectuals had maintained their faith, they would have been hard-pressed to communicate it. The readership of the political press has declined sharply, and the number of newspapers in circulation has fallen steadily; Parisian dailies, numbering ninety in the wake of the great press law of 1881, were at thirty-two in 1946. In the first year of the Mitterrand era they had slipped to a mere nineteen.[4] The "little" journals of the intelligentsia continue to come and go; but no one now waits with baited breath for the latest number of *Temps modernes* or *Tel quel*. As to the periodic efforts of Messrs. Jean-Edern Hallier and Bernard-Henri Lévy to establish glossy journals for the well-heeled thinking classes, these suffer from some of the defects of their postwar predecessors—self-importance, solipsism, and a slavish devotion to intellectual fashion—but lack most of their virtues. Television has perhaps given modern intellectuals more exposure but may thereby have served them ill, revealing to a wider public the faults and limitations of writers whose reputations might have been smaller but stronger in a more restricted milieu. It is not at all clear how well some of the great figures of earlier decades would have fared, condemned to regular appearances on "Apostrophes."

2. Elio Vittorini, in *Tempi moderni* 3/4 (1958).
3. See Pierre Rosanvallon, *L'État en France* (Paris, 1990), notably 9–16, 269–81.
4. Pascal Ory, *L'Entre-Deux-Mai* (Paris, 1983), 47.

Their standing was better assured when their public exposure was restricted to a brief appearance at a Montparnasse or Saint-Germain cafe table, enveloped in cups, paper, and cigarette smoke. In a student generation whose role-models in 1986 were Coluche and Renaud, the place of the intellectual is at a severe discount.

Then again, one must not speak of the intellectual as though this were some sort of timeless entity, Rodin's thinker musing his (or her) way through modern French history, always changing, always the same. The same transformation that passed largely unnoticed by most intellectuals during the fifties and sixties also affected the constitution of their own community, perhaps most of all. This matter has been discussed ad nauseam by its own subjects, and there is no need to rehearse it here.[5] What should be emphasized, however, is how the boom in higher education gave the university teacher back some of the status lost to philosophers and novelists in the years 1930–70. Although there are still today some prominent intellectuals whose renown and income derive largely from their journalism and books, the rise of the social sciences and the expansion of the tertiary sector in education have given professors a new lease on public life. They thus enter the intellectual arena as experts, even if they are then free to express an opinion on matters well beyond their professional range, most commonly in the pages of *Commentaire* or *Le Débat*. This encourages a degree of modesty and care, deriving from the typical professorial sense that it is one's colleagues rather than the world whom one has to convince. It also accounts for the reactions of people like Pierre Vidal-Naquet, Annie Kriegel, or even Pierre Bourdieu to the more traditional "interventions" of Régis Debray, Bernard-Henri Lévy, and their ilk. The former may publish and appear in a variety of different media, but their credibility (and their initial status) remains firmly grounded in an academic discipline, its rules, and its materials. The latter suffer no such constraints, and their casual, amateurish ventures into history, philosophy, aesthetics, or social theory seem superficial and pretentious by contrast.

This marks a distinct change from earlier decades, when the writings of Malraux, Camus, Sartre, Mounier, and their peers, often half-informed, frequently lazy and ignorant, provoked no such rebukes. These were, in the cliché of another time, "master thinkers," and their reflections on justice, violence, literature, capitalism, ethics, and anything else acquired weight simply by being theirs. Like the state, the major figures of French

---

5. See, for example, Régis Debray, *Le Pouvoir intellectuel;* and Alain Finkielkraut, *La Défaite de la pensée* (Paris, 1987).

intellectual life were the natural source of authority and legitimacy; with the decline of the state-as-provider has come the fall of its intellectual *doppelgänger*. In the civil society of today's intellectual community, the market operates with reasonable efficiency and the collective conscience of the elite has been "privatized," with some of the attendant discomfort and insecurity that accompanies the real thing further east. Left to their own devices, intellectuals are thus better placed to retain their local influence if they can point to the imprimatur of quality that comes with institutional attachment and disciplinary conventions. The correspondence between the decline of the great public intellectuals and the resurrection of the professors is thus no mere coincidence.

There have been two other important changes, both of which seem likely to endure. The attractions of violence, the seductive appeal of terror in all its forms, have finally waned. There does not appear to be any single efficient cause to which one can point, this transformation being instead the outcome of accumulated examples and lessons whose message seems finally to have been heard. Once again, however, history can play tricks upon memory. The charms of revolutionary terror did not die with Stalin, nor with Solzhenitsyn, nor even with the decision by post-'68 French Maoists to eschew the model of the Italian Red Brigades. Only between the fall of Pol Pot and the celebration of the bicentennial of the French Revolution did the idea take root that revolutionary terror might be an object of study rather than of emulation or admiration, encouraged by signs that the world's longest-lived advertisement for the efficacy of revolutionary terror was disappearing before one's eyes. There was thus laid to rest a literary and political trope that ran unbroken through French writings from Buonarotti to Sartre, sustained by a sort of scholarly descant chanted by five generations of historians, from Louis Blanc to Michel Vovelle, and given regular empirical credibility by the Manichaean division of French political culture. It is hard now to imagine a return to the almost erotic charge that an earlier generation of French intellectuals derived from their literary and philosophical reflections upon the appeal of violent action. On rereading their collective works, one is struck to see how little Sartre and Malraux have in common with younger writers today, and how much they shared, despite themselves, the sensibilities of Drieu or Brasillach.

The second change is related to the first. François Mauriac was one of many to record the astonishing influence of the Action française upon fifty years of French cultural and political life. Even its opponents paid it the inadvertent compliment of seeing republican politics through the

distorting prism of the lens supplied by the great reactionary journalists.[6] Its prewar influence was comparable to that of the PCF after
1945, and many of the intellectuals discussed in this book passed
through Maurras's movement before settling comfortably into place at
the opposite end of the spectrum. Even Sartre, who did not follow this
pattern, paid indirect homage to Maurras by adapting the latter's categories of "pays réel" and "pays légal," with the interests of the proletariat (as
endorsed by the PCF) standing in for the "pays réel" of Maurras's royalist
imaginings. Action française and Communists alike emphasized not only
change and violence but also commitment, efficacity, and the application of hyperrationality to the critique of public life. For the Communist
party to take the place of a discredited Action française as the institutional alternative to republican and bourgeois uncertainty after 1945
thus made sense, and in this light French intellectual life demonstrates a
continuity and a coherence stretching unbroken from the 1890s to the
1970s. That engaged intellectuals found themselves sometimes on the
Right, sometimes on the Left, can thus be attributed to accidents of
context, a point obscured by the inevitably leftward orientation of
intellectual life that followed the Liberation.

But whereas the Communists replaced the Action française, the two
of them together spanning the entire history of modern French intellectual life (and most of the lifespan to date of the word *intellectual* itself),
nothing has replaced the Communists, and it is not at all obvious that
anything will do so. Both movements, each in its way, assumed a set of
attitudes to France and French history, and a relationship of the intellectual elite to political culture that are now past, beyond recovery. Just as
the Communists appealed to the utopian vision of the nineteenth-
century radical conscience, so Maurras and Léon Daudet exercised a
magnetic attraction upon a class of persons no longer to be found in
French life: lay Catholic thinkers, whether orthodox or dissident. The
demise of the Catholic polemicist has passed mostly unnoticed; but the
absence of any legitimate heirs to the tradition of Bloy, Bernanos, and
Mauriac, although it is a normal and predictable consequence of the
decline in faith and the end of a national political cleavage shaped by religious affiliation, has left a marked vacuum. The determining element in
twentieth-century French intellectual life, after all, was faith, however
defined. The sudden withdrawal of the nation's major religions, secular

6. See Mauriac's comments on 17 February 1946, *Journal*, vol. 4 (Paris, 1950); and
10–11 March 1946, *Journal*, vol. 5 (Paris, 1953).

and Catholic alike, may not have deprived French political culture of its content, but it has largely shorn it of form.

These and other changes have had a more distinctive impact at home than abroad. No one in France doubts that intellectuals are in crisis, uncertain as to their identity, their function, their audience. The attitude adopted towards distant heroes from the past is either critical or at best dismissive, while more recent icons (Lacan, Foucault, Barthes, Derrida, and so on) have lost their charm and provoke little interest. The few domestic intellectuals who still arouse universal admiration are either old (Lévi-Strauss, Levinas), dead (Aron), or foreign-born (Kundera). Curiously, then, it is outsiders who now sustain the myth of the French intellectual. To some extent this was always the case: American, British, and Latin-American writers flocked to Paris in the fifties not, as in earlier decades, to become French intellectuals by some sort of ecological osmosis but simply to ogle the great men (and woman) as they sat and wrote. This exercise in self-denial, the abnegation of one's own culture in preference for an uncritical wallowing in the ambiance of another's, did not usually extend to the importation of French ideas, however. Today, though, things are very different.

In the United States, and to a distinctly lesser extent in Britain, Italy, Spain, and Latin America, the second generation of postwar Parisian intellectuals remains an admired and much-imitated group. Foreign universities are full of professors who not only study the works of Lacan, Foucault, Derrida, Barthes, Lyotard, Bourdieu, Baudrillard, and others, but apply their "methods" assiduously to their own research, in a bewildering array of disciplines. In Britain and the United States there are to be found persons not only calling themselves Marxists (this phenomenon, though rare, is still not unknown in France itself) but grimly clinging to their faith in Althusser and his science. Deconstruction, postmodernity, poststructuralism, and their progeny thrive, however implausibly, from London to Los Angeles. The late-lamented French Intellectual is alive and well and living everywhere . . . except Paris. With this difference: for good or ill, French intellectuals mattered, in their own culture and in the international culture of which it was the center. By contrast, their admirers and imitators, in the English-speaking universities in particular, matter not at all—which is precisely why they are able to continue playing with names and ideas whose time has gone. For them, a "Foucault reading group" not only stimulates the synapses but also simulates membership in an intellectual community of which they were never a part. Like light from a distant dead star, it shines for them even after the extinction of the original power source. But for their Parisian visitors, though, it is surely rather different, and there is something not quite right in the prospect of Jacques Derrida selling his wares on the sun-dappled streets of Irvine, California. It suggests a sort of patronizing self-exploitation, rather as though Maurice Merleau-Ponty had chosen to hawk paperback editions of *Humanism and Terror* among vacationing schoolteachers in an early Club Med.

Even in their frenzy of admiration for things French, foreign intellectuals today are markedly selective. Little attention is paid to Foucault's later concern, for example, with prisoners' or homosexuals' rights, or with Derrida's occasional forays into human rights debates. In part this is because these more recent sorts of political and ethical concerns contradict (to their credit), in their neo-Kantian emphases and their search for criteria with which to evaluate moral and political claims, the aggressively relativist stance with which these writers were first associated and for which they are most admired abroad. But this uninterest also arises from something else. For outsiders, French intellectuals were and are talking heads: ideas and categories that are contingently attached to a sometimes charismatic body but quite detached from the cultural and political context of France. Overseas admirers are thus sometimes at a loss to understand just what all the recent fuss in Paris is about, and why there has been such a rush to abandon old heroes and established ways of thinking; but these matters are rarely allowed to interfere with the imitation and application of timelessly Parisian ideologies and ideas. And thus it comes about that French scholars who travel in Britain, the United States, or elsewhere today sometimes have the uncomfortable sense that they have flown back into their own past, as they encounter critics for whom Sartre was the "conscience of his age," hear historians deconstructing the Middle Ages, meet literary theorists disquisitioning upon the death of the text and late-structuralist feminists sorting society into linguistically gendered spheres. But it is a two-dimensional past, where time and place have disappeared, where the body of French cultural and political life has faded away, and all that is left is a postmodern Cheshire Cat with a Ph.D., grinning.

For the foreigner, occasional forays into the rich treasure chest of French cultural discourse are a cost-free exercise. If we like what we find, we take it. If we find it disturbing, irrelevant, or simply uninteresting, we are at liberty to ignore it and leave it for the French to dispose of as they may. Like the Acropolis in the heyday of the Romantics, France is littered with cultural heirlooms, available for salvage and export by any aspirant professorial Elgin. But for the French, as for the Greeks, these are weightier matters. They are part of the past and *therefore* a constituent element of the present; they cannot be ignored, forgotten, selectively preserved, or given away. So it is with the years 1944–56 in French intellectual consciousness. The verbal actions of Sartre and his peers, the opinions and silences of a generation of Left intellectuals in the era of high Stalinism, are embossed in the collective identity and common memory of the French intelligentsia. Like it or not, and however significant the changes that have taken place, they are part of what it means, today, to be a French intellectual. No less than Victor Hugo's funeral or the battlefield at Verdun, they are a *lieu de mémoire*.[7]

In common with other such national heirlooms, the glory years of the French intellectual community are vulnerable to mismemory, exploitation, neglect, and misappropriation, according to present need. Because of their association with a style of thought and commitment now distinctly unfashionable, the years 1944–56 and the beliefs and writings associated with them are subject to a curious form of amnesia, in which writers fall over themselves to confess how awful things were, how guilty everyone was—and in so doing conveniently absolve themselves, and by implication anyone else, from personal responsibility for what was said or done. This exercise in collective self-absolution is all the more complex because for most intellectuals, this period is one in which embarrassment and nostalgia are mixed in equal part.

The conventional claim, already noted, is that *everyone* in postwar France was swept up into the vortex of communism and the attendant moral ambivalence. These, it is now widely believed, were years in which all young intellectuals were Communist or *Communisants,* so that not only can they not be blamed for having failed to see the light, but they would have been distinctly out of step with their generation (and perhaps the times) had they behaved otherwise.[8] This is a view that is likely to gather force in years to come, as today's leading scholars sit down to write their memoirs and give further credence to the impression that anyone who was anyone was at some time or another in the Communist fold. A random sampling of France's leading historians, for example,

---

7. For this way of thinking about the modern cultural history of France, I am indebted to a conversation with Professor Vinni Datta, of Wellesley College.

8. See the memoirs and autobiographies of Daix, Besançon, and Roy already cited. See also Emmanuel Le Roy Ladurie, *Paris-Montpellier: PC-PSU, 1945–1963* (Paris, 1982); Dominique Desanti, *Les Staliniens: Une Expérience politique, 1944–1956* (Paris, 1975); and many others. Also, in this respect, Edgar Morin, *Autocritique* (Paris, 1958), though in most other ways this is in a class of its own for insight and honesty.

seems to confirm such a reading: François Furet, Jacques and Mona Ozouf, Annie Kriegel, Maurice Agulhon, Madeleine Rebérioux, and Michelle Perrot are just a few of the persons whose early careers would appear to support this version of recent history.

Yet such evidence is misleading. These people were but students at the time, unknown, unpublished, without influence. Their generation, coming of age around 1950, certainly passed through the Communist mill but can hardly be said to represent the intellectual community as a whole, much less to have been an influence within it in the years that interest us here; furthermore, as historians, they do not even represent the community of humanist scholars and students as a whole but are in a discipline that in France as in Britain was peculiarly, perhaps uniquely, vulnerable to the appeals of Marxism in these years. Moreover, as Jean-François Sirinelli has shown, even among students at the École normale supérieure the percentage of party members at the end of the forties hovered around the 15 percent mark, many of them in the scientific disciplines.[9] It was certainly widely *believed* that the rue d'Ulm was a hot-bed of Communist plotting, but that is another matter.

As to the older generation, there too the myth of universal philocommunism is misleading. Most of the prominent intellectuals of the post-war years were never tempted to join the party; the main catchment area for the PCF was the "lumpen-intelligentsia." The sort of apologetics that form much of the subject-matter of this book, too, were the work of a minority. In this case the minority was astonishingly influential, to the point of blotting out of public memory the significant number of intellectuals who never shared the prejudices and blinkers of the editors of *Esprit* or *Temps modernes*. Nevertheless, the others were there, too, and this fact alone weakens the claim advanced by Pierre Emmanuel as early as December 1956; we were sleepwalkers, he asserted, "exuding ecstasy and anxiety," but our excuse is that "not one Frenchman" ("pas un français") remained untainted, uncaptivated by the Soviet mirage.[10] *Pas un français?*

The myth of universal intellectual sympathy for a certain kind of Left line, a sort of collective categorical mistake by France's educated elite, is not confined to those whose own biographies require that they explain themselves thus. The losers of these years, intellectuals outside of the charmed circle and whose impact and influence were at best a function of

9. Sirinelli, "Les Normaliens de la rue d'Ulm après 1945: Une Génération communiste?" *Revue d'histoire moderne et contemporaine* 33 (October–December 1986).

10. Pierre Emmanuel, "Les Oreilles du roi Midas," *Esprit*, December 1956, 780.

their very marginality, have similarly strong reasons to believe that the mood of the times was monopolized by a few dominant ideas and thinkers. In his memoirs, Jacques Laurent finds it convenient to affirm that Sartre "reigned at that time over French thought," a view in which he is supported by Pierre de Boisdeffre, who wrote in the early fifties of the "magistrature intellectuelle" exercised by Sartre and Camus at the time of their famous quarrel, a hegemony to which only that of Malraux in an earlier decade could begin to compare.[11] And perhaps this was true. But like most forms of divine monarchy, Sartre's reign depended in large part on the will to subservience of his subjects. If he and a few others did indeed dominate the scene, we must ask why this was so. The fact alone explains nothing.

This habit of assigning responsibility to the era has evolved into a shorthand, almost standardized version of the modern French intellectual autobiography: depending on his age, the protagonist passes through the thirties with increasing political awareness, drawn to Left or Right by an aesthetic disengagement from the world of the republican bourgeoisie. He (or occasionally she) is brought up short by the experience of 1940, discovering the facticity of life and history. There then follows the Resistance, Liberation, political engagement on the intellectual Left, and steady disenchantment with Stalinism, finally expressed in a burst of rejection and rebirth in 1956, after which the terms of analysis and the criteria for inclusion shift radically, and no further reference is made to those uncomfortable earlier experiences. Even the late Louis Althusser, who saw no reason to abandon or deny his earlier engagements, exploited this *Ur*-narrative for his own purposes: I joined the Communist party, he explained in the sixties, as a result of my youthful experience and observation of politics in the seminal period from the Popular Front to the Liberation.[12] No doubt, but then why wait until 1948, when Stalinism was already in full flow, the Liberation was four years old, and M. Althusser was already thirty? There is little doubt that the Marxist philosopher *thought* that he joined the party as the immediate result of his experience of war and Occupation, just as Pierre Emmanuel *thought* that every Frenchman (or at least every French intellectual) was captivated by communism. This version of their own story, and the story of their generation, has now long since replaced and overlaid messier and less convenient personal accounts.

11. Pierre de Boisdeffre, *Des vivants et des morts* (Paris, 1954), 249; see also Jacques Laurent, *Les Années 50* (Paris, 1989), 10.
12. Louis Althusser, *Pour Marx* (Paris, 1965), 11–21.

The story of these years is also subject, like much else in recent French history, to revision and selective exploitation. Until 1977 it lay half-buried in the collective memory, like the Vichy years that preceded it. These matters, it was felt, had been resolved, not least by Sartre himself, whose violent rejection of Soviet communism and all its works after 1968 comfortably obscured his earlier writings, now buried in unread volumes of yellowing journals. Like the collaborators of the Occupation years, the fellow-travelers of the postwar decade were an embarrassment; and like collaboration, they were thought to have been purged from the soul of the nation, the first by Resistance and heroic liberation, the second by the blood-letting of 1956 and the morally unassailable engagement over Algeria. Where this did not work, there was always the argument from history: whatever their later mistakes, Sartre, Bourdet, Mounier, and their colleagues had been on the side of the angels in a difficult time and could be forgiven their mistakes, committed anyway in the name of an anticapitalism whose appeal was not yet moribund.

After 1977, the perspective shifted. The new "philosophers" engaged in some public score-settling of a sub-Oedipal nature, condemning *all* the master thinkers of the past, bag and baggage. Burying their own Maoist peccadillos of the sixties in a lava torrent of accusations directed at their teachers, their indiscriminate dismissal of all holistic thought bundled Sartre and his generation into a single sack, with Althusser, Heidegger, Marx, Hegel, Rousseau, and others besides. All sorts of pasts thereby disappeared in this epistemological auto-da-fé, making distinctively contextual explanations of modern intellectual behavior impossible to articulate. The polemical value of such work was considerable. But the enduring effect has been to push "all that" even further away, distanced from us now by time, moral distaste, and philosophical dismissal alike.

For a curious instance of such absolution from a different quarter, one has only to look at the treatment recently accorded to Mounier and his circle. On the evidence of his own writings and those of his colleagues, Mounier and the *Esprit* group occupy an ambiguous place in modern French intellectual history. During the thirties a number of them were tempted by the radical Right and most of them were disenchanted with the Republic. In 1940 and for some months to come they were fascinated by the opportunities for rebirth apparently opened up by the Pétain regime. The Resistance record of Mounier and some of his friends is unimpressive at best, and for much of the rest of the forties their journal, although occasionally publishing important and courageous articles by men like Fejtö and Cassou, mostly devoted its editorial pages to embarrassing apologies for Stalinism, dialectical neo-Christian humbug at its most abject. Mounier's editorial successors continued to occupy ambivalent positions well into the fifties. Many of the younger Catholics, within *Esprit* itself and among its readers, however, were also the first to throw themselves into the Algerian fray. As a result, men like Jacques Julliard or Michel Winock see their own generation as one that, by drawing away from political affiliation with communism and "cleansing" itself in the struggle for Algerian independence, broke with the pattern set by earlier generations of intellectuals and represents "the end of the treason of the intellectuals."[13]

There is something disturbingly self-satisfied about this point of view, as though this generation were somehow uniquely morally superior, not tarred with the brush of debased engagement that colored the trajectory of those who came both before and after. It is also misleading, for if "the treason of the intellectuals" means anything at all then it assuredly describes many of the attitudes still prevalent around 1970 no less than 1950. More seriously, it casts a benevolent retrospective glow, anachronistically attributing to Mounier and *his* generation many of the intentions and attitudes that did indeed surface in the group that followed them. It is curious to note that the two important French studies of the *Esprit* group are both relatively generous towards their subject matter, whereas the full-length accounts by foreigners, though less sophisticated, are much more critical.[14]

Another distorting trait of recent French memory is the distinctive nostalgia that many feel for the postwar years, despite the stale air of moral ambivalence that surrounds them; it was, after all, a time when intellectuals, whatever their failings, had a place, an audience, and a role that, for all that it was self-ascribed, was also very real. Here, too, the analogy with another *lieu de mémoire* is revealing. The Resistance, like Vichy, has finally become an object of serious historical study. The *résistantialisme* of the postwar years, assiduously cultivated by Gaullists and Communists alike, has given way to judicious scholarly accounts of public opinion, studies of popular Pétainism, and acknowledgment of the marginality of Resistance movements for much of their short life.

13. Jacques Julliard, in *Le Débat* 50 (May–August 1988): 38–39; Michel Winock, "L'Âge d'or des intellectuels," *L'Histoire* 83 (November 1985).
14. Jean-Louis Loubet del Bayle, *Les Non-conformistes des années 30* (Paris, 1969); Michel Winock, *Histoire politique de la revue "Esprit," 1930–1950* (Paris, 1975); John Hellmann, *Emmanuel Mounier and the New Catholic Left, 1930–1950* (Toronto, 1981); William Rauch, *Politics and Belief in Contemporary France: Emmanuel Mounier and Christian Democracy, 1932–1950* (The Hague, 1972).

And yet, the rise of Le Pen, and the accompanying increase in nationalist rhetoric and racist or anti-Semitic incidents in recent times, have provoked an overhasty retreat to the easy nostrums of postwar "Resistance-kitsch," an exploitation of misleadingly simple Manichaean themes (them and us, good and evil, Pétainists and Resisters), invocations of 1940 and the need to speak out, take sides, and so forth. Such engagement hardly requires much courage in the France of 1991, nor did it in the late 1940s, the last time such a language was unwrapped for polemical use. This nostalgia for other people's experiences is difficult to condemn, invoked as it is in a good cause; but it is achieved at the expense of clarity and honesty not only about France's present social problems but also about a past whose alignments and affiliations were much more ambiguous than such uncomplicated analogies would suggest. In a similar manner, we are beginning to hear maudlin reminiscences of better days, when moral lines were clearly drawn and intellectuals had clearly assigned ontological duties. Newspaper advertisements for hastily written essays by aspirant heirs to the vacant chairs of the masters now promise that *this* is the book we have been awaiting, the work that will carve out anew a role for lost intellectuals.

This (mis)memory of French intellectuals' happier past entails a number of appropriations and distortions of the historical text. Not only were the years 1944–56 a trifle less glorious than has sometimes been thought, but upon closer inspection they stand if anything as an argument *against* the use to which latter-day nostalgics would put them. One of the most persistent complaints of intellectuals today is that they don't matter, that because their words have no weight, they are relieved of all responsibility; they suffer, as it were, from the unbearable lightness of their being. In earlier years, it is suggested, intellectuals not only mattered, but their words counted; they were *in* history; they bore responsibility for their actions. This is certainly the claim that Sartre, among others, made on his own behalf and in the name of all intellectuals: a writer, he asserted, is engaged by what he writes and must take responsibility for his words (and, implicitly, for his silences). This was the basis of his criticism of Flaubert and Goncourt for their failure to speak out against the repression of the Communards, and it was the source of Simone de Beauvoir's desire to see Brasillach shot for his journalistic collaboration.[15] The problem is that the argument was undermined by its

15. Jean-Paul Sartre, *Qu'est-ce que la littérature?* in *Situations,* vol. 2 (Paris, 1948); and "Présentation," *Les Temps modernes* 1 (October 1945); Simone de Beauvoir, "Oeil pour oeil," *Les Temps modernes* 5 (February 1946).

authors' own behavior; Sartre never spoke out against Soviet anti-Semitism or in defense of the victims of show trials, nor was he ever held to account by his followers and heirs for this, any more than for his more egregiously silly pronouncements from the early fifties.

In other words, the years 1944–56 were not a golden era of intellectual responsibility but quite the reverse; never were French intellectuals so *irresponsible,* saying and writing whatever they desired, pronouncing angrily on a subject one month, neglecting it thereafter for years to come, at no cost either to their reputations or their skins. Their engagements and affiliations smack less of a sense of collective moral responsibility or a desire to influence public sentiment than of the need to give themselves a clean social and political conscience. Nor can this be explained as a style of behavior attributable uniquely to the cataclysmic moral lessons of 1940; already in 1938 Denis de Rougemont was attacking "debased" forms of intellectual engagement on the part of the "angry sheep" who ever since 1934 had signed any and every petition: "In short, in the last four years nothing has happened in the world that has not been roundly denounced by 'French intellectuals.'"[16]

Rougemont's comments on the devaluation of the idea of responsibility and engagement could as well have been written in 1970, even later. They are thus a salutary reminder that if the immediate postwar years were in certain ways something special in the French experience, this was only because they saw intellectual confidence and self-promotion carried to unusual heights. The intellectual privilege associated with that era was not unique but was a constituent part of something else, something that characterized French public life for most of the past century and that is only contingently related to the intellectuals as such. When today's essayists agonize over the "end" of the intellectuals they are missing their target: what has actually been lost, and what has yet to be replaced, is the security that derives from a confident political culture, from the knowledge of certain simple "truths" about history and society. The normalization of French politics was long overdue, but it has brought new problems in its wake.

Although it is incontrovertible that the social and political world of Fourth Republic France lies in the distant past, transformed beyond recognition and recall, French thinkers have been perhaps a little too quick to suppose that the same is true of the habits of mind and word that were once the trademark of its cultural elite. There is today a wide-

16. Denis de Rougemont, *Journal d'une époque, 1926–1946* (Paris, 1968), 372.

spread assumption that we have seen some sort of irreversible epistemological break, that old ghosts have finally been laid and old patterns finally broken. In a number of respects this assumption is open to doubt.

It is a long-standing peculiarity, some would say virtue, of the French that they are, in the words of Caesar describing his Gallic subjects, *rerum novarum cupidi*. Thus the very urgency with which recent writings have sought to bury the radical nostrums of the fifties, the immoderate manner in which today's younger intellectuals have seized upon the novel charms of moderation, bespeaks a continuity with that same past. No one doubts for a minute that French intellectuals, as a community, have parted company from a certain set of beliefs. But the ways in which those beliefs, that past, are described and explained point to remarkable continuities of intellectual habit. Doing well what they do best, French writers have demonstrated brilliantly the relationship between knowledge and power in totalitarian societies; a totalizing *savoir* implies and requires a totalizing *pouvoir*, so that the discrediting of Marxism and the rejection of Stalinism and its heirs are necessarily conjoined. This is fine, and true. But it is *itself* a totalizing sort of analysis of a very traditional kind; what has been lacking in most modern French critiques of the defects of utopian social projects is any empirical or moral account of what these visions meant in practice, how they work and why they fail. For most intellectuals, they were either completely true or utterly false, in both cases *ex hypothesi*. In the event of their proving false, moreover, nothing remains to be salvaged, and nothing more needs to be said.

French intellectuals are thus never more faithful to their past than when they are breaking with it. Ever since the statutes of the University of Paris (A.D. 1215) required of them that its scholars work to found a "comprehensive theory of the world," the dominant characteristic of French intellectual discourse has been the drive to organize and contain knowledge within a single frame, and both the all-embracing metatheories of earlier decades and the antiholism of recent years are consistent with this style of reasoning, though the latter is an unstable form of it.[17] This habit of thought, moreover, is not transmitted by some mysterious collective gene, a cultural Lamarckian trait inherited by thirty generations of Sorbonnards. It is the product of a remarkably unbroken

17. See Louis Bodin, *Les Intellectuels* (Paris, 1964), 25; and Stephen Ferruolo, "Parisius-Paradisus: The City, Its Schools, and the Origins of the University of Paris," in Thomas Bender, ed., *The University and the City* (New York, 1988).

urban culture, that of the Parisian community of writers and scholars, unique in the Western experience. In spite of the changing media of communication and notwithstanding deep transformations of the educational system, the forms of intellectual intercourse in Paris, the fashions that dictate how an idea should be crafted and what sorts of ideas merit publication, have survived curiously untouched. The modern visitor to Paris would find little to alter in Goethe's comment to Eckermann, recorded in May 1827:

Imagine a city like Paris, where the best minds of the realm are all on one spot and instruct and excite one another by daily contact, conflict, and emulation.[18]

In such circumstances, we should not be surprised to find that the pattern of the fifties and sixties, whereby French intellectuals exploited the Soviet or third-world models of utopia to reflect critically upon their own society, is now being emulated by those who have turned to post-Communist East-Central Europe as a way of proclaiming the charms of liberalism. Indeed, the very critique of totalitarian rationality (Marxist or Heideggerian) is itself something periodically rediscovered by each succeeding generation (beginning at least with Sorel), a symbol of that peculiarly Parisian combination of long-term collective memory and short-term private amnesia. Fashion, too, has a long history: not any one fashion—quite the contrary—but the fashion for fashions. In the 1880s it was Russian literature, when translations of Tolstoy, Dostoyevsky, and lesser writers were eagerly sought out in the wake of de Vogüé's publication of *Le Roman russe* in 1886, which went through eleven editions in just twenty years. Before and since, there were enthusiasms for Polish writers, German metaphysicians, and, most recently, Anglo-American philosophers. Other nations have experienced comparable cultural fads, of course, but few with the intensity and the regularity of the French, and none with anything like the same capacity to incorporate and exploit the exotic for domestic cultural purposes with such enthusiasm, such depth of commitment, and for such short periods.[19]

This truly impressive capacity for innovation and incorporation and the way in which, in the confines of a few small districts of the capital city, such novelties communicate themselves to the whole intellectual

18. Johann-Peter Eckermann, Thursday, 3 May 1827, *Conversations avec Goethe* (Paris, 1930), vol. 2, 299.

19. On the Tolstoy craze, see Owen Chadwick, *The Secularisation of the European Mind in the Nineteenth Century* (Cambridge, 1975), 244.

milieu are achieved at a price. Innovation is almost exclusively linguistic, requiring a protean capacity to adapt language and categories to new materials and new shapes but for this very reason entailing little substantive change in the habits of mind. Commenting on the excessively abstract character of French historical and economic writing, Georges Sorel once wrote to Benedetto Croce, "We in France have the defect of seeking to see things from on high, à la Napoléon."[20] From such heights everything is clear, but not very much is visible.

One reason for this is that in a culture so confidently oriented towards the word, the conventional constraints on meaning are sometimes difficult to apply. In his inaugural lecture at the Collège de France, Roland Barthes made much play with his techniques for "liberating" people and concepts from power in all its forms: whatever controls, restricts, and whatever restricts is tyrannical, Fascist. Language controls and restricts, and is thus Fascist; the destruction of linguistic norms, by analogy, is a liberating exercise.[21] Propositions of this sort communicate through the ether with other concerns of the intellectual community, past and present: antifascism, Resistance, Liberation; and they do so in a manner consonant with the conventions of the high intelligentsia, substituting in time for the things themselves. Or, in Simone de Beauvoir's summary of Sartre's "praxis" as vouchsafed in *Qu'est-ce que la littérature?*: "To name is to unmask, and to unmask is to change."[22]

Hence the special appeal, for a few years, of Stalinism, which likewise operated from abstract a prioris, accumulating (or inventing) facts to suit its case. In his discussion of Merleau-Ponty's manner of defending the Russian trials, Louis Martin raised just this question: "What sort of a 'mentality' is it that needs to invent concrete facts in order to illustrate an abstraction [the objective utility of Trotskyism to the Nazis]?"[23] Today there is little need to invent facts or believe the inventions of others in order to marshal a case against totalitarianism, but it is indeed curious

20. Sorel to Croce, 20 December 1895, quoted in Schlomo Sand, *L'Illusion du politique: Georges Sorel et le débat intellectuel, 1900* (Paris, 1984), 74. Writing in the 1860s, another observer of French thought, foreign but distinctly sympathetic, found in the speculations of Auguste Comte "a monumental warning to thinkers on society and politics of what happens, when once men lose sight, in their speculations, of the value of Liberty and Individuality." See John Stuart Mill, *Autobiography* (New York, 1969), 127–28.

21. See Jerrold Seigel, "La Mort du sujet: Origines d'un thème," *Le Débat* 58 (January–February 1990): 169.

22. Simone de Beauvoir, *La Force des choses*, 146.

23. Louis Martin, "Psychologie de la pensée communiste," *Revue socialiste* 32 (December 1949): 1466, n. 3.

how little such a case, when made by most French writers, does in practice depend upon social or historical detail; in his 1981 essay on French intellectual life, Jean-Marie Domenach managed to give an account of the decline of Marxism couched exclusively in terms of high moral inadequacy and grand paradox, with no mention of the social or economic failures that constitute the efficient cause of communism's fall from grace. The only difference between Domenach's critique of Marxism and his own and others' defense of it thirty years before is the insertion of negative abstractions in place of the positive ones that determined his earlier desire to believe.[24]

Similar observations apply to the critique of Marx and Marxism that so preoccupied discussion during the decade following the publication in French of the *Gulag Archipelago*. The "new philosophers" and their successors added little if anything to the arguments of Albert Camus in *L'Homme révolté;* the energetic if somewhat undisciplined linking of Marx, Hegel, Rousseau, the Terror, Russian nihilism, and Stalin into a single unprepossessing package was both the strength and the weakness of Camus's work, and Francis Jeanson's observation that Camus was simply attacking Hegel for the "original sin" of deifying Man, could as well be made of Glucksmann and his successors.[25] Jeanson had motives of his own for dismissing such an approach, but it does have real limitations. Like analogous recent critiques of other German theorists, it disposes efficiently enough of a whole category of worldviews, but through an approach whose terms of reference leave little hope for any positive or productive alternative description of the human condition.[26]

In these circumstances we should not be surprised to find that a number of French writers in recent times have been falling back on another "deep structure" of French intellectual practice, the faith in republican universalism. As French society struggles to integrate a growing minority of persons of different color, faith, or nationality, conflicts over education, religious practices, and ethnic affiliations have come to the fore.

24. Jean-Marie Domenach, *Enquête sur les idées contemporaines* (Paris, 1981), 244ff.

25. Francis Jeanson, "Albert Camus ou l'âme révoltée," *Les Temps modernes* 79 (May 1952): 2080.

26. See Luc Ferry and Alain Renaut, *Heidegger et les Modernes* (Paris 1988). On the whole, Aron's observation applies as much today, *mutatis mutandis,* as it did when he reviewed Merleau-Ponty's *Aventures de la dialectique:* "Après avoir fourni à l'intelligentsia' de gauche sa caution philosophique, le professeur du Collège de France apparaît soudain libéré des superstitions qu'il a tant contribué à nourrir." See "Aventures et mésaventures de la dialectique," *Preuves* 59 (January 1956): 8.

This too is not something new—similar questions arose at the time of Jewish migration from eastern Europe before World War I and again during the great immigrant wave of the twenties and early thirties—but most of those now engaging with such matters are having to think about them for the first time. It is thus interesting to find many French thinkers responding to issues of Jewish or Moslem identity with an instinctive return to the dream of a secular, unitary Republic. Like the Abbé Grégoire and his many successors, they are happy to promise equality for all, but at the price of a denial of individual or communitarian identity. In spite of nearly two decades of debate over the need to deliver themselves once and for all from the irksome habit of treating human beings in the collective rather than the individual, many French intellectuals still instinctively gravitate towards the neo-Jacobin republicanism of Max Gallo or Jean-Pierre Chévènement, notwithstanding its relative unconcern for the sorts of individual liberties to which so much lip-service is now paid.

The fear recently expressed by Alain Finkielkraut—"the nation is being replaced by tribes"—not only reflects the anxieties of many of his fellow commentators but could have been lifted, unchanged, from similar warnings expressed by republicans in France from Robespierre to Ferry and beyond. This is not to say that the sectional and sectarian response to Le Pen on the part of some Jewish groups in particular does not occasion legitimate charges of overreaction. But all the same there is something profoundly atavistic in the views advanced by two writers in April 1990, commenting on the growing nervousness and retreat of French Jews following a spate of anti-Semitic incidents: "To take part in the national debate exclusively as a Jew and not as a Jewish Frenchman would be to begin a divorce from the Republic of incalculable consequences."[27]

From the expression of such sentiments, it is reasonable to conclude that a certain liberalism, for all its recent prominence as a category of public debate, has yet to take root as a political concept in France. Of the characteristic French attitude towards the implications of liberal thought, we might say with Camus (responding to Jeanson's review quoted above), "Your article appears to consent to a doctrine, while maintaining silence over its political implications."[28] The point is not

---

27. See Florence Assouline and Maurice Szafran, "Juifs de France: La Malaise," in *L'Évenement du Jeudi,* 19–25 April 1990; also Paul Yonnet, "La Machine Carpentras," *Le Débat* 61 (September–October 1990).

28. Albert Camus, "Révolte et servitude," letter to *Les Temps modernes,* reprinted in *Actuelles,* vol. 2 (Paris, 1953), 113.

that Republican diehards are altogether mistaken in their gloomy prog-
nostications: a society *can* be too atomized, with its constituent groups
defined more by mutual antagonism than by a common national culture, and this might be especially true in a nation like France, where the
expectations for national cohesion and common identity are set high.
But it is curiously solipsistic of French intellectuals to believe that *theirs*
is a state in which such thresholds of unacceptable heterogeneity are
being reached.

Liberalism, like liberty, is not, of course, an unproblematic or uncontested concept. Its origins in Enlightenment constructions of reason
make it no less vulnerable to conceptual (and real) tyranny than other
visions of human well-being: happiness, socialism, equality. But whatever liberalism's capacity to fall short of or contradict its own stated
intentions, it cannot even begin to become the organizing principle of
public thought and political practice unless two underlying premises are
accepted beyond question: first, the importance and primacy of the individual; and, second, the necessary and desirable complexity, plurality,
and indeterminacy of political life. Neither of these ideas has so far made
many inroads upon the French intellectual imagination, and Thomas
Pavel is quite correct to conclude that, for the French, liberalism has
been subverted and distorted into an uninvestigated telos: "The liberalism of the past decade is presented as the final accession to a state of grace
after long errors and penance."[29]

This is because the analysis of totalitarianism, although it has taken up
much space, has not bitten very deep. It is a rare French thinker who has
faced and engaged the real problem with totalitarianism, which is that it
is a logical and historical derivative of precisely that universalist vision of
republican democracy that still bedazzles so many French thinkers. With
due respect to Jean-Pierre Faye and his successors, totalitarianism is more
than just a set of languages.[30] To come to terms with the European
experience of totalitarianism, including those aspects of it that so
seduced Western intellectuals, it is not enough to proclaim the virtues of
democracy and the victory of liberal politics. One must first ask what it
is that distinguishes liberal democracy from its totalitarian relative, and
this entails transcending the various inherited categories of post-

29. Thomas Pavel, "Empire et paradigmes," *Le Débat* 58 (January–February 1990):
174. Pavel is here commenting on the material presented in "Notre Histoire: Matériaux
pour servir à l'histoire intellectuelle de la France, 1953–1987," *Le Débat* 50 (May–August
1988).

30. See Jean-Pierre Faye, *Langages totalitaires* (Paris, 1972).

Enlightenment social thought and engaging seriously with the rights and status of the individual.

It might be thought that this was something that French intellectuals had indeed been doing in recent years, with so much attention paid to the theory and practice of human rights. But here, too, the past has been overcome a trifle rapidly. It is good indeed to hear Jean-François Lyotard, among many others, expatiating on the Rights of Man. But one would be more convinced had he felt constrained to show how such high moral seriousness can be squared with his long-held theories about the heterogeneity and consequent indeterminacy of language. Consistency is not everything, but its absence cannot help but arouse suspicion.[31] It is hard to avoid the feeling that some French thinkers are not wholly *serious* about such matters—that this too may be a fashion and one in its turn altogether too dependent upon another fashion, that for eastern Europe. Despite recent enthusiasms for the work of Karl Popper, John Rawls, and others, the idea that in any compromise between private rights and public interest it is the latter that must make its case is not one with which modern French political thought is familiar. It is thus no accident that liberal political literature in France is still largely imported and no major local figure has yet emerged to ground liberal theory in domestic experience.[32]

The reference to eastern Europe in this context is not gratuitous. For understandable reasons, politicians and philosophers in Czechoslovakia, Hungary, and elsewhere have been inclined to treat liberalism as a uniquely desirable and unproblematic goal, the object of their efforts first as dissidents and now as nation-builders, and an uncontested political category. This has had the paradoxical and troubling consequence of turning liberalism into a project and making it function almost as a substitute utopia. Liberalism's *own* account of itself is incompatible with such a use of the term, and it is not at all clear just how one *constructs* a liberal society where the conditions for its emergence have never existed. In most important respects these are problems that France has been happily spared; but in certain ways the French share some of the eastern European difficulties. For the modern French intellectual also sees in liberalism something essentially utopian, a solution to the holistic

31. See the acerbic comments of Luc Ferry and Alain Renaut in *La Pensée 68* (Paris, 1985); and Ferry and Renaut, *68–88: Itinéraires de l'individu* (Paris, 1988). For Jean-François Lyotard, see *La Condition postmoderne* (Paris, 1979); and *Le Différend* (Paris, 1983).

32. The exception is Raymond Aron, but his own trajectory and the fact that he belongs to an earlier generation rather confirm the diagnosis.

detour taken by French life and thought in years past; it is as though the French were today experiencing in the world of ideas the lived history of East Europeans, much as left-wing intellectuals undertook to do in the postwar decade. This curious symbiosis may also have unfortunate consequences, as the post-Communist lands of eastern Europe fall into economic difficulties and ethnic and national conflict. When the French intelligentsia once again loses interest in these lands, now shorn of romantic appeal and with their formerly dissident leaders compromised by the realities of public life, what will remain of the liberal vision now associated with them and the language of rights and freedoms that they brought in their train?

The fragility of post-totalitarian thought in France is closely bound up with the odd use to which the rediscovery of liberalism is being put. For liberalism, as I noted above, is necessarily indeterminate. It is not about some sort of liberal project for society; it is about a society in which the messiness and openness of politics precludes the application of large-scale projects, however rational and ideal—especially, indeed, if they are rational and ideal. But it is just this that renders it so alien to French traditions of political reasoning. A liberal democracy is, and strives precisely to remain, an untidy compromise between competing claims, and its only consistent defense is that it interferes least in the affairs of each while simultaneously striving to meet the needs and defend the interests of all. Despite everything that has happened, and all the claims that have been made for the "end of French peculiarity," in its reluctance to engage with this messiness at the heart of liberalism, French political culture still stands quite distinctively apart from most of the Western tradition.[33] Even today, as political thinkers take it for granted that the old ideologies and systems are defunct, most of them continue to write as though it were not possible to think seriously about politics until one had generated a worthy replacement for these systems and doctrines, and in their own ambitious terms.

In the meantime, political reasoning in France sounds temporary, as though it were merely marking time between ideologies. The idea that the present indeterminacy not only is but should be the *natural* condition of public life, with politics no less than people treated as an end in

---

33. See Sunil Khilnani, "Un Nouvel Espace pour la pensée politique," *Le Débat* 58 (January–February 1990): 187. Exception should be made here for the work of François Furet, Marcel Gauchet, Pierre Manent, Pierre Rosanvallon and others at the École des hautes études and the Institut Raymond Aron. But they remain a tiny minority.

itself, remains troubling to many. Thus, few thinkers in France have so far undertaken to construct a moral vocabulary for liberal politics, an ethics, so to speak, of democracy. The discrete categories are present and frequently invoked: rights, freedom, duties, individuals, justice, and so forth. But for modern thinkers as for Sartre or Mounier, they seem to require some other-directed project, some *telos ex machina* in order to become operational. In the meantime we are still subject to political dissertations in the form of the most casual of random reflections, of which it would not be unfair to say, as Julien Benda once said of the enthusiasm for Péguy and Sorel, "We treat as genuine forms of philosophy the rattling of 'intuitions,' flung down with no order, no cohesion, no critical apparatus, a sort of verbal action and sometimes very seductive."[34]

In this long twilight of French political theory it comes as no real surprise to find that the attractions of German thought have survived unscathed their troubled passage through the middle years of this century. It is certainly true that the appeal of Hegel, Husserl, and Heidegger —not to mention Marx, Freud, and Nietzsche—is no longer what it once was. Yet even the best French writing in this field remains firmly and ironically shackled to a typically Germanic problematic. Thus Luc Ferry and Alain Renaut, who have been in the forefront of modern intellectual "detoxification," have concentrated their fire not only on the weaknesses of Heidegger but also on many of the fallacies contained in the whole post-Kantian German tradition of historical and social thought. But nowhere in their various histories of modern French philosophy or in their studies of French political theory do these authors, separately or together, abandon their characteristic fixation upon transcendental philosophy. The whole history of modern French thought is presented as though it were a syllabus of categorical errors and moral mistakes, most of them the outcome of the misapplication of Germanic epistemes. The authors evince virtually no interest in other things that have shaped and informed French political argument: religion, civil and political institutions, commerce, and social conflict. Even the Germans don't write intellectual history like this any more![35]

---

34. Julien Benda, *Belphégor: Essai sur l'esthétique de la société française dans la première moitié du vingtième siècle* (Paris, 1947), 152–53.

35. See the various works cited by Ferry and Renaut above. Also their *Philosophie politique* (Paris, 1985), in particular volume 3, *Des droits de l'homme à l'idée républicaine*. For commentaries, see, for example, Thomas Pavel, *Le Mirage linguistique* (Paris, 1988); and Mark Lilla, "The Making of the 'Me' Generation," *Times Literary Supplement*, 17–23 November 1989.

Here too, then, and in the very act of settling the score with a tradition of high German thought deemed responsible for the tragic deviations of two generations of French thinkers, a new generation of French intellectuals is reforging the chains of its own cultural dependence—if that is what it really was. Heidegger, who was by no means the only German philosopher to note that "when the French begin to think they speak German," thus has the last laugh. The very complexity and sophistication of French intellectuals' self-analysis has become its own self-defeating naiveté, with the overabstract historical account of past errors not only compensating for the disappointments of the present but depriving contemporaries of the skeptical distance necessary for a true appreciation of their own condition.

In the end, of course, that condition is not uniquely French. The loss of the great faiths, secular and religious alike, the apparent opacity of history and social relations, and the absence of a story for intellectuals to tell are contemporary commonplaces. Marcel Gauchet's version of the post-Marxist dilemma—"The more we are led to acknowledge a universal validity to the principles of Western modernity, the less we are able to ground them in a history of progress of which they represent the fulfillment"[36]—applies with equal force to the present state of moral and political thought in Britain, the United States, Germany, and elsewhere.[37] It was part of Marxism's special appeal that it posited a simple causal relationship between understanding, action, and outcome. Whoever mastered History in theory was sure to control it in practice; human well-being would inevitably ensue.

In such a way of thinking, the role of the intellectual was crucial, and it is incontrovertible that modern tyranny not only gave the intelligentsia a privileged place but was in certain important respects a tyranny *of* the intelligentsia.[38] Where the tyrant embodies reason, the role of the intellectual becomes vital in the transmission of that reason to the people

36. Marcel Gauchet, in *Le Débat* 50 (May–August 1988): 168.

37. See, for example, John Dunn, *Western Political Theory in the Face of the Future* (Cambridge, 1979), and *Rethinking Modern Political Theory* (Cambridge, 1985); Richard Rorty, *Philosophy and the Mirror of Nature* (Princeton, 1979); and Jürgen Habermas, *The Theory of Communicative Action*, 2 vols. (Boston, 1984, 1989), and *Moral Consciousness and Communicative Action* (Cambridge, Mass., 1990).

38. See Nicola Chiaromonte, *The Worm of Consciousness and Other Essays* (New York, 1976), and *Credere e non credere* (Milan, 1971). For a different but compatible account, see George Konrad and Ivan Szelenyi, *The Intellectuals on the Road to Class Power* (New York, 1979).

in whose name it is applied. Where once he or she sought to scourge tyrants, the modern intellectual finished by interpreting and serving them. Far from representing a deviation from the ideal—his own and that of others—Sartre is indeed, as was once believed, the very essence of the twentieth-century intellectual. For the intellectual must, as Sartre wrote, betray, if he is to be true to his calling. Efforts by Sartre's heirs to overcome this inherited traitorous role will only succeed if they can agree to abandon the very qualities that made twentieth-century intellectuals what they were. In the light of present longings for a recovery of the intellectuals' prestige, such an enlightened exercise in self-interested modesty seems unlikely.

The belief, born of the special circumstances of the Dreyfus Affair, that the ontological condition of the intellectual in modern times is that of a witness for freedom and progress is thus distinctly misleading. At best, in André Chamson's words, "The duty of the writer is to be tormented." In practice, the writer or scholar who aspires to that public position which defines intellectuals and distinguishes them from mere scribblers has always had to choose between being the apologist for rulers or an advisor to the people;[39] the tragedy of the twentieth century is that these two functions have ceased to exist independently of one another, and intellectuals like Sartre who thought they were fulfilling one role were inevitably drawn to play both. If their successors, in France as elsewhere, are truly to put this past behind them, it will not be enough to recognize past mistakes. It will also be necessary to accept that entailed in the very meaning for modern society of the term *intellectual* are a number of roles that writers and scholars today may no longer wish to fulfill; indeed, a *refusal* to occupy the post of the (engaged) intellectual may be the most positive of the steps modern thinkers can take in any serious effort to come to terms with their own responsibility for our common recent past.

This will be harder in France than elsewhere, for reasons that I hope I have succeeded in illustrating in the course of this book. No one should suppose that Parisian culture is about to divest itself of all those qualities that constitute at once its great appeal and fatal weakness. There will be French intellectuals for many years to come; all of them will say foolish things some of the time, and some of them will say foolish things all of the time. They will on periodic occasions be drawn to grand theory

---

39. A distinction we owe to Saint-Simon.

more than intellectuals elsewhere, and there will be those who listen to what they have to say about it. This is a form of power, which is why it is so appealing, and such verbal actions have consequences. The most that one may ask is that those who thus engage themselves in the public arena, and who place on the scales of political or moral choice the weight of their intellectual prestige, do so with more care, coherence, and responsibility than their predecessors, and that they measure the meaning and impact of the things they say and how they express them. "No one," wrote Montaigne, "is exempt from talking rubbish. The misfortune lies in the way it is said."[40]

40. "Personne n'est exempt de dire des fadaises. Le malheur est de les dire curieusement."

Suggestions for Further Reading

In what follows I have noted some of the more important, or useful, works dealing with French intellectuals in the period covered by this book. This subject has generated a substantial literature, both because of its intrinsic importance and because intellectuals are a subject of perennial fascination to themselves and to one another. I have not tried to present an exhaustive survey of the secondary literature, much less discuss the primary sources I have used, which would require a whole book in itself. Instead I have confined myself to books in French and English directly pertaining to the material treated in this study. Those readers seeking further reading in particular topics are referred to the notes of the present book and to the "Indications bibliographiques" in Pascal Ory and Jean-François Sirinelli, *Les Intellectuels en France, de l'affaire Dreyfus à nos jours* (Paris, 1986). For a detailed list of works dealing with intellectuals of the Left in the years from 1956 to the present, a theme not covered in this book, see the bibliographies in Tony Judt, *Marxism and the French Left* (New York, 1986), and Sunil Khilnani, *The Decline of the Intellectual Left in France, 1945–1985* (Cambridge, Mass., forthcoming).

Intellectuals and Politics

On the general question of the public role of intellectuals in our time and the moral dilemmas raised by writers' and artists' participation in social and political movements, see Philip Rieff, ed., *On Intellectuals* (New York, 1969), notably the contribution by J. P. Nettl, "Ideas, Intellectuals, and Structures of Dissent"; Bruce Mazlish, *The Revolutionary Ascetic* (New York, 1976); Lewis Coser, *Men of Ideas: A Sociologist's View* (New York, 1965); and Edward Shils, *The Intellectuals and the Powers and Other Essays* (Chicago, 1972). Useful studies of the opinions and activities of intellectuals in various contexts include Paul Hollander, *Political Pilgrims: Travels of Western Intellectuals to the Soviet Union, China, and Cuba, 1928–1978* (Oxford, 1981); James Wilkinson, *The Intellectual Resistance in Europe* (Cambridge, Mass., 1981); David Caute, *The Fellow Travellers: A Postscript to the Enlightenment* (New York, 1973); Stanley Weintraub, *The Last Great Cause: The Intellectuals and the Spanish Civil War* (London, 1968); and Alistair Hamilton, *The Appeal of Fascism: A Study of Intellectuals and Fascism, 1919–1945* (New York, 1971). For a broad-ranging discussion of the cohort of European intellectuals who passed through the experience of the First World War, see Robert Wohl, *The Generation of 1914* (Cambridge, Mass., 1979).

French Intellectuals (General)

In addition to the synoptic and rather breathless survey by Ory and Sirinelli already noted, see the works of H. Stuart Hughes: *Consciousness and Society: The Re-orientation of European Social Thought, 1890–1930* (New York, 1958), and *The Obstructed Path: French Social Thought in the Years of Desperation, 1930–1960* (New York, 1968). Unfortunately, the second of these, which is devoted exclusively to France, is also the weaker. The best overall account of intellectuals and politics in postwar France is now Ariane Chebel d'Appollonia, *Histoire politique des intellectuels en France, 1944–1954,* 2 vols. (Brussels, 1991). For a more literary survey see John Lough, *Writer and Public in France: From the Middle Ages to the Present Day* (Oxford, 1978). A racy but generally reliable account of the world of intellectual Paris can be found in Herbert Lottman, *The Left Bank* (London, 1982). The early years of the modern intellectual community in France are analyzed in a more scholarly fashion by Christophe Charle, *Naissance des "intellectuels": 1880–1900* (Paris, 1990); and Antoine Compagnon, *La Troisième République des lettres* (Paris, 1985); and, with attention to a more restricted theme, by Paul Bénéton, *Histoire des mots: "Culture" et "civilisation"* (Paris, 1975). For the close relationship between elite educational institutions and the intellectual community they spawned, see Robert J. Smith, *The École normale supérieure and the Third Republic* (Albany, 1982); and Jean-François Sirinelli, *Génération intellectuelle: Khâgneux et normaliens dans l'entre-deux-guerres* (Paris, 1988), though the latter is marred by excessive devotion to the organizing concept of its title.

Among the many recent essays dealing with the intellectual condition in modern France, the following are of more than passing interest: François Bourricaud, *Le Bricolage idéologique: Essai sur les intellectuels et les passions démocratiques* (Paris, 1980); Jean Belkhir, *Les Intellectuels et le pouvoir* (Paris, 1982); Jean-Paul Aron, *Les Modernes* (Paris, 1984); Louis Janover, *Les Intellectuels face à l'histoire* (Paris, 1980); Hervé Hamon and Patrick Rotman, *Les Intellocrates: Expédition en haute intelligentsia* (Paris, 1981); Pierre Bourdieu, *Homo Academicus* (Cambridge, 1988; orig. Paris, 1984); and Régis Debray, *Teachers, Writers, Celebrities: The Intellectuals of Modern France* (London, 1981; orig. Paris, 1979). The journal *Le Débat,* in its fiftieth issue (May–June 1988), provides a detailed chronology of postwar French intellectual and cultural history under the title "Notre Histoire: Matériaux pour servir à l'histoire intellectuelle de la France, 1953–1987." Special mention should be made of two earlier contributions of a different order: Louis Bodin, *Les Intellectuels* (Paris, 1964), one of the first serious attempts by a practicing historian to study the place of intellectuals in French society;, and George Lichtheim, *Marxism in Modern France* (New York, 1966), which covers an astonishing range in a short space and remains, nearly thirty years after its appearance, the most valuable single work on its subject.

The Thirties

The "nonconformist" intellectuals of the thirties were studied—and defined—by Jean-Louis Loubet del Bayle, *Les Non-conformistes des années 30* (Paris, 1969). See also the ambitious but tendentious synthesis in Zeev Sternhell, *Neither Right nor Left: Fascist Ideology in France* (Berkeley, 1986). An account of intellectual commitment in politics, based on a number of case studies from these years, can be found in David Schalk, *The Spectrum of Political Engagement* (Princeton, 1979); while the philosophical ambiance of the period is ably dissected by Michael Roth, *Knowing and History: Appropriations of Hegel in Twentieth-century France* (Ithaca, N.Y., 1988), a book that deals with postwar thought as well. For Georges Bataille and his circle, see Jean-Michel Besnier, *La Politique de l'impossible: L'Intellectuel entre révolte et engagement* (Paris, 1972); and Denis Hollier, *The College of Sociology* (1979; reprint Minneapolis, 1988). For more general background, see also Maurice Nadeau, *Histoire du sur-réalisme* (Paris, 1970). On the little groups of the official and unofficial Left in the Popular Front era, see Géraldi Leroy and Anne Roche, *Les Écrivains et le Front populaire* (Paris, 1986); and D. Bonnaud-Lamotte and J-L Rispail, eds., *Intellectuel(s) des années trente* (Paris, 1990). For the Communists, see Jean-Pierre Bernard, *Le Parti Communiste français et la question littéraire, 1921–1939* (Grenoble, 1972).

Resistance and Collaboration

Some of the best accounts of the mood of France and French intellectuals in the aftermath of defeat are to be found in the memoirs and autobiographies listed below. Of contemporary commentary, the best is that of Marc Bloch, *Strange Defeat* (London, 1949), invaluable in this as in so many respects. On the Uriage circle of moral renovators, see Pierre Bitoun, *Les Hommes d'Uriage* (Paris, 1988), and Antoine Delestre, *Uriage: Une Communauté et une école dans la tourmente, 1940–1945* (Nancy, 1989), as well as works by Hellman and Winock cited below. For the intellectual Resistance see the general study by James Wilkinson already cited (under "Intellectuals and Politics"); Roderick Kedward, *Resistance in Vichy France* (Oxford, 1978); Kedward and Roger Austin, eds., *Vichy France and the Resistance* (London, 1985); and Jacques Debû-Bridel, *La Résistance intellectuelle* (Paris, 1970), though the latter should be used with caution, given the author's Gaullist *parti pris* and his oversanguine account of popular anti-Pétainism. The older work by Henri Michel, *Les Courants de pensée de la Résistance* (Paris, 1962), is still informative and reliable.

For intellectual collaboration, see Pascal Ory, *Les Collaborateurs* (Paris, 1977); Claude Lévy, *"Les Nouveaux Temps" et l'idéologie de la collaboration* (Paris, 1974); and the collective work edited by Gerhard Hirschfeld and Patrick Marsh, *Collaboration in France: Politics and Culture during the Nazi Occupation, 1940–1944* (Oxford, 1989). Despite the recent spate of interesting studies of the Vichy years, there is still no outstanding general work covering the intellectual life of occupied France. But see Christian Faure, *Le Projet culturel de Vichy* (Lyon, 1989); Gérard Loiseaux, *La Littérature de la défaite et de la collaboration* (Paris, 1984); and an interesting case study by Jean-Michel Guiraud, *La Vie intellectuelle et artistique à Marseille à l'époque de Vichy et sous l'occupation (1940–1944)* (Marseille, 1987). On Fascist intellectuals see Pierre-Marie Dioudonnat, *Je suis partout, 1930–1944* (Paris, 1973); and W. R. Tucker, *The Fascist Ego: A Political Biography of Robert Brasillach* (Berkeley, 1975).

The Purge

The student of postwar events is altogether better served. For a general account of the *épuration*, see Peter Novick, *The Resistance versus Vichy: The Purge of Collaborators in Liberated France* (New York, 1968). A more popular but well researched account can be found in Herbert Lottman, *The Purge* (New York, 1986). Robert Aron's massive work, *Histoire de l'épuration*, 3 vols. (Paris, 1967–75), suffers from the same prejudices as his *Histoire de Vichy* (Paris, 1954) and should be read with critical care. For the treatment of writers and artists, see Pierre Assouline, *L'Épuration des intellectuels, 1944–45* (Brussels, 1985); and in part, Philippe Bourdrel, *L'Épuration sauvage: 1944–45* (Paris, 1988). Jean Paulhan's cautionary essay, *Lettre aux directeurs de la Résistance* (1951; reprint Paris, 1987) can still be read with profit. On the context of these events, see Georges Madjarian, *Conflits, pouvoirs, et société à la Libération* (Paris, 1980); and Fred Kupferman, *Les Premiers Beaux Jours, 1944–1946* (Paris, 1985).

Philosophy and Politics in Postwar France

The literature on "existentialism and politics" is enormous and for the most part useless. Although much of the French writing exhibits a marked *parti pris* for or against its subject, British and North American scholarship, especially that of the sixties and seventies, tended to take the claims of postwar French intellectuals altogether too seriously and somewhat out of context. For this reason books like that of Mark Poster, *Existentialist Marxism in Postwar France* (Princeton, 1975), although reasonably reliable as guides to the thought itself, show little appreciation of French circumstances or the larger historical developments from which postwar philosophical debate emerged. *Modern French Marxism,* by Michael Kelly (Oxford, 1982), does a better job with the philosophy but is even less concerned with the circumstances of its production. For these purposes the reader is better advised to refer to the work by Michael Roth, already cited ("The Thirties"), or that of Vincent Descombes, *Modern French Philosophy* (Cambridge, 1980; orig. Paris, 1979, *Le Même et l'autre*). For the writings of Merleau-Ponty, see Kerry Whiteside, *Merleau-Ponty and the Foundation of an Existentialist Politics* (Princeton, 1988). Studies of Sartre are too numerous to cite, and the reader should refer to the bibliography in Annie Cohen-Solal's biography (see below), as well as that in Judt, *Marxism and the French Left.* Among the most useful general accounts are Anna Boschetti, *Sartre et "Les Temps modernes"* (Paris, 1985); and Michel-Antoine Burnier, *Les Existentialistes et la politique* (Paris, 1966), although the former is spoiled by its obsession with models of "cultural force-fields" derived from the work of Pierre Bourdieu. Burnier has also published a dyspeptic little book, *Le Testament de Sartre* (Paris, 1983), which gleefully cites the great man's many contradictions and political gaffes. The issues dividing Camus and Sartre are laid out by Eric Werner in *De la violence au totalitarisme: Essai sur la pensée de Camus et Sartre* (Paris, 1972), with an avowed preference for the person and opinions of the former. There are some good discussions of Camus in Jean-Yves Guérin, ed., *Camus et la politique* (Paris, 1986).

For the circle around Mounier there is now a growing literature, much of it controversial. Michel Winock's *Histoire politique de la revue "Esprit," 1930–1950* (Paris, 1975), is informative but hopelessly handicapped by a sympathy for its subject that frequently blinds the author to the implications and incoherence of Mounier's writings. John Hellman's dispassionate study, *Emmanuel Mounier and the New Catholic Left, 1930–1950* (Toronto, 1981), lacks Winock's sophistication but takes a proper critical distance. Bernard-Henri Lévy's aggressive account of French Catholic thought in the twentieth century, which reduces it to a sort of moralizing neofascism and treats dismissively of popular icons like Charles Péguy and Emmanuel Mounier, is unreliable and simplistic as intellectual history; but it has yet to provoke a satisfactory defense from Mounier's defenders. Curiously, Mounier's philocommunism in the postwar years tends to confirm at least a part of Lévy's interpretation. See Bernard-Henri Lévy, *L'Idéologie française* (Paris, 1981). For a study of the wartime emergence of a Catholic strain in the Resistance, see Renée

Bédarida, *"Témoignage Chrétien," 1941–1944* (Paris, 1977); the concerns and house style of *Le Monde,* the most influential postwar daily and one deeply influenced by the ethos of social Catholicism, are sympathetically recounted in Jacques Julliard and Jean-Noel Jeanneney, *"Le Monde" de Beuve-Méry, ou le métier d'Alceste* (Paris, 1979).

Intellectuals and Communism

The obvious starting point for anyone seeking to understand the troubled relations between intellectuals and communism in postwar France is still the book by David Caute, *Communism and the French Intellectuals, 1914–1960* (London, 1964), although it is beginning to show its age. The standard accounts of intellectuals' relations with the PCF are now those of Jeannine Verdès-Leroux, *Au service du parti: Le Parti Communiste, les intellectuels et la culture (1944–1956)* (Paris, 1983), and *Le Réveil des somnambules: Le Parti Communiste, les intellectuels, et la culture (1956–1985)* (Paris, 1987), although they deal only with those who were party members. The farther reaches of self-abasement are chronicled in Bernard Legendre, *Le Stalinisme français: Qui a dit quoi, 1944–1956* (Paris, 1980); and analyzed in Natacha Dioujeva and François George, *Staline à Paris* (Paris, 1982). To understand just what it was that Sartre and his contemporaries were responding to, see, for example, Laurent Casanova, *Le Parti Communiste, les intellectuels, et la nation* (Paris, 1949). For an appreciation of the motivation and ambivalence of intellectual fellow-travelers, memoirs and autobiographies are the best source (see below); among contemporary polemics and commentaries, those of continuing interest include Pierre Naville, *L'Intellectuel communiste* (Paris, 1956), which deals with the problem of Sartre; Denys Mascolo, *Lettre polonaise sur la misère intellectuelle en France* (Paris, 1957); and Jules Monnerot, *La Sociologie du communisme* (Paris, 1949). The two classic analyses of the emotional and intellectual process by which intellectuals come to accept and embrace communism both date from this period: Czeslaw Milosz, *The Captive Mind* (New York, 1953); and, supremely, Raymond Aron, *The Opium of the Intellectuals* (London, 1957; orig. Paris, 1955). See also *Marxism in Modern France,* by George Lichtheim (already cited) and the same author's various essays collected in *From Marx to Hegel* (New York, 1971).

The Totalitarian Dilemma

There is no general account of the complex interactions, suspicions, and misunderstandings that have marked the relations between French intellectuals and the countries under Soviet domination in the years 1945–89. But see Peter Deli, *De Budapest à Prague: Les Sursauts de la Gauche française* (Paris, 1981), and Pierre Grémion, *Paris-Prague: La Gauche face au renouveau et à la répression tchécoslovaques, 1968–1978* (Paris, 1985), both of them covering the period after 1956, and Evelyne Pisier-Kouchner, ed., *Les Interprétations du Stalinisme* (Paris, 1983). For a brief discussion of the East European syndrome in French progressive thinking, see Tony Judt, "The Rediscovery of Central Europe," in Stephen Graubard, ed., *Eastern Europe . . . Central Europe . . . Europe* (Boulder, Co., 1991). For the show trials and political purges of the forties, see George Hodos, *Show Trials: Stalinist Purges in Eastern Europe, 1948–1954* (New York, 1987). The "French connection" is discussed in the memoirs of one of the Czech victims, Artur Londonin, *The Confession* (New York, 1970); see also François Fejtö, who wrote extensively on eastern European developments for the French press at this time. See his *Mémoires: De Budapest à Paris* (Paris, 1986).

For attitudes towards the Soviet Union, see M. Cadot, *La Russie dans la vie intellectuelle française* (Paris, 1967); Lily Marcou, ed., *L'URSS vue de gauche* (Paris, 1982); Fred Kupferman, *Au pays des Soviets* (Paris, 1979); Christian Jelen, *L'Aveuglement: Les Socialistes et la naissance du mythe soviétique* (Paris, 1984); and the various general works cited at the beginning of this essay. Concerning the events covered in this book the following are also of interest: Guillaume Malaurie, *L'Affaire Kravchenko* (Paris, 1982); Dominique Lecourt, *Proletarian Science? The Case of Lyssenko* (London 1977; orig. Paris, 1976); Denis Buican, *Lyssenko et le Lyssenkism* (Paris, 1988); and David Rousset, Gérard Rosenthal, and Théo Bernard, *Pour la vérité sur les camps concentrationnaires (un procès antistalinien à Paris)* (1951; revised edition Paris, 1990). Examples of the Communist party line as espoused and presented by its own intellectuals can be found in Dominique Desanti, *Masques et visages de Tito et des siens* (Paris, 1949); and Pierre Daix, *Pourquoi David Rousset a inventé les camps soviétiques* (Paris, 1949).

Anti-Americanism

The best introduction to the troubled theme of French attitudes towards America is Denis Lacorne, Jacques Rupnik, and Marie-France Toinet, eds., *L'Amérique dans les têtes* (Paris, 1986), which can be supplemented with David Strauss, *Menace in the West: The Rise of French Anti-Americanism in Modern Times* (Westport, Conn., 1978). Contemporary French attitudes are also discussed in Karl Deutsch, ed., *France, Germany, and the Western Alliance: A Study of Elite Attitudes on European Integration and World Politics* (New York, 1967). For a historical survey, see Jean-Baptiste Duroselle, *La France et les États-Unis des origines à nos jours* (Paris, 1976). The subject is also discussed in the works on the thirties listed above, as well as the general studies by Caute and Hollander. Because anti-Americanism not only meant dislike of the United States but also functioned on occasion as a blanket metaphor and excuse for antimodernism, anti-Semitism, xenophobia, and collective insecurity, these books might be supplemented with Ralph Schor, *L'Opinion française et les étrangers, 1919–1939* (Paris, 1985); René Girault and Robert Frank, eds., *La Puissance française en question, 1945–1949* (Paris, 1988); and Michel Winock, *Nationalisme, antisémitisme et fascisme en France* (Paris, 1982). On French anti-Semitism see also *La France et la question Juive* (Paris, 1981); Jeffrey Mehlman, *Legacies of Anti-Semitism in France* (Minneapolis, 1983); and Pierre Birnbaum, *Un Mythe politique: La "République Juive"* (Paris, 1988).

Liberalism, Republicanism, and Rights

For a survey of French political thought since the Revolution, see Jacques Droz, *Histoire des doctrines politiques en France* (Paris, 1971), or the older but still informative work by Albert Thibaudet, *Les Idées politiques en France* (Paris, 1927). Roy Pierce, *Contemporary French Political Thought* (Oxford, 1966), is useful but dated. The collection of short essays edited by Pascal Ory, *Nouvelle Histoire des idées politiques* (Paris, 1987), is of distinctly variable quality. For the history of republicanism in France, see Claude Nicollet, *L'Idée républicaine en France: Essai d'histoire critique* (Paris, 1982); and Luc Ferry and Alain Renaut, *Philosophie politique* (Paris, 1985), vol. 3, *Des droits de l'homme à l'idée républicaine*. François Furet's volume in the new *History of France* published by Hachette, *La Révolution: De Turgot à Jules Ferry, 1770–1880* (Paris, 1988), has many acute observations on this subject, as does Claude Lefort in *L'Invention démocratique* (Paris, 1981). On the subject of rights and their usage in early French republican language, see Marcel Gauchet, *La Révolution des Droits de l'Homme* (Paris, 1989); and many of the contributions to François Furet and Mona Ozouf, eds., *Critical Dictionary of the French Revolution* (Cambridge, Mass. 1989; orig. Paris, 1988), notably in chapter 4. The most accessible survey of the place of rights in French constitutional thought, from a rather legalistic perspective, is Jean Rivero, *Les Libertés publiques* (Paris, 1974), vol. 1, *Les Droits de l'homme*.

On the troubled history of liberalism and liberal thought in France there is now a growing literature of excellent quality, prompted by recent shifts in the French political and intellectual mood. For general accounts from a French perspective, see Pierre Manent, *Histoire intellectuelle du libéralisme: Dix Leçons* (Paris, 1987); and André Jardin, *Histoire du libéralisme politique: De la crise de l'absolutisme à la Constitution de 1875* (Paris, 1985). For the early years of French Liberal thought there are a number of specialized studies: Georges Gusdorf, *Les Sciences humaines et la pensée occidentale* (Paris, 1966–1985), vol. 8, *La Conscience révolutionnaire: Les Idéologues*; Stephen Holmes, *Benjamin Constant and the Making of Modern Liberalism* (New Haven, Conn., 1984); Pierre Rosenvallon, *Le Moment Guizot* (Paris, 1985). Also pertinent is Jean-Claude Lamberti, *Tocqueville et les deux démocraties* (Paris, 1983).

Algeria and After

A number of historians are currently at work preparing studies of the impact of the Algerian War on the French intellectual community. In the meantime, the best coverage is provided by the essays in Jean-Pierre Rioux and Jean-François Sirinelli, eds., *La Guerre d'Algérie et les intellectuels français* (Brussels, 1991), and in Rioux, ed., *La Guerre d'Algérie et les français* (Paris, 1990). The motives of those who intervened actively on the side of the Algerian nationalists are described in Hervé Hamon and Patrick Rotman, *Les Porteurs de valises: La Résistance française à la Guerre d'Algérie* (Paris, 1982). See also André Rezler, *L'Intellectuel contre l'Europe* (Paris, 1976). For the signatories of the various petitions in these years (but also covering the whole period since Dreyfus), see Jean-François Sirinelli, *Intellectuels et passions françaises: Manifestes et pétitions au XXe siècle* (Paris, 1990). For a broad but not very imaginative survey of the whole period, see Paul C. Sorum, *Intellectuals and Decolonization in France* (Chapel Hill, N.C., 1977).

There is no synoptic history of the French intellectual community in the Fifth Republic. For the New Left of the sixties and after, see Arthur Hirsh, *The French New Left: An Intellectual History from Sartre to Gorz* (Boston, 1981), or Keith Reader, *Intellectuals and the Left in France since 1968* (London, 1987), neither of which is better than serviceable. A superior work but on a more restricted theme is Sherry Turkle's *Psychoanalytic Politics: Freud's French Revolution* (London, 1979). French contributions have tended to the dismissive (see, for example, Serge Quadruppani, *Catalogue du prêt-à-penser français depuis 1968* [Paris, 1983]), or the chatty (Pascal Ory, *L'Entre-Deux-Mai: Histoire culturelle de la France, mai '68–mai '81* [Paris, 1983]). An exception to this is the work of Luc Ferry and Alain Renaut; see their *68–88: Itinéraire de l'individu* (Paris, 1987) and *La Pensée 68* (Paris, 1985), although all of their work is shaped by rigid interpretive paradigms and is for the most part restricted to the arena of philosophy. Those interested in Foucault, Derrida, and their thought may be further informed by Allan Megill, *Prophets of Extremity: Nietzsche, Heidegger, Foucault, Derrida* (Berkeley, 1985), and Mark Poster, *Foucault, Marxism, and History: Mode of Production versus Mode of Information* (Cambridge, 1984); for enlightenment they would do better to turn to John Sturrock, *Structuralism and Since: From Lévi-Strauss to Derrida* (Oxford, 1979), and José Guillherme Merquior, *Foucault* (Berkeley, 1985), and the same author's excellent discussion of this and much else in *From Prague to Paris* (London, 1986).

Among the essays and arguments that have marked French thought since 1968, the following are emblematic: Jean-Pierre Faye, *Langages totalitaires* (Paris, 1972); André Glucksmann, *The Master Thinkers* (Brighton, 1981; orig. Paris, 1977); Bernard-Henri Lévy, *La Barbarie à visage humain* (Paris, 1977); Jacques Julliard, *La Faute à Rousseau* (Paris, 1985). All these, in their various ways, manage to place the blame for the emergence of totalitarianism and totalitarian styles of thought upon the original sins of the great holistic thinkers of the late Enlightenment (Rousseau, Hegel, and so on) and their Romantic-era heirs. For a bright account of one of the journalistic forums in which their views reached a wider public and became the new orthodoxy, see Louis Pinto, *L'Intelligence en action: "Le Nouvel Observateur"* (Paris, 1984).

Biographies, Autobiographies, and Memoirs

The most comprehensive study of Sartre's life is that by Annie Cohen-Solal, *Sartre, 1905–1980* (Paris, 1985). What she lacks in philosophical acuity, Ms. Cohen-Solal more than makes up for in energy and information. See also Ronald Hayman, *Sartre: A Biography* (New York, 1987). For Simone de Beauvoir, see Deirdre Bair, *Simone de Beauvoir* (New York, 1990). Camus is well covered by Herbert Lottman's *Camus* (Garden City, N.Y., 1979). Neither Maurice Merleau-Ponty nor Raymond Aron has yet been the subject of a satisfactory biography. This may reflect both the more rigorous quality of their work and the less eventful shape of their private lives—they do not lend themselves to chatty, informative narratives. For Merleau-Ponty, see André Robinet, *Merleau-Ponty: Sa Vie, son oeuvre* (Paris, 1970); for Raymond Aron we must await the promised study by Ariane Chebel d'Appollonia. Emmanuel Mounier receives a near-hagiographical treatment from Jean-Marie Domenach, *Emmanuel Mounier* (Paris, 1972); for a more dispassionate analysis but limited to his thought and writings, see Gérard Lurol, *Mounier 1. Genèse de la personne* (Paris, 1990). François Mauriac has been the subject of a biography by Jean Lacouture: *François Mauriac* (Paris, 1980); of a good study by his son Claude: *François Mauriac* (Paris, 1985); and of an account covering the war years: Jean Touzot, *Mauriac sous l'Occupation* (Paris, 1990). For the troubled life of Louis Aragon see Pierre Daix, *Aragon: Une Vie à changer* (Paris, 1975).

The biography is not a well-developed genre in France, though things have changed in recent years. But self-studies—in the form of memoirs, diaries, or autobiographies—are an established and popular form of analysis, explanation, or exculpation. Virtually every person mentioned in this book has written an account of his or her life, with special reference to the years in which they said or did embarrassing things. Not all of these are interesting, and some of them are distinctly unreliable. What follows is a selection, divided into three groups: works of intrinsic literary, philosophical, or political interest; works directly relevant to the subject-matter of this book; and works of tangential or related interest.

In the first category, see the multivolume autobiography of Simone de Beauvoir, notably the two volumes covering the wartime and postwar years: *The Prime of Life* (Cleveland, 1962), and *Force of Circumstance* (New York, 1965). Although they sometimes lack psychological insight and show remarkable naiveté at times, they are honest and informative narratives of a high quality. For a higher order of self-analysis and an honesty unusual for someone with such a checkered past, see the three volumes by Claude Roy: *Moi, Je* (Paris, 1969); *Nous* (Paris, 1972); and *Somme tout* (Paris, 1976). The best and perhaps the most influential autobiography by an ex-Communist intellectual is that of Edgar Morin, *Autocritique,* first published in Paris in 1958. In a more analytical mode see the reflections of the Communist philosopher Henri Lefebvre: *La Somme et le reste* (Paris, 1959). At the extreme frontier of the genre, revealing almost nothing about his personal life and recounting his trajectory as a series of intellectual undertakings, there are the *Mémoires: 50 Ans de réflexion politique* of Raymond Aron (Paris, 1983). Despite their impersonality, or perhaps because of it, these are a hugely impressive and enlightening guide to the intellectual life of France since the thirties. Of comparable standing but in a very different vein are the *Mémoires politiques* of François Mauriac (Paris, 1967), which can be complemented by his multivolume *Journal* (Paris, 1937–53).

Of those works of secondary quality, the following are of relevance: for fellow travelers, see Julien Benda, *Les Cahiers d'un clerc, 1936–1949* (Paris, 1950); Jean Cassou, *La Mémoire courte* (Paris, 1953), and *Une Vie pour la liberté* (Paris, 1981); and Vercors (Jean Bruller), *For the Time Being* (London, 1960; orig. Paris, 1957, *Pour prendre congé*). Claude Bourdet was more of a "neutralist" than a fellow-traveler, although his journalism from the period often went to some lengths to justify the practices of the Stalinists. For his version of the choices of those years, see *L'Aventure incertaine* (Paris, 1975). From the other side, the memoirs of Bertrand de Jouvenel, *Un Voyageur dans le siècle* (Paris, 1979), are in some measure an apologia for his ambivalent stance in the thirties. Similarly troubled by its author's unhappy passage through Vichy is *Le Rouge et le blanc, 1928–1944* (Paris, 1977), by Pierre Andreu. But the largest and most interesting body of writing comes from ex-Communists, most of them born in the 1920s. See, for example, Pierre Daix, *J'ai cru au matin* (Paris, 1976); Alain Besançon, *Une Génération* (Paris, 1987); Emmanuel Le Roy Ladurie, *Paris-Montpellier: P.C.-P.S.U., 1945–1963* (Paris, 1982); Victor Leduc, *Les Tribulations d'un idéologue* (Paris, 1985); Annie Kriegel (formerly Annie Besse), *Ce que j'ai cru comprendre* (Paris, 1991); and Dominique Desanti, *Les Staliniens: Une Expérience politique, 1944–1956* (Paris, 1975). In their different ways these are all sincere attempts to come to terms with the conundrum of Stalinism. If they all in varying degrees fail to meet the challenge this should not be ascribed to bad faith; it seems reasonable to suggest that men and women who plunged into the totalitarian language and thought of the postwar decade have real difficulty, thirty or forty years later, remembering and understanding what they thought they were doing and why.

A third group of writings deals with the same or adjacent periods in French intellectual life but comes from people only peripherally concerned in the events described in this book. They are nonetheless of value for anyone seeking to understand the broader cultural and human context of the time. Among the more interesting are: Robert Aron, *Fragments d'une vie* (Paris, 1981); Jean Davray, *La Brûlure* (Paris, 1983), which deals with the anti-Semitism, as the author sees it, of major French Catholic and Protestant writers, Mauriac and Gide included; Clara Malraux, *Le Bruit de nos pas*. Vol. 6: *Et pourtant j'étais libre* (Paris, 1979); Henri Massis, *Au long d'une vie* (Paris, 1967), the autobiography of a major figure on the French intellectual Right during the first half of the century; Jacques Laurent, *Histoire égoïste* (Paris, 1976); Philippe Viannay, *Du bon usage de la France* (Paris, 1988); and Simone Signoret, *Nostalgia Isn't What It Used to Be* (New York, 1978), a readable autobiography by France's best-loved actress that is at the same time an acute analysis of the mind of a "pigeon," as the East Europeans dubbed their "cultural visitors" from the West.

Index

Compositor: **T·H** Typecast, Inc.
Text: 10/13 Galliard
Display: Galliard
Printer: Maple-Vail Book Mfg. Group
Binder: Maple-Vail Book Mfg. Group